# Gatsby: The Definitive Guide

*Build and Deploy Highly Performant
Jamstack Sites and Applications*

*Preston So*

Beijing · Boston · Farnham · Sebastopol · Tokyo

**Gatsby: The Definitive Guide**

by Preston So

Copyright © 2021 Preston So. All rights reserved.

Published by O'Reilly Media, Inc., 1005 Gravenstein Highway North, Sebastopol, CA 95472.

O'Reilly books may be purchased for educational, business, or sales promotional use. Online editions are also available for most titles (*http://oreilly.com*). For more information, contact our corporate/institutional sales department: 800-998-9938 or *corporate@oreilly.com*.

| | |
|---|---|
| **Acquisition Editor:** Amanda Quinn | **Indexer:** nSight, Inc. |
| **Development Editor:** Jeff Bleiel | **Interior Designer:** David Futato |
| **Production Editor:** Katherine Tozer | **Cover Designer:** Karen Montgomery |
| **Copyeditor:** Rachel Head | **Illustrator:** Kate Dullea |
| **Proofreader:** Stephanie English | |

September 2021:     First Edition

**Revision History for the First Edition**

2021-09-10:    First Release

See *http://oreilly.com/catalog/errata.csp?isbn=9781492087519* for release details.

The O'Reilly logo is a registered trademark of O'Reilly Media, Inc. *Gatsby: The Definitive Guide*, the cover image, and related trade dress are trademarks of O'Reilly Media, Inc.

978-1-492-08751-9

[LSI]

*For my father, with love.*

# Table of Contents

## Part II.    Data in Gatsby

# Part III.  Extending Gatsby

# Part IV.    Production Gatsby

## Part V.    Advanced Gatsby

# Foreword

Preston So is nothing if not thorough.

Where most people would be happy to speak more than one or two languages, Preston decided he'd go ahead and learn—as far as I can tell—all of them. If you ask him for a restaurant recommendation, he'll send you a full-fledged guide to dining out in New York. I've never seen Preston phone it in on a project. He's always fully engaged and ready to dive deep into whatever he's up against.

This book is no exception.

This is the first comprehensive book about Gatsby on the market. True to his nature, Preston nails the journey from initial exploration to deep understanding in a thorough, approachable manner.

Gatsby's part of the rise of the Jamstack architecture, and it's been cool to see the community embrace and expand the capabilities of the Jamstack over the last few years. We've seen Gatsby grow beyond a "static site generator" and become a full-fledged app-development tool. We're seeing everything from ecommerce stores to app dashboards to the ordering kiosks at fast food restaurants adopt the Jamstack, and many of those projects are powered by Gatsby.

I'm watching more and more of the largest companies out there adopting the Jamstack as a more scalable, maintainable, and cost-effective approach to building and shipping frontends at scale. If you're new to the Jamstack approach to building websites, welcome! You're arriving at a great moment!

But I'm off on a tangent; let's get back to Gatsby, Preston, and why this book is great.

Gatsby is a tough thing to teach. To really understand it, we need to dig into the technologies behind Gatsby, like React and GraphQL. The supporting technologies that power Gatsby are big enough topics to cover that each one has its own book (or, in the case of React, an entire wing of the bookstore) dedicated to teaching it.

Many folks who teach Gatsby—myself included—will start our introductions by saying, "You'll need at least a basic understanding of the underlying tools before we start." We just assume that someone has enough familiarity with these tools that we can skip ahead. That's the beauty of a good abstraction: it lets people be productive without needing to know the things that have been abstracted away.

But being able to use Gatsby is only the beginning. Anyone can use a tool, but a craftsperson understands the tool. That understanding unlocks possibilities that are otherwise hidden from view. The really interesting stuff happens when people who deeply understand their tools start to apply those tools to hard problems.

This book is a clearly marked map from zero to understanding. Whether you're looking to create your first ever Gatsby site or trying to gain deep insights into how to customize Gatsby for your specialized requirements, this book will get you where you want to go.

So tuck in, my friends! I can't wait to see what you build with your new knowledge!

*— Jason Lengstorf*
*VP of Developer Experience at Netlify*
*and host of Learn With Jason*

# Preface

Of all the technologies to emerge in the web development industry in recent years, perhaps none has generated as much attention and excitement as Gatsby, a static site generator based on React. Though Gatsby is touted for its ease of use, performance benefits, and versatility for use cases both simple and complex, it's equally vaunted for its developer experience advantages thanks to its use of GraphQL and high degree of extensibility.

When I first discovered Gatsby in 2017, the idea of the Jamstack, the architectural paradigm of which Gatsby is a prominent part, was still in its infancy. The concept of synthesizing new performance optimizations in browsers with a statically generated site hadn't yet taken the web development world by storm. In the years since, the pattern into which Gatsby fits has become a popular strategy emulated by other ecosystems in the JavaScript and static site generator landscape.

I also have a personal connection to Gatsby, having joined the core framework team and company in 2019 to lead product management for Gatsby Cloud, the hosting infrastructure underpinning many Gatsby sites. As of this writing, Gatsby has one of the most active and knowledgeable open source communities in existence, and I'm excited to see what's ahead in Gatsby's future. By the end of this book, you will be too!

## Who Should Read This Book

*Gatsby: The Definitive Guide* is a book that is intended to serve not only as an introduction to beginning, intermediate, and advanced use cases for developers working with Gatsby but also as a holistic reference to use while building Gatsby sites. To that end, it aims to be both edifying and exhaustive without veering too far to either extreme.

This book is intended for anyone in the web development world who is looking to work with Gatsby, whether you have experience with React or not. Though knowledge of JavaScript is helpful, many of the concepts that undergird Gatsby are understandable to those who have only previously worked in HTML and CSS, and *Gatsby: The Definitive Guide* provides a full introduction to the Jamstack pattern and an abridged primer on React and modern JavaScript.

If you're a web designer, a web developer, or even a programmer with limited knowledge of modern web development practices, this book is an ideal way to get started with Gatsby. But it also has plenty of new information for those already well versed in Jamstack and JavaScript technologies. And if you're looking to modernize your skill set in preparation for the coming decade of the web, this book is an excellent way to learn one of the technologies at the vanguard of frontend development.

# Why I Wrote This Book

*Gatsby: The Definitive Guide* isn't just the first book from O'Reilly on the topic of the Gatsby framework; it's also the first comprehensive guide to Gatsby, covering the foundations of what makes Gatsby great and the full range of what developers can achieve with Gatsby. It's the first-ever book that will give you a full understanding of both key elements of the Jamstack world and everything you need to equip yourself for success with Gatsby development.

As someone with a passion for both content management and modern web development, I authored this book with an eye toward enabling those who work at the intersection of cutting-edge digital experiences and leading frontend technologies. My own personal site has been powered by Gatsby for several years now, and both colleagues and casual observers have commented on its speed, despite the fact that it handles data originating from a variety of sources.

*Gatsby: The Definitive Guide* is my second book focused entirely on web development, following in the footsteps of my debut, *Decoupled Drupal in Practice* (Apress), which was the first comprehensive guide to decoupled Drupal. Just like that work, I wrote this book to provide others with the encyclopedic reference and comprehensive coverage I wish I had when I kicked off my own journey.

# Navigating This Book

*Gatsby: The Definitive Guide* consists of five overarching parts, each of which covers an essential facet of the Gatsby universe. The book is organized roughly as follows:

- Part I, *Elementary Gatsby* covers the foundational concepts behind Gatsby. Chapter 1 describes how to build your first Gatsby site and the what and why of Gatsby; Chapter 2 introduces the core elements of Gatsby; and Chapter 3 walks you through beginning use cases.

- Part II, *Data in Gatsby* covers the Gatsby data layer. Chapter 4 examines GraphQL and the Gatsby data layer; Chapters 5 through 7 introduce source plugins, programmatic page creation, and asset handling, respectively; and Chapter 8 guides you through intermediate data-driven use cases in Gatsby.

- Part III, *Extending Gatsby* explores the Gatsby ecosystem beyond the core framework. Chapter 9 delves into plugins and starters in greater depth, while Chapter 10 provides coverage of themes.

- Part IV, *Production Gatsby* illustrates what developers and architects need to know about taking Gatsby live in production. Chapter 11 dives into how best to debug and test Gatsby sites, and Chapter 12 tours various deployment options for Gatsby and a sampling of deployment approaches.

- Part V, *Advanced Gatsby* concludes the book with an array of advanced and expert-level topics. Chapter 13 covers advanced topics in Gatsby, such as schema customization and MDX, while Chapter 14 provides a brief tour of Gatsby's inner workings.

- The Appendices provide a quick and useful reference to some of the most important developer features in Gatsby, such as the command-line interface, component APIs, and configuration APIs.

# Conventions Used in This Book

The following typographical conventions are used in this book:

*Italic*
: Indicates new terms, URLs, email addresses, file and directory names, and file extensions.

`Constant width`
: Used for program listings, as well as within paragraphs to refer to program elements such as variable or function names, data types, environment variables, statements, and keywords.

**`Constant width bold`**
: Shows commands or other text that should be typed literally by the user. Also used for emphasis in program listings.

*`Constant width italic`*
: Shows text that should be replaced with user-supplied values or by values determined by context.

`>>>`
: Indicates code that wraps but should not be put on a new line.

This element signifies a tip or suggestion.

 This element signifies a general note.

 This element indicates a warning or caution.

# Using Code Examples

Supplemental material (code examples, exercises, etc.) is available for download online. The author's tutorial code is on GitHub (*https://github.com/prestonso/gtdg*). Illustrative code from *https://github.com/gatsbyjs/gatsby* is also included as guideposts or reference-only examples. You can find those file names at the beginning of code blocks.

If you have a technical question or a problem using the code examples, please email *bookquestions@oreilly.com*.

This book is here to help you get your job done. In general, if example code is offered with this book, you may use it in your programs and documentation. You do not need to contact us for permission unless you're reproducing a significant portion of the code. For example, writing a program that uses several chunks of code from this book does not require permission. Selling or distributing examples from O'Reilly books does require permission. Answering a question by citing this book and quoting example code does not require permission. Incorporating a significant amount of example code from this book into your product's documentation does require permission.

We appreciate, but do not require, attribution. An attribution usually includes the title, author, publisher, and ISBN. For example: "*Gatsby: The Definitive Guide*, by Preston So. Copyright 2021 Preston So, 978-1-492-08751-9."

If you feel your use of code examples falls outside fair use or the permission given above, feel free to contact us at *permissions@oreilly.com*.

## O'Reilly Online Learning

 For more than 40 years, *O'Reilly Media* has provided technology and business training, knowledge, and insight to help companies succeed.

Our unique network of experts and innovators share their knowledge and expertise through books, articles, and our online learning platform. O'Reilly's online learning platform gives you on-demand access to live training courses, in-depth learning paths, interactive coding environments, and a vast collection of text and video from O'Reilly and 200+ other publishers. For more information, visit *http://oreilly.com*.

## How to Contact Us

Please address comments and questions concerning this book to the publisher:

O'Reilly Media, Inc.
1005 Gravenstein Highway North
Sebastopol, CA 95472
800-998-9938 (in the United States or Canada)
707-829-0515 (international or local)
707-829-0104 (fax)

We have a web page for this book, where we list errata, examples, and any additional information. You can access this page at *https://oreil.ly/gatsby-guide*.

Email *bookquestions@oreilly.com* to comment or ask technical questions about this book.

For news and information about our books and courses, visit *http://www.oreilly.com*.

Find us on Facebook: *http://facebook.com/oreilly*

Follow us on Twitter: *http://twitter.com/oreillymedia*

Watch us on YouTube: *http://www.youtube.com/oreillymedia*

## Acknowledgments

Without the Gatsby community and my former colleagues at Gatsby, as well as personal connections around the world, this book would never have made it past the drawing board.

First and foremost, my fond thanks to my editor Jeff Bleiel, who has been a steadfast resource and sounding board throughout the entire writing process, even at the nadir of the still-ongoing coronavirus pandemic.

My gratitude also goes to Alexander Nnakuwe and David Mackey, the book's technical reviewers, whose comments have helped it attain a high level of quality and lasting relevance. In addition, Amanda Quinn was a spectacular resource at O'Reilly in working with me on the initial steps of this book, Katie Tozer has been fantastic to collaborate with as production editor, and Rachel Head gave this text an incredibly thorough review as copyeditor. Thanks also to proofreader Stephanie English and all of the O'Reilly production team for their stellar work.

Second, I'd be remiss not to thank my colleagues and friends at Gatsby, who made my time there edifying along multiple dimensions and helped me grow as a writer and a product leader. Big thanks must go to Sid Chatterjee, without whom this book would never have made it past the planning stage—his ideas and suggestions were instrumental to getting this process off the ground.

I also offer my profound gratitude to the Product and Design organization at Gatsby, who were among the finest teams I've ever had the privilege to work for and learn from: especially Marisa Morby, Florian Kissling, and Shannon Soper. Thanks also to my other colleagues at Gatsby, particularly Nat Alison, David Bailey, Chris Biscardi, Aisha Blake, Caitlin Cashin, Obinna Ekwuno, Kurt Kemple, Jason Lengstorf, Madalyn Parker, Amberley Romo, Marcy Sutton, and Hashim Warren, all of whom deeply inspired this project with their own work and left Gatsby in a better place in ways both human and technical.

Finally, thanks to all my former and current colleagues at companies including Time Inc., Acquia, and now Oracle who have been encouraging and understanding throughout this writing process. And a fond word of support to those, like me, who have felt excluded from many aspects of the technology industry due to systemic oppression in various forms—it's my hope that this work inspires you to contribute your important and much-needed voice to the discourse as well.

# PART I

# Elementary Gatsby

# CHAPTER 1

# Gatsby Fundamentals

Gatsby is an open source framework for building static sites, based on React. Commonly referred to as a *static site generator* (SSG), Gatsby is part of the Jamstack category of technologies, alongside other SSGs like Gridsome and JavaScript frameworks like Next.js, which also facilitates static site generation. Gatsby places particular emphasis on performance, scalability, and security, and it has a rich and growing ecosystem of plugins, themes, recipes, starters, and other contributed projects.

In this first chapter, we'll get acquainted with Gatsby. Though Gatsby's building blocks are pages and components, its internal data layer, made up of GraphQL and source plugins, acts as a bridge between data sources and the pages and components that are compiled at build time to produce a static site. Gatsby is built on React, so we'll also take a look at some JavaScript and React concepts that are essential for Gatsby developers to understand. Finally, we'll build our first Gatsby "Hello World" site, which will familiarize you with Gatsby's developer tooling.

## What Is Gatsby?

In short, Gatsby is a free and open source framework based on React for creating websites and web applications. But internally, its creator, Kyle Mathews, describes Gatsby as a complex and robust "web compiler"—a collection of building blocks that engage in data retrieval and rendering, page composition using components, linking across pages, and finally, compilation of components into a working static site.

In this section, we'll take a bird's-eye view of Gatsby's overarching architecture to help us understand its major components. In addition, we'll take a closer look at the three most important components of Gatsby: its basic building blocks (pages and components), the Gatsby data layer (GraphQL and source plugins), and the Gatsby ecosystem (plugins and themes that extend Gatsby's functionality).

# Gatsby Pages and Components

Gatsby leverages React components as its atomic unit for building websites. In other words, everything in Gatsby is built using components. To understand this more deeply, let's take a look at the typical Gatsby project structure:

```
/
|-- /.cache
|-- /plugins
|-- /public
|-- /src
    |-- /pages
    |    |-- index.js
    |-- /templates
    |    |-- article.js
    |-- html.js
|-- /static
|-- gatsby-config.js
|-- gatsby-node.js
|-- gatsby-ssr.js
|-- gatsby-browser.js
```

For the purposes of illustrating Gatsby's component-based architecture, let's imagine that this Gatsby project consists of a home page (*index.js*) that links to individual pages that adhere to an article template (*article.js*). This article template renders the full text of each article into a consistent template for individual articles. To simplify this example even further, let's assume that these articles are coming from an external database rather than from the local filesystem (something we'll cover in Chapters 4 and 5).

Gatsby has four main types of components, the first three of which we can readily identify in this sample project structure:

*Page components*

Page components become full-fledged Gatsby pages. Any component that is placed under *src/pages* becomes a page automatically assigned the path suggested by its name. For instance, if you place a *contact.js* or *contact.jsx* file containing a React component in *src/pages*, it will eventually be available at *<example.com>/ contact/*. In order for a file in *src/pages* to become a page, it must resolve to a string or React component.

*Page template components*

For relatively static pages, page components work well. But for pages that are templates, such as our article template, we need a reusable boilerplate according to which we'll render each article. It would be prohibitive to write a page component for each individual article, so instead of doing that, we prefer to write a single page template component through which all article data will flow. Page templates are located under the *src/templates* directory.

---

*The HTML component*

There is only one HTML component: *src/html.js*. This file is responsible for everything outside the area of the page that Gatsby controls. For instance, you can modify metadata contained in the `<head>` element and add other markup. Customizing this file is optional, as Gatsby also has a default *html.js* that it uses as a fallback.

*Non-page components*

These are the typical in-page React components. They are sections of a page, such as a header, that are embedded in a larger page component, forming a hierarchy. As we'll see later in the chapter, there are some non-page components that have greater importance, such as the layout component. I haven't included the *src/components* directory in our sample Gatsby codebase, but this is where our non-page components would appear.

The three types of components that Gatsby developers will spend the most time on are page components, page template components, and non-page components. But how does Gatsby know what data to use to populate the properties, or *props*, in those components? That's where GraphQL and Gatsby's data layer, which we'll explore in much more depth in Chapters 4 and 5, come in.

## Gatsby's Data Layer: GraphQL and Source Plugins

*GraphQL* is a query language that enables highly tailored queries. In the Representational State Transfer (REST) model, clients cannot define which data they receive from the server—that is a server-side responsibility. GraphQL takes a different approach, allowing clients to define their data requirements according to an arbitrary structure. The server then not only returns the needed data, but returns it according to the same structure the client sent in the request. This is the primary advantage of GraphQL.

For a full overview of GraphQL and how it works in Gatsby, consult Chapter 4. For now, this conceptual understanding is sufficient to understand GraphQL's role in Gatsby.

GraphQL is frequently used as a replacement or enhancement on top of APIs that use the REST paradigm, commonly known as *RESTful APIs* or *REST APIs*, which instead return data as defined by the server, not the client. In many content and commerce architectures, for example, GraphQL is used to retrieve data from third-party services and data providers such as databases and content management systems (CMSs) for use in an application. In these use cases, there is a GraphQL server that is constantly running, ready to respond to any incoming GraphQL query.

Gatsby, however, leverages GraphQL for an additional purpose: declarations of *internal* data requirements. Rather than consuming GraphQL from external sources as a client, Gatsby places GraphQL front-and-center to conduct data retrieval and handling at build time, not runtime. In other words, whereas many frameworks use GraphQL solely to consume data externally, Gatsby instead uses GraphQL internally so that many different data sources can be combined into a single GraphQL API.

A typical Gatsby site might pull from many different sources of data. The disparate data structures then need to be harmonized into a format that developers can easily consume in Gatsby. Gatsby might pull from an internal filesystem for data directly embedded in the Gatsby site, or it might perform API calls during the build process to a separate CMS or commerce platform. Gatsby could even pull from a GraphQL API to populate its own internal GraphQL API. And it can pull data from all of these sources at once into a single unified GraphQL API that makes the data easily accessible and straightforward to consume.

Each Gatsby component contains a GraphQL query that dictates the data that populates that component's props. Though you can certainly declare data directly within the component, chances are you have data from other sources you want to pull into your Gatsby site. How does Gatsby achieve this?

In Gatsby, *plugins* are additional functionality that can be layered on top of an existing Gatsby site. Certain plugins might extend Gatsby's core functionality, but there is one type of plugin that is particularly important due to its key role in the retrieval of data from external sources: *source plugins*.

In Gatsby, source plugins are Node.js packages that fetch data from its source, whatever that source may be. Gatsby offers many source plugins for a variety of systems that emit data, including APIs, databases, CMSs, commerce systems, and even local filesystems. For instance, `gatsby-source-filesystem` pulls data directly from the internal filesystem of Gatsby, whether it's Markdown or something else. Meanwhile, `gatsby-source-drupal` and `gatsby-source-contentful` pull content from the Drupal and Contentful CMSs, respectively.

We'll return to source plugins in short order, but first let's take a look at the Gatsby ecosystem, which includes source plugins and a variety of other add-ons that improve the Gatsby developer experience.

## The Gatsby Ecosystem

The *Gatsby ecosystem* encompasses all the community-contributed plugins and other modules that introduce new functionality to Gatsby. There are four types of projects in the Gatsby ecosystem:

*Plugins*

As we defined at a surface level in the previous section, plugins in Gatsby are Node.js packages that provide crucial functionality to Gatsby core. For instance, the `gatsby-image` plugin can be added to Gatsby sites by developers who need robust image handling. Gatsby plugins run the gamut from sitemap and RSS feed functionality to offline and search engine optimization (SEO) support.

*Themes*

A Gatsby theme is a kind of plugin that contains a *gatsby-config.js* file, just like a regular Gatsby site. This file provides arbitrarily defined configuration—prebuilt functionality, data sourcing in the form of source plugins, and interface code—to Gatsby sites. This means that a Gatsby site can become a Gatsby theme, which is installed as a package into another Gatsby site to extend it with reusable functionality.

*Starters*

In the Gatsby ecosystem, starters are boilerplate templates that developers can easily clone onto their own machines as a starting point for Gatsby development. Once modified by a developer, however, starters bear no ongoing relationship to their original state, unlike themes. Gatsby provides a long list of official starters for typical use cases, and it also has a rich process for building your own.

*Recipes*

New to Gatsby and still experimental, recipes are tools that are invoked in the Gatsby CLI to automate certain common responsibilities like creating pages, installing plugins, supporting TypeScript, and more. As of this writing, Gatsby has released roughly a dozen example recipes as well as information on how to write your own recipes.

We'll explore each of these types of Gatsby ecosystem projects, but now that you're equipped with a basic understanding of what Gatsby is, you may be wondering: Why should I use Gatsby? What's in it for me?

# Why Gatsby?

In this section, we'll analyze some of the unique advantages and rationales that motivate developers to choose Gatsby for their next website projects. Gatsby has gained a reputation in the JavaScript and Jamstack communities for its focus on four key pillars: performance, accessibility, developer experience, and security.

## Performance

Many websites today remain primarily server-driven, which means servers respond to each individual request issued by a browser. Gatsby, however, emphasizes performance enhancements at every level, including *payload optimization* (minimizing the size of the file sent down the wire to the browser) and *delivery optimization* (minimizing the time it takes to get there).

Here are the four primary means by which Gatsby enhances performance:

*Static site delivery*
When you perform a Gatsby build, the result is a collection of static assets that can be uploaded to any content delivery network (CDN), located in the *public* folder in the Gatsby project root. This means that Gatsby sites primarily consist of static HTML, which loads quickly in a browser. Only then is further client-side JavaScript, such as that provided by React, initialized.

*Build-time compilation*
Gatsby engages in build-time compilation to produce static files, rather than runtime compilation, which is much more granular and might render only a single page. Instead, build-time compilation renders a full set of static pages—this means requests to external data sources never introduce additional latency to the overall delivery time, because the result is a set of static files with data prepopulated, not a page that needs to retrieve and render data upon request. In this way, build-time compilation limits the amount of work servers usually need to perform for web applications that are chattier. Gatsby can leverage both build-time and runtime compilation, depending on which is more optimal for performance.

*Payload optimization*
Gatsby works hard to limit the size of the eventual payload delivered to users by reducing the sizes of images and JavaScript files, delaying the loading of any images below the fold (the unseen part of the browser viewport upon page load), and inlining CSS where necessary. Gatsby also includes automated route-based code splitting (so only code for a needed route is loaded), background prefetching (so assets can load in the background), and lazy loading of assets that aren't immediately needed.

*Delivery optimization*
Gatsby sites are optimized to be served from a CDN, which lends itself to faster delivery of deployed code. Depending on your requirements, this model can be a substantial improvement over the historical paradigm, in which every incoming request from a browser would need to return to the origin server and database (though extensive caching can mitigate this on non-Gatsby sites).

Thanks to static site delivery and build-time compilation, Gatsby sites consist mostly of HTML rather than a slew of JavaScript files. And thanks to payload optimization and delivery optimization, Gatsby sites load quickly at the edge and stay small.

# Accessibility

Once a fringe concern, accessibility is becoming an important consideration for businesses and organizations across the market. Single-page JavaScript applications have until recently been notorious for their poor support for assistive technologies and lack of consideration for different access needs. Gatsby treats accessibility as a first-class citizen by focusing on providing accessible markup and accessible routing, in addition to delivering static HTML rather than highly dynamic JavaScript:

*Accessible markup*
> Gatsby provides by default the `eslint-plugin-jsx-a11y` package, which is an accessibility linting tool for code. This package looks for missing alternative text for images and correct usage of Accessible Rich Internet Applications (ARIA) properties, among other potential issues.

*Accessible routing*
> Most JavaScript applications use dynamic page navigation to allow a user to click a link and see the page rerender immediately rather than incurring an additional page load by the browser. This dynamic routing, however, can be impossible for disabled users to use with the same convenience as normal hyperlinks. Gatsby ships with the `@reach/router` library, which supports scroll restoration and accessible dynamic navigation, and it also ensures that Gatsby links function accessibly.

 Web accessibility is becoming an increasingly pressing problem for many organizations. For more information about ARIA, consult the Web Accessibility Initiative's website (*https://oreil.ly/ku3Bv*). Gatsby has consistently expressed a commitment to better accessibility in its own ecosystem, including the publication of an accessibility statement (*https://oreil.ly/0jx6Q*) on its website.

# Developer Experience

To make development as seamless as possible, and to enable developers to save time when building websites, Gatsby offers a range of developer experience features (especially for repetitive tasks), including:

*Scaffolding with starters and minimal configuration*
> Gatsby starters allow for almost zero configuration and provide a fully scaffolded directory structure. All starters are fully functional Gatsby sites and can be immediately deployed. Though it's possible to create a Gatsby site from scratch, it's highly recommended to use one of the existing official starters, and that's the approach we take in this book.

*Local development environment with hot reloading*
> Gatsby provides a local development environment with hot reloading whenever code changes are saved. This facilitates a rapid feedback loop, where developers see their modifications immediately reflected in their working site. We'll return to Gatsby's local development environment in "Creating Your First Gatsby Site" on page 24.

*GraphiQL and GraphQL Explorer*
> In addition to providing GraphQL, Gatsby also provides, out of the box, developer tools that aid those who need to consume data through GraphQL. GraphiQL, a GUI that provides debugging, and GraphQL Explorer, a schema explorer for GraphQL, are both packaged with Gatsby by default.

*Built-in linting and testing*
> Gatsby also includes in its core package a variety of built-in tests and linting processes that allow you to check for concerns such as adherence to coding standards, loyalty to accessibility rules, and other issues of quality assurance that emerge during the development process.

*Continuous integration and continuous deployment (CI/CD)*
> Finally, Gatsby integrates gracefully with a variety of infrastructure providers that offer rich capabilities for continuous integration (CI) and continuous deployment (CD). Some of the most common hosts for Gatsby include Netlify, Vercel, and Gatsby Cloud.

## Security

These days, security is one of the most essential concerns plaguing traditional websites. Many websites still leverage monolithic architectures whose systems may be vulnerable to unmitigated access by attackers, especially when there is no protection between layers like databases and authentication providers. Others require actively running databases and servers, which can facilitate another vector for vulnerabilities if not architected carefully.

Because Gatsby delivers its sites as static HTML and not as dynamic code that includes information about the APIs or data sources it is consuming from, Gatsby automatically obfuscates external data sources, protecting them from unwanted eyes. For content and commerce system maintainers, this can be particularly useful, because those data sources can be shut down whenever they aren't needed by an ongoing Gatsby build or an editor who wishes to update data. Security is a multifaceted topic that we will return to throughout this book, but Gatsby's static site delivery ensures a rock-solid firewall between your markup and your data sources.

Now that you have a sense of some of the motivations behind why so many developers choose Gatsby, let's contextualize it within the larger landscape of architectural paradigms and JavaScript development with React.

While Gatsby is a standalone framework for building highly performant websites and web applications, it is part of a larger trend toward web frameworks that prize build-time rather than runtime compilation, serverless over server-dependent architectures, and performance optimizations across the stack. In the next section, we'll look at how Gatsby fits into the larger contexts of Jamstack architectures, JavaScript, and React.

 If you already understand the background behind Gatsby and the Jamstack and wish to get started immediately with code, you can skip to "Getting Going with Gatsby" on page 22.

# Gatsby and the Jamstack

We've covered the architectural underpinnings of why organizations have migrated to architectures that are less monolithic and more decoupled than before. But to understand why developers and engineering teams have made similar moves, we need to explore the *Jamstack* (also written *JAMstack*), an architectural paradigm that juggles JavaScript, APIs, and static markup to facilitate high-performance websites.

In this section, we'll first cover SSGs, which presaged the Jamstack by providing a build-time means of website deployment as opposed to runtime. Then, we'll cover distributed content and commerce, a contemporaneous paradigm shift occurring in content and commerce architectures. Finally, we'll combine SSGs and content and commerce architectures to define and outline what the Jamstack is and how Gatsby fits into the Jamstack landscape.

## Static Site Generators

At its most basic level, Gatsby is an SSG. SSGs are tools that generate static HTML files based on a template and data furnished by an external database or other source (such as a spreadsheet). Given this data input, they then apply styles and templates, which can be written in templating languages like Markdown, Liquid, or others, to the data based on logic written by the developer.

Unlike typical dynamic web applications, which usually require an actively running server and execute at runtime, SSGs yield a series of static files and assets that don't require anything more than a filesystem on a web server. Because they're run manually, typically through a terminal command, they execute at build time, which means that they only run when the state of the static assets needs updating.

The first wave of SSGs were primarily rooted in server-side technologies to perform static site generation and processing of data into templates. For instance, though the still-popular Jekyll and Hugo are written in server-only languages like Ruby and Go, other older SSGs, like Metalsmith, are written in Node.js and JavaScript. Though the first generation of SSGs were optimal for small websites with limited content and dynamism, they lacked entirely the interactivity found in JavaScript applications.

In recent years, a second generation of SSGs has emerged, particularly in the JavaScript ecosystem. These differ considerably from older tools like Jekyll and Hugo in that they connect static files to dynamic client-side JavaScript that injects asynchronous rendering and other mainstays of interactive JavaScript into normally unchanging static sites. Because they rely on the client-side capabilities of JavaScript frameworks, rather than being associated with server-side languages, these SSGs link themselves with JavaScript frameworks. Gatsby and Next.js, for example, fall into the category of React-powered SSGs, whereas Gridsome and Nuxt.js are part of the Vue ecosystem.

This brings us to the first of several definitions of the framework we cover in this book: Gatsby is first and foremost an SSG based on React. But to examine precisely why Gatsby emerged in the first place and the reasons behind its success, we need to zoom out to a much wider perspective on how Gatsby resolves many persistent issues surrounding content and commerce website implementations: through distributed content and commerce and through the Jamstack.

## Distributed Content and Commerce

In recent years, thanks to the emergence of frameworks like Gatsby, a new architectural paradigm has begun to emerge in the form of *distributed content and commerce* (the content variant of this is sometimes referred to as the "content mesh").

One of the most important issues facing any content and commerce implementation is the availability of third-party integrations and plugins or extensions that make those third-party integrations available to a website implementation. Many of these plugins handle small concerns important to content and commerce, such as a search tool or a checkout system. During the era of monolithic content and commerce, most plugin ecosystems were tightly contained, as shown in Figure 1-1. WordPress plugins, for instance, were never interchangeable with Drupal modules.

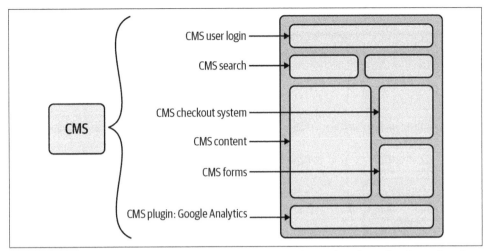

*Figure 1-1. Monolithic content and commerce systems have closed marketplaces for plu-gins that aren't interchangeable with other systems*

Another reason for the emergence of distributed content and commerce architectures was the increasing concern about the long-term maintenance of these plugins. If a checkout system maintainer decides to leave their open source project behind or to delist their plugin from a closed-source marketplace, the resulting disruption has an outsized impact on the ability of a user of that plugin to continue to make a checkout system available, especially if the plugin is proprietary. Often, the only solution is to rebuild the plugin from scratch or to architect a custom implementation.

In the last several years, as seen in Figure 1-2, interest has grown among developers in *interchangeable in-page services* that they can swap out as newer services emerge. A new class of startups offers in-page widgets and third-party services that are agnostic to content and commerce ecosystems, meaning that they can be used in any website implementation (though they still present long-term maintenance issues, in that they can also cease to exist). These companies include services like Algolia, which provides search features; Snipcart, which provides a shopping cart and checkout process; and Typeform, which offers easily managed webforms.

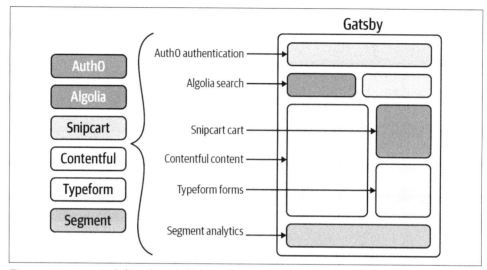

*Figure 1-2. A typical distributed CMS architecture, showing Gatsby containing a variety of interchangeable in-page services from third-party providers, thus preventing ecosystem lock-in*

Today, a content and commerce implementation might need to pull data from multiple sources in order to populate a website, with backend data providers being added and removed behind the scenes. Moreover, a content and commerce implementation might require a multifaceted combination of interchangeable in-page services that can be switched out as developers see fit. All this points to a more *distributed* future for content and commerce architectures that permits developers to leverage a diverse array of data sources, and just as diverse a range of third-party plugins and services.

## The Jamstack

Let's discuss the Jamstack in isolation before we turn to what makes Jamstack architectures so different from other (namely monolithic and decoupled) architectures.

Jamstack frameworks and methodologies introduce the notion of *build-time rendering*. In Jamstack architectures, an SSG is responsible for performing the rendering once a build begins. During a build, the SSG's *JavaScript* is responsible for retrieving data from *APIs* (such as content and commerce providers) and rendering that data into static markup. The result of the build is a collection of static assets that can be uploaded to any filesystem, rather than a constantly running database, web server, or server-side application.

Thereafter, developers can choose to place those statically generated assets on a CDN to ensure rapid delivery at the edge (i.e., as close as possible geographically to the user's location) and any required caching.

## Differences between Jamstack and other architectures

On the other hand, traditional architectures—especially monolithic and many decoupled content and commerce implementations—perform *runtime rendering*, which occurs only when a user requests a website page. Rather than a build, an underlying database, constantly humming along, receives a request and provides the necessary data to another actively running server-side application, which is then deployed to a constantly running web server. This undesirable behavior is mitigated in most implementations through aggressive caching and a CDN.

Before the emergence of Jamstack architectures, all server-side JavaScript applications leveraged a constantly running Node.js web server. And all monolithic content and commerce architectures follow this pattern. As for decoupled content and commerce architectures, it depends on whether build-time or runtime rendering is occurring. Though distributed content and commerce architectures lend themselves most favorably to build-time rendering, it's possible to implement runtime rendering as well.

The most important disadvantage of runtime rendering is that it produces only individual pages that are delivered on the wire. These pages can certainly be placed on a CDN and be aggressively cached, but each time a new page is requested that is unavailable in the CDN or in cached form, runtime rendering needs to occur all over again.

## Serverless infrastructure

Today, there are a wide range of infrastructure providers that provide build-time rendering and CDN support for Jamstack implementations, especially those in Gatsby. Collectively, these infrastructure providers are known as *serverless* because they do not rely on constantly running server instances to power functionality like runtime rendering, which doesn't occur in Jamstack implementations. Serverless hosts typically require three elements for a Jamstack deployment to succeed:

- A static site codebase, typically a repository in a source control system such as GitHub
- A build command, which triggers the build and rendering process conducted by the serverless host
- A deployment target, representing the URL where the statically generated assets will be placed

One of the most commonly used serverless infrastructure providers is Netlify. Others include Vercel (formerly Zeit), the creator of the Next.js framework; Amazon's AWS Amplify; and Gatsby Cloud, which specializes in Gatsby implementations.

Now that you have an understanding of some of the underpinnings of the Jamstack, let's take a look at how Gatsby fits in the larger world of JavaScript and how it leverages JavaScript and React, a JavaScript library for building UIs.

# JavaScript in Gatsby

A comprehensive overview of JavaScript's core concepts and history is outside the scope of this book, but let's highlight a few of the most salient concepts that are essential to working with Gatsby as a developer.

 This section is not intended as an end-to-end guide to JavaScript. It is geared toward developers who already have some experience with the language, but before the emergence of server-side JavaScript. For a more holistic approach to learning JavaScript, consult David Flanagan's *JavaScript: The Definitive Guide*, 7th edition (O'Reilly) or Kyle Simpson's *You Don't Know JavaScript*.

JavaScript is one of only two programming languages that can be executed in a web browser (the other, which as of this writing remains without widespread support, is WebAssembly). It's characterized by its imperative orientation, weak typing, prototype-based inheritance (though class-based inheritance is possible in newer iterations of JavaScript), and functional nature.

In the earliest years of JavaScript's history, it was used primarily to decorate static web pages with limited interactivity and asynchronous rendering. Today, however, JavaScript is among the most important languages in web development, and those who have worked with JavaScript in past decades, but not this one, will find that many aspects of the JavaScript developer experience have changed considerably—including CLIs and how modern JavaScript displays modularity.

## Command-Line Interfaces

CLIs are text-based interfaces that developers use to interact with filesystems on their local machines and to provide tooling for application development, dependency handling, and deployment. Though the earliest CLIs were written in low-level languages such as Shell or Bash, today, many of these interfaces are written in JavaScript through Node.js (or still other languages like Rust and Go).

Node.js, the JavaScript runtime used for server-side rendering (SSR) and universal JavaScript approaches, isn't just useful for JavaScript that needs to be executed outside the browser environment. It's also useful for JavaScript that needs to be executed on computers to manipulate files and perform other actions that are important to application development. For instance, many JavaScript applications require the download of many dependencies, often third-party libraries that are maintained by other developers in the JavaScript space.

Today, JavaScript dependencies are downloaded and managed by *package managers* that facilitate the retrieval of dependency libraries and their interpolation into an application that needs them. The most popular package managers are Node Package Manager (NPM) (*https://npmjs.org*) and Yarn (*https://yarnpkg.com*), which each provide a vast collection of packages. Though many of these packages can be dependencies that become small portions of application code, other packages contain CLIs that can be installed globally and whose commands can be invoked anywhere in the local filesystem.

The Gatsby CLI, which we cover in "Getting Going with Gatsby" on page 22, is an example of a JavaScript-driven CLI that is typically installed globally by invoking the command:

```
$ npm install -g gatsby-cli
```

NPM and Yarn are the most popular approaches to both dependency management and CLI installation in the JavaScript world.

## Modular JavaScript

JavaScript today exhibits considerable *modularity*, which wasn't the case when the language was first introduced in the 1990s. At the time, most JavaScript code was written either in a single embedded JavaScript file, which might have a colossal file size, or in multiple JavaScript files embedded in succession, indicating an order of execution. As JavaScript applications became more complex in the late 2000s and early 2010s, many developers recognized that a better approach to modularity was necessary.

*ES6* (ECMAScript 2015) was the first version of JavaScript to introduce the concept of *modules* natively. In short, modules are isolated JavaScript files that have relationships to other JavaScript files in the application by means of *exports* and *imports*. Consider two JavaScript files, one providing a module and the other consuming that module (this example is adapted from *Exploring ES6* by Axel Rauschmayer). Here's the first one:

```
// lib.js
export const sqrt = Math.sqrt
export function sq(x) {
  return x * x
}
export function diag(x, y) {
  return sqrt(sq(x) + sq(y))
}
```

If this is a library that we want to import as a module into another application, we can either import only the exported functions that we need by referring to them by name:

```
// app.js
import { sq, diag } from 'lib'
console.log(sq(5))
// 25
console.log(diag(4, 3))
// 5
```

Or we can import the entire module and refer to it under the namespace we assign:

```
// app.js
import * as lib from 'lib'
console.log(lib.sq(5))
// 25
console.log(lib.diag(4, 3))
// 5
```

Many JavaScript frameworks and JavaScript applications use modules to pass values, functions, and classes between one another so they can be invoked and used in other areas of the application. Gatsby is no exception, and neither is React, a declarative library in JavaScript for writing component-driven UIs. In the next section, we'll work through a rapid-fire introduction to the core React concepts you need to know to be successful with Gatsby and contextualize Gatsby within the larger React ecosystem.

 This was but a short introduction to ES6 modules and modular JavaScript in general; the full range of module syntax and approaches is outside the scope of this book. For a more comprehensive overview, I recommend *Exploring ES6 (https://oreil.ly/KHinP)* by Axel Rauschmayer or the Mozilla Developer Network's guide on modules (*https://oreil.ly/e6iLx*).

# React in Gatsby

React defines itself as a JavaScript library for building UIs, but it is perhaps better described as a declarative, component-based approach to writing interactive UIs. Originally created by Facebook, React is now one of the most popular libraries for building JavaScript applications in existence. Gatsby is built on top of React and inherits many of its concepts.

Providing a comprehensive overview of React would be impossible here, but throughout the book, we will deal with many React concepts. While there is much more to discover when it comes to React, the most important ideas to understand for now are declarative rendering, co-location of rendering and logic in React components, and passing values between React components by using React props.

This section is not intended as a full end-to-end guide to React. For a more holistic approach to learning React, consult *Learning React*, 2nd edition, by Alex Banks and Eve Porcello (O'Reilly).

## Declarative Rendering with JSX

*JSX* is the name given to a syntax extension that most React developers use to perform rendering in React. Consider, for instance, this "Hello World" example:

```
const el = <h1>Hello, world!</h1>
```

Though JSX is similar in appearance to HTML or a templating language, it is actually interpreted as JavaScript syntax by React. When executed, this code will construct an HTML element and prepare it for insertion into the Document Object Model (DOM). The actual insertion looks like this:

```
const el = <h1>Hello, world!</h1>

ReactDOM.render(
  el,
  document.getElementById('root')
)
```

Most React applications, before any rendering has taken place, consist solely of a `<div id="root"></div>` within the `<body>` element. React will render any elements declared in JSX within that HTML element.

JSX also allows for expressions within element declarations, unlike HTML:

```
const el =
  <h1>Hello, world! The current time is {Date().toLocaleString()}.</h1>

ReactDOM.render(
  el,
  document.getElementById('root')
)
```

Note that certain HTML attributes need to be named differently in JSX due to conflicts with existing keywords in JavaScript, or due to React's stylistic preference for `camelCase`:

```
const el = <div tabIndex="0"></div>
const el = <div className="hero-image"></div>
```

You can't use double quotes in JSX (as they are interpreted differently by JavaScript), so all string interpolation into JSX attributes should occur within curly braces:

```
const el = <img src={article.heroImageUrl} />
```

JSX can also allow for nested elements within others. For multiline element declarations, it's best to surround them in parentheses so JavaScript interprets them as expressions:

```
const el = (
  <div className="hero-image">
    <img src={article.heroImageUrl} />
  </div>
)
```

Let's see an example of how Babel, a compiler for JavaScript that can compile JSX into raw JavaScript, compiles JSX into JavaScript. The following code is equivalent to the code in the previous example:

```
const el = React.createElement(
  "div",
  {
    className: "hero-image"
  },
  React.createElement(
    "img",
    {
      src: article.heroImageUrl
    }
  )
);
```

Now that you have an understanding of how React utilizes JSX to perform declarative rendering, we can turn our attention to React's component-driven approach to UI development.

## React Components

React displays a clear preference for co-location of two primary concerns that are important to application development: markup and logic. Unlike many historical approaches, which separate markup and logic arbitrarily into distinct files, React instead operates on *components* that contain both the rendering code and the data management logic in order to promote co-locating both responsibilities in a single file. For this reason, the declarative rendering we saw in the previous section is typically accompanied in each file by logic that governs the data to be rendered.

You can define a component either as a function or as a class:

```
// Function component
function HeroImage(props) {
  return (
```

```
      <div className="hero-image">
        <img src={props.heroImageUrl} />
      </div>
    )
  }

  // Class component
  class HeroImage extends React.Component {
    render() {
      return (
        <div className="hero-image">
          <img src={this.props.heroImageUrl} />
        </div>
      )
    }
  }
```

Up until now, we've only employed standard HTML elements to define the internal declarative rendering that occurs within a component. But React allows for components to be reused after they are defined as new JSX elements. When React comes across a JSX element that is equivalent to a component rather than an existing HTML element, it will pass the attributes and children contained inside that element declaration to the component as an object known in React parlance as *props* (short for "properties").

## React Props

Consider the following example, where we have replaced the URL for the article's hero image with a new value contained within the props as we declare the element. Here, the resulting HTML is `<img src="https://img.example.com/hero.jpg" />`:

```
  class HeroImage extends React.Component {
    render() {
      return <img src={this.props.src} />
    }
  }

  const el = <HeroImage src="https://img.example.com/hero.jpg" />

  ReactDOM.render(
    el,
    document.getElementById('root')
  )
```

Most new React applications contain a single root-level App component that represents the entire application as well as the components contained therein. In this example, we create a new overarching App component that contains the other component we've just created:

```
class HeroImage extends React.Component {
  render() {
    return <img src={this.props.src} />
  }
}

class App extends React.Component {
  render() {
    return <HeroImage src="https://img.example.com/hero.jpg" />
  }
)

ReactDOM.render(
  <App />,
  document.getElementById('root')
)
```

Note that in React, props are read-only within components, regardless of whether they are defined as a function or a class. React has a strict rule that applies to all props: "All React components must act like pure functions with respect to their props." In other words, a component must not modify its own props; it must only use them to return a predictable result. Pure functions never modify their inputs.

 Some of the React syntax we've seen so far, including JSX and React's component-driven approach, bears quite a bit of resemblance to Web Components and custom elements. However, JSX and Web Components should not be conflated with one another as they are fundamentally incompatible. Web Components is now available in all modern browsers, but React requires the full scope of the React library to function properly. As of this writing, React facilitates the use of React in Web Components and vice versa, but they cannot be merged.

As new React concepts surface during our deep examination of Gatsby concepts, we'll explore them in the context of Gatsby rather than in isolation. Gatsby employs React extensively to power its underpinnings in terms of component and props handling. Now, let's build our first Gatsby site!

# Getting Going with Gatsby

Now that you have a full understanding of how Gatsby fits into the worlds of JavaScript and React, it's time to get started with our first Gatsby site. In this section, we'll focus solely on setting up a local development environment for Gatsby and creating a Gatsby site based on a starter, which as you saw earlier is Gatsby parlance for a boilerplate site template.

## The Command Line

Like many other web development tools, Gatsby makes extensive use of the com-mand line, the text-based interface that allows developers to manipulate files and folders within a computer rather than through graphical means. Also known as the *terminal*, the command line is the primary means of interacting with the local devel-opment environment that Gatsby provides as a foundation for implementation.

To find the command line on your local machine:

- On macOS, open the *Utilities* folder in *Applications*. Open the Terminal applica-tion.
- On Windows 10, click the Start button and type **cmd**. Then, select Command Prompt from the returned search results.
- On Linux, open the application menu on the desktop, type "Terminal" to search for applications, and select Terminal.

> If you're already familiar with the command line and have Node.js and Git installed, you can proceed to the next section.

On all three command lines, you can execute a command by typing the command (such as pwd, which prints the path to the current working directory into the termi-nal, or cd, which changes directories from where you executed the command to dive into a designated directory) and hitting the Enter key.

## Installing the Gatsby CLI

The Gatsby CLI is the primary instrument developers can use to interact with Gatsby sites. It's a tool that can scaffold and spin up Gatsby sites very quickly, and it contains various commands that are useful for developing Gatsby sites. It's published as an NPM package, so the Gatsby CLI can be installed on any computer with Node.js installed.

To install the Gatsby CLI, execute the following NPM command. It is highly recom-mended to install Gatsby CLI globally using the -g flag so you can scaffold new Gatsby sites anywhere in your local machine's filesystem:

```
$ npm install -g gatsby-cli
```

The first time you install the Gatsby CLI, a message will appear informing you about Gatsby telemetry, which collects anonymous usage data about Gatsby commands to guide future development of the framework. To avoid the gathering of telemetry data, opt out when the message appears using the following command:

```
$ gatsby telemetry --disable
```

To see all available executable commands represented in the Gatsby CLI, run the help command:

```
$ gatsby --help
```

 Some computers, especially work computers, restrict the ability for users to install NPM packages globally using the -g flag and to impersonate a root user using the sudo command. The Gatsby documentation recommends consulting one of the following guides to resolve permission issues that may arise due to how computers are configured:

- Resolve EACCES permissions errors when installing packages globally (*https://oreil.ly/kJ3TP*)
- Install NPM packages globally without sudo on macOS and Linux (*https://oreil.ly/pqikv*)

Now that you've successfully executed your first Gatsby command, you're ready to create your first Gatsby site using the Gatsby CLI. Instead of building the site from scratch, which can be time-consuming, we'll start with Gatsby's "Hello World" starter.

## Creating Your First Gatsby Site

Gatsby starters are boilerplate templates that contain partially implemented Gatsby sites with some initial configuration. Starters are designed to make it as painless and easy as possible to create a new site for a particular use case. The bare-bones "Hello World" starter contains the base-level requirements for a typical Gatsby site.

To create a new site based on the Gatsby "Hello World" starter, open your terminal and run the gatsby new command, which creates a new project in the directory you specify immediately afterward (if you execute the command without any arguments, the Gatsby CLI will open an interactive shell where you can supply certain parameters):

```
$ gatsby new hello-world \
  https://github.com/gatsbyjs/gatsby-starter-hello-world
```

You can supply an arbitrary directory name, since if it doesn't exist, the Gatsby CLI will go ahead and create the directory for you—for example:

```
$ gatsby new my-new-gatsby-site \
    https://github.com/gatsbyjs/gatsby-starter-hello-world
```

The final portion of the command beginning with `https://` is the URL at which the starter code is housed. Gatsby uses GitHub to manage its starter codebase repositories.

Now, you can change into the directory in which the "Hello World" starter was downloaded:

```
$ cd hello-world
```

If you gave the directory a different name, use that instead, as in:

```
$ cd my-new-gatsby-site
```

To see the files and directories encompassing the "Hello World" starter, you can issue the list command (`ls`). By executing the following command within the directory you've just changed into, you'll be able to see what the root folder of a typical Gatsby site looks like. The `-la` flag instructs the terminal to show all files, including those whose names begin with a period (`.`), and certain details about them:

```
$ ls -la
```

The output of this command is a list of the files and directories in the project:

```
total 1032
drwxr-xr-x   14 prestonso    staff      448 May 16 12:37 .
drwxr-xr-x    6 prestonso    staff      192 May 16 12:37 ..
drwxr-xr-x   12 prestonso    staff      384 May 16 12:37 .git
-rw-r--r--    1 prestonso    staff      974 May 16 12:37 .gitignore
-rw-r--r--    1 prestonso    staff       45 May 16 12:37 .prettierignore
-rw-r--r--    1 prestonso    staff       46 May 16 12:37 .prettierrc
-rw-r--r--    1 prestonso    staff      675 May 16 12:37 LICENSE
-rw-r--r--    1 prestonso    staff     5866 May 16 12:37 README.md
-rw-r--r--    1 prestonso    staff      177 May 16 12:37 gatsby-config.js
drwxr-xr-x 1051 prestonso    staff    33632 May 16 12:37 node_modules
-rw-r--r--    1 prestonso    staff      822 May 16 12:37 package.json
drwxr-xr-x    3 prestonso    staff       96 May 16 12:37 src
drwxr-xr-x    3 prestonso    staff       96 May 16 12:37 static
-rw-r--r--    1 prestonso    staff   492120 May 16 12:37 yarn.lock
```

But we're not done! Simply seeing a list of the files and directories of a Gatsby site isn't enough—we want to see it in a browser. However, to view our Gatsby site in a browser environment when it's still offline, we'll need to spin up a local development server. We'll do that next.

## Starting a Development Server

To view a Gatsby site that isn't yet online in a web browser, we need to find some way for the browser to be able to access that Gatsby site. This means that we need to set up a *local development server* that can mimic a website that's online and can approximate as closely as possible the experience of visiting our Gatsby site in a browser.

The Gatsby CLI contains a development mode that starts up a new local development server on your behalf. To enter development mode and start the local development server, execute the following command in the root directory of your Gatsby site:

```
$ gatsby develop
```

As part of the messages the terminal will display from the Gatsby CLI, you will see a URL such as *http://localhost:8000*. Here, *localhost* means that we are accessing the Gatsby "Hello World" site we scaffolded on our local machine rather than fetching it from an external URL online somewhere. This means that we don't need an internet connection to access *localhost* URLs.

Open the browser of your choice and navigate to *http://localhost:8000* or the URL indicated in your terminal. There, you'll see a message saying "Hello world!" Nice work—you've just built your first Gatsby site, as you can see in Figure 1-3!

```
success createSchemaCustomization - 0.005s
success Checking for changed pages - 0.005s
success source and transform nodes - 0.118s
success building schema - 0.341s
info Total nodes: 18, SitePage nodes: 1 (use --verbose for breakdown)
success createPages - 0.010s
success Checking for changed pages - 0.002s
success createPagesStatefully - 0.070s
success update schema - 0.043s
success write out redirect data - 0.004s
success onPostBootstrap - 0.006s
info bootstrap finished - 5.072s
success onPreExtractQueries - 0.003s
success extract queries from components - 0.127s
success write out requires - 0.008s
success run page queries - 0.045s - 2/2 44.28/s

You can now view gatsby-starter-hello-world in the browser.

  http://localhost:8000/

View GraphiQL, an in-browser IDE, to explore your site's data and schema

  http://localhost:8000/___graphql

Note that the development build is not optimized.
To create a production build, use gatsby build

success Building development bundle - 6.839s
```

*Figure 1-3. Our first Gatsby site! Note the localhost URL and the "Hello world!" text.*

Back in the terminal, notice that `gatsby develop` is still running; the command has not terminated, as shown in Figure 1-4. This is to enable you to continue using the local development server for as long as needed. The Gatsby CLI supports *hot reloading*, which is a feature that enables Gatsby sites to update immediately when you modify code. For as long as `gatsby develop` is running, the local development server will be available at the *localhost* URL, and the vast majority of changes you make to the code will be reflected immediately in the browser.

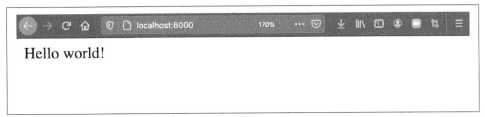

*Figure 1-4. Our local development environment remains running until we decide to shut it down, so any code changes are reflected immediately in the browser*

To see hot reloading in action, try opening *src/pages/index.js* and modifying the "Hello world!" text to something else. If you save your file while `gatsby develop` is still running, you'll see the change take effect immediately without having to incur a browser reload!

To stop running the development server, in the terminal window, type Ctrl-C (hold down the Control key and press C). This will terminate the command, shut down the local development server, and make the site inaccessible through the browser. To restart the local development server, execute `gatsby develop` again.

## Creating a Production Build

Though we've built our first Gatsby site, our work isn't done yet. So far, we've managed to get a website running locally on a development server, but that doesn't mean that our website is online. For that, we need to deploy our Gatsby site to a *production environment*, a publicly accessible web server where anyone can access the site. In addition, we need to perform a Gatsby *build*, which makes a Gatsby site production-ready and as small as possible so there aren't any performance issues down the line.

Creating a production build means converting a development-ready Gatsby site into a production-ready static Gatsby site that consists of static HTML, CSS, JavaScript, and static assets such as images. To create a production Gatsby build, run the following command in the root of your Gatsby site directory:

```
$ gatsby build
```

This command will deposit the built and processed static files, ready for deployment to a production environment, into the *public* directory of your Gatsby codebase.

## Serving the Production Build Locally

Now, we can either deploy this static site to an infrastructure provider of our choosing, or deploy the production Gatsby site locally so we can view it in a browser. To view your production site locally, run the following command, which spins up a local development server:

```
$ gatsby serve
```

The site will be viewable at *https://localhost:9000* (note the difference from `gatsby develop`'s local development server), unless you're already using that port for something else. There you have it—your first Gatsby site, ready for local development or for production deployment!

# Conclusion

In this chapter, we've covered considerable ground. First, we linked the distinct trends of evolution in content and commerce architectures and evolution in developer experience and web architectures that coalesced in the form of the Jamstack and SSGs. This allows us to define Gatsby explicitly as an SSG and part of the Jamstack range of technologies, positioning it alongside similar serverless technologies.

Then we pivoted to the technical side of Gatsby, exploring core technologies essential to Gatsby development and how changes in both JavaScript and React have made Gatsby an even better choice for developers. Finally, we took a rapid-fire tour through installing Gatsby dependencies, working with the Gatsby CLI, and creating a new Gatsby "Hello World" site using a starter template, all of which has set us up nicely for a more comprehensive examination of Gatsby's fundamentals.

In the next chapter, we'll turn our attention to the core building blocks and elements of Gatsby, including starters, Gatsby pages and components, accessibility, CSS, and Gatsby's plugin ecosystem.

# CHAPTER 2

# Core Elements of Gatsby

In Chapter 1, we covered some of the most important foundations you'll need to be familiar with as you begin working with Gatsby and walked through creating a rudimentary "Hello World" site in Gatsby in your local development environment. In this chapter, we'll dive into what we covered at the end of Chapter 1 in more detail. I'll provide more information about the Gatsby CLI, working with starters, how Gatsby pages and components work, the layout component, CSS in Gatsby, and how to add plugins to your site.

We explored the Gatsby CLI at some length at the end of Chapter 1, because it is the primary conduit by which you, as a Gatsby developer, will interact with your Gatsby sites. Many common tasks for Gatsby development can be performed with the Gatsby CLI, and we'll return frequently to Gatsby CLI commands throughout this book. For this reason, it's only logical that we start with a closer look at CLI and what it can do to accelerate your Gatsby development workflows.

## The Gatsby CLI

As you saw in Chapter 1, the Gatsby CLI is the primary means by which developers interact with Gatsby sites during development. It's the main way to set up a new Gatsby application through scaffolding (generation of files and directories adhering to a boilerplate template) and to run a development server for debugging. In this overview of the Gatsby CLI, we'll take another look and discuss some of the most important commands.

### Installing and Configuring the Gatsby CLI

The Gatsby CLI is an executable JavaScript package named `gatsby-cli` that you can leverage from anywhere in your filesystem if you install it globally, though some commands will work only in directories where there is a Gatsby codebase present. As we covered briefly in Chapter 1, the Gatsby CLI is available in the NPM registry, and it's recommended that all users install (i is shorthand for install) it globally by running:

```
$ npm i -g gatsby-cli
```

To see a list of commands and a help mode to help you navigate the internals of the Gatsby CLI, you can run the following help command, which begins with the word gatsby, as all Gatsby CLI commands do:

```
$ gatsby --help
```

Some starters wrap their Gatsby CLI commands in NPM scripts, which are executable commands that can be defined within a *package.json* file. In NPM projects, the *package.json* file contains information about the project in question and all of its dependencies, along with other important information such as commands specific to the project.

Now that we've covered the Gatsby CLI installation process and help mode, we'll turn to some of the most frequently invoked commands in the Gatsby CLI and why they are relevant to your own work.

> In certain scenarios, you may wish to use NPM scripts to execute Gatsby CLI commands. To allow developers to create aliases to use NPM scripts to execute Gatsby CLI commands on your behalf, add the following to your *package.json* file. Check to make sure that another NPM script isn't already present; if one is, add this alongside the existing script:
>
> ```
> {
>   "scripts": {
>     "develop": "gatsby develop"
>   }
> }
> ```
>
> Now, instead of running gatsby develop to access the gatsby develop command, you can also run the following command according to the defined NPM script:
>
> ```
> $ npm run develop
> ```

## gatsby new

The gatsby new command is responsible for the creation of new Gatsby sites based on specific parameters. It takes the following format:

```
$ gatsby new [site-name [starter-url]]
```

The gatsby new command accepts two arguments:

*site-name*

Your Gatsby site name. This is also used as the name for your new project directory.

*starter-url*

A URL pointing to a Gatsby starter or to a local filepath. If you don't supply a *starter-url* argument, the Gatsby CLI will supply `gatsby-starter-default` by default.

 The *site-name* argument must only contain letters and numbers, and the `gatsby new` command will throw an error if you specify `.`, `./`, or a space in your site name argument.

To create a new Gatsby site named `my-great-gatsby-site` with the default starter, you can execute the `gatsby new` command without providing a *starter-url* argument:

```
$ gatsby new my-great-gatsby-site
```

To create a new Gatsby site with a specific starter, you can supply the URL or local file path to the starter as the *starter-url* argument. In this example, we're using `gatsby-starter-blog` as the starter of choice:

```
$ gatsby new my-great-gatsby-site \
  https://github.com/gatsbyjs/gatsby-starter-blog
```

You can also refer to a starter by using just a GitHub username and repository. Here is an example of the same command using this approach:

```
$ gatsby new my-great-gatsby-site gatsbyjs/gatsby-starter-blog
```

To supply your own local custom starter located on your machine's filesystem, use:

```
$ gatsby new my-great-gatsby-site ~/path/to/my/custom/starter
```

If you decide not to supply either of the two arguments, the Gatsby CLI will prompt you to supply them through an interactive shell interface that looks like the following:

```
$ gatsby new
create-gatsby version 1.3.0


                 Welcome to Gatsby!


This command will generate a new Gatsby site for you in
/Users/prestonso/projects with the setup you select. Let's answer some
questions:

What would you like to call your site?
? > My Gatsby Site
```

The gatsby new command is the quickest entry point to start developing a Gatsby site out of the box with minimal overhead. Though you can certainly write your own Gatsby site from scratch, you will find it much easier to use one of the existing default starters and adapt it to your needs rather than kicking off a new codebase from scratch.

Now that we've covered how the Gatsby CLI supports site creation, we'll turn to more details about gatsby develop, the command you executed to see your site in a browser at the end of Chapter 1.

## gatsby develop

The gatsby develop command can be executed within the root directory of any Gatsby project:

```
$ gatsby develop
```

Once you've created your new Gatsby site, you can change directories (cd) into the root of the project and execute gatsby develop immediately:

```
$ gatsby new my-great-gatsby-site
$ cd my-great-gatsby-site
$ gatsby develop
```

The gatsby develop command initializes a local development server that includes hot reloading (automatic browser refreshing) when your code is updated. This means you can keep gatsby develop running indefinitely while you modify your code and preview the changes in your browser. To exit and shut down the local development server, simply press Ctrl-C.

The gatsby develop command accepts several options:

--host *or* -H

This sets the host for your gatsby develop command and defaults to localhost for local development.

--port *or* -p

This sets the port for your local development server and defaults to env.PORT (if you have environment variables defined) or 8000 (if none is set).

--open *or* -o

This opens the site in your default browser on your behalf without any manual action on your part.

--https *or* -S

This instructs the server to use HTTPS to set up an HTTPS development server.

The `gatsby develop` command can also be used with the host option (`--host` or `-H`) to access your development environment from other devices that are on the same network. To do this, execute the following command:

```
$ gatsby develop -H 0.0.0.0
```

The terminal output will then log information as normal, and it will also provide you with a URL that you can share with those using other devices:

```
You can now view gatsbyjs.com in the browser.

  o o
  o o
  o o

Local:            http://0.0.0.0:8000/
On Your Network:  http://192.168.0.212:8000/
```

Navigate to that URL within a device on the same network to see how the site renders outside your local machine.

 When previewing code changes on your local machine instead of for other devices, with this host set, you have the option to use *http://localhost:8000* or the URL listed alongside "On Your Network" to see your Gatsby site in action.

# gatsby build

The `gatsby build` command is used to compile a complete Gatsby site and ready it for deployment to production (such as to a CDN). Generally speaking, it's the last step you'll take before making your site available for access on the web:

```
$ gatsby build
```

The `gatsby build` command must be executed in the root directory of your project and accepts several options. Note here that one of the options, `--prefix-paths`, relies on information from *gatsby-config.js*, which we'll discuss after this exploration of the Gatsby CLI:

`--prefix-paths`
: Build the site with all links prefixed (by setting `pathPrefix` in your Gatsby configuration).

`--no-uglify`
: Build the site without uglifying JavaScript bundles (this makes it much easier to debug generated bundles).

`-profile`
: Build the site with React's profiling API enabled to examine site performance.

`--open-tracing-config-file`
> Build the site and open a tracer configuration file that is OpenTracing-compatible. This is for performance tracing, a topic we'll return to in Chapter 14.

`--graphql-tracing`
> Build the site and open a trace for every GraphQL resolver. This option can be detrimental to site performance.

`--no-color` *or* `--no-colors`
> Build the site but disable color-coded terminal output.

 In addition to these options to cater your Gatsby build process to your needs, there are optional *build environment variables* that allow you to influence the outcome of your command. If you're familiar with environment variables (if not, we'll cover them in Chapter 12), you can set `CI=true` as an environment variable to cater to dumb terminals that aren't as robust as modern terminals. You can also set `NO_COLOR` as an environment variable to disable color-coded terminal output.

## gatsby serve

The `gatsby serve` command is used to serve the production build of your site from a local development server so you can see the production version of your site in a browser:

```
$ gatsby serve
```

The `gatsby serve` command must be executed in the root directory of your project and accepts several options:

`--host` *or* `-H`
> This sets the host to the host of your choosing. It defaults to `localhost`.

`--port` *or* `-p`
> This sets the port to the port of your choosing. It defaults to `9000`.

`--open` *or* `-o`
> This will open the site in your default browser on your behalf without any manual action on your part.

`--prefix-paths`
> This serves the Gatsby site with link paths prefixed according to the `pathPrefix` you configure in your Gatsby configuration.

These are the major commands you will use on a regular basis when interacting with your Gatsby site.

---

# Other Useful Gatsby CLI Commands

There are several other Gatsby commands that are useful for Gatsby development but might not be used as frequently as the others. These commands often are responsible for displaying information about a site, clearing the cache folder (*.cache*) for a site, and directing you to documentation about plugins.

## gatsby info

The `gatsby info` command is used to deliver helpful information about the environment in which a Gatsby site is displayed so that when a bug is reported, Gatsby's maintainers can reproduce the situation that led to the issue:

```
$ gatsby info
```

The `gatsby info` command must be executed in the root directory of your project and accepts one option: `--clipboard` or `-C`, which automatically copies the environment information displayed in terminal output to your clipboard so you can send it to others.

## gatsby clean

The `gatsby clean` command is used to wipe out any items in Gatsby's *.cache* folder, its internal cache, and public directories where compiled files are delivered:

```
$ gatsby clean
```

The `gatsby clean` command must be executed in the root directory of your project and is most useful as a last resort when your codebase seems to be having issues such as the following:

*Stale data*
> Sometimes Gatsby's internal cache can get out of sync with certain files or resources used to populate your site's data. If a particular file or resource isn't appearing, or if you aren't seeing data that should be loaded in, clearing the internal Gatsby cache may resolve the issue.

*GraphQL errors*
> If you have included a GraphQL resource but it is not appearing, executing `gatsby clean` can ensure that GraphQL accounts for all new resources.

*Dependency problems*
> If you are seeing a dependency with a different version from what was intended or incomprehensible errors in the terminal that have to do with a dependency that doesn't exist, your cache may need to be cleaned.

*Plugin problems*

If you are developing a local plugin (see Chapter 9) and your changes and feature additions are not taking effect, clean the cache.

The `gatsby clean` command can be useful in a variety of situations that may surface during Gatsby development, and we'll return to examine some of these in later chapters.

### gatsby plugin

The `gatsby plugin` command  is used to execute commands that are relevant to Gatsby plugins, add-ons from the Gatsby ecosystem. Executing `gatsby plugin docs` will transport you to documentation about how to use, install, and write plugins:

```
$ gatsby plugin docs
```

### gatsby repl

The `gatsby repl` command  is used to open a Node.js read–eval–print loop (REPL) within the context of your Gatsby environment:

```
$ gatsby repl
```

As you interact with `gatsby repl`, Gatsby will prompt you to type in certain commands and explore by displaying:

```
$ gatsby >
```

You can then type in a REPL command to understand more about how your site data is used within Gatsby.

# Starters

As we saw briefly in Chapter 1, *starters* are boilerplate Gatsby site templates managed by the Gatsby community that are intended to get you started quickly with Gatsby development. When you execute a `gatsby new` command with a starter URL, it clones that boilerplate starter's repository, installs any required dependencies, and clears its Git commit history so you can start with a clean slate.

## Official and Community Starters

The Gatsby ecosystem offers a range of *official starters*, which are maintained by the Gatsby project team. Many new Gatsby developers begin with the `gatsby-starter-hello-world` starter, as we did in Chapter 1, before moving on to the `gatsby-starter-default` starter.

Table 2-1 lists the official starters and their most salient features. We'll cover the starters for Gatsby themes in later chapters.

*Table 2-1. The list of official starters maintained by the Gatsby project team*

| Starter | GitHub URL | Use case | Features |
|---|---|---|---|
| gatsby-starter-default | *https://github.com/gatsbyjs/gatsby-starter-default* | Adequate for most use cases | Baseline Gatsby site |
| gatsby-starter-blog | *https://github.com/gatsbyjs/gatsby-starter-blog* | Create a rudimentary blog | Blog post pages and blog post listings |
| gatsby-starter-hello-world | *https://github.com/gatsbyjs/gatsby-starter-hello-world* | Get started with Gatsby | Bare essentials of a Gatsby site |
| gatsby-starter-blog-theme | *https://github.com/gatsbyjs/gatsby-starter-blog-theme* | Create a blog with blog posts and pages | Gatsby themes |
| gatsby-starter-theme-workspace | *https://github.com/gatsbyjs/gatsby-starter-theme-workspace* | Get started with Gatsby themes | Gatsby themes |

The `gatsby-starter-default` starter is the most common starting point for Gatsby developers beginning a site implementation from scratch. During our upcoming inspection of Gatsby's page strategy, I'll talk more about key concepts such as pages, templates, and components.

Gatsby also allows for community contributors to submit starters for inclusion in the community *starter library (https://www.gatsbyjs.com/starters)*, a compendium of starters built by members of the Gatsby community. We'll return to the topic of how to create your own custom starter for yourself or for the community in Chapter 9.

## Modifying Starters

All Gatsby starters are fully functional websites off the shelf, but the vast majority of Gatsby developers will wish to modify a starter and customize it according to their needs. For this reason, it's important to select a starter that satisfies your requirements, whether you're building a blog, a heavy-duty content or commerce site, or something else. There are four major areas within a given starter where you will need to do work:

*The gatsby-config.js file*
> The Gatsby configuration file identifies the codebase as a Gatsby site. In order to provide a unique name for the Gatsby site and other critical information, one of the first files developers modify after cloning a starter is the *gatsby-config.js* file.

*Pages, templates, and components in JSX*
> Chances are that the predefined structure of Gatsby's pages and components isn't in full sync with how you prefer to arrange them or with your organization's needs. Because Gatsby employs JSX as its primary syntax for components, you'll need some proficiency with JSX. In addition, for pages with a similar structure, you will need templates, which we'll cover in Chapter 6.

*Data from external or internal sources*
> Whether your data is housed in the filesystem where your Gatsby site is located or in a separate CMS or commerce system located on a different server, you'll need to substitute the dummy data in the starter with your own authentic data. We'll cover this in Chapters 4 and 5.

*Cascading Style Sheets (CSS) files*
> CSS is the canonical language for style and presentation on the web, and all Gatsby sites leverage CSS to add important aesthetic elements such as color, layout, and typography to a given Gatsby page. Gatsby is unopinionated about how you approach your CSS and makes a variety of approaches available for use, such as Emotion and Styled Components (discussed in "CSS-in-JS" on page 51).

With the exception of data from external and internal sources, which deserves a much deeper dive, let's look at each of these typical areas in turn. We'll create a new project that will guide us through the remainder of Chapter 2 as we explore the *gatsby-config.js* file, Gatsby pages and components, Gatsby's layout component, and using CSS with Gatsby.

# Creating a New Project from a Starter

In your terminal, execute the following command:

```
$ gatsby new gtdg-ch2-pages-components gatsbyjs/gatsby-starter-hello-world
```

Note here that we are creating a new directory, *gtdg-ch-2-pages-components*, to contain our new Gatsby site, and we're using the GitHub username and repository strategy to retrieve the Gatsby starter repository. Next, change into this directory:

```
$ cd gtdg-ch2-pages-components
```

and open the *gatsby-config.js* file in the code editor of your choice. For example, to open the file in Visual Studio Code, use:

```
$ code gatsby-config.js
```

and for Atom, use:

```
$ atom gatsby-config.js
```

Gatsby has no opinion about what code editor you use in developing a Gatsby site. Many developers prefer Visual Studio Code or Atom due to their rich capabilities for language- and framework-specific extensions and debugging tools. These code editors also have the benefit of being openable with a single command.

## The gatsby-config.js File

If you followed the steps to open *gatsby-config.js* in the code editor of your choice, you'll see the following contents:

```
/**
 * Configure your Gatsby site with this file.
 *
 * See: https://www.gatsbyjs.com/docs/gatsby-config/
 */

module.exports = {
  /* Your site config here */
  plugins: [],
}
```

This empty *gatsby-config.js* file has no configuration options set and no plugins loaded. The very first step to make your Gatsby site your own is to add some information about the site, specifying the page title and other page metadata. Add a new `siteMetadata` object to the top of your *gatsby-config.js* file, and add some information about your site. You can use this example to get some ideas:

```
// gatsby-config.js
module.exports = {
  siteMetadata: {
    title: `My New Gatsby Site`,
    description: `Check out Gatsby with this easy-to-use site.`,
    author: `@prestonso`,
  },
  plugins: [],
}
```

Congratulations! You've now made your first Gatsby site your very own by identifying it as a unique Gatsby site with your own information. Now, let's turn our attention to what's happening inside the Gatsby site—and that means opening up one of the pages in our starter.

# Gatsby Pages and Components

Pages and components are typical entry points for developers when building a Gatsby site. Pages are the higher-level components that Gatsby uses to build a site, while components can be nested within those pages and in each other. Any time you add a new page, Gatsby will automatically recognize it and incorporate it into your site build.

So how exactly does this work? In this section, we'll take a close look at Gatsby pages, Gatsby components, and how to link between Gatsby pages.

## Pages

We'll begin with the most important atomic unit of Gatsby sites: the page. In Gatsby, any React component defined with a name in the form *src/pages/\*.js* will automatically be recognized by Gatsby as a page and will be rendered as such. In our "Hello World" starter, we already have one page in *src/pages*, named *index.js*.

A typical need for any bona fide website is an about page, so let's add an about page that contains a bit of information about the site. Because Gatsby recognizes any new file named *src/pages/\*.js* as a new component, we can simply create a file named about.js and place it in that directory.

First, create a new file located at *src/pages/about.js*, and paste the following inside:

```
// src/pages/about.js
import React from "react"

export default function About() {
  return (
    <div>
      <h1>About us</h1>
        <p>Welcome to our about page! Here is some info about us.</p>
    </div>
  )
}
```

Then, if you aren't already running `gatsby develop`, go ahead and start your development server from the root of the project:

```
$ gatsby develop
```

Now, if you navigate to *https://localhost:8000/about*, you'll see your new about page. And you didn't have to do any work besides adding a file to the *pages* directory!

There's much more to know about pages, including how Gatsby generates pages, how Gatsby builds pages from components, and how to hook into the page-building process. In addition, some pages have *templates*, a shared format across pages that is used to programmatically render pages of a certain category (such as individual blog articles or product pages). For now, however, this is an adequate introduction to pages in Gatsby and allows us to proceed to Gatsby components.

## Components

In Gatsby, *components* are just like React components in the traditional sense: they are portions of a page or repeatable code that needs to be placed in a separate file for reuse in multiple places, or simply to make the code more maintainable. In the context of a Gatsby page, a component might be a header, footer, or sidebar. It could also be a lead generation form or a contact form, or it could simply introduce additional code that is important to the site, such as an embedded Google Analytics snippet.

Let's create a footer component that will be used across both our home page and our about page. First, create a new directory located at *src/components*. Create a file in that directory named *footer.js* and insert the following code:

```
// src/components/footer.js
import React from "react"

export default function Footer() {
  return <p>&copy; 2020 My Gatsby Site. All rights reserved.</p>
}
```

Now, let's modify each of the pages to use our new footer component. First, let's add the footer to our about page by adding an additional `import` statement and invoking the component in our JSX:

```
// src/pages/about.js
import React from "react"
import Footer from "../components/footer"

export default function About() {
  return (
    <div>
      <h1>About us</h1>
      <p>Welcome to our about page! Here is some info about us.</p>
      <Footer />
    </div>
  )
}
```

Now we'll do the same in *src/pages/index.js*:

```
// src/pages/index.js
import React from "react"
import Footer from "../components/footer"

export default function Home() {
  return (
    <div>
      <p>Hello world!</p>
```

```
        <Footer />
      </div>
    )
  }
```

React allows us to define what properties (props) a component should have by adding attributes to JSX elements. Instead of using the same copyright text on both pages, let's have the page define what year the copyright statement should have, rather than the footer component itself. Modify *src/components/footer.js* to the following:

```
// src/components/footer.js
import React from "react"

export default function Footer(props) {
  return <p>&copy; {props.copyrightYear} My Gatsby Site. All rights reserved.</p>
}
```

Now, on our about page, let's provide the prop that our footer needs to fill in the missing copyright year:

```
// src/pages/about.js
import React from "react"
import Footer from "../components/footer"

export default function About() {
  return (
    <div>
      <h1>About us</h1>
      <p>Welcome to our about page! Here is some info about us</p>
      <Footer copyrightYear="2020" />
    </div>
  )
}
```

Now when you navigate to the about page at *https://localhost:8000/about*, you'll see the same copyright message, but this time you're defining that prop within your use of the footer component rather than in the footer component itself. Do the same thing in *index.js* by adding the prop and its value to the use of the footer component there.

 There is a special type of component that exists in Gatsby known as the *layout component*, which is commonly used to define shared behavior across pages. We'll discuss this in "The Layout Component" on page 44.

# Linking Between Pages

Now that you have a rudimentary understanding of pages and components and how they interrelate, we can turn our attention to another type of component that exists in Gatsby and is, in fact, unique to the framework: the Gatsby <Link /> component, which facilitates linking between Gatsby pages. Let's take a look at how Gatsby performs routing between individual Gatsby pages.

First, let's open our home page and add in a <Link /> component to our about page. Note that we need to import the <Link /> component from Gatsby and use it in our page:

```
// src/pages/index.js
import React from "react"
import { Link } from "gatsby"
import Footer from "../components/footer"

export default function Home() {
  return (
    <div>
      <p>Hello world!</p>
      <p><Link to="/about/">About</Link></p>
      <Footer copyrightYear="2020" />
    </div>
  )
}
```

Now, let's add a link back to the home page from our about page:

```
// src/pages/about.js
import React from "react"
import { Link } from "gatsby"
import Footer from "../components/footer"

export default function About() {
  return (
    <div>
      <h1>About us</h1>
      <p>Welcome to our about page! Here is some info about us.</p>
      <p><Link to="/">Home</Link></p>
      <Footer copyrightYear="2020" />
    </div>
  )
}
```

Success! Now we have linking between two distinct Gatsby pages using the Gatsby <Link /> component.

The Gatsby `<Link />` component should be used for any linking between Gatsby pages. For external links or for anchor links, you should still use the HTML `<a>` tag rather than `<Link />`. `<Link />` does not work for external URLs outside the immediate Gatsby site, as external URLs are not part of Gatsby's purview.

## The Layout Component

Before we turn our attention to CSS, we need to cover one of the most important components in Gatsby, which has a considerable impact on how we leverage CSS. *Layout components* are sections of your Gatsby site that should be shared across multiple Gatsby pages and that are most frequently used to provide styling across those pages (unlike the footer component we created in the previous section).

By default, Gatsby never applies a particular layout to pages, because it adheres to React's compositional approach of importing and using nestable components. Component nestability allows for rich hierarchies within layouts on Gatsby sites, and you can create a header and footer that appear on every page, as well as certain components that should only appear on certain pages. Because all Gatsby components are React components, passing data between layout and page components is a trivial problem to solve.

Layout components are important in Gatsby because they are how we, as Gatsby developers, can indicate to Gatsby that pages with different layouts should display different components. On the main page of a Gatsby site, for instance, a global footer and header might be present, but developers may wish to add an additional sidebar with a menu on internal pages.

Gatsby strongly recommends placing your layout components alongside your other Gatsby components within the same directory, such as *src/components/*. Here's an example of a rudimentary layout component adapted from the Gatsby documentation, which we would place into a file located at *src/components/layout.js*:

```
// src/components/layout.js
import React from "react"
export default function Layout({ children }) {
  return (
    <div style={{ margin: `0 auto`, maxWidth: 960, padding: `0 1.5rem` }}>
      {children}
    </div>
  )
}
```

Note here that we're using inline styles on the surrounding `<div>` element to indicate certain styles, but we'll soon refactor this code.

You should recast CSS property names that contain hyphens from `kebab-case` to `camelCase` in JSX, because `kebab-case` can lead to issues later on in JavaScript.

Now, we can return to our home page and apply this layout to the page's contents such that all of the markup on the page is surrounded by our layout component. Any page or template we want to have this layout should use the `<Layout>` component we've defined. Note here that we're importing the layout we just created into our home page:

```
// src/pages/index.js
import React from "react"
import { Link } from "gatsby"
import Footer from "../components/footer"
import Layout from "../components/layout"
export default function Home() {
  return (
    <Layout>
      <p>Hello world!</p>
      <p><Link to="/about/">About</Link></p>
      <Footer copyrightYear="2020" />
    </Layout>
  );
}
```

And now that we have our first layout component, we can define our first global stylesheet.

Because Gatsby does not normally surround pages in a layout component by default, the top-level component is the page component itself. This means that when the page component updates during route changes, React will perform asynchronous rendering of all child components contained therein. If you're using shared components in your layout, such as a navigation menu, those components will unmount and remount in React, thereby breaking CSS transitions or interrupting React state management in those shared components. To avoid this issue, you can wrap page components that shouldn't get unmounted on page changes with the `wrapPageElement` API, which is one of Gatsby's Browser APIs (*https://oreil.ly/v0smp*), or the `gatsby-plugin-layout` plugin, which implements `wrapPageElement` for you.

# Using CSS in Gatsby

There are several different styling approaches in Gatsby that allow you to adjust the typography, colors, and layout of your Gatsby website. In this section, we'll cover each of the three CSS approaches that Gatsby makes available:

*Global styling*

> In many uses of CSS, a single stylesheet (CSS file) is downloaded and used to style a website. Gatsby also allows you to provide a single CSS file with global scope according to all the usual rules of CSS, or to provide a variety of CSS files that are associated with a component but whose styles still apply globally. Note, however, that without postprocessing the CSS to strip out unused styles, you may have some dead CSS within your global stylesheet. This is the traditional approach that most web developers are already familiar with.

*Modular styling*

> Gatsby also provides modular stylesheets that allow you to scope CSS declarations to individual Gatsby components. In this model, CSS is written traditionally within Gatsby components but processed by JavaScript. This allows for local scoping and avoids unintended consequences elsewhere. Gatsby offers this CSS paradigm off the shelf.

*CSS-in-JavaScript (CSS-in-JS)*

> In recent years, a new paradigm for CSS in JavaScript applications, CSS-in-JS, has emerged. With this approach, CSS declarations are still locally scoped and consumed in JavaScript, but because JavaScript manages the CSS entirely, dynamic styling based on asynchronous events is possible. This approach requires the use of third-party dependencies.

It's important to note that Gatsby has no opinion on or prescription for which CSS paradigm you should use, and use of all three is widespread in the Gatsby community. In addition, all three of these options have both official and community plugins that can help you avoid any headaches around dependency management. Let's take a closer look at each.

## Global Styling

In traditional CSS approaches, globally scoped CSS is found in external stylesheets that have the *.css* extension, according to standard CSS specificity and inheritance. There are two ways to use global stylesheets in Gatsby: without a layout component and with a layout component.

## Global styling with a layout component

Applying global styles with a layout component is the quickest way to apply an already existing CSS stylesheet to a Gatsby site or to write CSS that adheres to traditional CSS approaches and will work in every browser.

To use global CSS styles with a layout component, we can add a shared layout component that surrounds all shared components across the site, including styles, header and footer components, and other common components like sidebars and navigation menus. Gatsby's default starter uses this same approach, but to learn how the layout component works with global styles, we'll use the "Hello World" starter instead.

Create a new Gatsby site on your local machine. Note here that we're using the GitHub username/repository strategy to target the correct starter:

```
$ gatsby new gtdg-ch2-global-styling-with-layout \
  gatsbyjs/gatsby-starter-hello-world
$ cd gtdg-ch2-global-styling-with-layout
```

Next, create a new directory located at *src/components* and create two new files named *layout.js* and *layout.css* within it. The *layout.js* file represents our layout component, while the *layout.css* file represents the styles associated with that layout component.

Now, we can take the same styles we defined inline in the previous section and add them to *src/components/layout.css*:

```
/* src/components/layout.css */
div {
  margin: 0 auto;
  max-width: 960px;
  padding: 0 1.5rem;
}
```

For good measure, let's also add a readily identifiable CSS rule that will be noticeable as soon as we load the page:

```
/* src/components/layout.css */
div {
  /* Previous lines of CSS */
  background-color: blue;
}
```

Now, inside *src/components/layout.js*, let's import the stylesheet we just created at *src/components/layout.css* and export the layout component so any other component can use it as well:

```
// src/components/layout.js
import React from "react"
import "./layout.css"
export default function Layout({ children }) {
  return <div>{children}</div>
}
```

Note that our `<div>` element no longer needs any inline styles because we've applied our global styles to the layout component.

The last step is to update our home page in Gatsby with our layout component so that the home page uses the layout component as well as its associated styles:

```
// src/pages/index.js
import React from "react"
import Layout from "../components/layout"
export default function Home() {
  return <Layout>Hello world!</Layout>
}
```

If we now run `gatsby develop` in the root of our project, we'll see our page containing a `<div>` that has a blue background color:

```
$ gatsby develop
```

There are situations, however, where using the layout component may not be preferable. Next, we'll discuss how to write global stylesheets without leveraging the layout component.

### Global styling without the layout component

There are situations where you won't want to use a layout component to drive global styles, whether due to the way you've architected components in your Gatsby site or because another element of your Gatsby site prevents the use of the layout component. Fortunately, you can hook into Gatsby's browser API to include a global stylesheet separately from the React paradigm.

There is no way to apply styles globally without the layout component *and* leverage CSS-in-JS at the same time. You will need to use shared components (like the layout component) in order to share styles across components in CSS-in-JS.

Let's spin up a new "Hello World" Gatsby site to take a look at how we can leverage *gatsby-browser.js* instead of a layout component to drive global styling. First, let's create a new copy of the "Hello World" starter:

```
$ gatsby new gtdg-ch2-global-styling-without-layout \
  gatsbyjs/gatsby-starter-hello-world
$ cd gtdg-ch2-global-styling-without-layout
```

Now, let's create a stylesheet and save it to *src/styles/global.css* to reflect our new global stylesheet:

```
/* src/styles/global.css */
div {
  margin: 0 auto;
```

```
    max-width: 960px;
    padding: 0 1.5rem;
    background-color: blue;
  }
```

Then we'll create a new file named *gatsby-browser.js* in the root folder of our project, and import our global stylesheet into *gatsby-browser.js*:

```
// gatsby-browser.js
import "./src/styles/global.css"
```

 You can use `require` instead if you prefer, as in `require('./src/styles/global.css')`. In addition, Gatsby has no opinion about where you place a global stylesheet with this approach, so the path *src/styles/global.css* is arbitrary.

While global stylesheets are the primary means by which developers have written CSS for many years, there are significant disadvantages to global styles, including conflicts between names and instances of unintended inheritance. That's where component stylesheets can help.

### Global styling with component stylesheets

While many Gatsby developers use global stylesheets to keep all their styles in one place, others prefer to split their CSS into component-level CSS files or even individual class declaration blocks that apply to a single Gatsby component. You can decompose your global stylesheet into multiple constituent stylesheets to allow team members to work separately without running into each other, only importing those CSS files that you need for a particular page, template, or component.

For instance, you can create individual CSS files for different components in the *components* directory (for better organization) and import them into your components. Go back to the previous example, *gtdg-ch2-pages-components*, to proceed into global styling with component stylesheets, since we have a footer component defined there. Consider a scenario where you need to import a "footer" component that has the same styles that we already applied previously:

```
/* src/components/footer.css */
p {
  margin: 0 auto;
  max-width: 960px;
  padding: 0 1.5rem;
  background-color: blue;
}
```

Now, back in our footer component, all we need to do is to import the CSS file:

```
// src/components/footer.js
import React from "react"
```

```
import "./footer.css"

export default function Footer(props) {
  return <p>© {props.copyrightYear} My Gatsby Site. All rights reserved.</p>
}
```

 While this form of using CSS files can lead to independent work streams thanks to the separation of concerns in stylesheets, it doesn't take advantage of some of the most important ways Gatsby improves CSS performance, because it doesn't use the layout component strategy, and Gatsby doesn't manage the styles itself. Leveraging this approach to importing CSS files will remove your ability to take advantage of CSS performance enhancements such as dead code elimination.

Because these stylesheets still require global namespaces, as a *footer.css* file using global selectors will have its styles apply across the entire site as opposed to being scoped solely to a footer component, they can present many of the same issues as global stylesheets do. In the next sections, we'll discuss how JavaScript can help us scope our CSS locally instead of globally with CSS Modules and CSS-in-JS.

## Modular Styling with CSS Modules

Gatsby offers two approaches to writing CSS that is scoped to components: CSS Modules and CSS-in-JS (discussed in the next section). Scoping CSS to individual components permits Gatsby developers to write traditional CSS that is portable and more maintainable. Styles that apply to only a single component will never infiltrate a different component or change how other components are styled.

CSS Modules is a well-known way to write component-scoped CSS. In short, an individual CSS Module is a CSS stylesheet where all class names (and animation names) are scoped locally out of the box. In CSS Modules, CSS styles become JavaScript objects that are passed between components. Because CSS Modules automatically assign unique names to classes and animations, there is no risk of incurring a collision between two identically named selectors across discrete components.

To illustrate this, let's return to the *gtdg-ch2-pages-components* example in the previous section—a case of traditional CSS being imported into a Gatsby component—and convert it into a CSS Module being imported into the same Gatsby component. All we need to do to our CSS file is rename it and move it to *src/components/footer.module.css*.

Also, for the purposes of this look at CSS Modules, let's select a class name rather than a <div> element:

```
/* src/components/footer.module.css */
.footer {
  margin: 0 auto;
  max-width: 960px;
  padding: 0 1.5rem;
  background-color: blue;
}
```

Now, modify the code in *src/components/footer.js* to use the CSS Modules paradigm instead of a direct import of the CSS stylesheet:

```
// src/components/footer.js
import React from "react"
import * as footerStyles from "./footer.module.css"

export default function Footer(props) {
  return
    <p className={footerStyles.footer}>
    © { props.copyrightYear} My Gatsby Site. All rights reserved.</p>
}
```

Note the syntax in our `className` value that allows us to drill down into our footer styles and find the specific class name we're looking for: `.footer`. Because we've used an import, we can use any of the styles contained in that stylesheet within the component, and no style will ever escape the scope of the component. CSS Modules will render the class name into a dynamic CSS class name such as `footer-module--container--2KckL`.

Next, we'll take a look at how to locally style components with CSS-in-JS.

 The Gatsby documentation recommends using CSS Modules if Gatsby developers are interested in the benefits of properly scoping CSS to individual components, as it allows you to take advantage of performance enhancements such as dead code elimination and better portability.

# CSS-in-JS

CSS-in-JS is a very different approach from CSS Modules in that it focuses on the idea of writing CSS in JavaScript rather than in external CSS files. When using this approach, it's important to note that some of the traditional syntax of CSS cannot be written in the same way in JavaScript (e.g., `backgroundColor` is `camelCase` in JavaScript, whereas `background-color` in CSS is `kebab-case`).

CSS-in-JS is a paradigm that emphasizes scoped styling, dead code elimination, and better performance when dynamic styling gets involved. It has the following characteristics:

*Component-driven*

Because CSS-in-JS uses the same component methodology as React and Gatsby—all CSS comes in the form of components—you'll often find CSS-in-JS to be more graceful than other methods.

*Scoped locally*

Like CSS Modules, CSS-in-JS is scoped to individual components by default.

*Styled dynamically*

If you need asynchronous changes to styles because of client-side changes in component state, you can integrate JavaScript variables that depend on that state into your CSS-in-JS so the value can change based on its surroundings.

*Performance-tuned*

CSS-in-JS libraries generate unique class names that don't collide, thus supporting easier caching, automated vendor prefixing, quick loading of the most important CSS styles, and other features.

While CSS-in-JS is very popular in the JavaScript community to handle CSS, it isn't so straightforward for those coming from traditional CSS, and it can be time-consuming to refactor traditional CSS into CSS-in-JS and vice versa. And because Gatsby has no opinion about which CSS strategy you use, CSS-in-JS invariably requires the introduction of an additional dependency in the form of a CSS-in-JS library.

There are two CSS-in-JS libraries commonly used with Gatsby, and we'll cover both of them here: Emotion and Styled Components.

## Emotion

Emotion is a CSS-in-JS library that builds on other preexisting libraries and allows you to add styles to applications using string or object style declarations. Emotion leverages predictable composition of styles to avoid some of the specificity concerns that accompany traditional CSS use. In addition, Emotion uses source maps and labels to offer a better debugging experience and better caching for performance.

In order to use Emotion, we need to install our first plugin, which we'll do here after setting up another "Hello World" starter:

```
$ gatsby new gtdg-ch2-css-in-js-emotion gatsbyjs/gatsby-starter-hello-world
```

Now that we have our site scaffolded, let's change directories into the site and add the dependencies that are required for Emotion using NPM:

```
$ cd gtdg-ch2-css-in-js-emotion
$ npm install gatsby-plugin-emotion @emotion/react @emotion/styled
```

Our final step is to open *gatsby-config.js* and add the plugin to the list of plugins there. If you have no other plugins installed, your *gatsby-config.js* section for plugins will need to look like the following:

```
// gatsby-config.js
module.exports = {
  plugins: ['gatsby-plugin-emotion'],
}
```

Now, let's introduce styles for a header component into our Emotion page. Note that Emotion prefers to co-locate styles in the same file as the logic defining how those styles will take effect on JSX elements:

```
// src/pages/index.js
import React from "react"
import styled from "@emotion/styled"
import { css } from "@emotion/react"

const Header = styled.div`
  margin: 0 auto;
  max-width: 960px;
  padding: 0 1.5rem;
  background-color: blue;
  color: white;
`

export default function Home({ children }) {
  return (
    <Header>
      <div>Welcome to my Gatsby site!</div>
    </Header>
  )
}
```

As you can see, here we're using a multiline string to define the CSS rules for our header.

Emotion also allows us to add arbitrary declarations that can be used to style individual JSX elements. In the following example, we apply a text-transform property to ensure that the header will be in uppercase on the home page by applying a chunk of CSS to the element:

```
// src/pages/index.js
import React from "react"
import styled from "@emotion/styled"
import { css } from "@emotion/react"

const Header = styled.div`
  margin: 0 auto;
  max-width: 960px;
  padding: 0 1.5rem;
  background-color: blue;
```

```
  color: white;
`

const uppercase = css`
  text-transform: uppercase;
`

export default function Home({ children }) {
  return (
    <Header>
      <div css={{uppercase}}>Welcome to my Gatsby site!</div>
    </Header>
  )
}
```

When we run `gatsby develop`, we can see our newly Emotion-styled Gatsby site, as depicted in Figure 2-1.

## WELCOME TO MY GATSBY SITE!

*Figure 2-1. Our Gatsby home page styled with Emotion, with styles pulled in through the* css *tag*

One of the most important benefits of Emotion and other CSS-in-JS techniques is the placement of CSS directly within the definition of your component in JavaScript. But you can also use Emotion to apply global styling to your Gatsby site by adding Emotion as a dependency and using it within your layout component. Using Emotion for global styling with a layout component would obviate the need for a separate *layout.css* file.

 Server-side rendering, or the prerendering of HTML before it reaches the client side (see Chapter 3 for more information on this), functions off the shelf in Emotion. You can choose to use React's `renderToString` method or `renderToNodeStream` method without any additional configuration. Meanwhile, the `extractCritical` feature deletes unused CSS rules (dead code elimination) so pages can load faster down the line.

### Styled Components

Styled Components is another CSS-in-JS library that allows Gatsby developers to write actual CSS inside components, just like Emotion. And like Emotion, Styled Components eliminates the possibility of name collisions and dead code appearing in your production CSS.

Let's take a look at the exact same example we went through with Emotion to see how Styled Components offers a similar approach. To use Styled Components, we need to install its plugin, which we'll do here after setting up yet another "Hello World" starter:

```
$ gatsby new gtdg-ch2-css-in-js-styled-components \
  gatsbyjs/gatsby-starter-hello-world
```

With our site scaffolded, let's change directories into the site and add the dependencies that are required for Styled Components using NPM:

```
$ cd gtdg-ch2-css-in-js-styled-components
$ npm install gatsby-plugin-styled-components styled-components \
  babel-plugin-styled-components
```

Next, we'll open *gatsby-config.js* and add the plugin to the list of plugins there. If you have no other plugins installed, your *gatsby-config.js* section for plugins will look like the following:

```
// gatsby-config.js
module.exports = {
  plugins: [`gatsby-plugin-styled-components`],
}
```

Our *index.js* will look similar to the Emotion example and produce the same result, as seen in Figure 2-2:

```
// src/pages/index.js
import React from "react"
import styled from "styled-components"

const Header = styled.div`
  margin: 0 auto;
  max-width: 960px;
  padding: 0 1.5rem;
  background-color: blue;
  color: white;
`

export default function Home({ children }) {
  return (
    <Header>
      <div>Welcome to my Gatsby site!</div>
    </Header>
  )
}
```

*Figure 2-2. Our Gatsby home page styled with Styled Components—this library allows us to apply styles directly to elements without having to refer to them as we do in Emotion*

Just like with Emotion, it's possible to apply global styles to our layout component, but Styled Components takes a slightly different tack. Styled Components offers a `createGlobalStyle` method that defines globally scoped styles. This method should be invoked within Gatsby's layout component to ensure that it's shared across all pages using that layout component.

Here's an example of a layout component that uses a `GlobalStyle` object, adapted from the Gatsby documentation. Note here that according to our layout component's state, we are toggling between two different background colors:

```
// src/components/layout.js
import React from "react"
import { createGlobalStyle } from "styled-components"
const GlobalStyle = createGlobalStyle`
 body {
   background-color: ${props => (props.theme === "blue" ? "blue" : "white")};
 }
`

export default function Layout({ children }) {
 return (
   <React.Fragment>
     <GlobalStyle theme="blue" />
   </React.Fragment> )
}
```

Both Emotion and Styled Components are commonly found in Gatsby implementations. But it's perfectly fine to use global styling and traditional CSS as well, and Gatsby makes no assumptions about which paradigm of CSS you prefer to use with your site build!

As you probably noticed, we just installed our first two Gatsby plugins. Our next step is to explore Gatsby's plugin ecosystem and how to extend the core functionality of the Gatsby framework with community plugins.

# Extending Gatsby with Plugins

In Gatsby, plugins are Node.js packages that introduce additional functionality that implements Gatsby's APIs (Gatsby functionality that developers can hook into to implement their own custom code). Plugins are particularly useful because they can help you modularize functionality into tightly scoped chunks of logic. Gatsby plugins run the gamut of use cases, including SEO, responsive image support, Sass and LESS support for CSS, offline support, sitemaps and RSS feeds, TypeScript and CoffeeScript compilation, Google Analytics embeds, and more.

You can also create your own custom plugins, which we'll cover in Chapter 9.

As you saw when we installed the Emotion and Styled Components plugins, the authoritative way to install a new Gatsby plugin is to use the NPM installation process to add the dependency to your *package.json* file. However, Gatsby also requires you to add the plugin explicitly to *gatsby-config.js* so Gatsby's aware of it too.

There are several broad categories of plugins that exist in the Gatsby ecosystem:

*Source plugins*
These plugins are responsible for introducing external data or content from an arbitrary source, whether it is a CMS, a commerce system, static files on the local filesystem, or a web service such as a REST API or GraphQL API (which expose data and are covered at length in Chapter 5). Source plugins translate external data into data consumable through Gatsby's internal GraphQL API.

*Transformer plugins*
Transformer plugins are responsible for converting data in one format to another, especially to JSON. For instance, some external data arrives in the form of Markdown, YAML, CSV, or XML, all serialization formats that are ill suited to use in JavaScript. Transformer plugins for each individual format convert other formats into JSON for Gatsby.

*External service plugins*
Broadly speaking, any plugin that embeds or adds in third-party functionality is an external service plugin that pulls information or code directly from a third party such as Google Analytics, Segment, or Algolia. Though these plugins are very common, they also tend to be much smaller in size than source plugins or transformer plugins.

There are also many plugins that don't fit into a clear category. To get an idea of what's available, check out the Gatsby Plugin Library (*https://oreil.ly/CFZbr*).

Themes are also a type of Gatsby plugin, but they require a full discussion in their own right. We'll return to them in Chapter 10.

It's also important to note where plugins are *not* necessary. Though plugins introduce additional functionality to Gatsby sites, not all additional functionality needs to be added via a Gatsby plugin. For instance, if you wish to use JavaScript packages that provide developer utilities, like `lodash` or `axios`, or that integrate libraries that are essential to the functioning of a component, like d3 for visualization, it's generally best to import the package directly as a dependency in *package.json* rather than as a plugin. This means that you would install the library normally as an NPM package but refrain from editing anything in *gatsby-config.js* to reflect the new library's presence.

As a general rule, to help you decide whether some piece of functionality should be a plugin or a separate library, if the functionality does not hook into or implement Gatsby's APIs in any way, it's generally safe to import it solely as a dependency and not write or search for a plugin that contains it. In some cases, however, you can choose between an existing Gatsby plugin and a library: for example, you could use either `gatsby-plugin-styled-components`, which offers a deeper integration with Gatsby APIs, or the `styled-components` package itself, which you would need to implement yourself in Gatsby where you wish to use it.

## Installing Gatsby Plugins

Recall from our examination of Emotion and Styled Components how the installation process for plugins works. Let's revisit it here with a typical plugin. To keep things simple, we'll use `gatsby-plugin-google-analytics`, which allows us to embed Google Analytics code into our Gatsby site.

You can install a plugin from the root directory of your Gatsby site, and you can install a plugin at any time—at the very start of the development process when your site has just been scaffolded, or well into the project timeline when your site is full of other installed plugins. To install a plugin, run this command, substituting the plugin name for a name of your choosing:

```
$ npm install gatsby-plugin-google-analytics
```

In your *gatsby-config.js* file, ensure that your plugin is represented in the `plugins` array. If you're adding a plugin for the first time, you may need to add the `plugins` array yourself. If you already have plugins in your configuration, you can simply add it as a member to the existing array:

```
// gatsby-config.js
module.exports = {
  plugins: [`gatsby-plugin-google-analytics`],
}
```

You'll follow this exact process every single time you need to introduce another plugin into your Gatsby site.

Some plugins also accept options in their definitions in *gatsby-config.js*. This is usually to configure key parameters specifying how the plugin should behave or credentials that are required for an external service. For instance, a typical `options` object for `gatsby-plugin-google-analytics` looks like this:

```
// gatsby-config.js
module.exports = {
  plugins: [
    {
      resolve: `gatsby-plugin-google-analytics`,
      options: {
        // The property ID; the tracking code won't be generated without it
        trackingId: "YOUR_GOOGLE_ANALYTICS_TRACKING_ID",
        // Defines where to place the tracking script - `true` in the head
        // and `false` in the body
        head: false,
        // Setting this parameter is optional
        anonymize: true,
        // Setting this parameter is also optional
        respectDNT: true,
        // Avoids sending pageview hits from custom paths
        exclude: ["/preview/**", "/do-not-track/me/too/"],
        // Delays sending pageview hits on route update (in milliseconds)
        pageTransitionDelay: 0,
        // Enables Google Optimize using your container Id
        optimizeId: "YOUR_GOOGLE_OPTIMIZE_TRACKING_ID",
        // Enables Google Optimize Experiment ID
        experimentId: "YOUR_GOOGLE_EXPERIMENT_ID",
        // Set Variation ID. 0 for original 1,2,3....
        variationId: "YOUR_GOOGLE_OPTIMIZE_VARIATION_ID",
        // Defers execution of google analytics script after page load
        defer: false,
        // Any additional optional fields
        sampleRate: 5,
        siteSpeedSampleRate: 10,
        cookieDomain: "example.com",
      },
    },
  ],
}
```

Depending on the nature of your plugin, it may or may not require options.

## Loading Local Plugins

It's also possible to load plugins from your local filesystem, in much the same way you might derive data from the filesystem. Gatsby is able to load plugins from your Gatsby codebase as long as you place them in a top-level *plugins* directory alongside the *src* directory. Local plugins are valuable for cases where you may need to introduce proprietary code to a Gatsby codebase or you wish to write your own custom plugins.

The Gatsby documentation provides an example of a project structure that would leverage a local plugin called gatsby-local-plugin:

```
/my-gatsby-site
└─ /src
    └─ /pages
    └─ /components
└─ /plugins
    └─ /gatsby-local-plugin
        └─ /package.json
        └─ /gatsby-node.js
└─ gatsby-config.js
└─ gatsby-node.js
└─ package.json
```

 You can add any number of local plugins to this folder, as long as they all have distinct names.

With local plugins, you don't need an NPM installation command, but you do need to configure the plugin in *gatsby-config.js* so that Gatsby is aware of it:

```
module.exports = {
  plugins: [`gatsby-local-plugin`]
}
```

To verify your plugin is loading correctly in your Gatsby site, you can add a *gatsby-node.js* file to the *plugins* directory (we'll cover what this file does in Chapter 6) and add a line to the terminal output that is printed when you run either gatsby develop or gatsby build. This line should use one of Gatsby's build hooks, such as onPreI nit (before any other step), which we'll also discuss in more detail in Chapter 6:

```
// plugins/gatsby-local-plugin/gatsby-node.js
exports.onPreInit = () => {
  console.log("Hey, I'm a local plugin that just got loaded! Look at me!")
}
```

In your terminal output, the next time you run gatsby develop or gatsby build, you will see the following:

```
success open and validate gatsby-configs - 0.053s
success load plugins - 1.036s
Hey, I'm a local plugin that just got loaded! Look at me!
success onPreInit - 0.025s
...
```

You can also load a local plugin from outside the *plugins* folder. I'll cover that approach when we look at writing custom plugins in Chapter 9.

# Conclusion

In this chapter, we examined several of the most important foundational concepts in Gatsby in detail to prepare us for an examination of common use cases in Chapter 3. In addition, we inspected the Gatsby CLI commands you'll use most frequently in the day-to-day work of implementing Gatsby, whether that involves spinning up starters quickly, facilitating the use of CSS-in-JS libraries, or installing new plugins.

We also explored the structure of Gatsby projects in terms of pages and components to support your journey into new Gatsby implementations. Because CSS is a baseline requirement for websites today, we also walked through the many possible ways to introduce CSS to your Gatsby site.

In the next chapter, we'll build on this conceptual foundation and begin to work with common use cases to build certain functionality into a boilerplate Gatsby site, including analytics, form handling, contact forms, SEO, 404 pages, and other common requirements in web development today. In the process, we'll find practical applications for all of the underpinnings we covered in this chapter.

# CHAPTER 3

# Adding Features to Gatsby Sites

Now that you're equipped with an understanding of Gatsby fundamentals and core elements, including the Gatsby CLI, starters, pages, components, CSS, and plugins, we can direct our attention to how to introduce and implement certain key features that are common on websites.

In this chapter, we'll take a brief detour from the conceptual underpinnings of Gatsby to focus on real-world use cases and requirements that many Gatsby developers encounter when developing websites. Adding critical features to Gatsby sites such as analytics, authentication, and form handling will help you hone your React and Gatsby skills. In this chapter, we'll build a basic Gatsby site with all of these features, putting what you've learned so far to use.

## Pages and Routing in Gatsby

One of the primary selling points of Gatsby is that it is an SSG, as we discussed in Chapter 1. Nonetheless, thanks to Gatsby's dependency on React, a library for building interactive UIs, Gatsby sites can blur the line between static sites and more dynamic applications. This is a general trend in websites today, with dynamic forms and dynamic search becoming more common than search features and contact forms that require a full-page refresh, and Gatsby follows suit. Once a static rendering of the site is made available to the browser, Gatsby passes the baton to React, which performs all further dynamic or asynchronous operations that need to occur to decorate and enrich the static site with more interactive behavior.

In this section, we won't be adding new features just yet. Instead, we'll establish the background you need to understand how to implement different features in Gatsby, including some of the key ways in which Gatsby allows developers to add those features, whether they are static or dynamic in nature.

# Rehydration

Once Gatsby's generated static files are flushed (i.e., transmitted) to the browser, Gatsby sites perform *rehydration,* a process common in universal JavaScript (Java-Script that can run both on the client and the server) in which static HTML that was rendered through ReactDOM APIs on the server is bound to dynamic JavaScript initialized through the client-side React bundle. Rehydration occurs in the following sequence:

1. First, Gatsby builds and renders static HTML through ReactDOM APIs on the server side, with the retrieval of content and pages occurring during build-time compilation. This is initiated by execution of the `gatsby build` command, which launches a Node.js server to render HTML into static files in the */public* folder.

2. Next, Gatsby invokes ReactDOM's `hydrate` method to pick up any further rendering from where the static HTML left off. `ReactDOM.hydrate()` is used for those areas whose HTML contents were rendered by `ReactDOMServer`.

3. Finally, Gatsby transfers rendering to the React reconciler, which performs rehydration of the Gatsby-generated static site. The React reconciler is also responsible for tracking changes in the DOM tree and implementing updates as needed based on state and props changes.

In other words, Gatsby allows rendering to happen arbitrarily in two locations: build-time compilation on the server side is responsible for generating the initial static HTML, and React reconciliation and rehydration on the client side are responsible for any further dynamic behavior the page requires. In this way, Gatsby sites can make calls for dynamic data and perform asynchronous actions like user authentication without requiring the use of a completely separate development paradigm.

Gatsby makes three types of routes (equivalent to pages in Gatsby) available: static, dynamic (client-only), and a hybrid of the two. We'll cover each of them in turn in the coming three sections.

# Static Pages

*Static pages* are the primary approach to working with Gatsby. As you saw in the previous chapters, Gatsby automatically detects new JavaScript files that are located in the *src/pages* folder in order to convert them into static pages. Later in the book, you'll see that programmatic page creation also follows this pattern to generate static pages based on particular parameters.

Figure 3-1 shows how Gatsby can automatically create pages from files placed in *src/pages* as well as programmatically create pages through the `createPages` API, which we cover at length in Chapter 6.

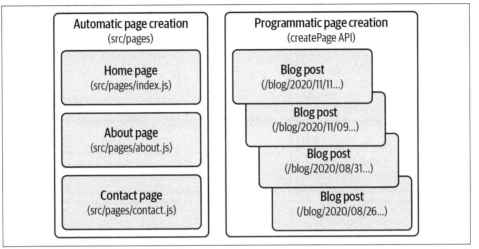

Figure 3-1. An illustration of the difference between static page creation, driven by developers placing a page in the src/pages directory, and programmatic page creation through the createPages API

> Gatsby plugins and themes can also implement the createPages API and create Gatsby pages on your behalf programmatically. We cover this workflow in Chapter 6.

## Hybrid Application Pages

In Gatsby, *hybrid application pages* are pages that contain both static HTML generated by Gatsby and dynamic HTML and JavaScript, which means they connect to external services and APIs serving data asynchronously through API requests. We call these pages "hybrid" because they leverage Gatsby's performance benefits in the form of static site performance and the client-side benefits of greater interactivity and dynamism in the browser.

Figure 3-2 depicts how Gatsby can provide static HTML that outlines the initial markup for a form, with a subsequent asynchronous POST request occurring once the form is submitted.

Note that any asynchronous API requests can be realized through this paradigm, including GET requests to populate a section of the page that requires much more "live" or "real-time" data than Gatsby's build-time compilation would be able to facilitate. Though this paradigm depends on the constant availability of backend services, which isn't the case in static pages, these more dynamic integrations are often of critical importance for business logic.

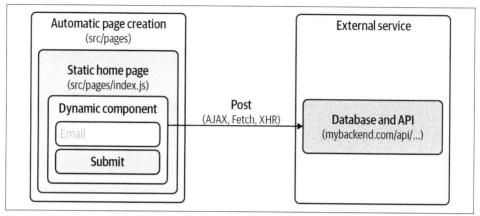

*Figure 3-2. In hybrid application pages, a static page contains a dynamic component that issues an asynchronous POST request to communicate with an external service*

## Client-Only Routes

Because Gatsby is built on top of React, it's possible to leverage React's client-side router to provide *client-only routes* that don't represent a full static page or a full hybrid application page. Gatsby ships with the accessible router @reach/router, now part of the core React Router library, which allows you to refrain from introducing other routing dependencies from the React ecosystem. In short, client-only routes made available by React on the client side are not registered among the statically rendered files or pages created during Gatsby's build-time compilation.

Figure 3-3 shows an example of how client-only routes can enrich static Gatsby sites with dynamic and asynchronous routing based on information such as the logged-in user's profile or a response in a form field earlier in the page.

To allow users to bookmark or link to the URL for a client-only route directly, you will need to use a plugin to create those pages under Gatsby's purview so Gatsby is aware of them.

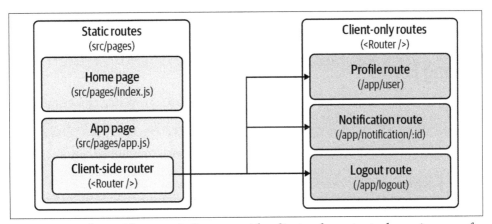

*Figure 3-3. A client-side router in React provides client-only routes to dynamic areas of the site where authentication is needed or where a static page isn't possible; in this scenario, Gatsby delegates client-only routes to React*

## Differences Between Gatsby Sites and React Applications

This section covers the differences between React development paradigms like the Create React App (CRA) project and Gatsby. Though a site built with React's official CRA boilerplate can easily be ported to Gatsby, it's important to recognize these differences, particularly for developers context-switching between the two approaches.

Gatsby differs from normal CRA applications in a few crucial ways:

1. *React uses App.js; Gatsby uses pages.* Instead of a single global *App.js* component, which is common in CRA and registers all client routes on that component, Gatsby delivers a collection of multiple pages that can be either hybrid or static.

2. *React requires routers; Gatsby automates routing.* Instead of creating pages through setting up a React-compatible router, Gatsby provides automatic and programmatic ways to generate pages that represent routes. When files are placed into the *src/pages* directory, Gatsby generates fixed URLs for each based on the component name. For client-side routing, developers can introduce routing driven by React on the client side.

Porting CRA applications to Gatsby sites is beyond the scope of this book, but the documentation includes a guide to migrating CRA implementations to Gatsby (*https://oreil.ly/KOvRj*).

Now that you understand how implementing additional features in Gatsby often requires distinct approaches to pages and routing, we can move ahead to adding key features to our sites. Remember that many of these implementations will require some combination of static pages, hybrid application pages, and dynamic (client-only) routes, depending on the desired user experience.

# Adding Forms

One of the most common needs in any website is HTML forms that collect information from users, whether that data is intended for authentication or for some response from an external service. Because Gatsby is built on top of React, many of the same approaches used to build and handle forms in React carry over into Gatsby.

## Basic Forms

Let's take a look at how we can introduce basic form markup and handling into any Gatsby site. To begin, we'll create another version of the Gatsby default starter (we'll build on top of the default starter throughout the remainder of this chapter, ending up with a Gatsby site with a variety of features):

```
$ gatsby new gtdg-ch3-features gatsbyjs/gatsby-starter-default
$ cd gtdg-ch3-features
```

Let's add another page named *src/pages/basic-form.js* with the following code. Note that here we're introducing several state props that we want to ensure Gatsby tracks, so we are instantiating a new class based on `React.Component`:

```
// src/pages/basic-form.js
import React from "react"
import { Link } from "gatsby"

import Layout from "../components/layout"
import Seo from "../components/seo"

export default class BasicFormPage extends React.Component {
  state = {
    firstName: "",
    lastName: "",
    country: "",
    city: "",
  }
  render() {
    return (
      <Layout>
        <Seo title="Basic form" />
        <h1>Hi from the basic form page</h1>
        <p>Welcome to the basic form page</p>
        <Link to="/">Go back to the homepage</Link>
      </Layout>
    )
  }
}
```

Now, we can add several HTML <input> elements to render a form on the basic form page. As you can see, we've replaced the "Welcome to the basic form page" paragraph with an HTML form:

```
// src/pages/basic-form.js
export default class BasicFormPage extends React.Component {
  state = {
    firstName: "",
    lastName: "",
    city: "",
    country: "",
  }
  render() {
    return (
      <Layout>
        <Seo title="Basic form" />
        <h1>Hi from the basic form page</h1>
        <form>
          <label>
            First name
            <input type="text" name="firstName" />
          </label>
          <label>
            Last name
            <input type="text" name="lastName" />
          </label>
          <label>
            City
            <input type="text" name="city" />
          </label>
          <label>
            Country
            <input type="text" name="country" />
          </label>
          <button type="submit">Submit</button>
        </form>
        <Link to="/">Go back to the homepage</Link>
      </Layout>
    )
  }
}
```

In React, one of the key tenets of state management is that any change to user input in a form element should result in an update to the state props we've defined (first Name, lastName, city, and country). To handle changes to input, let's add an onChange prop to each <input> element and a value prop to keep the input up to date:

```
// src/pages/basic-form.js
export default class BasicFormPage extends React.Component {
  state = {
```

```
    firstName: "",
    lastName: "",
    city: "",
    country: "",
}

handleInputChange = event => {
  const target = event.target
  const value = target.value
  const name = target.name

  this.setState({
    [name]: value,
  })
}

render() {
  return (
    <Layout>
      <Seo title="Basic form" />
      <h1>Hi from the basic form page</h1>
      <form>
        <label>
          First name
          <input
            type="text"
            name="firstName"
            value={this.state.firstName}
            onChange={this.handleInputChange}
          />
        </label>
        <label>
          Last name
          <input
            type="text"
            name="lastName"
            value={this.state.lastName}
            onChange={this.handleInputChange}
          />
        </label>
        <label>
          City
          <input
            type="text"
            name="city"
            value={this.state.city}
            onChange={this.handleInputChange}
          />
        </label>
        <label>
          Country
          <input
```

```
              type="text"
              name="country"
              value={this.state.country}
              onChange={this.handleInputChange}
            />
          </label>
          <button type="submit">Submit</button>
        </form>
        <Link to="/">Go back to the homepage</Link>
      </Layout>
    )
  }
}
```

 This example does not use React Hooks, a common paradigm Gatsby developers can use to replace class-based components. We'll see some examples of its use in the next chapter.

Now, whenever we change any of the contents of the <input> elements on the page, our state will update with the new values in those form elements. But what happens when we submit the form? Currently, because we haven't added an onSubmit event handler, the submit button won't work as expected.

What we need to do is add another method right underneath handleInputChange that handles our submit event: handleSubmit. For brevity's sake, the following example shows just the definitions of handleInputChange and handleSubmit:

```
// src/pages/basic-form.js
// ...

  handleInputChange = event => {
    const target = event.target
    const value = target.value
    const name = target.name

    this.setState({
      [name]: value,
    })
  }

  handleSubmit = event => {
    event.preventDefault()
    alert(`
      Howdy ${this.state.firstName} ${this.state.lastName}
      from ${this.state.city}, ${this.state.country}
    `)
  }
```

```
// ...
```

We also need to invoke the `handleSubmit` handler when the form is submitted, which we do by adding an `onSubmit` attribute to the form element:

```
<form onSubmit={this.handleSubmit}>
```

Now, our basic form performs a submit action by displaying an alert message containing our newly input values. But now that we have a submission handler, how do we extend it so that we can pass user input on to an external service as needed?

 The React ecosystem has several libraries that make developing forms much easier in React applications and Gatsby sites, such as Formik (*https://oreil.ly/uDXNq*) and Final Form (*https://oreil.ly/uY65J*).

## Handling Form Submissions

In many traditional websites, whenever a form is submitted, the contents of the user-provided inputs are passed to a server, which handles the data and responds in some fashion. In the example from the previous section, we wrote some rudimentary logic for an alert message to display the user-submitted data.

If the logic handling form submissions is all housed within the confines of your React application, you'll write React code to control what happens when the user submits a form. But in the case of common forms like contact forms, you'll want to store that information somewhere else, such as in an external database or CRM system. Let's copy the contents of *src/pages/page-2.js* into another file named *src/pages/contact.js*. Replace the paragraph element again with a form whose purpose is to request a name, an email address, and a message:

```
// src/pages/contact.js
import React from "react"
import { Link } from "gatsby"

import Layout from "../components/layout"
import Seo from "../components/seo"

export default class ContactPage extends React.Component {
  render() {
    return (
      <Layout>
        <Seo title="Contact" />
        <h1>Hi from the contact page</h1>
        <form method="post" action="#">
          <label>
            Name
            <input type="text" name="name" id="name" />
```

```
        </label>
        <label>
          Email
          <input type="email" name="email" id="email" />
        </label>
        <label>
          Message
          <textarea name="message" id="message" rows="6" />
        </label>
        <button type="submit">Submit</button>
        <input type="reset" value="Reset" />
      </form>
      <Link to="/">Go back to the homepage</Link>
    </Layout>
  )
 }
}
```

There are four ways to handle form submissions in Gatsby:

1. Getform

2. Netlify Forms

3. Formspree

4. Roll your own server

We'll cover the first three in the next three sections. The final approach, setting up your own form handler in an HTTP server, is well beyond the scope of this book. If you have a working form handler, the value of the `action` attribute becomes the endpoint at which your server accepts form submissions:

```
<form method="post"
      action="https://my-form-handler-wxyz789.vercel.app/contact">
```

Getform, Netlify Forms, and Formspree all offer code examples for common requirements such as Ajax-based form submissions and reCAPTCHAs to prevent spam.

## Getform

*Getform* is a backend form service that offers a free tier for handling form submissions that originate from static sites. As you can see here, you need to make only one small modification to the form we wrote earlier:

```
// src/pages/contact.js
import React from "react"
import { Link } from "gatsby"
```

```
import Layout from "../components/layout"
import Seo from "../components/seo"

export default class ContactPage extends React.Component {
  render() {
    return (
      <Layout>
        <Seo title="Contact" />
        <h1>Hi from the contact page></h1>
        <form
          method="post"
          action="https://getform.io/your-getform-endpoint-here" ❶
        >
          <label>
            Name
            <input type="text" name="name" id="name" />
          ></label>
          <label>
            Email
            <input type="email" name="email" id="email" />
          ></label>
          <label>
            Message
            <textarea name="message" id="message" rows="6" />
          ></label>
          <button type="submit">Submit></button>
          <input type="reset" value="Reset" />
        ></form>
        <Link to="/">Go back to the homepage></Link>
      ></Layout>
    )
  }
}
```

❶  Point the value of the action attribute to your unique Getform endpoint.

Then, once the changes are applied and your Getform endpoint is configured, you'll begin to see your Getform dashboard populated with the form submissions.

 For more information about Getform, consult the Getform website (*https://getform.io*).

## Netlify Forms

*Netlify Forms* is a form submission collection feature available for free on the Netlify hosting platform, which offers infrastructure for static sites. Netlify has its own form-handling feature that works similarly to Getform and again requires only a few updates to the original form:

```
// src/pages/contact.js
import React from "react"
import { Link } from "gatsby"

import Layout from "../components/layout"
import Seo from "../components/seo"

export default class ContactPage extends React.Component {
  render() {
    return (
      <Layout>
        <Seo title="Contact" />
        <h1>Hi from the contact page</h1>
        <form
          method="post"
          netlify-honeypot="bot-field"       ❶
          data-netlify="true"
          name="contact"
        >
          <input type="hidden" name="bot-field" />    ❷
          <input type="hidden" name="form-name" value="contact" />
          <label>
            Name
            <input type="text" name="name" id="name" />
          </label>
          <label>
            Email
            <input type="email" name="email" id="email" />
          </label>
          <label>
            Message
            <textarea name="message" id="message" rows="6" />
          </label>
          <button type="submit">Submit</button>
          <input type="reset" value="Reset" />
        </form>
        <Link to="/">Go back to the homepage</Link>
      </Layout>
    )
  }
}
```

❶ Add Netlify's required form attributes.

❷ Add Netlify's two required hidden input fields.

Once Netlify recognizes the form, you'll see your Forms dashboard in Netlify being populated with form submissions.

 For more information about Netlify Forms, consult the Netlify Forms documentation (*https://oreil.ly/cmgiV*).

### Formspree

*Formspree* differs from both Getform and Netlify Forms in that it provides a free tier for form submissions to be delivered to an email address rather than a web dashboard. All form submissions will be sent to the configured address:

```
// src/pages/contact.js
import React from "react"
import { Link } from "gatsby"

import Layout from "../components/layout"
import Seo from "../components/seo"

export default class ContactPage extends React.Component {
  render() {
    return (
      <Layout>
        <Seo title="Contact" />
        <h1>Hi from the contact page</h1>
        <form
          method="post"
          action="https://formspree.io/email@me.com" ❶
        >
          <label>
            Name
            <input type="text" name="name" id="name" />
          </label>
          <label>
            Email
            <input type="email" name="_replyto" id="email" /> ❷
          </label>
          <label>
            Message
            <textarea name="message" id="message" rows="6" />
          </label>
          <button type="submit">Submit</button>
          <input type="reset" value="Reset" />
```

```
        </form>
        <Link to="/">Go back to the homepage</Link>
      </Layout>
    )
  }
}
```

❶  Point the value of the form's `action` attribute to your email address.

❷  Add the Formspree-specific value of the `name` attribute (`_replyto`) on the `<input>` element collecting a visitor's email address.

Also note that while Formspree comes with reCAPTCHA enabled by default, you can also enable spam filtering through Honeypot by adding a hidden `<input>` element with the name `_gotcha`, similarly to how Netlify Forms includes hidden `<input>` elements to prevent spam:

```
<input type="hidden" name="_gotcha" />
```

> For more information about Formspree, consult the Formspree website (*https://formspree.io*).

# Adding Localization and Internationalization

For Gatsby sites with multiple audiences, whether that means different regions or different language communities, *localization* (l10n) and *internationalization* (i18n) comprise essential functionality. Generally speaking, the processes of localization and internationalization entail providing translations of text, date formats, numbers, and other elements that adhere to the expectations of a user's location. As an example, though dates in the United States follow the *MM/DD/YYYY* date format, Japanese users follow the *YYYY-MM-DD* format.

The React ecosystem makes available several different packages for internationalization, each with its own advantages and disadvantages. For this reason, it's best to evaluate each package based on factors such as whether you are already using that internationalization package on other projects, how well it serves your users' requirements, and how well documented and well maintained the package is.

In this section, we cover three of the available packages, starting with the Gatsby ecosystem's own internationalization plugin.

## gatsby-plugin-i18n

The `gatsby-plugin-i18n` plugin integrates directly with the `react-intl` and `react-i18next` libraries (discussed next) to facilitate integration with Gatsby sites. Though `gatsby-plugin-i18n` itself does not perform any translation or reformatting, it uses Gatsby's built-in page system to create routes for each localization or internationalization and to permit layout changes (e.g., for right-to-left languages). Once you install `gatsby-plugin-i18n`, your localized or internationalized versions of Gatsby pages will adhere to the format in Table 3-1.

*Table 3-1. How page filenames and resulting URLs change based on the use of the gatsby-plugin-i18n plugin*

| Scenario | Page filename | Page URL |
| --- | --- | --- |
| No localization or internationalization | *src/pages/contact.js* | *mygatsbysite.com/contact* |
| With localization or internationalization | *src/pages/contact.**en**.js* | *mygatsbysite.com/**en**/contact* |

## react-intl

The `react-intl` library, part of the FormatJS collection of internationalization libraries, is based on JavaScript's standard Internationalization API and offers built-in support for more than 150 languages. `react-intl` uses React context and higher-order components (HOCs) in React to provide translations. In React parlance, this means that you can dynamically load language modules as you require them and remove them from bundles when they aren't needed. `react-intl` integrates with `gatsby-plugin-i18n` and a polyfill for browsers that don't yet support the JavaScript i18n API.

## react-i18next

The `react-i18next` library is built on top of the `i18next` framework and leverages components to ensure that translations are rendered where needed and to dynamically update page content when the user selects a new language. `react-i18next` can be more flexible than `react-intl` depending on your needs, especially if they involve caching, server-side translations, and bundling translations using Webpack. The `react-i18next` library also makes use of modern React APIs such as the Suspense API and React Hooks.

Examining these React libraries would require considerable discussion of projects specific to the React ecosystem and be well outside the scope of this book, so we'll end our exploration of localization and internationalization here. Just be aware that because multilingual and multilocale capabilities remain in significant flux in both the React and Gatsby ecosystems, the Gatsby community has not yet unified around a standard set of best practices.

---

For more comprehensive information about these libraries, consult the respective documentation for `gatsby-plugin-i18n` (*https://oreil.ly/ebKP0*), `react-intl` (*https://oreil.ly/FaAkO*), and `react-i18next` (*https://react.i18next.com*). A tutorial by Samuel Goudie called "Building i18n with Gatsby" (*https://oreil.ly/fXngM*) is also available in the Gatsby blog.

# Adding an XML Sitemap

In traditional websites, *sitemaps* are important means for visitors to understand the overarching structure and information architecture as quickly as possible. Generally, XML sitemaps display the website's most critical pages and ensure that search engines discover them all. In other words, sitemaps are like maps for your website.

Gatsby has an official plugin, `gatsby-plugin-sitemap`, which provides automatic generation of XML sitemaps on every Gatsby build. To install `gatsby-plugin-sitemap`, change directories to the root of your Gatsby project and execute one of the following commands:

```
# If using NPM
$ npm install gatsby-plugin-sitemap

# If using Yarn
$ yarn add gatsby-plugin-sitemap
```

Then, in your *gatsby-config.js* file housing site information and plugins, add `gatsby-plugin-sitemap` to the `plugins` array:

```
module.exports = {
  siteMetadata: {
    siteUrl: `https://www.mygatsbyurl.com`,
  },
  plugins: [`gatsby-plugin-sitemap`],
}
```

The `gatsby-plugin-sitemap` plugin requires the `siteUrl` value to be populated and not empty in order to function properly. In addition, `gatsby-plugin-sitemap` has a variety of options that can be overridden based on configuration in *gatsby-config.js*. For a full account of the options, consult the plugin documentation (*https://oreil.ly/usUew*).

Now, when you run a production build (with `gatsby build` or `npm run build`), `gatsby-plugin-sitemap` will automatically generate a new sitemap based on the current state of your pages located at */sitemap.xml* (Figure 3-4).

```
-<urlset>
  -<url>
      <loc>https://www.mygatsbyurl.com/basic-form/</loc>
      <changefreq>daily</changefreq>
      <priority>0.7</priority>
  </url>
  -<url>
      <loc>https://www.mygatsbyurl.com/contact/</loc>
      <changefreq>daily</changefreq>
      <priority>0.7</priority>
  </url>
  -<url>
      <loc>https://www.mygatsbyurl.com/</loc>
      <changefreq>daily</changefreq>
      <priority>0.7</priority>
  </url>
  -<url>
      <loc>https://www.mygatsbyurl.com/page-2/</loc>
      <changefreq>daily</changefreq>
      <priority>0.7</priority>
  </url>
  -<url>
      <loc>https://www.mygatsbyurl.com/using-typescript/</loc>
      <changefreq>daily</changefreq>
      <priority>0.7</priority>
  </url>
</urlset>
```

*Figure 3-4. The sitemap generated by the `gatsby-plugin-sitemap` plugin upon execution of the gatsby build command*

To avoid any unexpected surprises, it's important to note that `gatsby-plugin-sitemap` always excludes these pages: */dev-404-page* (Gatsby's development 404 page), */404* (a developer-defined 404 page), and */offline-plugin-app-shell-fallback* (an offline fallback). These cannot be modified; we'll discuss the first two in the next section.

> A `gatsby-plugin-advanced-sitemap` plugin is available that offers more configuration possibilities and options to generate single or multiple sitemaps that contain XSL templates for better formatting. For more information, consult the plugin page (*https://oreil.ly/eDwG4*) and Aileen Nowak's blog post (*https://oreil.ly/Bcy5t*) about its usage.

# Adding a 404 Page

One of the most important error pages in any website is the 404 page, which handles 404 Not Found errors for users who have clicked a broken link or entered a nonexistent URL. The most common and straightforward method to add a 404 page to a Gatsby website is to simply create a new page at *src/pages/404.js*.

Because many static hosting platforms default to sending users to a *404.html* page, naming your 404 page in this way will ensure that Gatsby automatically detects it and places it in the expected location in the */public* directory. Fortunately, our Gatsby default starter already creates a 404 page for us. Open the file *src/pages/404.js*, and you'll see the following code:

```
// src/pages/404.js
import React from "react"

import Layout from "../components/layout"
import Seo from "../components/seo"

const NotFoundPage = () => (
  <Layout>
    <Seo title="404: Not found" />
    <h1>404: Not Found</h1>
    <p>You just hit a route that doesn't exist...the sadness.</p>
  </Layout>
)

export default NotFoundPage
```

You can replace this with your own desired 404 page content, such as a link back to the home page or a list of common destinations for users who have landed in the wrong place. When you deploy your Gatsby site online, whenever you type in a URL absent from the site, the 404 page will display (Figure 3-5).

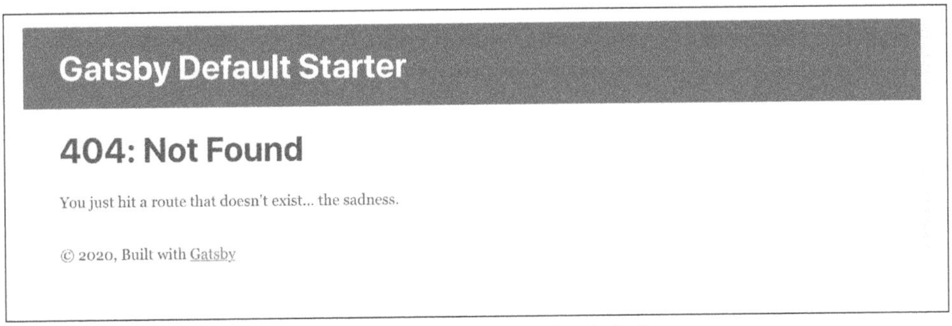

*Figure 3-5. The default 404 page built into the Gatsby default starter*

If you have a local development server running with `gatsby develop`, Gatsby will override your custom 404 page with its own internal "Gatsby.js development 404 page," which provides some useful developer actions. It also makes a "Preview custom 404 page" button available so you can still access your custom 404 page from the Gatsby development server's own 404 page.

# Adding Analytics

Often one of the aspects of web development left to the end of the implementation process, *analytics* is one of the best ways to gain insights into how your visitors and users interact with your website, including which areas are the most visited, where users are coming across your site, and at what times they come by.

Though there are a variety of analytics services available, the most commonly used with Gatsby sites is Google Analytics, which provides a free tier for up to 10 million hits per month per Tracking ID (a single Google Analytics property).

Once you've set up a Google Analytics account (if you don't have one already), you'll be prompted by the interface to create a new *property*, which is associated with a single Tracking ID. Each website will generally need a separate Tracking ID to avoid corrupting the incoming data. Tracking IDs have the format *UA-XXXXXXXXX-X*.

Now, we'll add Google Analytics support to our Gatsby site using the `gatsby-plugin-gtag` plugin, which can be installed using the following commands:

```
# If using NPM
$ npm install gatsby-plugin-gtag

# If using Yarn
$ yarn add gatsby-plugin-gtag
```

In *gatsby-config.js*, add your plugin to the `plugins` array and configure it by adding an `options` object that contains your own `trackingId` from Google Analytics:

```
// gatsby-config.js
module.exports = {
  plugins: [
    {
      resolve: `gatsby-plugin-gtag`,
      options: {
        trackingId: `UA-XXXXXXXX-X`,
      },
    },
  ],
}
```

Now, when you check your Google Analytics dashboard for your Gatsby property, you'll begin to see analytics data streaming in.

# Conclusion

In this chapter, we took a closer look at some of the most common requirements that web developers face when implementing a new website, including form handling, localization and internationalization, analytics, and necessities like an XML sitemap and a 404 page. In the process, we revisited many of the concepts from the first two chapters, including the Gatsby CLI, JSX in Gatsby, Gatsby pages and components, and working with Gatsby plugins. We also implemented a variety of forms, sitemaps, 404 pages, and analytics.

Though this chapter involved many interactions with external services and use cases that may be less useful for your purposes, it allowed us to engage in a comprehensive review of some of the foundational concepts in Chapters 1 and 2. This is important because in Chapters 4 and 5 we'll move into the Gatsby data layer, GraphQL, and source plugins, which interact in rich ways to facilitate the retrieval and management of external data. With a few more features in our Gatsby site, we can begin to substitute hardcoded content and data for real-world information coming from disparate sources.

# PART II

# Data in Gatsby

# CHAPTER 4

# GraphQL and the Gatsby Data Layer

Up until now, all of our work on implementing Gatsby has focused on use cases that don't require data retrieval and processing. Before we turn our attention to how Gatsby integrates with external data, in this chapter we'll cover the data layer in Gatsby, whether data comes from files in your Gatsby site (the local filesystem) or from external sources such as CMSs, commerce systems, or backend databases (external data sources that require a source plugin, discussed in more detail in Chapter 5).

Within Gatsby's data layer, GraphQL mediates the relationship between Gatsby pages and components and the data that populates those pages and components. Though GraphQL is popular in web development as a query language, Gatsby uses it *internally* to provide a single unified approach to handling and managing data. With data potentially originating from a variety of disparate sources, Gatsby flattens the differences between discrete serialization formats (forms of articulating data) and thus third-party systems by populating a GraphQL API that is accessible from any Gatsby page or component.

In this chapter, we'll explore the foundations of GraphQL that apply to any GraphQL API before switching gears to look at how Gatsby uses GraphQL specifically in its data layer and in page and component queries.

# GraphQL Fundamentals

GraphQL is a query language that provides client-tailored queries. That is, unlike REST APIs, which adhere to the requirements dictated by the server, GraphQL APIs respond to client queries with a response that adheres to the shape of that query. Today, GraphQL APIs are commonplace for backend database access, headless CMS consumption, and other cross-system use cases, but it's still quite rare to find GraphQL used internally within a framework.

GraphQL has become popular thanks to the flexibility it provides developers and the more favorable developer experience it facilitates through client-driven queries. Common motivations for using it include:

*Avoiding response bloat*
> GraphQL improves query performance by only serving that data that is necessary to populate the response according to the client-issued query. In traditional REST APIs, response payload sizes can be larger than necessary, or additional requests may be required to acquire the needed information.

*Query-time data transformations*
> In many JavaScript implementations, data postprocessing needs to occur to harmonize data formats or to perform a sort operation. GraphQL offers means to perform data transformations on the fly at query time through the use of explicitly defined arguments within a GraphQL API.

*Offloading request complexity*
> In many JavaScript implementations, correctly issuing a query often requires a complex interplay between promises, XMLHttpRequest implementations, and waiting for the requested data to arrive. Because GraphQL only requires a query, as opposed to a particular URL (and potentially headers and request bodies), it may provide a smoother developer experience.

Using GraphQL does have some disadvantages, too—notably, GraphQL APIs can be difficult to scale due to the need to serve a response that is tightly tailored to the client's query. Fortunately, because Gatsby uses GraphQL during development and build-time compilation, that latency only impacts the build duration rather than the end user's time to first interaction.

To get you up to speed, in the coming sections we'll cover GraphQL queries, fields, arguments, query variables, directives, fragments, and finally schemas and types.

## GraphQL Queries

The primary means of interacting with a GraphQL API from the client is a *query*, which is a declarative expression of data requirements from the server.

Consider the following example GraphQL query, which in Gatsby returns the title of the Gatsby site from its metadata:

```
{
  site {
    siteMetadata {
      title
    }
  }
}
```

Gatsby's internal GraphQL API will return the following response to this query:

```
{
  "data": {
    "site": {
      "siteMetadata": {
        "title": "A Gatsby site!"
      }
    }
  },
  "extensions": {}
}
```

Notice how the GraphQL query and response are structurally identical: they share the same hierarchy and the same sequence of names. In other words, a typical GraphQL query issued by a client outlines the shape that the GraphQL response issued by the server should take. The pseudo-JSON structure of the GraphQL query becomes a valid JSON object in the GraphQL response.

The preceding GraphQL query is anonymous; it lacks an explicit name. But in GraphQL, you can identify queries with an *operation type* and an *operation name*. Here, query is the operation type, and GetSiteInfo is the operation name:

```
query GetSiteInfo {
  site {
    siteMetadata {
      title
    }
  }
}
```

You can also identify the operation type without an operation name, if you wish to write an anonymous query. This and the previous query return identical responses:

```
query {
  site {
```

```
    siteMetadata {
      title
    }
  }
}
```

 GraphQL queries are read operations; they retrieve data. There is another operation type, mutation, which handles write operations. However, Gatsby does not provide mutation support within its internal GraphQL API due to its impact on how Gatsby functions, so we do not cover mutations here. For more information about GraphQL beyond Gatsby, including GraphQL mutations, consult *Learning GraphQL* by Eve Porcello and Alex Banks (O'Reilly).

## GraphQL Fields

Let's take another look at the anonymous version of the query:

```
{
  site {
    siteMetadata {
      title
    }
  }
}
```

In GraphQL, each of the words contained within the query (site, siteMetadata, title) that identify inner elements are known as *fields*. Those fields located at the top level (e.g., site) are occasionally referred to as *root-level fields*, but keep in mind that all GraphQL fields behave identically, and there is no functional difference between fields at any point in a query's hierarchy.

GraphQL fields are crucial because they tell the GraphQL API what information the client desires for further processing and rendering. In GraphQL APIs outside Gatsby, the client and server are generally distinct from an architectural perspective. But in Gatsby, the GraphQL server and client are contained within the same framework; for our purposes, React and Gatsby components are our GraphQL clients.

Fields can take *aliases*, which allow us to arbitrarily rename any GraphQL field in the schema to something else in the resulting response from the API. In the following example, though the title field is identified as such in the schema, we've aliased it to siteName in our query, so the server will return a JSON object containing siteName as the identifier rather than title:

```
{
  site {
    siteMetadata {
      siteName: title
```

```
      }
    }
  }
```

Aliases can be particularly useful when you wish to serve the same data multiple times but in a different form, since GraphQL prohibits repeating the same field name twice in a single query:

```
{
  defaultSite: site {
    siteMetadata {
      title
    }
  }
  aliasedSite: site {
    metadata: siteMetadata {
      siteName: title
    }
  }
}
```

 Gatsby structures its data according to common GraphQL conventions. Each individual data object in Gatsby is a *node*. In Gatsby's GraphQL API, nodes are connected through *edges*, which are ranges that represent all the nodes returned for a given query.

## GraphQL Arguments

In GraphQL, *arguments* are used to apply certain criteria to the fields in the response. These can be as simple as sort criteria, such as ascending or descending alphabetical order, or as complex as date formatters, which return dates according to the format stipulated by an argument applied to a field.

Let's take a look at a more complex query to understand how to refine the sort of response that comes back through arguments applied to fields—we'll discuss many of the unfamiliar aspects of this query in subsequent chapters:

```
query {
  site {
    siteMetadata {
      title
    }
  }
  allMarkdownRemark {
    nodes {
      excerpt
      fields {
        slug
      }
      frontmatter {
```

```
        date(formatString: "MMMM DD, YYYY")
        title
        description
      }
    }
  }
}
```

In this anonymous query, we see an example of an argument on the date field, named formatString:

```
date(formatString: "MMMM DD, YYYY")
```

In many databases and servers, dates are stored as Unix timestamps or in a machine-friendly format rather than a human-readable format. To display a date like 2021-11-05 in a more user-friendly form in the response, we can use a GraphQL argument on the date field to perform query-time date formatting. In this example, the date would be formatted as:

```
"November 5, 2021"
```

In addition to providing a date format to the formatString argument on the date field, we can also define a locale to adapt the outputted date to the preferred locale or language, which will have different names for months and days of the week. For example:

```
date(
  formatString: "D MMMM YYYY"
  locale: "tr"
)
```

Because tr represents the Turkish language and region, our date will have the Turkish name for the month of November (note that we've also supplied a formatString appropriate to the region):

```
"5 Kasım 2021"
```

As mentioned previously, aliases allow us to serve multiple dates in different formats in the same response without running afoul of GraphQL's prohibition of repeated field names in a single query:

```
englishDate: date(formatString: "MMMM DD, YYYY")
turkishDate: date(
  formatString: "D MMMM YYYY",
  locale: "tr"
)
```

You can also use fromNow, which returns a string showing how long ago or how far in the future the returned date is, and difference, which returns the difference between the date and current time in the specified unit (e.g., days or weeks):

```
firstDate: date(fromNow: true)
secondDate: date(difference: "weeks")
```

 Gatsby depends on a library known as Moment.js to format dates. The Moment.js documentation has a full accounting of tokens for date formatters (*https://oreil.ly/HPZQv*). Note that to introduce locales unavailable by default (Moment.js ships with English–US locale strings by default), you will need to load the locale into Moment.js (*https://oreil.ly/sfVww*).

Though string formatters are a common type of argument found in GraphQL APIs, other arguments influence not only the field they are attached to but also all fields nested within. For instance, given a query that returns multiple objects of a given type, GraphQL arguments exist that allow you to arbitrarily limit, skip, filter, or sort the objects returned in the response.

 The group field in GraphQL also accepts an arbitrary field argument by which to group results. For an illustration of using group, see Chapter 8.

### limit and skip

In the following query, we have added a `limit` argument to ensure that only four items are returned:

```
{
  allMarkdownRemark(limit: 4) {
    edges {
      node {
        frontmatter {
          title
        }
      }
    }
  }
}
```

The response to this query will contain only four items, even if there are more than four present.

In the following query, we've added a `skip` argument so the GraphQL API excludes the first five items from the list and returns only four items from that point onward:

```
{
  allMarkdownRemark(limit: 4, skip: 5) {
    edges {
      node {
```

```
        frontmatter {
          title
        }
      }
    }
  }
}
```

The response to this query will contain only four items, having skipped the first five in the list. Assuming there are at least nine items available, the response will contain items six through nine.

### filter

In the following query, we've added a `filter` argument that uses the `ne` (not equal) operator to ensure that the `title` field within the `frontmatter` field will be excluded from the response if it contains no content:

```
{
  allMarkdownRemark(
    filter: {
      frontmatter: {
        title: {
          ne: ""
        }
      }
    }
  ) {
    edges {
      node {
        frontmatter {
          title
        }
      }
    }
  }
}
```

The response to this query will exclude any items in which the `title` field is empty.

Gatsby uses a package known as *Sift* to perform filtering through a MongoDB-like syntax that will be familiar to developers who routinely work with MongoDB databases. Therefore, Gatsby's GraphQL API supports common operators such as `eq` (equal), `ne` (not equal), `in` (is this item in an arbitrary list?), and `regex` (arbitrary regular expressions). You can also filter on multiple fields, as in the following example, which checks for an item that contains the `title` "Their Eyes Were Watching God" and does not have an empty `date`:

```
allMarkdownRemark(
  filter: {
    frontmatter: {
```

```
      title: {
        eq: "Their Eyes Were Watching God"
      }
      date: {
        ne: ""
      }
    }
  }
)
```

These operators can even be combined on the same field. This example filters for items containing the string "Watching" but excludes "Their Eyes Were Watching God" from the returned results:

```
allMarkdownRemark(
  filter: {
    frontmatter: {
      title: {
        regex: "/Watching/"
        ne: "Their Eyes Were Watching God"
      }
    }
  }
)
```

Thanks to Sift, Gatsby provides a variety of useful operators for filter arguments (see Table 4-1).

*Table 4-1. A full list of operators that can be used in Gatsby's GraphQL API for filtering*

| Operator | Meaning | Definition |
|---|---|---|
| eq | Equal | Must match the given data exactly |
| ne | Not equal | Must differ from the given data |
| regex | Regular expression | Must match the given regular expression (in Gatsby 2.0, backslashes must be escaped twice, so /\+/ must be written as /\\\\+/) |
| glob | Global | Permits the use of * as a wildcard, which acts as a placeholder for any nonempty string |
| in | In array | Must be a member of the array |
| nin | Not in array | Must not be a member of the array |
| gt | Greater than | Must be greater than the given value |
| gte | Greater than or equal | Must be greater than or equal to the given value |
| lt | Less than | Must be less than the given value |
| lte | Less than or equal | Must be less than or equal to the given value |
| elemMatch | Element match | Indicates that the field being filtered will return an array of individual elements, on which filters can be applied with the preceding operators |

## sort

Just as the `filter` argument can ensure the inclusion or exclusion of certain data in a query response, the `sort` argument can reorder or resequence the data returned. Consider the following query, in which we're sorting the returned data in ascending alphabetical order (ASC):

```
allMarkdownRemark(
  sort: {
    fields: [frontmatter___title]
    order: ASC
  }
) {
  edges {
    node {
      frontmatter {
        title
        date
      }
    }
  }
}
```

Note here that we've used three underscores in succession within the `fields` value to identify a *nested field* within the `frontmatter` field (`frontmatter___title`).

We can also sort according to multiple fields, as in the following query, which sorts the items by `title` in ascending alphabetical order before sorting by `date` in ascending chronological order:

```
allMarkdownRemark(
  sort: {
    fields: [frontmatter___title, frontmatter___date]
    order: ASC
  }
) {
  edges {
    node {
      frontmatter {
        title
        date
      }
    }
  }
}
```

If we want to sort by title in ascending alphabetical order but sort by date in descending chronological order, we can use the `order` argument to identify how the two fields should influence the sort distinctly. Note the addition of square brackets:

```
allMarkdownRemark(
  sort: {
    fields: [frontmatter___title, frontmatter___date]
    order: [ASC, DESC]
  }
) {
  edges {
    node {
      frontmatter {
        title
        date
      }
    }
  }
}
```

 By default, the sort keyword will sort fields in ascending order
when no order is indicated. The sort keyword can be used only
once on a given field, so multiple sorts need to occur through successive field identifications, as shown in the preceding example.

## GraphQL Query Variables

Though GraphQL query arguments are common for typical limit, skip, filter, and sort
operations, GraphQL also provides a mechanism for developers to introduce *query
variables* at the root level of the query. This is particularly useful for situations where
a user defines how a list should be sorted or filtered, or what items in the list should
be skipped. In short, query variables allow for us to provide user-defined arguments
as opposed to static arguments that don't change.

Consider the following example query, which leaves it up to the query variables to
determine how the results should be limited and filtered:

```
query GetAllPosts(
  $limit: Int
  $sort: MarkdownRemarkSortInput
  $filter: MarkdownRemarkFilterInput
) {
  allMarkdownRemark {
    edges {
      node {
        frontmatter {
          title
        }
      }
    }
  }
}
```

In order for this query to function properly, we need to provide values for each of these query variables in the form of a JSON object containing each of these variable names:

```
{
  "limit": 4,
  "sort": {
    "fields": "frontmatter___title",
    "order": "ASC"
  },
  "filter": {
    "frontmatter": {
      "title": {
        "regex": "/Watching/"
      }
    }
  }
}
```

As you can see, query variables can take the place of query arguments when we need to provide arbitrarily defined limits, skips, filters, and sorts. Note, however, that the query must be named and cannot remain anonymous when using query variables.

 Query variables in GraphQL can be either scalar values or objects, as you can see in this example. GraphiQL, a query editor and debugger we'll cover in "The Gatsby Data Layer" on page 103, contains a Query Variables pane where developers can input arbitrary query variable values.

## GraphQL Directives

GraphQL query variables allow us to designate arbitrary arguments that apply to fields, but what if we want to define actual logic that conditionally includes or excludes certain fields at query time based on those query variables? For that, we need *directives*. GraphQL makes two directives available:

- The `@skip` directive indicates to GraphQL that based on a Boolean value defined by a query variable, the field carrying the directive should be excluded from the response.

- The `@include` directive indicates to GraphQL that based on a Boolean value defined by a query variable, the field carrying the directive should be included in the response.

Consider the following example query, which defines a query variable `$includeDate` with a default value of `false`. If the query variable is set to `true`, then the response to the query will include items that have dates as well as titles:

```
query GetAllPosts(
  $includeDate: Boolean = false
) {
  allMarkdownRemark {
    edges {
      node {
        frontmatter {
          title
          date @include(if: $includeDate)
        }
      }
    }
  }
}
```

The @skip directive works similarly and is useful for cases where you want to leave out certain information, such as when rendering solely item titles for a list view rather than the full item for the individual item view:

```
query GetAllPosts(
  $teaser: Boolean = false
) {
  allMarkdownRemark {
    edges {
      node {
        frontmatter {
          title
          date @skip(if: $teaser)
        }
      }
    }
  }
}
```

GraphQL directives are particularly useful for situations where you wish to perform conditional rendering of only certain data pertaining to a component, and when you prefer not to overload GraphQL API responses to keep payload sizes small. The @skip and @include directives can be added to any field, as long as the query variable is available.

## GraphQL Fragments

Sometimes our GraphQL queries can become overly verbose, with multiple hierarchical levels and many identified fields. This often necessitates the extraction of certain parts of the query into separate, reusable sets of fields that can be included where needed in a more concise form. In GraphQL, these repeatable sets of fields are known as *fragments*.

Consider a scenario where we want to reuse the `frontmatter` portion of the following query, shown in bold, in other queries:

```
query {
  site {
    siteMetadata {
      title
    }
  }
  allMarkdownRemark {
    nodes {
      excerpt
      fields {
        slug
      }
      frontmatter {
        date(formatString: "MMMM DD, YYYY")
        title
        description
      }
    }
  }
}
```

To define this as a fragment, we can separate out the portion of the query we wish to turn into a reusable field collection and identify it as a fragment separately from the query. In addition, we can then include the fragment within a query by referring to the name we give it when we define the fragment:

```
query {
  site {
    siteMetadata {
      title
    }
  }
  allMarkdownRemark {
    nodes {
      excerpt
      fields {
        slug
      }
      ...MarkdownFrontmatter
    }
  }
}

fragment MarkdownFrontmatter on MarkdownRemark {
  frontmatter {
    date(formatString: "MMMM DD, YYYY")
    title
    description
```

```
    }
  }
```

As you can see in this example, to use our newly created fragment within the query, we simply reference it with an ellipsis prefix (...) and the name of the fragment (MarkdownFrontmatter). Now we can potentially reuse this fragment in any other query where we need the same data to be extracted.

Fragments can also be *inline*, where we provide the fragment's contents directly where the fragment is invoked. The following query is identical to the previous one, and the ellipsis here represents an anonymous fragment that is defined immediately rather than in a separate fragment definition. This approach allows you to include fields by type without resorting to the use of a fragment outside the query itself, which can improve readability:

```
query {
  site {
    siteMetadata {
      title
    }
  }
  allMarkdownRemark {
    nodes {
      excerpt
      fields {
        slug
      }
      ... on MarkdownRemark {
        frontmatter {
          date(formatString: "MMMM DD, YYYY")
          title
          description
        }
      }
    }
  }
}
```

But there's an outstanding question that we need to answer: what exactly is the Mark downRemark name that comes after the fragment name, if included, and the keyword on in the fragment definition? To answer that question, we need to dig a little deeper into GraphQL's inner workings and take a look at schemas and types.

## GraphQL Schemas and Types

Because GraphQL queries are fundamentally about retrieving data that adheres to a shape desired by the client, those writing queries need to have some awareness of what shapes the GraphQL API can accept. Just like databases, GraphQL has an internal *schema* that assigns *types* to fields. These types dictate what responses look like for a given field. Most GraphQL schemas are manually written by architects, but Gatsby *infers* a GraphQL schema based on how it handles data internally and how it manages data from external sources.

A GraphQL schema consists of a series of type definitions that define what a field returns in the form of an object (e.g., a string, a Boolean, or an integer), as well as possible arguments for that object (e.g., ASC or DESC for ascending or descending sort order, respectively). For example, consider a GraphQL response that looks like this:

```
{
  "title": "Good trouble"
}
```

In the associated GraphQL schema to which all fields adhere, the type for the `title` field would be identified as follows—this explicitly limits the type of object issued by the GraphQL API in response to the `title` field to be a string and nothing else:

```
title: String
```

Let's take another look at the query and fragment we wrote in the previous section:

```
query {
  site {
    siteMetadata {
      title
    }
  }
  allMarkdownRemark {
    nodes {
      excerpt
      fields {
        slug
      }
      ...MarkdownFrontmatter
    }
  }
}

fragment MarkdownFrontmatter on MarkdownRemark {
  frontmatter {
    date(formatString: "MMMM DD, YYYY")
    title
    description
  }
}
```

In this fragment definition, we're also indicating under which field types the fragment can be applied. In this case, the `allMarkdownRemark` field accepts inner fields of type `MarkdownRemark`. Because the `excerpt`, `fields`, and `frontmatter` fields are all represented as possible fields within the `MarkdownRemark` type, we know that our fragment containing a top-level `frontmatter` field will be applicable for all objects of type Mark downRemark. Every fragment must have an associated type so that a GraphQL API can validate whether that fragment can be interpreted correctly or not.

But how do we introspect our GraphQL schema to understand how types relate to one another in type definitions, like the relationship between MarkdownRemark and the fields excerpt, fields, and frontmatter? And how do we know what type each individual field is within a given GraphQL query? To answer those questions, we'll explore the foundational role GraphQL plays in Gatsby and how Gatsby makes available GraphQL tooling that offers query debugging and schema introspection capabilities.

# The Gatsby Data Layer

The *Gatsby data layer* encompasses both Gatsby's internal GraphQL API and source plugins, which together collect data and define a GraphQL schema that traverses that data. Whether this data comes from the surrounding filesystem in the form of Markdown files or from a REST or GraphQL API in the form of WordPress's web services, Gatsby's internal GraphQL API facilitates the single-file co-location of data requirements and data rendering, as all Gatsby GraphQL queries are written into Gatsby components.

A common question asked by Gatsby novices is why GraphQL is necessary in the first place. After all, Gatsby is primarily about generating static sites; why does it need an internal GraphQL API? Because Gatsby can pull in information from so many disparate sources, each with its own approach to exposing data, a unified data layer is required. For this reason, it's common to hear the word *data* in Gatsby defined as "anything that doesn't live in a React or Gatsby component."

Before we jump into the sorts of GraphQL queries Gatsby's GraphQL API makes available, we'll first explore Gatsby's developer ecosystem for GraphQL. This includes tools such as GraphiQL, GraphQL Explorer, and GraphQL Playground, all of which are useful means for Gatsby developers to test queries and introspect schemas.

 Though Gatsby's internal GraphQL API is the easiest way to retrieve and manipulate data within Gatsby, you can also use unstructured data and consume it through the createPages API, which we discuss in Chapter 6.

## GraphiQL

There's no requirement to install a GraphQL dependency or otherwise configure GraphQL when you start implementing a Gatsby site. As soon as you run gatsby develop or gatsby build at the root of your codebase, Gatsby will automatically infer and create a GraphQL schema. Once the site is compiled by running gatsby develop, you can explore Gatsby's data layer and GraphQL API by navigating to the URL *https://localhost:8000/___graphql* (note the three underscores).

To see this in action, clone a new version of the Gatsby blog starter and run `gatsby develop`. Once the development server is running, navigate to *https://localhost:8000/___graphql*:

```
$ gatsby new gtdg-ch4-graphiql gatsbyjs/gatsby-starter-blog
$ cd gtdg-ch4-graphiql
$ gatsby develop
```

At this URL, you'll see a two-sided UI consisting of a query editor on the lefthand side and a response preview pane on the righthand side (Figure 4-1). This is *Graph-iQL*, an interactive GraphQL query editor that allows developers to quickly test queries. Figure 4-1 also shows the Documentation Explorer, accessed by clicking "Docs," expanded.

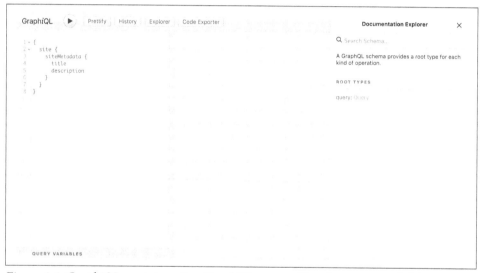

*Figure 4-1. GraphiQL, an interactive GraphQL query editor for testing and debugging queries according to a given schema*

To see GraphiQL in action, let's try inserting a simple GraphQL query to extract some information about the site:

```
{
  site {
    siteMetadata {
      title
      description
    }
  }
}
```

After the `description` field, try hitting the Enter key and typing Ctrl-Space or Shift-Space. You'll see an autocomplete list appear with fields that are valid for insertion at that point, including `author` and `siteUrl` (Figure 4-2). This autocomplete feature is one way to insert fields into GraphiQL; you can also enter them manually.

*Figure 4-2. GraphiQL's autocomplete feature can be activated at any point by typing Ctrl-Space (or Shift-Space) to see what fields can be inserted at that point in the query*

Now, type Ctrl-Enter to run the query (or click the Play button in the header). You'll see the response in the righthand pane, expressed in valid JSON (Figure 4-3). As you can see, GraphiQL will run the query against Gatsby's internal GraphQL schema and return a response based on that schema. Testing our queries with GraphiQL, therefore, gives us full confidence that queries running correctly there will work properly within our code as well.

The Documentation Explorer on the right is GraphiQL's internal schema introspection system, which allows you to search the GraphQL schema and to view what types are associated with certain fields. The information served by the Documentation Explorer matches the information displayed when you hover over a field in the query editor on the lefthand side. To open the Documentation Explorer while it is toggled closed, click the "Docs" link in the upper righthand corner of GraphiQL.

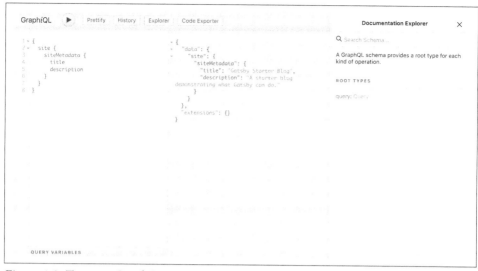

*Figure 4-3. To run a GraphQL query in GraphQL, click the Play button or press Ctrl-Enter; you'll see the response in the preview pane*

## GraphiQL Explorer

Packaged with GraphiQL's query editor is *GraphiQL Explorer*, a convenient introspection interface for developers to see what fields are available for a given query, along with nested fields within them. You can also use GraphiQL Explorer to construct a query by clicking on available fields and inputs, rather than writing out the query by hand. For developers who prefer more of a graphical query building experience, GraphiQL Explorer is a convenient tool (see Figure 4-4).

GraphiQL Explorer is particularly useful for advanced queries that require complex logic—especially unions, which are generally left up to the GraphQL implementation and lack a unified standard, and inline fragments, which can be frustrating for developers new to GraphQL to work with. GraphiQL Explorer lists all the available union types within the Explorer view and makes it easy to test inline fragments.

Gatsby also includes support for code snippet generation based on GraphiQL Explorer through GraphiQL's *Code Exporter*. Rather than generating just the GraphQL query, which needs to be integrated with a Gatsby component, the Code Exporter is capable of generating a Gatsby page or component file based on a query constructed in GraphiQL Explorer.

> For more information about GraphiQL Explorer and GraphiQL's Code Exporter, consult Michal Piechowiak's blog post on the subject (*https://oreil.ly/6QD60*).

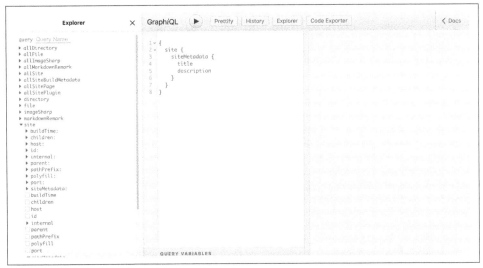

*Figure 4-4. In GraphiQL Explorer, built into the GraphiQL interface, you can click on fields represented in the Explorer view to construct queries without typing them by hand*

## GraphQL Playground

Though GraphiQL is useful for most developers' requirements, sometimes it's important to have a more fundamental understanding of a GraphQL schema, at the level of how data is served to the schema by external data sources through source plugins. Exploring how schemas are constructed for GraphQL can help identify deeper-seated issues that require work within external data sources rather than within the schema itself.

*GraphQL Playground*, developed by Prisma, is an integrated development environment (IDE) for GraphQL queries that provides much more power than GraphiQL. It considers the logic of how data enters GraphQL schemas, rather than just allowing query testing like GraphiQL, but it requires installation and isn't available out of the box in Gatsby. GraphQL Playground provides a range of useful tools, but for the time being it remains an experimental feature in Gatsby.

To use GraphQL Playground with Gatsby, add the `GATSBY_GRAPHQL_IDE` flag to the value associated with the `develop` script in your Gatsby site's *package.json* file:

```
"develop": "GATSBY_GRAPHQL_IDE=playground gatsby develop",
```

Now, instead of running `gatsby develop`, run the following command, and when you visit the URL *https://localhost:8000/___graphql* you'll see the GraphQL Playground interface instead of GraphiQL (Figure 4-5):

```
$ npm run develop
```

If you're developing Gatsby sites on Windows, you will first need to install `cross-env` (**npm install --save-dev cross-env**) and change the value associated with the `develop` script in your *package.json* to the following instead:

```
"develop": "cross-env GATSBY_GRAPHQL_IDE=playground
gatsby develop",
```

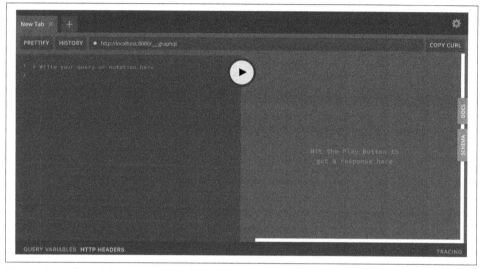

*Figure 4-5. The initial state of GraphQL Playground when you enable it in Gatsby*

Now that you have a solid understanding of the available developer tools for working with GraphQL in Gatsby, we can finally turn our attention to Gatsby's page and component queries, the most important GraphQL building blocks in Gatsby.

To continue using `gatsby develop` to instantiate your local development environment instead of `npm run develop`, add the `dotenv` package to your *gatsby-config.js* file and, separately, add an environment variable file. Because we are concerned with the development environment here, name the file *.env.development*, and add the following line to it:

```
GATSBY_GRAPHQL_IDE=playground
```

# Page and Component Queries

As we've seen in previous chapters, Gatsby works with both pages and components. Up to now, when exploring how we can build pages and components for Gatsby sites, we've always explicitly provided the data within the JSX that renders that data rather than pulling data from external sources or from the surrounding filesystem.

In this chapter's introduction, we defined Gatsby's data layer as the mediator between data, whether it originates from the local filesystem or from an external source like a database or CMS, and the rendering that occurs within Gatsby's pages and components. Now, we can connect the dots and see how this rendering happens.

Whenever Gatsby sees a GraphQL query conforming to Gatsby's standard GraphQL approach, it will parse, evaluate, and inject the query response into the page or component from which the query originates.

For the remainder of this chapter, we'll focus our attention primarily on GraphQL queries that work with the surrounding filesystem, as Gatsby can pull data from Markdown or other files that it can access. In Chapter 5, we'll discuss source plugins, which Gatsby employs to retrieve data from external systems and to populate a GraphQL schema.

## Page Queries

In Gatsby, pages can be rendered using no data at all (if the data is hardcoded) or using data brought in via GraphQL queries. GraphQL queries in Gatsby pages are known as *page queries*, and they have a one-to-one relationship with a given Gatsby page. Unlike Gatsby's static queries, which we'll examine in the following sections, page queries can accept GraphQL query variables like those we saw in "GraphQL Query Variables" on page 97.

Gatsby makes available a `graphql` tag for arbitrary GraphQL queries defined within a Gatsby page or component. To see this in action, let's create a new Gatsby blog based on the Gatsby blog starter. Because it already comes with a source plugin enabled, we can jump right in and look at some of the GraphQL queries contained in its pages:

```
$ gatsby new gtdg-ch4-graphql gatsbyjs/gatsby-starter-blog
$ cd gtdg-ch4-graphql
```

Open *src/pages/index.js*, one of our Gatsby pages, and let's go through it step by step:

```
// src/pages/index.js
import React from "react"
import { Link, graphql } from "gatsby"  ❶

import Bio from "../components/bio"
import Layout from "../components/layout"
import SEO from "../components/seo"

const BlogIndex = ({ data, location }) => {  ❷
  const siteTitle = data.site.siteMetadata?.title || `Title`
  const posts = data.allMarkdownRemark.nodes

  if (posts.length === 0) {
    return (
      <Layout location={location} title={siteTitle}>
```

```
        <SEO title="All posts" />
        <Bio />
        <p>
          No blog posts found. Add Markdown posts to "content/blog" (or the
          directory you specified for the "gatsby-source-filesystem" plugin in
          gatsby-config.js).
        </p>
      </Layout>
    )
  }

  return ( ❸
    <Layout location={location} title={siteTitle}>
      <SEO title="All posts" />
      <Bio />
      <ol style={{ listStyle: `none` }}>
        {posts.map(post => {
          const title = post.frontmatter.title || post.fields.slug

          return (
            <li key={post.fields.slug}>
              <article
                className="post-list-item"
                itemScope
                itemType="http://schema.org/Article"
              >
                <header>
                  <h2>
                    <Link to={post.fields.slug} itemProp="url">
                      <span itemProp="headline">{title}</span>
                    </Link>
                  </h2>
                  <small>{post.frontmatter.date}</small>
                </header>
                <section>
                  <p
                    dangerouslySetInnerHTML={{
                      __html: post.frontmatter.description || post.excerpt,
                    }}
                    itemProp="description"
                  />
                </section>
              </article>
            </li>
          )
        })}
      </ol>
    </Layout>
  )
}

export default BlogIndex
```

```
export const pageQuery = graphql` ❹
  query { ❺
    site {
      siteMetadata {
        title
      }
    }
    allMarkdownRemark(sort: { fields: [frontmatter___date], order: DESC }) {
      nodes {
        excerpt
        fields {
          slug
        }
        frontmatter {
          date(formatString: "MMMM DD, YYYY")
          title
          description
        }
      }
    }
  }
`
```

❶ This import statement brings in Gatsby's <Link /> component and graphql tag.

❷ Here the connection is made between our GraphQL query and the data variable, which is populated with the props generated by the response to our GraphQL query, and in the same shape as our query.

❸ This code performs all of our rendering in JSX.

❹ Note that we are using an export statement to ensure that Gatsby is aware of our GraphQL query. The name of the constant (here, pageQuery) isn't important, because Gatsby inspects our code for an exported graphql string rather than a specific variable name. Many page queries in the wild are simply named query. Only one page query is possible per Gatsby page. Also note that we are using a tagged template surrounded by backticks, allowing for a multiline string that contains our GraphQL query and is indicated by Gatsby's graphql tag. The contents of these backticks must be a valid GraphQL query in order for Gatsby to successfully populate the data in the page.

❺ This is the GraphQL query that populates the home page of our Gatsby blog starter.

Let's focus on that second section:

```
// src/pages/index.js
const BlogIndex = ({ data, location }) => {
  const siteTitle = data.site.siteMetadata?.title || `Title`
```

Rather than hardcoding data like we did in earlier chapters, we can now dig further into our `data` object to access all the data we need. Let's see this in action with a simple example that pulls from our Gatsby site information in *gatsby-config.js*. Change the preceding lines to use our description from *gatsby-config.js* instead:

```
// src/pages/index.js
const BlogIndex = ({ data, location }) => {
  const siteTitle = data.site.siteMetadata?.description || `Description`
```

We also need to update our `pageQuery` GraphQL query to retrieve the site description as well as the title:

```
// src/pages/index.js
export const pageQuery = graphql`
  query {
    site {
      siteMetadata {
        title
        description
      }
    }
    allMarkdownRemark(sort: { fields: [frontmatter___date], order: DESC }) {
      nodes {
        excerpt
        fields {
          slug
        }
        frontmatter {
          date(formatString: "MMMM DD, YYYY")
          title
          description
        }
      }
    }
  }
`
```

Now, when you save the file and execute `gatsby develop`, you'll see that the blog title has been updated to reflect the description text ("A starter blog demonstrating what Gatsby can do.") rather than the title ("Gatsby Starter Blog").

Page queries make up the majority of GraphQL queries you'll construct while building rudimentary Gatsby sites. But what about GraphQL queries contained within components that aren't pages? We'll look at that next.

# Component Queries with StaticQuery

As of Gatsby v2, Gatsby also allows individual components contained within a page to retrieve data using a GraphQL query through the StaticQuery API. This is particularly useful when you split out a component from a surrounding page but require external data for just that component. We call these *component queries*.

Though StaticQuery is capable of handling most of the use cases page queries already address, including fragments, static queries differ from page queries in several critical ways:

- Although page queries can accept query variables, they do not function outside of Gatsby pages.
- Static queries cannot accept query variables (this is why they're called "static"), but they can be used in both pages and in-page components.
- The StaticQuery API does not work properly with React.createElement invocations that fall outside of JSX's purview. For these cases, Gatsby recommends using JSX and, if needed, explicitly using StaticQuery in a JSX element (<Static Query />).

Static queries share one characteristic with page queries: only one static query can be used per component, just as only one page query can be used per page. Therefore, if you have separate data requirements in another portion of the component, you will need to split that logic out into another component before adding a new static query.

Importantly, static queries provide the same benefits of co-location within components that page queries do within pages. Using the StaticQuery API allows you to both issue a query and render the data from the response in a single JSX element. Consider the following example, which demonstrates this co-location:

```
// src/components/header.js
import React from "react"
import { StaticQuery, graphql } from "gatsby"

export default function Header() {
 return (
   <StaticQuery
     query={graphql`
       query {
         site {
           siteMetadata {
             title
           }
         }
       }
     `}
     render={data => (
```

```
      <header>
        <h1>{data.site.siteMetadata.title}</h1>
      </header>
    )}
  />
  )
}
```

As you can see, using the `<StaticQuery />` JSX element gives us the `query` attribute, whose value is our component query, and the `render` attribute, whose value represents how we want the response data from the component query to figure into our component's rendering within a function.

Now that we have a means of issuing component queries, not just page queries, we're all set! But there is one outstanding question remaining, particularly for developers who have adopted the React Hooks paradigm: how can we use a React hook to define a component query rather than a JSX element?

 If you are performing type checking through `PropTypes`, a common API in React applications, using the `<StaticQuery />` JSX element will break this. For an example of how to restore `Prop Types` type checking, consult the Gatsby documentation (*https:// oreil.ly/iKYTO*).

## Component Queries with the useStaticQuery Hook

As of Gatsby v2.1.0, a separate means of accessing component queries is available in the form of the `useStaticQuery` hook. For readers unfamiliar with the React Hooks paradigm, *React hooks* are methods to access state information and other key React features without having to create a class. In short, the `useStaticQuery` hook accepts a GraphQL query and returns the response data. It can be used in any component, including pages and in-page components.

The `useStaticQuery` hook has a few limitations, just like `<StaticQuery />`:

- The `useStaticQuery` hook cannot accept query variables (again, this is why it is called "static").

- As with page queries and static queries, only one `useStaticQuery` hook can be used per component.

You must have React and ReactDOM 16.8.0 or later to use the useStaticQuery hook. If you're using an older version of Gatsby, run this command to update your React and ReactDOM versions to the appropriate version:

```
$ npm install react@^16.8.0 react-dom@^16.8.0
```

Let's take another look at the example component from the previous section. This time we'll use the useStaticQuery hook instead of <StaticQuery />:

```
// src/components/header.js
import React from "react"
import { useStaticQuery, graphql } from "gatsby"

export default function Header() {
 const data = useStaticQuery(graphql`
   query {
     site {
       siteMetadata {
         title
       }
     }
   }
 `)
 return (
   <header>
     <h1>{data.site.siteMetadata.title}</h1>
   </header>
 )
}
```

React hooks have become popular because developers can easily use them to create chunks of repeatable functionality, much like helper functions. Because useStatic Query is a hook, we can leverage it to compose and also recycle blocks of reusable functionality rather than invoking that functionality every time.

One common example of this is to create a hook that will provide data for reuse in any component so that the query is only issued once. This shortens the build duration and means that our Gatsby site can deploy slightly faster. For instance, we may want to only query for our site title once. In the following hook definition, we've created a React hook that can be reused in any component:

```
// src/hooks/use-site-title.js
import { useStaticQuery, graphql } from "gatsby"

export const useSiteTitle = () => {
 const { site } = useStaticQuery(
   graphql`
     query {
       site {
         siteMetadata {
```

```
            title
          }
        }
      }
    }
  )
  return site.siteMetadata
}
```

Now, we can import this React hook into our header component and invoke it there to get our Gatsby site title:

```
// src/components/header.js
import React from "react"
import { useSiteTitle } from "../hooks/use-site-title"

export default function Header() {
 const { title } = useSiteTitle()
 return (
   <header>
     <h1>{title}</h1>
   </header>
 )
}
```

> Consult the React documentation (*https://oreil.ly/1FtyJ*) for more information about React Hooks.

Equipped with an understanding of page queries and component queries using either `<StaticQuery />` or the `useStaticQuery` hook, we now have a variety of approaches to query data from within our Gatsby pages and components.

> For more information about Gatsby's GraphQL APIs, which are inspectable in the GraphiQL interface, consult the GraphQL API (*https://oreil.ly/VVfP2*), query options (*https://oreil.ly/G89wO*), and the Node model (*https://oreil.ly/W6hO8*) and `Node` interface documentation (*https://oreil.ly/JxEAE*).

# Conclusion

This chapter introduced GraphQL and Gatsby's internal data layer, covering both the principles underlying GraphQL queries and APIs and how GraphQL appears in Gatsby in the form of page and component queries. Though it's possible to use Gatsby without GraphQL, this is where much of the power inherent to Gatsby comes from, because it mediates the relationship between data—whether it originates from an external source or a local filesystem—and its rendering.

The way we write GraphQL queries in Gatsby with the `graphql` tag and exported queries is by design when it comes to a favorable developer experience and separation of concerns. Because GraphQL queries usually sit alongside rendering code in Gatsby components, Gatsby's internal data layer also facilitates the sort of co-location of data requirements and rendering logic that many React developers consider just as much a best practice as testing your queries in GraphiQL or GraphQL Playground.

But where exactly does all this data come from? What does Gatsby do to retrieve data from disparate external sources or the filesystem and populate its internal GraphQL schema? How can we connect CMSs and commerce systems to our Gatsby sites? Next, we cover source plugins and sourcing data—all of the ways Gatsby gets its hands on external data.

# CHAPTER 5

# Source Plugins and Sourcing Data

Among the most important features of Gatsby is its ability to retrieve and handle data from a variety of disparate sources, such as WordPress, Shopify, other GraphQL APIs external to Gatsby, and the local filesystem. Through its plugin ecosystem, Gatsby makes available a wide spectrum of backend services from which to pull data into a Gatsby site.

In Gatsby's data layer, *source plugins* are responsible for retrieving data either internally from a local filesystem or externally from APIs, databases, third-party services, and especially content management and commerce systems. Regardless of what they're responsible for, source plugins can be combined arbitrarily as part of Gatsby's data layer, which contains data originating from many different sources. In this chapter, we'll explore source plugins and how to use them to derive a range of data from the systems you want to pull from.

## Using Source Plugins

Source plugins are similar to the other Gatsby plugins you'll see in Chapter 9. Unlike plugins that govern CSS or features like analytics, however, source plugins serve as the intermediary between a data source, such as a local filesystem or an external service, and the Gatsby site presenting that data. They are Gatsby's canonical data retrieval system for data beyond that provided within the *pages* directory.

When you run the `gatsby develop` or `gatsby build` command, your source plugins will issue queries against the data source to retrieve the desired data. Gatsby will then populate its GraphQL API with the data retrieved and make it available to any page or component within the Gatsby site, as well as to other Gatsby plugins.

The Gatsby Plugin Library (*https://oreil.ly/wXPJb*) contains both officially maintained and community plugins.

## Installing Source Plugins

The installation process for source plugins is the same as for other plugins, as we've seen in the previous chapters. In the Gatsby plugin ecosystem, feature plugins use the prefix `gatsby-plugin-`, while source plugins have the prefix `gatsby-source-`. Installing a source plugin requires executing the same command used for other plugins, where *{source-name}* is the unique identifier of the plugin:

```
# If using NPM
$ npm install --save gatsby-source-{source-name}

# If using Yarn
$ yarn add gatsby-source-{source-name}
```

From this point forward, in most cases, only NPM installation scripts will be included in the text for brevity, but you can use either NPM or Yarn to manage your dependencies. For more information about how to migrate from NPM to Yarn, including Yarn equivalents for NPM commands, consult the Yarn documentation's migration guide (*https://oreil.ly/8PQec*).

## Setting Up Source Plugins

All source plugins share a required initial step, just like all other Gatsby plugins. After installation, for Gatsby to recognize and enable the plugin's functionality you'll need to add it to your *gatsby-config.js* file. Whenever you complete installation of a new source plugin, open this file and add the new member to the `plugins` array, as follows:

```
// gatsby-config.js
module.exports = {
  siteMetadata: {
    title: `My Awesome Gatsby Site`,
  },
  plugins: [
    {
      resolve: `gatsby-source-{source-name}`,
    },
  ],
}
```

Many plugins require only the `resolve` key in their object, but source plugins are different. We must explicitly define where the data is coming from and provide any additional information that is required for us to be able to access that data.

Every source plugin also includes an `options` object that identifies these key inputs (the source URL, API version, API token, etc.), and each source plugin's documentation identifies what information should be supplied to the `options` object. Consider this example from a *gatsby-config.js* file that defines options for `gatsby-source-filesystem`:

```
// gatsby-config.js
module.exports = {
  siteMetadata: {
    title: `My Awesome Gatsby Site`,
  },
  plugins: [
    {
      resolve: `gatsby-source-filesystem`,
      options: {
        name: `src`,
        path: `${__dirname}/src/`,
      },
    },
  ],
}
```

To get a sense for what we need to supply in the `options` object, let's turn our attention to some commonly used source plugins in Gatsby. We'll first look at how to source data from the surrounding filesystem, before moving on to source plugins for databases, third-party services, and other software systems and APIs.

## Using Environment Variables with Source Plugins

Many data sources, particularly CMSs and database systems, require some form of authentication token in order to access their data. This is sensitive information that you may wish not to expose to public eyes, particularly if you are using a source repository that is publicly accessible on a platform like GitHub.

*Environment variables* are variables that can be injected at certain points in the application depending on the environment in which code using them is executed. They are the primary way in which sensitive credentials such as authentication tokens can be used by Gatsby without being revealed publicly. Some data sources will have their own best practices for handling external authentication by source plugins, but environment variables are the most common mechanism.

Consider a hypothetical source plugin with one option, `authToken`, which represents a sensitive credential:

```
// gatsby-config.js
module.exports = {
  siteMetadata: {
    title: `My Awesome Gatsby Site`,
  },
  plugins: [
    {
      resolve: `gatsby-source-mydatasource`,
      options: {
        authToken: `sensitive-token`
      },
    },
  ],
}
```

Instead of placing the value for that token into *gatsby-config.js* and potentially checking it into source control, exposing it publicly, you can obfuscate it using a library known as `dotenv` (*https://oreil.ly/nqmcO*), which allows you to load environment variables into a Node.js process from a *.env* file that is not committed to a code repository:

```
// gatsby-config.js
require('dotenv').config()

module.exports = {
  siteMetadata: {
    title: `My Awesome Gatsby Site`,
  },
  plugins: [
    {
      resolve: `gatsby-source-mydatasource`,
      options: {
        authToken: process.env.MYDATASOURCE_AUTH_TOKEN
      },
    },
  ],
}
```

In this example, we require and configure the `dotenv` library, which grants the application access to environment variables through `process.env`, an object that will contain `MYDATASOURCE_AUTH_TOKEN` when provided in a *.env* file. To access this on your local machine, create a new file named *.env* in your project root containing the following:

```
MYDATASOURCE_AUTH_TOKEN=sensitive-token
```

Many infrastructure providers offer environment variable configuration in their UIs, allowing you to maintain a *.env* file on your local system for development and use configured environment variables for production. See Chapter 12 for more information about deployment with environment variables.

# Sourcing Data from the Filesystem

gatsby-source-filesystem is the source plugin responsible for retrieving data from the Gatsby site's surrounding filesystem. Much like other SSGs, such as Jekyll, that can derive data from surrounding directories, Gatsby offers the same option for developers who wish to retrieve only local data rather than external data. Of course, gatsby-source-filesystem can be used in conjunction with other source plugins to retrieve both local and external data. In the next few sections, we'll install and configure gatsby-source-filesystem and examine how to work with arbitrary directories.

## Setting Up gatsby-source-filesystem

Installing gatsby-source-filesystem works the same way as with any other plugin:

```
$ npm install --save gatsby-source-filesystem
```

Where things differ is in the options object in *gatsby-config.js*. To ensure that Gatsby understands where our files are coming from, we need to identify the name of the directory containing the files we want to work with as well as the path to that directory (usually some variation of the path to the directory containing the Gatsby site):

```
// gatsby-config.js
module.exports = {
  siteMetadata: {
    title: `My Awesome Gatsby Site`,
  },
  plugins: [
    {
      resolve: `gatsby-source-filesystem`,
      options: {
        name: `src`,
        path: `${__dirname}/src/`,
        ignore: [`**/\.*`],
      },
    },
  ],
}
```

In this example, the directory name we are targeting is *src*, and the path to that directory is the path to the working Gatsby directory (*${__dirname}*) and onward to the directory we need (*/src/*). Finally, we also include an ignore key that identifies any files we wish to ignore, such as those starting with a dot, in arbitrary regular expressions within an array.

One of the unique traits of `gatsby-source-filesystem` is that it can be used multiple times within a single Gatsby site, and therefore within a single *gatsby-config.js* file. For instance, you may wish to pull data from multiple local directories that are in separate locations—say, if you have some data serialized as JSON and other data serialized as CSV that you want to combine in a single site.

In the following example *gatsby-config.js* file, we have two instances of the source plugin pulling from discrete directories:

```
// gatsby-config.js
module.exports = {
  siteMetadata: {
    title: `My Awesome Gatsby Site`,
  },
  plugins: [
    {
      resolve: `gatsby-source-filesystem`,
      options: {
        name: `json`,
        path: `${__dirname}/src/data/json`,
        ignore: [`**/\.*`],
      },
    },
    {
      resolve: `gatsby-source-filesystem`,
      options: {
        name: `csv`,
        path: `${__dirname}/src/data/csv`,
        ignore: [`**/\.*`],
      },
    },
  ],
}
```

In addition to those specified by the regular expressions you provide as members of the ignore array, Gatsby also ignores the following files by default when retrieving data:

- **/*.un~
- **/.DS_Store
- **/.gitignore
- **/.npmignore
- **/.babelrc
- **/yarn.lock
- **/node_modules
- ../**/dist/**

## Working with Files from the Filesystem

As we saw in Chapter 4, GraphQL is the primary means in Gatsby's data layer to access and read the data our source plugins retrieve. The gatsby-source-filesystem plugin takes the files that you've identified and converts the data they contain into *file* nodes in the GraphQL API. To see this in action, clone another version of the Gatsby blog starter, which uses gatsby-source-filesystem to retrieve its internal Markdown files:

```
$ gatsby new gtdg-ch5-filesystem gatsbyjs/gatsby-starter-blog
$ cd gtdg-ch5-filesystem
$ gatsby develop
```

Now, open up the GraphQL API by navigating to *http://localhost:8000/___graphql*. If you look at the initial autocomplete list provided for an empty query (Figure 5-1), you'll see that two additional GraphQL fields have been added at the top thanks to the gatsby-source-filesystem plugin: allFile (for all file objects) and file (for individual file objects).

*Figure 5-1. Gatsby sites that use `gatsby-source-filesystem` will have two new GraphQL fields available in the GraphQL API: `file` and `allFile`*

Now, if we issue the following query, which is the base-level `allFile` query, we get a list of universally unique identifiers (UUIDs), as Figure 5-2 shows:

```
{
  allFile {
    edges {
      node {
        id
      }
    }
  }
}
```

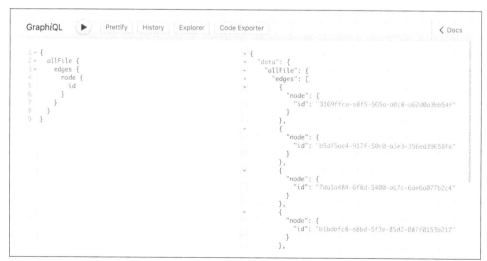

*Figure 5-2. The result of our initial query on `allFile` shows a list of `File` nodes, each identified with a UUID*

What we've generated here through our GraphQL API is an array consisting of `File` nodes, each of which contains a variety of GraphQL fields that we can now retrieve as well. These include metadata such as the file's extension, size, and relative path, as Figure 5-3 shows, as well as the file's contents, which may require further transformation to be ready for prime time in Gatsby:

```
{
  allFile {
    edges {
      node {
        relativePath
        extension
        size
      }
    }
  }
}
```

 In many cases, the data contained within individual files in a file-system might not be in the format you need for Gatsby. Rather than performing the required postprocessing when rendering the data, Gatsby recommends using *transformer plugins*, covered in Chapter 9, to convert `File` nodes into more consumable formats such as JSON.

*Figure 5-3. The result of another query on* `allFile` *showing a list of* `File` *nodes identified by relative path, extension, and file size*

# Working with Multiple Directories in the Filesystem

As we saw earlier, it's possible to pull data from multiple discrete directories by using multiple instances of the `gatsby-source-filesystem` plugin. But how do we access these individual directories uniquely within our GraphQL queries?

Gatsby's internal GraphQL API uses the `filter` argument, which we covered in Chapter 4, to identify which individual `gatsby-source-filesystem` plugin's configured directory to use. For instance, here we issue two separate queries that retrieve files from the two distinct directories we configured in "Sourcing Data from Database Systems" on page 129:

```
{
  allFile(filter: {
    sourceInstanceName: {
      eq: "json"
    }
  }) {
    edges {
      node {
        relativePath
        extension
        size
      }
    }
  }
}

{
  allFile(filter: {
    sourceInstanceName: {
      eq: "csv"
    }
  }) {
    edges {
      node {
        relativePath
        extension
        size
      }
    }
  }
}
```

Working with multiple directories requires us to filter based on the `sourceInstance Name` field, which is available on individual `File` nodes.

More information about the `gatsby-source-filesystem` plugin can be found in its documentation page (*https://oreil.ly/xtRFQ*) on the Gatsby website.

# Sourcing Data from Database Systems

Another important source of data for Gatsby sites is external databases, which either operate as standalone database systems or connect with other third-party systems. Retrieving data by querying a database rather than through APIs often provides greater flexibility in terms of data processing. The Gatsby plugin ecosystem provides integrations with some of the most well-known and commonly used database systems, including proprietary database systems and open source solutions like MongoDB and MySQL.

In addition to plugins designed to work with a specific database system, the `gatsby-source-sql` plugin allows the connection of arbitrary SQL databases (including not only MySQL/MariaDB and PostgreSQL but also Amazon Redshift, SQLite3, Oracle, and MSSQL) to Gatsby.

Whether you're working with a MongoDB database, a MySQL database, a PostgreSQL database, or any other SQL-based database, you can use any of the available source plugins for SQL databases and for MongoDB, MySQL, and PostgreSQL for maximum flexibility when it comes to retrieving the data you'll need in your Gatsby site.

For more information about these database source plugins, consult the respective source plugin documentation pages for MongoDB (*https://oreil.ly/1Ku1i*), MySQL (*https://oreil.ly/hwg0a*), PostgreSQL (*https://oreil.ly/8Q5rB*), and other SQL databases (*https://oreil.ly/MJMQ6*).

## MongoDB

MongoDB is a NoSQL database with a focus on documents rather than tables. Because the `gatsby-source-sql` plugin is solely for SQL databases, we need a distinct MongoDB-oriented source plugin to work with this data source. In the Gatsby source plugin ecosystem, `gatsby-source-mongodb`, an officially supported plugin, will do the trick.

We can install the MongoDB source plugin in the usual way:

```
$ npm install --save gatsby-source-mongodb
```

Then, in our `plugins` array in *gatsby-config.js*, we define some key information that MongoDB needs from us as well as the query that we wish to issue. The following MongoDB query requests documents that are more current than the indicated Unix timestamp:

```
// gatsby-config.js
plugins: [
  {
    resolve: `gatsby-source-mongodb`,
    options: {
      dbName: `local`,
      collection: `documents`,
    },
    query: {
      documents: {
        as_of: {
          $gte: 1606850284
        }
      }
    }
  },
]
```

If you need to query from more than one collection, in your `options` object, add the additional collection as a second member of an array:

```
// gatsby-config.js
options: {
  dbName: `local`,
  collection: [`documents`, `products`]
},
```

Within the `options` object, Gatsby's MongoDB source plugin offers a range of configuration options that relate to particular aspects of your MongoDB database, as Table 5-1 shows.

> For more information about `extraParams` and `clientOptions` values, consult the MongoDB documentation for query parameters (*https://oreil.ly/wEGyQ*) and `MongoClient` (*https://oreil.ly/FjIka*).

*Table 5-1. Configuration options for gatsby-source-mongodb*

| Option | Description |
| --- | --- |
| connectionString | MongoDB Atlas and later versions of MongoDB require a connection string that represents the full connection path; e.g., mongodb+srv://<USERNAME>:<PASSWORD>@<SERVERNAME>-fsokc.mongodb.net (for earlier versions, use dbName and extraParams for those respective values). This value should be obfuscated as an environment variable using a library such as dotenv. |
| dbName | The MongoDB database name. |
| collection | The name of the collection (or collections) to access within the MongoDB database; accepts a single string or an array of values. |
| query | The MongoDB database query. Keys represent collection names, and values represent query objects. |
| server | MongoDB server information. Defaults to a local running server on the default port; e.g.:<br><br>`server: {`<br>`    address: `ds143532.mlab.com`,`<br>`    port: 43532`<br>`}` |
| auth | An authentication object to authenticate into a MongoDB collection; e.g.:<br><br>`auth: {`<br>`    user: `root`,`<br>`    password: `myPassword``<br>`}` |
| extraParams | Additional parameters for the connection that can be appended as query parameters to the connection URI; examples include authSource, ssl, or replicaSet. |
| clientOptions | Additional options for creating a MongoClient instance, specific to certain versions of MongoDB and MongoDB Atlas. |
| preserveObjectIds | A Boolean to preserve nested ObjectIDs within documents. |

Once your MongoDB source plugin is configured appropriately, you can query MongoDB document nodes within Gatsby's GraphQL API as follows. Here, we're accessing a database named Cloud and a collection named products:

```
{
  allMongodbCloudProducts {
    edges {
      node {
        id
        name
        url
      }
    }
  }
}
```

Next, we'll take a look at the two SQL databases that Gatsby offers official source plugins for: MySQL and PostgreSQL.

# MySQL

Though the general SQL source plugin (which we'll look at shortly) offers features that are agnostic to any SQL database, there are scenarios where, as a developer, you'll prefer to use a source plugin that is more oriented toward those who are familiar with the inner workings of a particular database system. The `gatsby-source-mysql` source plugin works specifically with MySQL databases and allows developers to insert MySQL queries directly into the *gatsby-config.js* file. To install the MySQL source plugin, run:

```
$ npm install --save gatsby-source-mysql
```

Then, within your *gatsby-config.js* file, you'll need to provide details for connecting to the database as well as any queries you wish to issue:

```
// gatsby-config.js
plugins: [
  {
    resolve: `gatsby-source-mysql`,
    options: {
      connectionDetails: {
        host: `localhost`,
        user: `root`,
        password: `myPassword`,
        database: `user_records`
      },
      queries: [
        {
          statement: `SELECT user, email FROM users`,
          idFieldName: `User`,
          name: `users`
        }
      ]
    }
  },
]
```

You can issue multiple queries inside a single plugin object. To do this, simply add a second member to the `queries` array containing a unique `name` to differentiate this second query from the first:

```
// gatsby-config.js
queries: [
  {
    statement: `SELECT user, email FROM users`,
    idFieldName: `User`,
    name: `users`
  },
  {
    statement: `SELECT * FROM products`,
    idFieldName: `ProductName`,
```

```
      name: `products`
    }
  ]
```

As you can see in Table 5-2, the MySQL source plugin offers a variety of MySQL-specific configuration options within each individual query object.

*Table 5-2. Query options (for each query object) for `gatsby-source-mysql`*

| Options | Required? | Description |
|---------|-----------|-------------|
| `statement` | Required | The SQL query statement to be executed (stored procedures are supported) |
| `idFieldName` | Required | A column that is unique for each record; this column must be part of the returned statement |
| `name` | Required | A name for the SQL query, used by Gatsby's GraphQL API to identify the GraphQL type |
| `parentName` | Optional | A name for the parent entity, if any (relevant for joins) |
| `foreignKey` | Optional | The foreign key to join the parent entity (relevant for joins) |
| `cardinality` | Optional | The cardinality relationship between the parent and this entity (e.g., OneToMany, OneToOne; defaults to OneToMany); relevant for joins |
| `remoteImageField Names` | Optional | An array of columns containing image URIs that need to be downloaded for further image processing |

 A full accounting of joins in MySQL queries is beyond the scope of this book, but the Gatsby documentation contains a description of how to use the `parentName`, `foreignKey`, and `cardinality` keys to perform a join (*https://oreil.ly/rfHKs*).

Now, you can query the results of your MySQL queries within the GraphQL API internal to Gatsby:

```
{
  allMysqlUsers {
    edges {
      node {
        email
        id
      }
    }
  }
}
```

Note here that the name that follows `allMysql` is the same as the name you defined in the query object (`Users`).

## PostgreSQL

As mentioned earlier, you can use `gatsby-source-sql` to retrieve PostgreSQL data for common requirements, but a more specialized plugin is available for PostgreSQL databases. The `gatsby-source-pg` plugin's goal is to retrieve results from a PostgreSQL database with as little overhead as possible.

To install the PostgreSQL source plugin, execute the following command:

```
$ npm install --save gatsby-source-pg
```

Now, configure the plugin in *gatsby-config.js* to ensure Gatsby can import the database to make the data available through the GraphQL API:

```
// gatsby-config.js
plugins: [
  {
    resolve: `gatsby-source-pg`,
    options: {
      connectionString: `postgres://user:pass@host/dbname`,
      schema: `public`,
      refetchInterval: 60
    }
  }
],
```

Here, `connectionString` represents any valid PostgreSQL connection string (and should be obfuscated in an environment variable using a library such as `dotenv`), and `refetchInterval` represents the interval on which data should be retrieved again from the PostgreSQL database in question when the data needs to be updated.

Once you've configured your PostgreSQL options, you can access the entire database from within your GraphQL API using the `postgres` top-level field:

```
{
  postgres {
    allArticlesList {
      id
      title
      authorId
      userByAuthorId {
        id
        username
      }
    }
  }
}
```

A working example of thePostgreSQL source plugin is available on GitHub (*https://oreil.ly/R9H5k*), and information about customizing the PostgreSQL source plugin is available on the Gatsby website (*https://oreil.ly/pBDQz*).

## Amazon Redshift, SQLite3, Oracle, and MSSQL

Though Gatsby's ecosystem provides source plugins specifically targeting well-known SQL databases like MySQL and PostgreSQL, the `gatsby-source-sql` plugin also contains out-of-the-box support for both of these and other SQL databases like MariaDB, Amazon Redshift, SQLite3, Oracle, and MSSQL. (The dedicated source plugins for MySQL and PostgreSQL offer a different feature set.)

To install `gatsby-source-sql`, execute the following command in the root of your Gatsby site:

```
$ npm install --save \
  git+https://github.com/mrfunnyshoes/gatsby-source-sql.git
```

Depending on the database you wish to integrate with, you'll need to add the corresponding knex-compliant plugin (knex is the library `gatsby-source-sql` uses to work with databases directly):

```
$ npm install --save mysql
$ npm install --save mysql2
$ npm install --save pg
$ npm install --save sqlite3
$ npm install --save oracle
$ npm install --save mssql
```

To configure `gatsby-source-sql` in *gatsby-config.js*, you use the normal approach of adding the source plugin to the `plugins` array. However, the `options` object in this case requires three things: a `typeName` string (describing each individual row in the results table), a `fieldName` string (in a future version of the plugin, this will determine the field name in Gatsby's GraphQL API), and a `dbEngine` object. Consider the following example `plugins` array in *gatsby-config.js*:

```
// gatsby-config.js
module.exports = {
  siteMetadata: {
    title: `gatsby-source-sql demo`,
  },
  plugins: [
    {
      resolve: `gatsby-source-sql`,
      options: {
        typeName: "User",
        fieldName: "postgres",
        dbEngine: {
```

```
      client: 'pg',
      connection: {
        host: 'my-db.my-host-sql.com',
        user: 'root',
        password: 'zs8Jy0DGg0kTlKUD',
        database: 'user_records'
      }
    },
  }
},
],
}
```

Notice the typeName defined as the string User in this example configuration. When you issue your first GraphQL query within Gatsby's GraphQL API, the typeName string becomes the name that comes after the prefix all:

```
{
  allUser {
    ...
  }
}
```

The dbEngine object accepts a knex configuration object, which contains key information about the database system. For example, if you're using gatsby-source-sql to retrieve data from a MySQL database, certain information is required in order to connect to the database:

```
// gatsby-config.js
dbEngine: {
  client: 'mysql',
  connection: {
    host : 'my-db.my-host-sql.com',
    user : 'root',
    password : 'zs8Jy0DGg0kTlKUD',
    database : 'user_records'
  }
}
```

 Because this configuration involves highly sensitive database credentials, it's strongly recommended to use environment variables to provide these values to *gatsby-config.js*.

The gatsby-source-sql plugin works a bit differently from the gatsby-source-filesystem plugin we reviewed earlier. Each database connection is the source plugin's only opportunity to retrieve the data needed for the Gatsby site from the database, so each use of gatsby-source-sql in *gatsby-config.js* must also carry with it the database query you wish to issue. The results returned from the query will then populate the GraphQL API.

In *gatsby-config.js*, we need to add a `queryChain` function to identify the query we want to issue to the database. Keep in mind that this query must adhere to the specification of the database's internal workings and not the GraphQL specification in Gatsby. Only the results of the database query enter the Gatsby GraphQL API; to retrieve additional results, another instance of the plugin is required in *gatsby-config.js*.

For example, to issue the following two MySQL queries on a MySQL database:

```
SELECT user, email FROM users;
SELECT user FROM users WHERE user.name = 'admin'
```

We would need to define two source plugins with distinct `queryChain` functions:

```
// gatsby-config.js
plugins: [
  {
    resolve: `gatsby-source-sql`,
    options: {
      typeName: `User`,
      fieldName: `mysqlUser`,
      dbEngine: {
        client: 'mysql',
        connection: {
          host : 'my-db.my-host-sql.com',
          user : 'root',
          password : 'zs8Jy0DGg0kTlKUD',
          database : 'user_records'
        }
      },
      queryChain: function (x) {
        return x.select('user', 'email').from('users')
      }
    }
  },
  {
    resolve: `gatsby-source-sql`,
    options: {
      typeName: `Admin`,
      fieldName: `mysqlAdmin`,
      dbEngine: {
        client: 'mysql',
        connection: {
          host : 'my-db.my-host-sql.com',
          user : 'root',
          password : 'zs8Jy0DGg0kTlKUD',
          database : 'user_records'
        }
      },
```

```
      queryChain: function (x) {
        return x
          .select('user', 'email')
          .from('users')
          .where('user.name', '=', 'admin')
      }
    }
  },
]
```

In the `queryChain` function definitions shown here, the argument x represents a database connection object. Because we're solely concerned with retrieving data, the `gatsby-source-sql` plugin enables only read operations, not write operations.

The knex library is used by the `gatsby-source-sql` source plugin as a utility for issuing queries to databases of various types. The documentation (*https://knexjs.org/#Builder*) contains a full accounting of how to write queries in JavaScript according to various specifications.

# Sourcing Data from Third-Party SaaS Services

Though heavy-duty databases are often appropriate for data destined for Gatsby sites, many developers prefer third-party hosted software-as-a-service (SaaS) services that limit the amount of upkeep required. Three of the most popular SaaS services used for Gatsby sites today are Airtable, AWS DynamoDB, and Google Docs. Each of these has its own Gatsby source plugin.

Some CMSs and commerce systems are SaaS services too, rather than being built on dedicated servers; we'll cover those in the next section.

## Airtable

*Airtable* is a quick-and-easy solution for rudimentary data storage and management that's quickly gaining popularity among developers. The `gatsby-source-airtable` source plugin offers a range of features that allow you to retrieve data arbitrarily from any Airtable base tables.

To install the Airtable source plugin, execute the following command:

```
$ npm install --save gatsby-source-airtable
```

Now you need to configure your Airtable source plugin. Airtable provides an API key through which data is accessed, located at Help→API Documentation within the

Airtable interface. Because this API key is highly sensitive information, it's strongly recommended that you inject it into your configuration using an environment variable, as described in "Using Environment Variables with Source Plugins" on page 121. Though you can hardcode your API key during development, for production your configuration should instead look like this:

```
plugins: [
  {
    resolve: `gatsby-source-airtable`,
    options: {
      apiKey: process.env.AIRTABLE_API_KEY,
    },
  },
],
```

Within the `options` object, the Airtable source plugin also needs information about the tables you wish to query within Airtable. This takes the form of a `tables` array that can contain multiple table objects. Additionally, in Airtable, every individual table can have one or more named *views*, which allow for arbitrary filtering and sorting to occur before the data arrives in Gatsby's data layer. If you don't specify a view by setting `tableView`, you'll simply receive raw data with no set order.

The following example demonstrates the retrieval of data from two separate tables. The `concurrency` value, by default set to 5, indicates how many concurrent requests the Airtable source plugin should issue to avoid overloading Airtable's servers:

```
// gatsby-config.js
plugins: [
  {
    resolve: `gatsby-source-airtable`,
    options: {
      apiKey: process.env.AIRTABLE_API_KEY,
      concurrency: 5,
      tables: [
        {
          baseId: `myAirtableBaseId`,
          tableName: `myTableName`,
          tableView: `myTableViewName`,
        },
        {
          baseId: `myAirtableBaseId`,
          tableName: `myTableName`,
          tableView: `myTableViewName`,
        }
      ],
    },
  },
],
```

Each table object in the `tables` array can take a variety of options (Table 5-3).

*Table 5-3. Table options for `gatsby-source-airtable`*

| Option | Required? | Description |
|---|---|---|
| `baseId` | Required | Your Airtable base identifier. |
| `tableName` | Required | The name of the table within your Airtable base. |
| `tableView` | Optional | The name of the view for a given table; if unset, raw data is returned unsorted and unfiltered. |
| `queryName` | Optional | A name to identify a table. If a string is provided, recasts all records in this table as a separate node type (useful if you have multiple bases with identical table or view names across bases). Defaults to `false`. |
| `mapping` | Optional | Accepts a format such as `text/markdown` for easier transformation of columns. Requires a column name; e.g.:<br>`mapping: {`<br>`  myColumnName: ` `` `text/markdown` `` `<br>`}` |
| `tableLinks` | Optional | An array of field names identifying a linked record matching the name shown in Airtable; setting this creates nested GraphQL nodes from linked records, allowing deep linking to records across tables. |
| `separate NodeType` | Optional | A Boolean describing whether there are two bases with a table having the same name and whether query names should differ from the default of `allAirtable` or `airtable` (this requires `queryName` to be set). Defaults to `false`. |
| `separate MapType` | Optional | A Boolean describing whether a Gatsby node type should be created for each type of data (such as Markdown or other attachment types) to avoid type conflicts. Defaults to `false`. |

Once you have your Airtable source plugin populating your GraphQL API, you can start retrieving data from your Airtable tables. To retrieve all records from a given table `myTableName` where `myField` is equal to `myValue`, you can use a filter operation:

```
{
  allAirtable(
    filter: {
      table: {
        eq: "myTableName"
      }
      data: {
        myField: {
          eq: "myValue"
        }
      }
    }
  ) {
    edges {
      node {
        data {
          myField
        }
      }
    }
  }
}
```

To retrieve a single record from a given table—i.e., an individual table row where myField is equal to myValue—you can use the airtable field instead:

```
{
  airtable(
    table: {
      eq: "myTableName"
    }
    data: {
      myField: {
        eq: "myValue"
      }
    }
  ) {
    data {
      myField
      myOtherField
      myLinkedField {
        data {
          myLinkedRecord
        }
      }
    }
  }
}
```

In this example, note that we're also accessing a linked record that assumes the table Links key is defined in *gatsby-config.js*.

 GraphQL has different limitations on acceptable characters from Airtable. Because Airtable allows spaces in field names but GraphQL does not, the Airtable source plugin automatically rewrites keys such as column names without spaces: for example, a column named My New Column becomes My_New_Column in GraphQL. Full gatsby-source-airtable documentation (*https://oreil.ly/n0r42*) can be found on the Gatsby website.

## AWS DynamoDB

Another hosted SaaS database solution, Amazon's AWS DynamoDB, is also gaining traction among developers (particularly among architects who prefer AWS products). To install the AWS DynamoDB source plugin, execute the following command:

```
$ npm install --save gatsby-source-dynamodb
```

Just like with other source plugins, to use the DynamoDB source plugin you'll need to configure it in your Gatsby configuration file. As with other sensitive information, it's strongly recommended to use environment variables to inject the values for your AWS credentials:

```
// gatsby-config.js
plugins: [
  {
    resolve: `gatsby-source-dynamodb`,
    options: {
      typeName: `myGraphqlTypeName`,
      accessKeyId: `myAwsAccessKeyId`,
      secretAccessKey: `myAwsSecretAccessKey`,
      region: `myAwsRegion`,
      params: {
        TableName: `myTableName`,
      },
    },
  },
],
```

 More information is available in the AWS DynamoDB documentation about setting AWS credentials for IAM users (*https://oreil.ly/
3sfIE*), configuring permissions for IAM users (*https://oreil.ly/
w0GE8*), and available parameters on DynamoDB queries (*https://
oreil.ly/cT3ML*). Full documentation for the `gatsby-source-`
`dynamodb` plugin (*https://oreil.ly/58RUv*) is also available on the
Gatsby website.

## Google Docs

In recent years, Google Docs has become a compelling solution for developers who
don't wish to configure and maintain a full CMS or database. Though it's not an optimal data source for heavy-duty content or commerce implementations due to possible long build times, it can be useful for smaller sites and blogs.

The Google Docs source plugin in Gatsby relies on two additional plugins known as
*transformer plugins*, which we cover at length in the next chapter. For now, all you
need to know about them is that transformer plugins handle the processing of images
within a Google Docs document.

You can install the `gatsby-source-google-docs` source plugin in the usual way:

```
$ npm install --save gatsby-source-google-docs gatsby-transformer-remark
```

Next, you need to generate an OAuth token. To make this process easier, the source
plugin exposes an additional script that you can use to generate a token. To do this,
execute the following command in the root of your Gatsby project:

```
$ gatsby-source-google-docs-token
```

Alternatively, you can add the token generation script to your NPM or Yarn scripts:

```
// package.json
"scripts": {
```

```
    "token": "gatsby-source-google-docs-token"
  }
```

You can then generate a token by executing one of the following commands:

```
# If using NPM
$ npm run token

# If using Yarn
$ yarn token
```

The next step is to create three environment variables that identify your Gatsby site to the Google Docs service and save them into a *.env* file :

```
GOOGLE_OAUTH_CLIENT_ID=myGoogleOauthSubdomain.apps.googleusercontent.com
GOOGLE_OAUTH_CLIENT_SECRET=myGoogleOauthClientSecret
GOOGLE_DOCS_TOKEN={"access_token":"myAccessToken",
  "refresh_token":"myRefreshToken",
  "scope":"https://www.googleapis.com/auth/drive.metadata.readonly
          https://www.googleapis.com/auth/documents.readonly",
  "token_type":"Bearer","expiry_date":1606850284}
```

 There are two approaches available for using Google Sheets as the data source for your Gatsby site. The Gatsby blog contains a tutorial on using Google Sheets directly as a data source (*https://oreil.ly/ XLJlg*).

Finally, you can configure the Google Docs source plugin within your Gatsby configuration file. The first plugin object contains a `folder` option, which represents *{folder_id}* in the Google Drive folder URI, *https://drive.google.com/drive/folders/ {folder_id}*. The second plugin object in the `plugins` array configures `gatsby-transformer-remark`, which the Google Docs source plugin uses to process images embedded in Google Docs documents:

```
// gatsby-config.js
plugins: [
  {
    resolve: `gatsby-source-google-docs`,
    options: {
      folder: `{folder_id}`,
    },
  },
  {
    resolve: `gatsby-transformer-remark`,
    options: {
      plugins: [`gatsby-remark-images`],
    },
  },
],
```

# Sourcing Data from CMSs and Commerce Systems

For most developers, interacting with data sources requires interacting with a system that is oriented not only toward developers but also toward content editors, commerce site maintainers, and marketing teams. Many organizations use CMSs to work with content, while commerce systems are used to interact with commerce data such as product and pricing information.

Whereas many traditional CMSs and commerce systems have added APIs for data retrieval and management on top of their existing architectures, some newer CMS and commerce upstarts, commonly known as *headless* vendors, focus more of their attention on the APIs and software development kits (SDKs) that developers use to retrieve data. In this section, we cover a variety of both traditional and headless content management and commerce systems and their respective source plugins.

## Contentful

Contentful is a headless CMS that offers rich data retrieval and management capabilities through its API. In addition, Contentful offers a first-class integration with Gatsby Cloud, a hosting provider for Gatsby. Today, Contentful is commonly used by developers who need a headless CMS without the overhead of some traditional CMS features.

To install the Contentful source plugin, `gatsby-source-contentful`, execute the following command:

```
$ npm install --save gatsby-source-contentful
```

Now, you can configure the source plugin in your Gatsby configuration file. The two most important items you need from Contentful are the `spaceId`, representing the Contentful space you wish to query, and the `accessToken`, which is available in Contentful's settings. As always, with this sensitive information, remember to use environment variables rather than hardcoding the values into your configuration.

To use Contentful's Content Delivery API, which exposes published content for production, add this to your *gatsby-config.js*:

```
// gatsby-config.js
plugins: [
  {
    resolve: `gatsby-source-contentful`,
    options: {
      spaceId: `mySpaceId`,
      accessToken: process.env.CONTENTFUL_ACCESS_TOKEN,
    },
  },
],
```

To use Contentful's Content Preview API instead, which allows you to access unpublished content that isn't ready for production, use this:

```
// gatsby-config.js
plugins: [
  {
    resolve: `gatsby-source-contentful`,
    options: {
      spaceId: `mySpaceId`,
      accessToken: process.env.CONTENTFUL_ACCESS_TOKEN,
      host: `preview.contentful.com`,
    },
  },
],
```

To pull from multiple Contentful spaces, simply add another plugin object to identify the second space to Contentful:

```
// gatsby-config.js
plugins: [
  {
    resolve: `gatsby-source-contentful`,
    options: {
      spaceId: `myFirstContentfulSpaceId`,
      accessToken: process.env.CONTENTFUL_ACCESS_TOKEN,
    },
  },
  {
    resolve: `gatsby-source-contentful`
    options: {
      spaceId: `mySecondContentfulSpaceId`,
      accessToken: process.env.CONTENTFUL_ACCESS_TOKEN,
    },
  },
],
```

The Contentful source plugin offers a variety of configuration options in the `options` object, as Table 5-4 shows.

*Table 5-4. Plugin options for `gatsby-source-contentful`*

| Option | Required? | Description |
| --- | --- | --- |
| spaceId | Required | The space identifier for a Contentful space. |
| accessToken | Required | The API key for the Contentful Content Delivery API; if using the Content Preview API, use the Preview API key instead. |
| host | Optional | The base host for all API requests. Defaults to `cdn.contentful.com`; for the Preview API, use `preview.contentful.com`. |
| environment | Optional | The Contentful environment from which to retrieve content. |
| download Local | Optional | A Boolean that indicates whether all Contentful assets should be downloaded and cached to the local filesystem rather than referred to by CDN URL; defaults to `false`. |

| Option | Required? | Description |
|---|---|---|
| `localeFilter` | Optional | A function that limits the number of locales and nodes created in GraphQL for given Contentful locales in order to reduce memory usage. Defaults to `() => true` `localeFilter: local => locale.code === ` `tr-TR` `.` |
| `forceFull` `Sync` | Optional | A Boolean that prohibits the use of sync tokens upon accessing the Contentful API, preventing a full synchronization of content; defaults to `false`. |
| `proxy` | Optional | An object containing Axios (promise library) proxy configuration; defaults to `undefined`. |
| `useNameForId` | Optional | A Boolean indicating whether the content type's name should be used to identify an object in the GraphQL schema instead of the content's internal identifier; defaults to `true`. |
| `pageLimit` | Optional | The number of entries to pull from Contentful; defaults to `100`. |
| `assetDown` `loadWorkers` | Optional | The number of workers to use to download assets from Contentful; defaults to `50`. |

The Contentful source plugin makes available two node types in Gatsby's GraphQL API:

- Asset nodes, representing assets in Contentful, are created in the GraphQL schema under the fields `contentfulAsset` (single asset) and `allContentfulAs set` (all assets).

- ContentType nodes, representing content items in Contentful, are created in the GraphQL schema under the fields `contentful{TypeName}` (single content item) and `allContentful{TypeName}` (all content items), where `{TypeName}` is the content type's name, unless you have configured `useNameForId`.

To query for all Asset nodes, you can use the `allContentfulAsset` field:

```
{
  allContentfulAsset {
    edges {
      node {
        id
        file {
          uri
        }
      }
    }
  }
}
```

To query for all content items of the content type `BlogPost`, you can use the `allCon tentfulBlogPost` field, which takes this name unless you've set `useNameForId`, in which case it adopts that configured name:

```
{
  allContentfulBlogPost {
    edges {
      node {
        title
      }
    }
  }
}
```

To query for a single content item of the content type `BlogPost` whose title matches a particular string, you can use the `contentfulBlogPost` field:

```
{
  contentfulBlogPost(
    filter: {
      title: {
        eq: "My Blog Post"
      }
    }
  ) {
    title
  }
}
```

 Contentful offers rich text capabilities (*https://oreil.ly/ZSYHQ*) for formatted text fields. A working live example (*https://oreil.ly/ qDN0X*) of Gatsby with Contentful is available, and you can find full documentation about the `gatsby-source-contentful` plugin on the Gatsby website (*https://oreil.ly/YArTA*).

# Drupal

Drupal is a well-established CMS that powers more than 2% of the entire web. After several decades as a monolithic CMS, Drupal has recently introduced headless CMS capabilities in an architectural paradigm known as *decoupled Drupal*. Drupal offers rich content modeling capabilities as well as an administrative interface that is user-friendly for editorial and marketing teams.

To install the Drupal source plugin, execute this command:

```
$ npm install --save gatsby-source-drupal
```

You then need to configure the plugin in your Gatsby configuration file. The only required option is `baseUrl`:

```
// gatsby-config.js
plugins: [
  {
    resolve: `gatsby-source-drupal`,
    options: {
```

```
      baseUrl: `https://my-drupal-site.com`,
    },
  },
],
```

The Drupal source plugin also accepts a variety of additional options to allow developers to have full access to the features of the JSON:API specification (*https://jsonapi.org*), on which Drupal's REST API is based. Remember that sensitive information in these options should be obfuscated through environment variables using a library such as dotenv. The options are summarized in Table 5-5.

*Table 5-5. Configuration options in `gatsby-source-drupal`*

| Option | Required? | Description |
| --- | --- | --- |
| baseUrl | Required | A string containing the full URL to the Drupal site. |
| apiBase | Optional | A string containing the relative path to the root of the API; defaults to `jsonapi`. |
| filters | Optional | An object containing filter parameters based on content item collections, which are then supplied to the query as query parameters (see below for more information). |
| basicAuth | Optional | An object containing Basic Authentication credentials (username and password); e.g.:<br>`basicAuth: {`<br>`    username: process.env.DRUPAL_BASIC_AUTH_USERNAME,`<br>`    password: process.env.DRUPAL_BASIC_AUTH_PASSWORD,`<br>`}` |
| fastBuilds | Optional | A Boolean indicating whether fast builds should be enabled on the Drupal site. The Gatsby Drupal module (*https://oreil.ly/yPn4d*) and an authenticated user with the "Sync Gatsby Fastbuild log entities" permission are required for this functionality. Defaults to `false`. |
| headers | Optional | An object containing any request headers required for the query; e.g.:<br>`headers: {`<br>`    Host: `https://my-host.com`,`<br>`}` |
| params | Optional | An object containing any additional required parameters for GET requests against Drupal; e.g.:<br>`params: {`<br>`    "api-key": "myApiKeyHeader"`<br>`}` |
| skipFileDownloads | Optional | A Boolean indicating whether Gatsby should refrain from downloading files from your Drupal site for future image processing; defaults to `true`. |
| concurrent FileRequests | Optional | A number indicating how many simultaneous file requests should be made to the Drupal site; defaults to 20. |
| disallowed LinkTypes | Optional | An array containing strings representing JSON:API link types that should be skipped, such as `self` and `describedby`. E.g.:<br>`disallowedLinkTypes: [`<br>`    `self`,`<br>`    `describedby`,`<br>`    `action--action``<br>`],` |

Drupal uses the JSON:API specification to drive its REST API, which makes available rich filtering capabilities based on JSON:API syntax. Consider an example in Drupal where the primary endpoint of our JSON:API-compliant API returns a series of collections:

```
// Response to GET https://my-drupal-site.com/jsonapi
{
  // ...
  links: {
    articles: "https://my-drupal-site.com/jsonapi/articles",
    products: "https://my-drupal-site.com/jsonapi/products",
    // ...
  }
}
```

The JSON:API specification defines filtering through query parameters, with nested fields exposed in square brackets. For instance, to target only products that are tagged with the Drupal tag "Holiday," our Gatsby configuration file needs to contain an additional `filters` option defining the collection and the filter that should be applied to it:

```
// gatsby-config.js
plugins: [
  {
    resolve: `gatsby-source-drupal`,
    options: {
      baseUrl: `https://my-drupal-site.com`,
      filters: {
        // Collection: Filter criteria
        products: `filter[tags.name][value]=Holiday`,
      },
    },
  },
],
```

Now, we can issue queries in the Gatsby GraphQL API to populate Gatsby pages and components. Note that because of the way Drupal handles content types, collections are accessed through the field `allNode{TypeName}` and individual items are accessed through the field `node{TypeName}`, where *{TypeName}* is the name of the Drupal content type. To retrieve articles in the collection, we can issue this query, which limits the returned results to 50 items:

```
{
  allNodeArticle(limit: 50) {
    edges {
      node {
        title
        created(formatString: "MMM-DD-YYYY")
      }
    }
```

```
    }
  }
```

To retrieve only a single article, we can issue a query that targets only a single content item:

```
{
  nodeArticle(
    uuid: {
      eq: "49346fb8-3574-11eb-adc1-0242ac120002"
    }
  ) {
    title
    uuid
    created(formatString: "MMM-DD-YYYY")
  }
}
```

 Full documentation about the `gatsby-source-drupal` plugin is available on the Gatsby website (*https://oreil.ly/icKbJ*). For more information about Drupal's JSON:API implementation and filtering capabilities, see my book *Decoupled Drupal in Practice* (Apress).

## Netlify CMS

Another popular CMS for developers working with Gatsby sites is Netlify CMS, a free and open source application that facilitates editing of content and data directly in a Git repository. One of the traits that makes Netlify CMS unique is the fact that it is a Git-based CMS. This means that all content and data updates are implemented not through database operations but through source control and code commits.

The primary advantage of using a system like Netlify CMS is its suitability for SSGs like Gatsby. Because Netlify CMS merely provides a UI that lies above code commits, it's a compelling solution for content editors and marketers who need granular control over content changes. As one might expect, Netlify CMS works a bit differently from the other headless CMSs discussed in this section.

Unlike the other source plugins we've covered so far, Gatsby provides a full-fledged plugin for Netlify CMS that goes well beyond data retrieval use cases, due to the fact that Netlify CMS and Gatsby are capable of deeper levels of integration through an editorial interface built as a React application. For this reason, you may wish to install `netlify-cms-app`, the Netlify CMS interface, alongside the canonical Gatsby plugin for Netlify CMS, `gatsby-plugin-netlify-cms`:

```
$ npm install --save netlify-cms-app gatsby-plugin-netlify-cms
```

Now, add the plugin to the `plugins` array in your Gatsby configuration file. Note that here, we are solely providing the plugin name as a string rather than placing it inside a `resolve` object with a nested `options` object:

```
// gatsby-config.js
plugins: [
  `gatsby-plugin-netlify-cms`,
],
```

Together, the `netlify-cms-app` and `gatsby-plugin-netlify-cms` plugins will create a Netlify CMS application in your browser at the path */admin/index.html*, where content editors can modify their content. Because Gatsby copies everything in the */static* directory (where static assets unmanipulated by Gatsby are placed) to the */public* folder, you'll also need to create a Netlify CMS configuration file located at */static/admin/config.yml*.

Your Netlify CMS configuration YAML file will look something like the following:

```
# static/admin/config.yml
backend:
  name: my-netlify-cms-repo

media_folder: static/assets
public_folder: /assets

collections:
  - name: blog
    label: Blog
    folder: blog
    create: true
    fields:
      - { name: path, label: Path }
      - { name: date, label: Date, widget: datetime }
      - { name: title, label: Title }
      - { name: body, label: Body, widget: markdown }
```

Once you save this file, you'll be able to run `gatsby develop` and access the Netlify CMS editorial interface at *https://my-gatsby-site.com/admin/* (the trailing slash is required). With the Netlify CMS application now running, you can make arbitrary edits to create and modify content. However, further authentication will be required in order to connect the Netlify CMS application with a working Git repository.

Because Netlify CMS will store any content you create as files that are committed to source repositories rather than to a database, your Netlify CMS "database" is in fact your local filesystem. Therefore, the queries you'll issue within the Gatsby GraphQL API will match those implemented for `gatsby-source-filesystem`, which should also be installed and included in your Gatsby configuration if you wish to include Netlify CMS content within your Gatsby site. When you configure the source plugin, the path to your Markdown files should be defined as ${__dirname}/blog to adhere to the preceding configuration.

 Gatsby has gatsby-plugin-netlify-cms plugin documentation online (*https://oreil.ly/BbjIE*). Because approaches differ across providers, describing how to integrate Netlify CMS with Git source control providers is outside the scope of this book. The Netlify CMS documentation (*https://oreil.ly/ba0b8*) contains information about integrations with GitHub and GitLab (*https://oreil.ly/Dl9td*).

## Prismic

Prismic is a hosted headless CMS available as a SaaS solution for content management. As a CMS for both editorial teams and developer teams, Prismic makes available an editorial interface as well as an API. In addition to its core feature set of custom content modeling, content scheduling and versioning, and multilingual support, Prismic also offers a feature known as Content Slices, which facilitates the creation of dynamic layouts.

Once you've populated your Prismic content repository with some content, you can acquire an API access token by navigating to Settings→API & Security in the Prismic interface, creating a new application (the Callback URL field can remain empty), and clicking "Add this application." Then, install the Prismic source plugin as usual:

```
$ npm install --save gatsby-source-prismic
```

Next, add the Prismic source plugin to your *gatsby-config.js* file in order to register it. As always, store your sensitive credentials as environment variables using a library such as dotenv whenever you're using them in your Gatsby configuration file:

```
// gatsby-config.js
plugins: [
  {
    resolve: `gatsby-source-prismic`,
    options: {
      repositoryName: `myPrismicRepositoryName`,
      accessToken: process.env.PRISMIC_API_KEY,
      schemas: {
        page: require(`./src/schemas/page.json`),
        article: require(`./src/schemas/article.json`),
      },
    },
  },
],
```

Note that the repositoryName and schemas options are the only required options if your Prismic API does not require authentication; otherwise, the accessToken option is also required. Schemas are available by navigating to the "JSON editor" feature in the Prismic Custom Type Editor and copying the contents into the appropriate required files. Table 5-6 summarizes all of the configuration options available for the Prismic source plugin.

*Table 5-6. Configuration options for `gatsby-source-prismic`*

| Option | Required? | Description |
|---|---|---|
| `repositoryName` | Required | A string containing the name of your Prismic repository (e.g., `my-prismic-site` if your *prismic.io* address is *my-prismic-site.prismic.io*). |
| `accessToken` | Optional | A string containing the API access token for your Prismic repository. |
| `releaseId` | Optional | A string containing a specific Prismic release, which is a collection of changes intended for preview within Gatsby Cloud. |
| `linkResolver` | Optional | A function determining how links in content should be processed in order to generate the correct link URL. The document node, field key (API ID), and field value are provided; e.g.:<br><br>`linkResolver: ({ node, key, value }) => (doc) => {`<br>`    // Link resolver logic`<br>`}` |
| `fetchLinks` | Optional | An array containing a list of links that should be retrieved and made available in the link resolver function so you can fetch multiple fields from a linked Prismic document; defaults to `[]`. |
| `htmlSerializer` | Optional | A function determining how fields with rich text formatting should be processed to generate correct HTML. The document node, field key (API ID), and field value are provided; e.g.:<br><br>`htmlSerializer: ({ node, key, value }) => (`<br>`    type,`<br>`    element,`<br>`    content,`<br>`    children,`<br>`) => {`<br>`    // HTML serializer logic`<br>`}` |
| `schemas` | Required | An object containing custom types mapped to Prismic schemas; e.g.:<br><br>`schemas: {`<br>`    page: require(`./src/schemas/page.json`),`<br>`    article: require(`./src/schemas/article.json`),`<br>`}` |
| `lang` | Optional | A string containing a default language code for retrieving documents; defaults to `*`, which retrieves all languages. |
| `prismicToolbar` | Optional | A Boolean indicating whether the Prismic Toolbar script should be added to the site; defaults to `false`. |
| `shouldDownloadImage` | Optional | A function determining whether images should be downloaded locally for further processing. The document node, field key (API ID), and field value are provided; e.g.:<br><br>`shouldDownloadImage: ({ node, key, value }) => {`<br>`    // Return true to download`<br>`    // Return false to skip`<br>`}` |

| Option | Required? | Description |
|---|---|---|
| imageImgix Params | Optional | An object containing a set of Imgix (a library for image processing) image transformations for future image processing; e.g.:<br><br>```<br>imageImgixParams: {<br>  auto: `compress,format`,<br>  fit: `max`,<br>  q: 50,<br>}<br>``` |
| imagePlace holderImgix Params | Optional | An object containing a set of Imgix image transformations applied to placeholder images for future image processing; e.g.:<br><br>```<br>imagePlaceholderImgixParams: {<br>  w: 50,<br>  blur: 20,<br>  q: 100,<br>}<br>``` |
| typePathsFile namePrefix | Optional | A string containing prefix for filenames where type paths for schemas are stored, including the MD5 hash of your schemas after the prefix; defaults to `prismic-typepaths---{repositoryName}`, where *{repositoryName}* is your Prismic repository name. |

With the Prismic source plugin configured, you can now issue queries against the Gatsby GraphQL API to retrieve your Prismic data within Gatsby pages and components. To retrieve all content items of type `Article` from Prismic, you can issue a query like the following:

```
{
  allPrismicArticle {
    edges {
      node {
        id
        first_publication_date
        last_publication_date
        data {
          title {
            text
          }
          content {
            html
          }
        }
      }
    }
  }
}
```

You can also retrieve an individual content item by issuing a query like the following, with an argument supplied:

```
{
  prismicArticle(
```

```
      id: {
        eq: "My Prismic Article"
      }
    } (
      id
      first_publication_date
      last_publication_date
      data {
        title {
          text
        }
        content {
          html
        }
      }
    }
  }
}
```

 More example queries are available on the NPM package page (*https://oreil.ly/8AByW*), and Gatsby provides full documentation about the gatsby-source-prismic plugin (*https://oreil.ly/5N3cI*).

# Sanity

Sanity is a hosted service providing backends for structured content, together with a free and open source editorial interface built in React. With a focus on real-time APIs for retrieving and managing data, Sanity is a potential candidate as a headless CMS for developers working with Gatsby sites. To use Sanity as a data source for Gatsby, you'll need to configure an instance of Sanity Studio (a React application for interacting with your Sanity content) and a GraphQL API that exposes your Sanity dataset. To install the Sanity source plugin, execute the following command:

```
$ npm install --save gatsby-source-sanity
```

Then configure the plugin in your Gatsby configuration file. As always, any sensitive information should be provided as environment variables through dotenv:

```
// gatsby-config.js
plugins: [
  {
    resolve: `gatsby-source-sanity`,
    options: {
      projectId: `mySanityProjectId`,
      dataset: `mySanityDataset`,
    },
  },
],
```

The Sanity source plugin makes available a range of additional configuration options within the `options` object, apart from the required `projectId` and `dataset` options, as Table 5-7 shows.

*Table 5-7. Configuration options for `gatsby-source-sanity`*

| Option | Required? | Description |
| --- | --- | --- |
| projectId | Required | A string containing the Sanity project identifier. |
| dataset | Required | A string containing the name of the Sanity dataset. |
| token | Optional | A string containing the authentication token for retrieving data from private datasets (or when using `overlayDrafts`). |
| overlay Drafts | Optional | A Boolean indicating whether drafts should replace published versions in delivery. Defaults to `false`. |
| watchMode | Optional | A Boolean indicating whether a listener should be kept open and provide the latest changes in real time. Defaults to `false`. |

 Full documentation regarding the `gatsby-source-sanity` plugin is available on the Gatsby website (*https://oreil.ly/UY8NA*).

With the configuration done, you can query your Sanity data within the Gatsby GraphQL API by using the top-level field `allSanity{TypeName}` (all items) or `sanity{TypeName}` (individual items), where *{TypeName}* is a Sanity document type name. For instance, if you have a Sanity document type known as `article`, you can retrieve data for all articles with this query:

```
{
  allSanityArticle {
    edges {
      node {
        title
        description
        slug {
          current
        }
      }
    }
  }
}
```

And you can retrieve an individual article with a query like this:

```
{
  sanityArticle(
    title: {
      eq: "My Sanity Article"
    }
```

```
  ) {
    title
    description
    slug {
      current
    }
  }
}
```

# Shopify

Shopify is a popular commerce system for building online storefronts. With the Shopify source plugin, Gatsby sites can retrieve data from the Shopify Storefront API and populate the internal GraphQL API. The `gatsby-source-shopify` plugin provides public shop data and also supports both the `gatsby-transformer-sharp` and `gatsby-image` plugins for image handling (covered at greater length in Chapter 7).

To install the Shopify source plugin, use this command:

```
$ npm install --save gatsby-source-shopify
```

To access the Shopify Storefront API, you need to acquire an access token that is permissioned such that your source plugin can read products, variants, and collections; read product tags; and read shop content such as articles, blogs, and comments. As always, this access token should be provided as an environment variable through the dotenv library to avoid revealing sensitive credentials. Once you have the access token, you can add the plugin to your Gatsby configuration file:

```
// gatsby-config.js
plugins: [
  {
    resolve: `gatsby-source-shopify`,
    options: {
      password: process.env.SHOPIFY_ADMIN_PASSWORD
      storeUrl: process.env.SHOPIFY_STORE_URL,
    },
  },
],
```

Though these are the only required options for the Shopify source plugin, there are a variety of additional options that can be configured in the `options` object, as Table 5-8 shows.

*Table 5-8. Configuration options for* `gatsby-source-shopify`

| Option | Required? | Description |
|---|---|---|
| password | Required | A string containing the administrative password for the Shopify store and application you are using. |
| storeUrl | Required | A string containing your Shopify store URL, such as `my-shop.myshopify.com`. |
| shopifyConnections | Optional | An array consisting of additional data types to source, such as `orders` or `collections`. |
| downloadImages | Optional | A Boolean that, when set to `true`, indicates that images should be downloaded from Shopify and processed during the build (the plugin's default behavior is to fall back to Shopify's CDN). |
| typePrefix | Optional | A string containing an optional prefix to add to a node type name (e.g., when set to MyShop, node names will be under `allMyShopShopifyProducts` instead of `allShopifyProducts`). |
| salesChannel | Optional | A string containing an optional channel name (e.g., `My Sales Channel`) whose active products and collections will be the only data sourced. The default behavior is to source all that are available in the online store. |

For more information about the `gatsby-source-shopify` plugin and example queries, consult the documentation on the Gatsby website (*https://oreil.ly/CGj86*).

Once you've included the Shopify source plugin in your Gatsby configuration file, you can query Shopify data through the Gatsby GraphQL API. To query all Shopify nodes, you can issue a query such as the following:

```
allShopifyProduct(
  sort: {
    fields: [publishedAt],
    order: ASC
  }
) {
  edges {
    node {
      id
      storefrontId
    }
  }
}
```

# WordPress

WordPress is a well-known free and open source CMS that is used by many websites on the internet. For developers building Gatsby sites, WordPress offers two means of retrieving data: WP-API, which is WordPress's native REST API, and WPGraphQL, which is a GraphQL API contributed to the WordPress ecosystem (in addition to another, known as the GraphQL API for WordPress). In the Gatsby plugin ecosystem, the `gatsby-source-wordpress` source plugin is responsible for retrieving data through WPGraphQL and making it available to Gatsby's internal GraphQL API.

To install the WordPress source plugin, use this command:

```
$ npm install --save gatsby-source-wordpress
```

As with the other source plugins, you will need to add the plugin to your Gatsby configuration:

```
// gatsby-config.js
plugins: [
  {
    resolve: `gatsby-source-wordpress`,
    options: {
      url: process.env.WPGRAPHQL_URL,
    },
  },
],
```

The `url` option is the only required key in the `options` object, but there are many other optional configuration options that the WordPress source plugin makes available. Table 5-9 shows a subset of these.

*Table 5-9. Configuration options for `gatsby-source-wordpress`*

| Option | Type | Description |
|---|---|---|
| url | String | The full URL of the WPGraphQL endpoint (required) |
| verbose | Boolean | Indicates whether the terminal should display verbose output; defaults to `true` |
| debug | Object | Commonly used debugging options (others include `preview`, `timeBuildSteps`, `disableCompatibilityCheck`, and `throwRefetchErrors`). <br> `graphql`: Object containing GraphQL debugging options: <br> • `showQueryVarsOnError`: Boolean indicating whether query variables used in the query should be logged; defaults to `false` <br> • `panicOnError`: Boolean indicating whether or not to panic when a GraphQL error is thrown; defaults to `false` <br> • `onlyReportCriticalErrors`: Boolean indicating whether noncritical errors should be logged; defaults to `true` <br> • `writeQueriesToDisk`: Boolean indicating whether all internal GraphQL queries generated during data sourcing should be written out to *.graphql* files; defaults to `false` |
| develop | Object | Options related to `gatsby develop`: <br> • `nodeUpdateInterval`: Integer indicating how many milliseconds Gatsby should wait before querying WordPress to see if data has changed; defaults to `5000` <br> • `hardCacheMediaFiles`: Boolean indicating whether media files should be cached outside the Gatsby cache to prevent redownloading when the Gatsby cache is cleared; defaults to `false` <br> • `hardCacheData`: Boolean indicating whether WordPress data should be cached outside the Gatsby cache to prevent redownloading when the Gatsby cache is cleared; defaults to `false` |

| Option | Type | Description |
|---|---|---|
| auth | Object | Options related to authentication:<br>htaccess: Object containing htaccess authentication information:<br>• username: String containing username for an .htpassword-protected site; defaults to null<br>• password: String containing password for an .htpassword-protected site; defaults to null |
| schema | Object | Commonly used options related to retrieving the remote schema (others include queryDepth, circularQueryLimit, requestConcurrency, and previewRequestConcurrency):<br>• typePrefix: String containing a prefix for all types derived from the remote schema to prevent name conflicts; defaults to Wp<br>• timeout: Integer indicating the amount of time in milliseconds before a GraphQL request should time out; defaults to 30000<br>• perPage: Integer indicating the number of nodes to retrieve per page during the sourcing process; defaults to 100 |
| exclude<br>Field<br>Names | Array | A list of field names to exclude from the newly generated schema; defaults to [ ] |
| html | Object | Options related to processing of HTML fields:<br>• useGatsbyImage: Boolean indicating whether Gatsby-driven images should replace HTML images; defaults to true<br>• imageMaxWidth: Integer indicating the maximum width for an image; defaults to null<br>• fallbackImageMaxWidth: Integer indicating the fallback maximum width if the HTML does not provide it; defaults to 100<br>• imageQuality: Integer indicating image quality that Sharp (an image processor covered in Chapter 7) will use to generate thumbnails; defaults to 90<br>• createStaticFiles: Boolean indicating whether URLs that contain the string /wp-content/uploads should be transformed into static files and have their URLs rewritten accordingly; defaults to true |
| type | Object | Options related to types in the remote schema:<br>• [TypeName]: Object containing options pertaining to individual types, falling under type[TypeName].{option}:<br>— exclude: Boolean indicating whether a type should be excluded from the newly generated schema; defaults to undefined<br>— excludeFieldNames: Array indicating fields that should be excluded from a type; defaults to undefined<br>• __all: Object containing a special type setting applied to all types in the generated schema; accepts same options as [TypeName] and defaults to undefined<br>• RootQuery: Object containing fields that are made available under the root wp field; accepts the same options as [TypeName] and defaults to { excludeFieldNames: [`viewer`, `node`, `schemaMd5`], }<br>• MediaItem: Object containing options pertaining to media items<br>— lazyNodes: Boolean indicating whether media items should be fetched through other nodes rather than fetching them individually; defaults to false<br>— localFile.excludeByMimeTypes: Array indicating that certain MIME types should be excluded; defaults to [ ]<br>— localFile.maxFileSizeBytes: Number indicating the file size above which files should not be downloaded; defaults to 15728640 (15 MB) |

Once you've saved your Gatsby configuration file, you'll be able to issue queries against the Gatsby GraphQL API to extract data from your WordPress site. Because the configuration options determine to a great extent how your queries appear, it isn't possible to provide a full accounting of all querying possibilities with the WordPress source plugin. For this reason, the `gatsby-source-wordpress` documentation recommends examining the wide range of examples that consume WordPress data.

 Full documentation for the `gatsby-source-wordpress` plugin is available on GitHub (*https://oreil.ly/uLlga*). There's also a WordPress plugin (*https://oreil.ly/sXksC*) that optimizes WordPress sites to work as data sources for Gatsby.

# Sourcing Data from Other Sources

Sometimes, you may need to pull directly from data that is serialized as JSON or YAML and isn't included in a database. In other cases, you may need to pull directly from other GraphQL APIs. For pulling from GraphQL APIs you need a GraphQL source plugin, but for JSON and YAML you need to use a different approach to import the data. In this section, we'll cover sourcing data from GraphQL APIs first before turning our attention to data housed in JSON and YAML documents.

## Sourcing Data from GraphQL APIs

It's often the case that you'll need to retrieve data from other GraphQL APIs to populate Gatsby's internal GraphQL API. To accomplish this, the `gatsby-source-graphql` source plugin is capable of *schema stitching*, a process in which multiple external GraphQL schemas are combined to form a single cohesive schema.

The GraphQL source plugin creates an arbitrary type name that surrounds the schema's overarching query type, while the external schema becomes available under a field within Gatsby's GraphQL API.

Installing the GraphQL source same way as with other source plugins:

```
$ npm install --save gatsby-source-graphql
```

Then, as usual, you need to configure the GraphQL source plugin within your Gatsby configuration file. The following example shows what a simple GraphQL source plugin configuration object might look like. The only required options are `typeName` (an arbitrary name that identifies the remote schema's `Query` type), `fieldName` (the Gatsby GraphQL field under which the remote schema will be available), and `url` (the URL of the GraphQL endpoint):

```
// gatsby-config.js
plugins: [
```

```
  {
    resolve: `gatsby-source-graphql`,
    options: {
      typeName: `myGraphqlName`,
      fieldName: `contentGraphql`,
      url: `https://my-graphql-api.com/graphql`,
    },
  },
],
```

Some remote GraphQL APIs require authentication to access their data. Always remember to store sensitive credentials as environment variables and inject those values into your configuration file through a library such as dotenv. In the following more complex example, we see an HTTP header used to provide the authentication:

```
// gatsby-config.js
plugins: [
  {
    resolve: `gatsby-source-graphql`,
    options: {
      typeName: `GitHub`,
      fieldName: `github`,
      url: `https://api.github.com/graphql`,
      headers: {
        Authorization: `Bearer ${process.env.GITHUB_ACCESS_TOKEN}`,
      },
    },
  },
],
```

The headers object also accepts functions as an alternative, which means it's possible to use an async function to provide the credentials, such as a getGithubAuthToken() function defined in the same file:

```
// gatsby-config.js
headers: async () => {
  return {
    Authorization: await getGithubAuthToken(),
  }
},
```

The options object accepts several other configuration options, which are listed in Table 5-10.

 Transforming schemas and configuring data loader options are for advanced GraphQL requirements. For more details about schema wrapping and why the transformSchema option is useful, consult the graphql-tools documentation (*https://oreil.ly/5hCOU*). For a full list of available dataLoaderOptions, see the graphql/data loader documentation (*https://oreil.ly/4zhdz*).

*Table 5-10. Configuration options for `gatsby-source-graphql`*

| Option | Required? | Description |
|---|---|---|
| typeName | Required | A string containing an arbitrary name for the remote schema Query type. |
| fieldName | Required | A string containing an arbitrary name under which the remote schema will be made available in the Gatsby GraphQL API. |
| url | Required | A string containing the URL for the GraphQL endpoint of the remote GraphQL API. |
| headers | Optional | Accepts two types:<br><br>• An object containing HTTP headers to be provided as part of the request.<br>• A function handling HTTP headers provided by a method or utility. |
| fetch Options | Optional | An object containing additional options to pass to the node-fetch library (*https://oreil.ly/ctnKD*) that the GraphQL source plugin uses. Defaults to {}. |
| fetch | Optional | A function providing a fetch-compatible API to use when issuing requests; e.g.:<br><br>```\nfetch: (uri, options = {}) => {\n  fetch(uri, { ...options, headers:\n    sign(options.headers) }),\n},\n``` |
| batch | Optional | A Boolean indicating whether queries should be batched to improve query performance rather than being executed individually in separate network requests; defaults to false. |
| dataLoader Options | Optional | An object containing GraphQL data loader options, including:<br>maxBatchSize: A number indicating how many queries the GraphQL source plugin should batch; defaults to 5. |
| createLink | Optional | A function providing the manual creation of an Apollo Link (Apollo Link is a library that offers fine-grained control over HTTP requests issued by Apollo Client) for Apollo users; e.g.:<br><br>```\ncreateLink: pluginOptions => {\n  return createHttpLink({\n    uri: `https://api.github.com/graphql`,\n    headers: {\n      Authorization: `Bearer\n        ${process.env.GITHUB_ACCESS_TOKEN}`,\n    },\n    fetch,\n  })\n},\n``` |

| Option | Required? | Description |
|---|---|---|
| create Schema | Optional | A callback function providing an arbitrary schema definition (e.g., schema SDL or introspection JSON). Returns a `GraphQLSchema` instance or a `Promise` resolving to a `GraphQLSchema`; e.g.: <br><br>```<br>// Dependencies<br>const fs = require(`fs`)<br>const { buildSchema, buildClientSchema } =<br>  require(`graphql`)<br><br>// Inside plugin options:<br><br>// Create schema from introspection JSON<br>createSchema: async () => {<br>  const json = JSON.parse(<br>    fs.readFileSync(`${__dirname}/introspection.json`)<br>  )<br>  return buildClientSchema(json.data)<br>},<br><br>// Create schema from schema SDL<br>createSchema: async () => {<br>  const sdl = fs.readFileSync(`${__dirname}/schema.sdl`).toString()<br>  return buildSchema(sdl)<br>},<br>``` |
| transform Schema | Optional | A function providing an arbitrary schema based on inputs from an object argument containing schema (introspected remote schema), `link` (default link), `resolver` (default resolver), `defaultTransforms` (array containing default transforms), and `options` (plugin options); e.g.: <br><br>```<br>// Dependencies<br>const { wrapSchema } = require(`@graphql-tools/wrap`)<br>const { linkToExecutor } = require(`@graphql-tools/links`)<br><br>// Inside plugin options:<br>transformSchema: ({<br>  schema,<br>  link,<br>  resolver,<br>  defaultTransforms,<br>  options,<br>}) => {<br>  return wrapSchema(<br>    {<br>      schema,<br>      executor: linkToExecutor(link),<br>    },<br>    defaultTransforms<br>  )<br>},<br>``` |
| refetch Interval | Optional | A number indicating how many seconds the GraphQL source plugin should wait before refetching the data (by default, it only refetches data when the server is restarted). |

Now, you can query the GraphQL API using queries that match the `fieldNames` you've defined in your Gatsby configuration file. And by using multiple plugin definitions, as you've seen in previous sections, you can make both datasets available to the GraphQL API in Gatsby, as follows:

```
// gatsby-config.js
plugins: [
  {
    resolve: `gatsby-source-graphql`,
    options: {
      typeName: `myGraphqlName`,
      fieldName: `remoteGraphql`,
      url: `https://my-graphql-api.com/graphql`,
    },
  },
  {
    resolve: `gatsby-source-graphql`,
    options: {
      typeName: `GitHub`,
      fieldName: `github`,
      url: `https://api.github.com/graphql`,
      headers: {
        Authorization: `Bearer ${process.env.GITHUB_ACCESS_TOKEN}`,
      },
    },
  },
],
```

With both GraphQL APIs now represented in your Gatsby GraphQL API, you can query both APIs in one GraphQL query, like this:

```
{
  remoteGraphql {
    allArticles {
      title
    }
  }
  github {
    viewer {
      email
    }
  }
}
```

 Full documentation for the `gatsby-source-graphql` plugin is available on the Gatsby website (*https://oreil.ly/ypUJy*).

## Sourcing Data from JSON and YAML

Sometimes, you have raw data that isn't in a database or other system; in fact, it's simply a YAML file or JSON file that contains data you need to use to populate your Gatsby site. For raw JSON and YAML data housed in files, we can't use a normal source plugin that retrieves data from external sources. Nor can we use `gatsby-source-filesystem`, because our data is stored in one file rather than in multiple files across directories.

Though this section is entitled "Sourcing Data from JSON and YAML," in fact the approach required to import raw JSON and YAML data into a Gatsby site for use in Gatsby pages and components is a direct import that bypasses Gatsby's GraphQL API entirely. Suppose you already have a YAML or JSON file containing data, in a format similar to one of the following:

```
# content/data.yaml
title: My YAML data
content:
  - item:
      Lorem ipsum dolor sit amet
  - item:
      Consectetur adipiscing elit
  - item:
      Curabitur ac elit erat

// content/data.json
{
  "title": "My JSON Data",
  "content": [
    {
      "item": "Lorem ipsum dolor sit amet"
    },
    {
      "item": "Consectetur adipiscing elit"
    },
    {
      "item": "Curabitur ac elit erat"
    }
  ]
}
```

You can create a new page component in *src/pages* that directly consumes the data in that file. If you're importing YAML data, your `import` statements will look like the following:

```
// src/pages/direct-import-example.js
import React from "react"
import ExternalData from "../../content/data.yaml"
```

For JSON data, refer to the JSON data file instead:

```
// src/pages/direct-import-example.js
import React from "react"
import ExternalData from "../../content/data.json"
```

Now, you can create a rudimentary Gatsby page that generates a list of content based on the data you've retrieved from that file:

```
// src/pages/direct-import-example.js
const DirectImportExample = () => (
  <div>
    <h1>{ExternalData.title}</h1>
    <ul>
      {ExternalData.content.map( (data, index) => {
        return <li key={`content-item-${index}`}>{data.item}</li>
      } )}
    </ul>
  </div>
)

export default DirectImportExample
```

After saving this page and running `gatsby develop`, you'll see your Gatsby page populated with the data you imported. Note in this example that we've bypassed the GraphQL API internal to Gatsby entirely in favor of directly importing our data as a dependency.

 It's also possible to build a Gatsby site entirely based on a YAML data manifest, but that is beyond the scope of this book. For more on this approach, consult the Gatsby documentation (*https://oreil.ly/dkJMx*).

# Conclusion

Source plugins, one of the most important aspects of the Gatsby ecosystem, are essential to the functioning of your Gatsby site because they are the conduit by which data from a local filesystem or external service or database is made available for use. This chapter covered only a selection of popular source plugins and sourcing approaches, but there's an infinite supply of potential services to interact with. The Gatsby plugin ecosystem contains a wide variety of additional source plugins with guides for integration with many other services beyond those represented here.

Source plugins are also fundamental for Gatsby developers because they determine how Gatsby builds pages programmatically using templates and arbitrarily sourced data. We've focused primarily on how to source data with source plugins so that we can interact with that data in GraphQL queries within Gatsby pages and components.

Next, we'll turn our attention to connecting the dots between the `createPages` API, which generates programmatic Gatsby pages based on data and logic in the *gatsby-node.js* file; the GraphQL queries enabled by our newly configured source plugins; and the templates determining how those pages ought to look.

# CHAPTER 6

# Programmatic Page Creation

In the previous chapter, we took a close look at how Gatsby enables the retrieval of arbitrary data from a variety of sources, whether that means a local filesystem, an external database or service, or a CMS or commerce platform. Thanks to source plugins, we can easily populate our Gatsby pages and components with external data.

But it's often the case that we want the creation of our Gatsby pages to be dictated by the data rather than manually creating the pages first and populating them with data later. What happens when the pages in our Gatsby site depend on the data we retrieve in order to exist? How do we take GraphQL data and *generate* pages based on arbitrary response data?

One of Gatsby's most important features, and one of the chief reasons for its success, is its capacity to perform *programmatic page creation*, in which pages depend on and are created according to GraphQL data. For instance, the home page of a blog might be manually created, but its archive pages and individual article pages likely rely on external data. As such, as developers, we can't predict how many pages there might be, since the number of blog posts is arbitrary.

Thanks to the *gatsby-node.js* file and the `createPages` API, we can now create not only manual pages that contain data but also generated pages that depend on external data to exist. Through these mechanisms, we can implement rich Gatsby sites that don't just contain static content; they also dynamically adjust to the data that we present them, becoming truly data-driven sites in the process.

Programmatic page creation involves a combination of the *gatsby-node.js* file, the `cre atePages` API, and, optionally, Gatsby templates. We'll cover each of these in turn in this chapter, in addition to introducing another type of Gatsby plugin: transformer plugins. To connect the dots between our explorations of GraphQL and the discussion of source plugins in the previous chapter, let's first revisit how to create a Gatsby page that depends on GraphQL data. Then, we'll examine transformer plugin usage before delving into the central file where programmatic page creation takes place: *gatsby-node.js*.

# Traversing GraphQL Data in Pages

In this section, we'll walk through building a rudimentary Gatsby site using a source plugin instead of using data hardcoded into the Gatsby configuration file (as our site name was). This means we'll be introducing a page that relies entirely on data made available through a source plugin, rather than from *gatsby-config.js* or from JSX we write.

To begin, clone a new version of the default starter for Gatsby:

```
$ gatsby new gtdg-ch6-programmatic-pages gatsbyjs/gatsby-starter-default
$ cd gtdg-ch6-programmatic-pages
```

Then install the `gatsby-source-filesystem` source plugin, which will allow you to access your filesystem through Gatsby's internal GraphQL API (see "Sourcing Data from the Filesystem" on page 123 if you need a refresher). In this walkthrough, we'll build a basic catalog of the files in our codebase. Fortunately, Gatsby's default starter comes with `gatsby-source-filesystem` preconfigured for us.

Next, create a file named *file-list.js* in the *src/pages* directory, and copy the contents of *src/pages/page-2.js* into it. Then change the contents of that file to the following to distinguish it from *src/pages/page-2.js*:

```
// src/pages/file-list.js
import React from "react"
import { Link } from "gatsby"

import Layout from "../components/layout"
import SEO from "../components/seo"

const FileListPage = () => (
  <Layout>
    <SEO title="File list" />
    <h1>Hi from the file list page</h1>
    <p>Welcome to the file list page</p>
    <Link to="/">Go back to the homepage</Link>
  </Layout>
)

export default FileListPage
```

Open GraphiQL in your browser by executing `gatsby develop` and navigating to *https://localhost:8000/___graphql*. You can issue a simple test query—the very first one we issued in Chapter 4—to make sure the GraphiQL interface is working properly:

```
{
  site {
    siteMetadata {
      title
    }
  }
}
```

Running this query in GraphiQL will give you the following JSON response:

```
{
  "data": {
    "site": {
      "siteMetadata": {
        "title": "Gatsby Default Starter"
      }
    }
  },
  "extensions": {}
}
```

Now you have your site title, which is provided by the Gatsby configuration file. Let's try a new query, this time using the GraphQL data retrieved from the filesystem source plugin. In this example, the `fromNow` argument indicates that the `birthTime` (time at which the file was created) and `modifiedTime` (time at which the file was modified) should be returned as a string, like "8 minutes ago" or "in 8 minutes":

```
{
  allFile {
    edges {
      node {
        relativePath
        birthTime(fromNow: true)
        modifiedTime(fromNow: true)
        extension
        prettySize
      }
    }
  }
}
```

You can see the result of the query we just issued to GraphiQL in Figure 6-1.

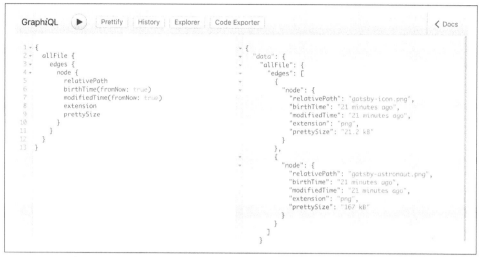

*Figure 6-1. The result of our GraphiQL request, with the JSON response matching the structure of the query we provided*

As you can see, according to the configuration in *gatsby-config.js* (scan for files in *src/ images/*), we now have a list of the two files returned by the source plugin, *gatsby-icon.png* (the favicon for Gatsby) and *gatsby-astronaut.png* (the astronaut image we see on the home page when spinning up any Gatsby default starter):

```
{
  "data": {
    "allFile": {
      "edges": [
        {
          "node": {
            "relativePath": "gatsby-icon.png",
            "birthTime": "21 minutes ago",
            "modifiedTime": "21 minutes ago",
            "extension": "png",
            "prettySize": "21.2 kB"
          }
        },
        {
          "node": {
            "relativePath": "gatsby-astronaut.png",
            "birthTime": "21 minutes ago",
            "modifiedTime": "21 minutes ago",
            "extension": "png",
            "prettySize": "167 kB"
          }
        }
      ]
    }
  },
```

```
        "extensions": {}
}
```

Back in our file list page, we can now add the query to our file. To make GraphQL queries available to our Gatsby pages, we need to declare a dependency on the graphql tag in Gatsby by adding to the Gatsby import statement:

```
// src/pages/file-list.js
import React from "react"
import { graphql, Link } from "gatsby"

import Layout from "../components/layout"
import SEO from "../components/seo"
```

Let's also add a console.log() statement that allows us to preview the data that we've just retrieved from the GraphQL API. Here is the rest of the file after the import statements:

```
// src/pages/file-list.js
const FileListPage = ({ data }) => {
  console.log(data)
  return (
    <Layout>
      <SEO title="File list" />
      <h1>Hi from the file list page</h1>
      <p>Welcome to the file list page</p>
      <Link to="/">Go back to the homepage</Link>
    </Layout>
  )
}

export const query = graphql`
  {
    allFile {
      edges {
        node {
          relativePath
          birthTime(fromNow: true)
          modifiedTime(fromNow: true)
          extension
          prettySize
        }
      }
    }
  }
`

export default FileListPage
```

We've now brought our GraphQL query in as an additional export, which Gatsby makes available to our page via the data variable, which we need to add as an argument to the `FileListPage` function. If you inspect the console at *http://localhost: 8000/file-list/*, you'll see the JSON object printed there, as illustrated in Figure 6-2.

*Figure 6-2. The result of our GraphQL query as a JSON object representing the data variable, inspected in the Firefox developer console*

Now, let's go ahead and replace the page's contents with some more compelling information about the files themselves, pulling from the data we now have available to us from the GraphQL API. In the process, let's add a table that identifies our two files. In this example, I show only the `const` definition of the `FileListPage` function:

```
// src/pages/file-list.js
const FileListPage = ({ data }) => {
  return (
    <Layout>
      <SEO title="File list" />
      <h1>Hi from the file list page</h1>
      <table>
        <thead>
          <tr>
            <th>Relative path</th>
            <th>Created</th>
            <th>Modified</th>
            <th>Extension</th>
            <th>Pretty size</th>
          </tr>
        </thead>
        <tbody>
          {data.allFile.edges.map( ({ node }, index) => (
            <tr key={index}>
              <td>{node.relativePath}</td>
              <td>{node.birthTime}</td>
              <td>{node.modifiedTime}</td>
              <td>{node.extension}</td>
              <td>{node.prettySize}</td>
            </tr>
```

```
      ))}
    </tbody>
  </table>
  <Link to="/">Go back to the homepage</Link>
</Layout>
  )
}
```

Figure 6-3 shows the result of our new file list page.

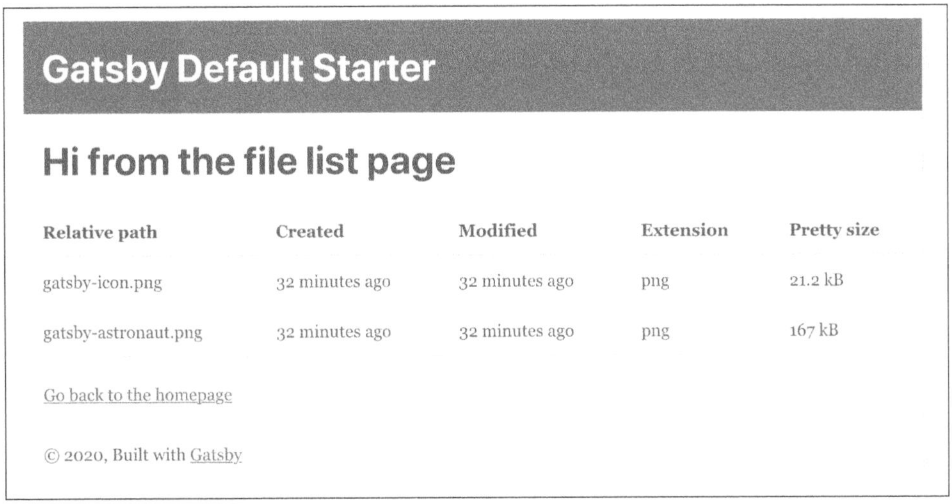

**Gatsby Default Starter**

## Hi from the file list page

| Relative path | Created | Modified | Extension | Pretty size |
|---|---|---|---|---|
| gatsby-icon.png | 32 minutes ago | 32 minutes ago | png | 21.2 kB |
| gatsby-astronaut.png | 32 minutes ago | 32 minutes ago | png | 167 kB |

Go back to the homepage

© 2020, Built with Gatsby

*Figure 6-3. The final result of the file list page, containing a full accounting of the files in src/images/ based on the results of a GraphQL query issued against data from gatsby-source-filesystem*

Now that we've reviewed how to construct pages that use data in GraphQL queries (like a blog home page), we can begin our examination of how to generate pages based on GraphQL data (like an individual blog post page). The question we now need to answer is: if we wanted to generate pages for each of the files displayed in our file list page, how would we go about doing that, given that there may be an arbitrary number of files in our Gatsby site?

# Working with Transformer Plugins

Before we get into working with *gatsby-node.js* and the `createPages` API, let's discuss a category of Gatsby plugin that is critical for a variety of use cases: *transformer plugins*. In many cases, you'll find that the raw data brought in by source plugins from filesystems or from external sources isn't quite appropriate for your needs.

Transformer plugins help Gatsby developers recast that data so it's more usable. Thus, we can think of programmatic page creation involving externally sourced data as a three-step process: sourcing the data itself through source plugins, transforming it so Gatsby can comprehend it through transformer plugins, and generating Gatsby pages based on those data structures through the *gatsby-node.js* file.

## Adding Transformer Plugins

Transformer plugins are installed in exactly the same way as source plugins and other Gatsby ecosystem plugins:

```
# If using NPM
$ npm install gatsby-transformer-remark

# If using Yarn
$ yarn add gatsby-transformer-remark
```

And they are also configured the same way in *gatsby-config.js*. For example, to use gatsby-transformer-remark, which is responsible for transforming Markdown into HTML, you need to include only the new plugin in your configuration file. Follow these steps:

1. Add gatsby-transformer-remark as a plugin alongside gatsby-source-filesystem, and then expand the scope of gatsby-source-filesystem to fetch from ${__dirname}/src/, replacing ${__dirname}/src/images/.

2. Change options.name to src, not images.

Now you'll be able to retrieve files from anywhere in the filesystem. Here's what your *gatsby-config.js* should look like:

```
// gatsby-config.js
plugins: [
  `gatsby-plugin-react-helmet`,
  `gatsby-plugin-image`,
  {
    resolve: `gatsby-source-filesystem`,
    options: {
      name: `src`,
      path: `${__dirname}/src/`,
    },
  },
  `gatsby-transformer-remark`,
  `gatsby-transformer-sharp`,
// ...
```

# Transforming Markdown into Data and HTML

Earlier, we ingested data from the surrounding filesystem by using the `gatsby-source-filesystem` source plugin. But although we have data about our files, to use what's contained in those files, we need a transformer plugin to interpret their contents. Many blogs and static sites on the web use Markdown, a text format, but for Gatsby to construct a page containing Markdown, it needs to be transformed into HTML first.

To try this out, let's create an arbitrary Markdown file, *src/posts/lorem-ipsum.md*, representing a sample Markdown blog post. Inside, we'll include some Markdown text. The top of the Markdown file containing keys and values is known as *frontmatter*, and we'll refer to it this way later:

```
---
title: "Lorem ipsum dolor sit amet"
date: "2021-08-04"
---

Lorem ipsum dolor sit amet.

Consectetur adipiscing elit.

- Sed et gravida lacus
- Duis lorem massa

Egestas quis sapien fringilla.
```

Now let's add a second Markdown file, *src/posts/consectetur-adipiscing.md*:

```
---
title: "Consectetur adipiscing elit"
date: "2021-09-05"
---

Donec lacinia vulputate porttitor.

Duis lacinia venenatis mi eget posuere.

- Phasellus rutrum dolor at lectus imperdiet
- At condimentum leo dapibus

Morbi fringilla tincidunt aliquam.
```

Now, navigate to *https://localhost:8000/file-list* again and you'll see all of our files represented, including the Markdown files we just created. Let's take a quick look at our GraphQL API now that we have these new Markdown files in place. When we write a new query in GraphiQL and open the autocomplete pulldown, we can see two new fields: `allMarkdownRemark` (for all Markdown files) and `markdownRemark` (for individual Markdown files). Issue the following query to see our Markdown files represented as JSON, as seen in Figure 6-4:

```
{
  allMarkdownRemark {
    edges {
      node {
        id
        frontmatter {
          date(fromNow: true)
          title
        }
        excerpt
        html
      }
    }
  }
}
```

The result of the query also shows the HTML that `gatsby-transformer-remark` has generated based on the Markdown in our Markdown files.

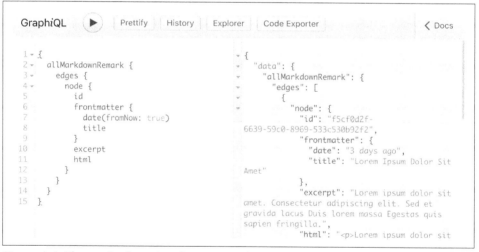

*Figure 6-4. The result of our GraphQL query showing information from the Markdown files as well as their transformation into HTML*

## Adding a List of Markdown Pages

Now, copy the contents of *src/pages/page-2.js* to create another page, *src/pages/blog.js*, where we'll display a list of Markdown posts. Here, we'll create a list of Markdown files that will give our example code some characteristics of a blog. Change the contents of *src/pages/blog.js* to the following:

```
// src/pages/blog.js
import * as React from "react"
import { graphql, Link } from "gatsby"

import Layout from "../components/layout"
import SEO from "../components/seo"

const BlogPage = ({ data }) => (
  <Layout>
    <SEO title="Blog" />
    <h1>Blog</h1>
    {data.allMarkdownRemark.edges.map( ({ node }) => (
      <div key={node.id}>
        <h2>{node.frontmatter.title}</h2>
        <p>{node.excerpt}</p>
        <p><em>{node.frontmatter.date}</em></p>
      </div>
    ))}
    <Link to="/">Go back to the homepage</Link>
  </Layout>
)

export const query = graphql`
  {
    allMarkdownRemark {
      edges {
        node {
          id
          frontmatter {
            date(fromNow: true)
            title
          }
          excerpt
        }
      }
    }
  }
`

export default BlogPage
```

When you save this file with the development server running, you'll see the blog page update with the contents of your Markdown files, though they're out of order. To fix this, let's add a sort criterion to the GraphQL query. Here's the new export statement:

```
// src/pages/blog.js
export const query = graphql`
  {
    allMarkdownRemark(
      sort: {
        fields: [frontmatter___date],
        order: DESC
```

```
        }
    ) {
      edges {
        node {
          id
          frontmatter {
            date(fromNow: true)
            title
          }
          excerpt
        }
      }
    }
  }
`
```

The resulting list of Markdown pages, now sorted in descending order by date, is shown in Figure 6-5.

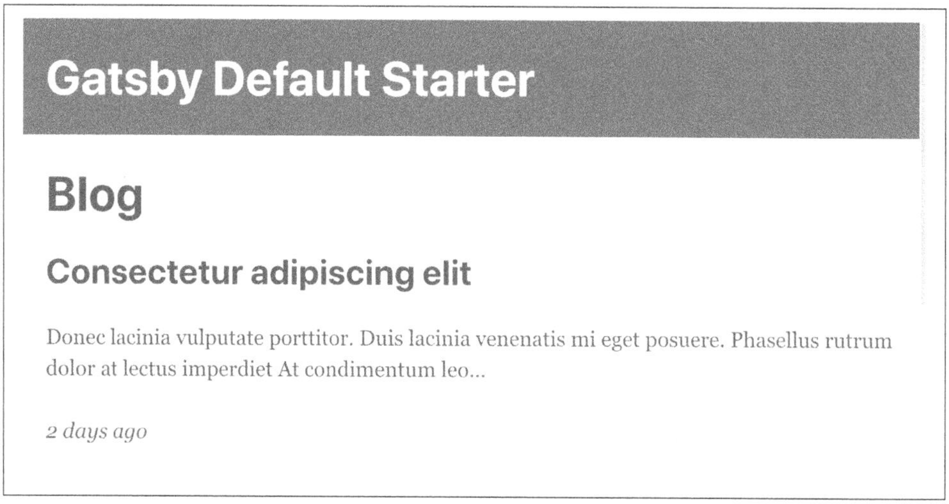

**Gatsby Default Starter**

# Blog

## Consectetur adipiscing elit

Donec lacinia vulputate porttitor. Duis lacinia venenatis mi eget posuere. Phasellus rutrum dolor at lectus imperdiet At condimentum leo...

*2 days ago*

*Figure 6-5. Our new blog page, containing information from each Markdown blog post we created, accessed through the filesystem plugin and transformed by the* `gatsby-transformer-remark` *transformer plugin*

Great! We have the beginnings of a working blog. But we're still missing one of the critical aspects of any blog: the individual blog post pages for each Markdown page we've created. In addition, we need to link to those pages from our list of blog posts. The solution to this problem lies in Gatsby's programmatic page creation.

# Working with gatsby-node.js

The most important element of Gatsby for generating pages programmatically is the *gatsby-node.js* file, which contains logic for implementing the `createPages` API, a set of methods that Gatsby developers can interact with to generate pages. When used in combination with Gatsby template files, programmatic page creation in Gatsby represents one of the most important features of the framework, because it allows developers to query data and map that data to pages at build time.

## Creating Slugs for Markdown Pages

To create our pages, one of the things we'll need is a *slug*, a unique name for each post that can identify them in URLs. We've already created implicit slugs through the naming of our Markdown files: *lorem-ipsum.md* and *consectetur-adipiscing.md*. Some data sources might provide their own slugs as fields in API responses, in which case we don't need to generate slugs based on the blog post titles.

### Using onCreateNode

Every time we create a new page, we need to do two things:

1. Generate the filepath or slug for the page.
2. Create the page itself, usually based on a template.

To create the slugs, we'll need to use a new file we haven't seen before, the *gatsby-node.js* file, and the `onCreateNode` API. Gatsby calls each `onCreateNode` function we export each time a new node is created or updated. To try out `onCreateNode`, let's open the currently empty *gatsby-node.js* file in our codebase and add these lines:

```
// gatsby-node.js
exports.onCreateNode = ({ node }) => {
  console.log(`Node created of type "${node.internal.type}"`)
}
```

Now, restart your Gatsby development server, which is a required step as you've modified the *gatsby-node.js* file. Watch the log output as it registers each and every node it creates based on the data returned by the filesystem source plugin, as seen in Figure 6-6.

```
info Total nodes: 54, SitePage nodes: 1 (use --verbose for breakdown)
success createPages - 0.003s
success Checking for changed pages - 0.001s
Node created of type "SitePage"
Node created of type "SitePage"
Node created of type "SitePage"
Node created of type "SitePage"
Node created of type "SitePage"
Node created of type "SitePage"
Node created of type "SitePage"
Node created of type "SitePage"
success createPagesStatefully - 0.098s
success update schema - 0.033s
success write out redirect data - 0.002s
success Build manifest and related icons - 0.154s
success onPostBootstrap - 0.163s
info bootstrap finished - 7.966s
success onPreExtractQueries - 0.003s
success extract queries from components - 0.496s
```

*Figure 6-6. Each onCreateNode event is logged in the terminal output when the Gatsby development starter is started, indicating the creation of a new node*

### Using createNodeField

Now, modify the contents of *gatsby-node.js* to use createNodeField, one of the actions available in onCreateNode. The createNodeField function allows us to arbitrarily add new fields on nodes that are created by other plugins. If you don't have control over how the node is provided within the source plugin's configuration in the *gatsby-config.js* file, you have to use *gatsby-node.js* to bolt on additional fields.

We'll add a new field called slug. In the process, we'll use a function available in the gatsby-source-filesystem source plugin, createFilePath, to create slugs based on filenames. The createFilePath function automatically accesses the parent File node and creates the slug on our behalf. We'll use the filenames we gave our Markdown files before and convert them into slugs:

```
// gatsby-node.js
const { createFilePath } = require(`gatsby-source-filesystem`)

exports.onCreateNode = ({ node, getNode, actions }) => {
  const { createNodeField } = actions
  if (node.internal.type === `MarkdownRemark`) {
    const slug = createFilePath({ node, getNode, basePath: `posts` })
    createNodeField({
      node,
      name: `slug`,
      value: slug,
    })
  }
}
```

Once you've made these changes, save *gatsby-node.js* again, restart the development server, and run the following query in GraphiQL:

```
{
  allMarkdownRemark {
    edges {
      node {
        fields {
          slug
        }
      }
    }
  }
}
```

You'll now see our slugs represented within each individual Markdown node, as shown in Figure 6-7.

Now that we've created slugs that go with our blog posts, we can create pages programmatically based on those slugs.

*Figure 6-7. The result of the preceding GraphQL query, containing a reference to our newly created field within each individual Markdown file node*

## Adding a Template

One of the things we need to generate pages programmatically based on GraphQL data is a *template* through which we can run data. A template in Gatsby is often important, because it indicates to our Gatsby site how data should be rendered within programmatically created pages. It wouldn't make sense to place all of this logic in *gatsby-node.js*, especially if we have multiple templates.

Create a new file named *src/templates/post.js*, which will contain our blog post template. Add the following code—as you can see, we're using a GraphQL query to get the information we need from our Markdown files:

```
// src/templates/post.js
import React from "react"
import { graphql } from "gatsby"
import Layout from "../components/layout"

export default function Post({ data }) {
  const post = data.markdownRemark
  return (
    <Layout>
      <h1>{post.frontmatter.title}</h1>
      <div dangerouslySetInnerHTML={{ __html: post.html }} />
    </Layout>
  )
}

export const query = graphql`
  query($slug: String!) {
    markdownRemark(
      fields: {
        slug: {
          eq: $slug
        }
      }
    ) {
      html
      frontmatter {
        date(fromNow: true)
        title
      }
    }
  }
`
```

 The dangerouslySetInnerHTML attribute (*https://oreil.ly/4mCBz*) in React indicates that the HTML string defined as the value of __html should be inserted as is. It is named this way to clearly indicate the risk of doing this, which could expose your site to cross-site scripting (XSS) attacks. Because we control the contents of the Markdown files, we can rest assured in this case that it's safe.

As you can see, one of the main differences between this query and the others is that we're also retrieving the full HTML generated by gatsby-transformer-remark from our Markdown. Now that we've created a template for each individual blog post, we need to write the logic that will generate the pages based on the slugs we've now provided to our GraphQL API and the template we've just created.

## Adding Markdown Pages with createPages

To finish our blog, we need to use Gatsby's `createPages` API to generate pages that use our slugs and template. We'll use the Node.js `path` library to handle the path to our blog post template, so we need to add it as a dependency at the top of the file:

```
// gatsby-node.js
const path = require(`path`)
const { createFilePath } = require(`gatsby-source-filesystem`)
```

Below the `onCreateNode` function we added previously, add a new `createPages` function, as shown here:

```
// gatsby-node.js
const path = require(`path`)
const { createFilePath } = require(`gatsby-source-filesystem`)

exports.onCreateNode = ({ node, getNode, actions }) => {
  const { createNodeField } = actions
  if (node.internal.type === `MarkdownRemark`) {
    const slug = createFilePath({ node, getNode, basePath: `posts` })
    createNodeField({
      node,
      name: `slug`,
      value: slug,
    })
  }
}

exports.createPages = async ({ graphql, actions }) => {
  const { createPage } = actions  ❶
  const result = await graphql(`
    {
      allMarkdownRemark {  ❷
        edges {
          node {
            fields {
              slug
            }
          }
        }
      }
    }
  `)

  result.data.allMarkdownRemark.edges.forEach( ({ node }) => {
    createPage({  ❸
      path: `/blog` + node.fields.slug,
      component: path.resolve(`./src/templates/post.js`),
      context: {  ❹
        slug: node.fields.slug,
      },
```

```
    })
  })
}
```

❶ Invoke the individual `createPage` function from the `actions` (a collection of functions used to manipulate state in a Gatsby site) available in the `createPages` API.

❷ Define the GraphQL query we need to generate pages.

❸ Add the page generation logic just below the `const` definitions, before closing out the `createPages` function.

❹ When we invoke `createPage`, we also provide `context`, which represents data made available as GraphQL query variables in page queries.

Now when you navigate to *http://localhost:8000/blog/lorem-ipsum*, you'll see one of our blog posts represented, as illustrated in Figure 6-8.

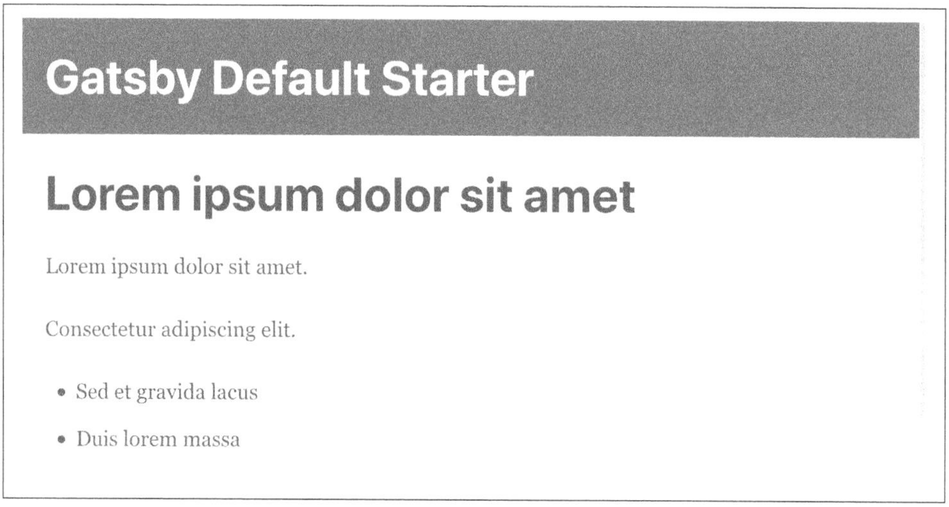

## Gatsby Default Starter

# Lorem ipsum dolor sit amet

Lorem ipsum dolor sit amet.

Consectetur adipiscing elit.

* Sed et gravida lacus
* Duis lorem massa

*Figure 6-8. An individual blog post located at /blog/lorem-ipsum, demonstrating that our blog post is correctly using our template via gatsby-node.js*

The final step is to link back to our blog posts from the blog page. Let's go back to *src/pages/blog.js* and add links to each individual blog post. First, we'll add a link to each of the blog post teasers that displays on the blog page:

```
// src/pages/blog.js
const BlogPage = ({ data }) => (
  <Layout>
    <SEO title="Blog" />
    <h1>Blog</h1>
```

```
      {data.allMarkdownRemark.edges.map( ({ node }) => (
        <div key={node.id}>
          <h2>
            <Link to={`/blog${node.fields.slug}`}>
              {node.frontmatter.title}
            </Link>
          </h2>
          <p>{node.excerpt}</p>
          <p><em>{node.frontmatter.date}</em></p>
        </div>
      ))}
      <Link to="/">Go back to the homepage</Link>
    </Layout>
  )
```

Second, we need to update the GraphQL query at the bottom to include our newly created slug field:

```
// src/pages/blog.js
export const query = graphql`
  {
    allMarkdownRemark(
      sort: {
        fields: [frontmatter___date],
        order: DESC
      }
    ) {
      edges {
        node {
          id
          frontmatter {
            date(fromNow: true)
            title
          }
          fields {
            slug
          }
          excerpt
        }
      }
    }
  }
`
```

The result of these changes can be seen in Figure 6-9, and our completed *src/pages/ blog.js* is as follows:

```
// src/pages/blog.js
import React from "react"
import { graphql, Link } from "gatsby"

import Layout from "../components/layout"
import SEO from "../components/seo"
```

```
const BlogPage = ({ data }) => (
  <Layout>
    <SEO title="Blog" />
    <h1>Blog</h1>
    {data.allMarkdownRemark.edges.map( ({ node }) => (
      <div key={node.id}>
        <h2>
          <Link to={`/blog${node.fields.slug}`}>
            {node.frontmatter.title}
          </Link>
        </h2>
        <p>{node.excerpt}</p>
        <p><em>{node.frontmatter.date}</em></p>
      </div>
    ))}
    <Link to="/">Go back to the homepage</Link>
  </Layout>
)

export const query = graphql`
  {
    allMarkdownRemark(
      sort: {
        fields: [frontmatter___date],
        order: DESC
      }
    ) {
      edges {
        node {
          id
          frontmatter {
            date(fromNow: true)
            title
          }
          fields {
            slug
          }
          excerpt
        }
      }
    }
  }
`

export default BlogPage
```

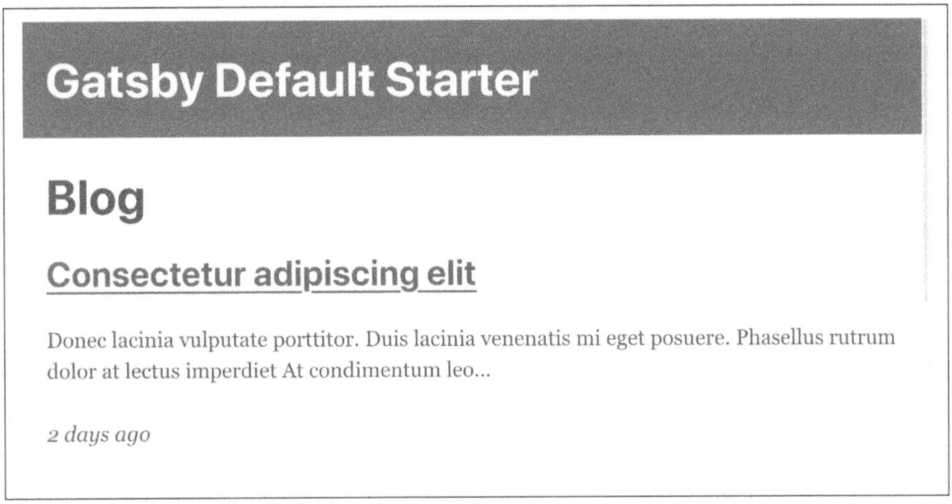

**Gatsby Default Starter**

## Blog

### <ins>Consectetur adipiscing elit</ins>

Donec lacinia vulputate porttitor. Duis lacinia venenatis mi eget posuere. Phasellus rutrum dolor at lectus imperdiet At condimentum leo...

*2 days ago*

*Figure 6-9. The completed blog, with each blog post title correctly leading to its individual page based on its slug*

There you have it! A blog powered by Gatsby's programmatic page creation.

# Conclusion

Programmatic page creation is one of the most fundamental aspects of Gatsby, and it's deeply powerful because it's capable of rendering data originating from disparate sources. In this chapter, we first revisited how to traverse GraphQL data in Gatsby pages to prepare ourselves for programmatic page creation. Another prerequisite was the use of transformer plugins, which are used to make external data understandable to the Gatsby framework. Finally, we used *gatsby-node.js* to generate a set of pages based on our transformed data.

While data from external sources is critical for the success of many Gatsby sites, there is another type of data that Gatsby's GraphQL API handles: assets, especially media assets, which may be images, videos, or audio files. To come full circle with our examination of Gatsby's data processing layer and how our Gatsby pages and components interact with its various elements, we'll now focus our attention on assets and how to handle these often-fickle files (and file sets) in our Gatsby sites.

# CHAPTER 7

# Assets in Gatsby

While creating and generating pages is one of the aspects of Gatsby that receives the most attention, Gatsby's asset handling capabilities are also highly robust. After all, when building Gatsby sites, it's not just text we're concerned with; often, as developers, we must also juggle images, videos, fonts, and other file assets that don't fit neatly into our sites. Complicating matters further is the fact that today's users demand highly performant and optimized image and video delivery.

There are a variety of plugins and APIs available to interact with different assets you might want to include in your Gatsby site, be they photographs, video streams, web fonts, or PDF documents. We'll look at the best practices Gatsby offers for specific asset types (images, videos, and fonts), but we'll begin with an overview of how to work with assets in general in Gatsby: by importing them into Webpack as part of the module system or importing them on their own as static assets.

## Working with Assets

In Gatsby, an *asset* is loosely defined as any file that needs to be used anywhere in a Gatsby site, whether that means in a Gatsby page, a React component, or a Markdown file. Assets can run the gamut from images in JPEG and PNG formats to animated GIFs as well as videos, fonts, and other static files with arbitrary extensions.

### Types of Assets in Gatsby

Before we get into the two approaches for importing assets, let's briefly examine which types of assets (which Gatsby also calls media content) Gatsby can handle natively and which ones require additional plugins or custom handling.

Aside from image assets that can be imported through the two paradigms we'll cover shortly, and excluding videos that require separate handling, there are other assets that Gatsby can accept in its pages and components. These include:

*Scalable vector graphics (SVG) images*
> There are two approaches for embedding SVG images in Gatsby. Because SVGs contain markup, they can often be embedded as-is into JSX components through an SVG-to-JSX converter like Transform (*https://transform.tools*). Alternatively, they can be embedded directly in an `<img>` tag or as a CSS background.

*Canvas and WebGL scenes*
> Two- and three-dimensional scenes are represented by the HTML5 `<canvas>` element and the WebGL standard, respectively. The React ecosystem provides two libraries for interacting with the two types of scenes: `react-konva` (*https://oreil.ly/LYDpi*) (for drawing canvas graphics) and Three.js (*https://threejs.org*) (for working with WebGL).

*PDF documents*
> PDF documents can be particularly vexing when it comes to accessibility. Gatsby recommends as a best practice that developers managing PDF files embed an image of the PDF together with alternative text. In addition, Gatsby advises that developers provide a link to download a tagged PDF for users working with assistive technologies.

For all other asset types we cover in this chapter—namely, images, videos, and fonts— there is either a native Gatsby API or a Gatsby plugin available.

> If you use Cloudinary as an external hosting service for your media assets, the Gatsby documentation provides a separate guide for Cloudinary-specific considerations (*https://oreil.ly/9cIQd*).

## Importing Assets Directly with Webpack

The easiest way to get access to images, fonts, and other files in a Gatsby site is to import the files and make them available to your Gatsby pages, components, and templates. When we import a file, a string is returned that represents the path at which the file is referenceable. We use this string to identify the file in the `src` attribute for an `<img>` element or the `href` attribute for an `<a>` element.

For performance reasons and to reduce round trips to the server, Webpack, which Gatsby uses to handle imports, will automatically return a data URI (a URI that provides the file data within the URI itself) instead of a path for files that are less than

10,000 bytes in size. This means that images such as favicons and other small images will have the entirety of their data represented rather than solely a path reference.

 Webpack provides this behavior for files with the following extensions: *.svg*, *.jpg*, *.jpeg*, *.png*, *.gif*, *.mp4*, *.webm*, *.wav*, *.mp3*, *.m4a*, *.aac*, and *.oga*.

Let's see how this works. We'll begin by cloning the "Hello World" starter:

```
$ gatsby new gtdg-ch7-importing-assets gatsbyjs/gatsby-starter-hello-world
$ cd gtdg-ch7-importing-assets
```

Then we'll import an image to include in our home page. We'll use *gatsby-astronaut.png*, provided in Gatsby's default starter (`gatsby-starter-default`) under *src/images*. Add it to the *src/pages* directory, then modify the contents of *src/pages/index.js* to the following to import the PNG image into the page:

```
// src/pages/index.js
import React from "react"

// Indicate to Webpack that this module uses this image.
import astronaut from "./gatsby-astronaut.png"

console.log(astronaut)

export default function Home() {
  return <img src={astronaut} alt="The Gatsby astronaut" />
}
```

When you save the home page and run `gatsby develop`, you'll see the image in Figure 7-1. You'll also notice in the browser's developer console that the referenceable path to the image, maintained by Webpack, is something like */static/gatsby-astronaut-6d91c86c0fde632ba4cd01062fd9ccfa.png*. This indicates that Webpack has successfully registered the image, moved it into Gatsby's *public* folder, and provided you with an accurate path for the image.

If you're using Webpack to manage image imports, you can also use Webpack's intelligent file tracking to reference images within CSS. For instance, if you write the following CSS, Webpack will replace the reference to the background image with the correct path when the site is built:

```
/* global.css */
.astronaut {
  background-image: url(./gatsby-astronaut.png);
}
```

*Figure 7-1. The new state of our Gatsby "Hello World" starter after replacing the default content with an image imported through Webpack*

When you run `gatsby develop` or `gatsby build`, Webpack will grab all of the relative module references in CSS (starting with the string `./`) and substitute them for the final paths from the combined bundle. If you delete a file or misspell a filename, Webpack will throw a compilation error. When the content of the file changes, Webpack assigns it a different name in production builds to avoid the need for long-term asset caching.

> If you're using a css preprocessor such as Sass (SCSS), all image imports are relative to the entry SCSS file (e.g., *main.scss*), so you'll need to pay close attention to those path references in certain circumstances (depending on how those SCSS files interact with each other).

## Querying for Assets with gatsby-source-filesystem

Importing assets directly into Gatsby pages and components through Webpack is an efficient way of managing them, but Gatsby's internal GraphQL API, together with the `gatsby-source-filesystem` plugin, can also provide a pleasant developer experience, especially if you're already using the source plugin to power the transformation of Markdown files.

In this section, we'll inspect two distinct approaches to querying for files: queries in Gatsby pages and components, and queries in Gatsby templates for Markdown and other formats.

## Querying for assets in Gatsby pages and components

When we query for files in Gatsby's internal GraphQL API, Gatsby will automatically copy those files to the *public* directory when it performs a build. Thanks to this functionality, we can use Gatsby's GraphQL API to retrieve the eventual public URL of any asset and use that in our Gatsby pages and components.

To demonstrate this, let's add another image to our *src/pages* directory, such as the *gatsby-icon.png* file that comes with the Gatsby default starter (in *src/images*). If you've followed the steps in the previous section to the letter, you will now have two images represented in your *src/pages* directory: *gatsby-astronaut.png* and *gatsby-icon.png*.

You'll need to install the `gatsby-source-filesystem` plugin as a dependency:

```
# If using NPM
$ npm install --save gatsby-source-filesystem

# If using Yarn
$ yarn add gatsby-source-filesystem
```

And add it to your *gatsby-config.js* file, configuring the source plugin in the process:

```
// gatsby-config.js
plugins: [
  {
    resolve: `gatsby-source-filesystem`,
    options: {
      name: `pages`,
      path: `${__dirname}/src/pages/`,
    },
  },
]
```

Now, run `gatsby develop`, navigate to *https://localhost:8000/___graphql*, and issue the following query as a test:

```
{
  allFile(
    filter: {
      extension: {
        eq: "png"
      }
    }
  ) {
    edges {
      node {
        publicURL
      }
    }
  }
}
```

As you can see in Figure 7-2, when you run this query you'll receive a response containing the two public URLs for your two images (*gatsby-astronaut.png* and *gatsby-icon.png*). You can now refer to these public URLs within your Gatsby pages and components to work with these image assets.

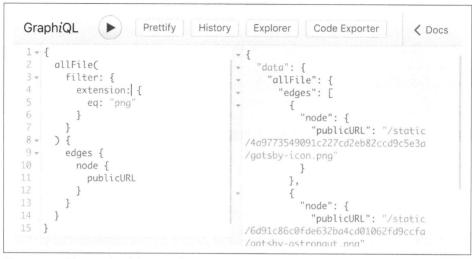

*Figure 7-2. The result of the GraphQL query requesting the public URLs for each of the images represented in the filesystem*

Now that you know how to return public URLs from a GraphQL query, you can create a rudimentary list of files within your home page. Replace the contents of *src/pages/index.js*, which still contains the code from the previous section, with the following:

```
// src/pages/index.js
import React from "react"
import { graphql } from "gatsby"

export default function Home( { data } ) {
  return (
    <>
      <h1>List of PNG images</h1>
      <ul>
        {data.allFile.edges.map( (file, index) => {
          return (
            <li key={`png-${index}`}>
              <a href={file.node.publicURL} download>
                {file.node.name}
              </a>
            </li>
          )
        })}
      </ul>
```

```
      </>
    )
  }

export const query = graphql`
  {
    allFile(
      filter: {
        extension: {
          eq: "png"
        }
      }
    ) {
      edges {
        node {
          name
          publicURL
        }
      }
    }
  }
  `
```

 In React and Gatsby, it's possible to indicate an empty JSX element by using the pair <> and </>, which will instruct JSX to treat the elements within as children but not to render any markup for the empty JSX element. Use of the empty element is often required because JSX accepts only a single element rather than multiple sibling elements.

As you can see in Figure 7-3, we've inserted the GraphQL query (along with one additional field, name—e.g., gatsby-icon and gatsby-astronaut) into the page query for the Gatsby page, along with rendering code that ensures our PNG image assets get referenced in an unordered list.

## List of PNG images

- gatsby-icon
- gatsby-astronaut

*Figure 7-3. The unordered list generated from the PNG files available in the filesystem— each link allows the user to download the file from the public URL*

The approach for GraphQL queries we've taken in this Gatsby page differs from that for Gatsby components, which need to use static queries instead. Refer back to Chapter 4 for more information about Gatsby page and component queries.

### Querying for assets in Markdown files

So far, we've focused on how to acquire image assets for direct use in Gatsby pages and components. It requires a slightly different workflow, but you can also use these image assets in Markdown files that you use to generate your Gatsby pages.

Suppose you're building a Gatsby blog that generates article pages according to a Gatsby template and Markdown files. One of your articles might have the following frontmatter, referring to two images that are referenced by a relative path to the Markdown file itself, like this modified example from Chapter 6. Note the additional attachments field in the frontmatter and the newly referenced file assets:

```
---
title: "Consectetur adipiscing elit"
date: "2020-12-05"
attachments:
  - "./gatsby-astronaut.png"
  - "./gatsby-icon.png"
---

Donec lacinia vulputate porttitor.

Duis lacinia venenatis mi eget posuere.

- Phasellus rutrum dolor at lectus imperdiet
- At condimentum leo dapibus

Morbi fringilla tincidunt aliquam.
```

Now, within the blog post template, you can refer to the images contained within the frontmatter field by using your Markdown transformer and querying the fields that result. Take the final state of your *src/templates/post.js* file from Chapter 6 and modify it to match the following:

```
// src/templates/post.js
import React from "react"
import { graphql } from "gatsby"
import Layout from "../components/layout"

export default function Post({ data }) {
  const post = data.markdownRemark
  return (
    <Layout>
      <h1>{post.frontmatter.title}</h1>
      {post.frontmatter.attachments.map( (image, index) => {
```

```
          return (
            <div key={`image-${index}`}>
              <img src={image.publicURL} /> ❶
            </div>
          )
        })}
        <div dangerouslySetInnerHTML={{ __html: post.html }} />
      </Layout>
    )
  }

  export const query = graphql`
    query($slug: String!) {
      markdownRemark(
        fields: {
          slug: {
            eq: $slug
          }
        }
      ) {
        html
        frontmatter {
          date(fromNow: true)
          title
          attachments { ❷
            publicURL
          }
        }
      }
    }
  `
```

❶ Modify the rendering code so that the images will display.

❷ Add the new file attachments in the Markdown file to the GraphQL query.

When you run `gatsby develop` with this template saved and image handling added (which we discuss in "Working with Images" on page 201), Gatsby will retrieve the images when it renders the post template.

## Importing Assets with the static Folder

Apart from adding assets to the filesystem and importing them through Webpack or retrieving data about them through Gatsby's GraphQL API, there's a third approach you can take to importing assets that's especially useful when you need to maintain a file outside of the module system. This approach imports assets using the *static* folder.

Before proceeding, it should be noted that Gatsby strongly recommends using one of the other two approaches (it refers to this final prong in the trio of asset import methods as an "escape hatch" for unmanaged file assets). This is because many of Gatsby's performance optimizations, including bundling and minification of scripts and stylesheets and content hashes for compiled filenames, rely on you using Gatsby's recommended paradigms. In addition, because missing files won't be available when compilation occurs, your users will encounter 404 errors when they attempt to access them.

### Motivations for using the static folder

Nonetheless, there are a variety of reasons why you as a Gatsby developer might want to use the *static* folder. Here are some example scenarios where it provides a useful workaround:

- A file with a specific name is required in the build output for specific clients, such as *manifest.webmanifest* for progressive web applications (PWAs) rendered as native applications.
- Hundreds or thousands of images need dynamic references to their paths, rather than content hashes that make those images more difficult to reference.
- A small library or utility needs to be added outside of the bundled code, such as `pace.js`, a progress bar for web pages.
- Some JavaScript libraries, especially older ones, are incompatible with Webpack and must be embedded in a `<script>` element rather than bundled with other code.
- You need to import JSON data that does not adhere to a consistent schema, such as TopoJSON, which is a format that translates poorly to GraphQL schemas. In these situations, it's highly recommended to move the JSON file to the *static* folder and to dynamically import the file in React's `useEffect` hook (*https://oreil.ly/6iZMR*) (`import(`/static/topojson.json`)`) to limit the bundle size.

Now that you have an idea of what it's useful for, let's take a look at how to reference a file asset within the *static* folder.

### Referencing a static asset

To reference a static asset, simply create a new directory called *static* in the root of your project, *outside the src directory* (i.e., create */static* as a sibling directory to */src*, not *src/static*).

Each and every file you place in that directory will be copied by Gatsby as is into the *public* folder. For example, if you copy *gatsby-astronaut.png* into */static/gatsby-astronaut.png*, during the next build Gatsby will copy that file, intact, to *public/gatsby-astronaut.png*.

Then, you can reference your static asset within your code. Consider the following example, adapted from the Gatsby "Hello World" starter:

```
// src/pages/index.js
import React from "react"

export default function Home() {
  // Uses the static folder, Gatsby's escape hatch for asset imports.
  return <img src={`/gatsby-astronaut.png`} alt="The Gatsby astronaut" />
}
```

There you have it! Now you can import assets using Gatsby's best practices—using Webpack as a file manager or querying the filesystem with GraphQL—or with its "escape hatch," the *static* folder.

# Working with Images

Of all the assets that we need to deal with and manage as Gatsby developers, perhaps none are as vexing or as complex as images. Though we've seen multiple examples of image importing so far in this chapter, all the approaches we've covered apply just as neatly to videos, fonts, and other assets, such as PDFs. In addition to these more generic approaches, Gatsby also provides a full-featured plugin, `gatsby-plugin-image` (a replacement for Gatsby 2.0's `gatsby-image` component), that allows us to perform a variety of operations on images and enables performance enhancements.

In this section, we'll cover both Gatsby 3.0's `gatsby-plugin-image` plugin and Gatsby 2.0's `gatsby-image` component in detail. I'll show you how to use them not only for images that Gatsby manages but also for externally hosted images that need optimization.

 For developers who haven't yet made the move from `gatsby-image` to `gatsby-plugin-image`, the two can be used interchangeably, and the Gatsby documentation has a migration guide available (*https://oreil.ly/iuZ4V*).

Using Gatsby's image plugin or component provides three main advantages:

- It uses the `InteractionObserver` API in browsers in order to lazy-load images inexpensively.
- It retains an image's position so that a user never experiences jumpiness as images load.
- It enables the use of placeholders such as a gray background or a blurred version of the image.

Gatsby's image plugin/component is helpful for optimizing the performance of large, unwieldy images, which are some of the biggest causes of slowdowns in page loads. Over the years, many web developers have employed best practices to limit image bloat, including various combinations of the following:

- Large images should be resized to just-right dimensions that don't exceed the dimensions required by a design.

- Multiple image versions should be generated so that lower-bandwidth devices such as smartphones and tablets refrain from downloading desktop-optimized images.

- All unnecessary metadata should be stripped from images, and JPEG and PNG compression should be optimized.

- On the client side, images should be efficiently lazy-loaded to accelerate the initial page load and to limit bandwidth usage.

- More recently, using a "blur-up" technique or a "traced placeholder" SVG image to show a rough preview of an image as it loads has become increasingly popular.

- Retaining the image's soon-to-be occupied position so that the page doesn't perceivably jump while images load is another recent user experience enhancement.

In many situations, repeating all of these steps without the aid of automated task runners, a plugin, or a ready-made image component in React is simply too burdensome, especially in teams where images undergo regular revisions. Fortunately, Gatsby's image plugin/component can help automate many of the most tedious optimization tasks and alleviate much of the complexity around image management and performance optimization.

Animated GIFs differ from other image formats and require special handling. Due to the specific nature of animated GIFs, Gatsby recommends importing these assets with Webpack, using the approach described in "Working with Assets" on page 191. You should not use the gatsby-image component to process animated GIFs, as it is optimized for static images. In addition, you should generally use animated GIFs with caution as they may cause motion sickness in some users, and you should disable autoplay through a client-only package such as react-gif-player.

# The gatsby-plugin-image Plugin (Gatsby 3.0)

The `gatsby-plugin-image` plugin available in Gatsby 3.0 combines the native image processing capabilities available in Gatsby with modern image loading techniques in order to optimize the loading of images in your Gatsby site. It replaces the deprecated `gatsby-image` component from v2.0, which we'll discuss in the next section.

## Using gatsby-plugin-image

To keep things simple, let's explore the `gatsby-plugin-image` plugin in a small-scale Gatsby site where we can limit complexity. To begin, clone another Gatsby "Hello World" starter:

```
$ gatsby new gtdg-ch7-gatsby-plugin-image gatsbyjs/gatsby-starter-hello-world
$ cd gtdg-ch7-gatsby-plugin-image
```

Then install the plugin and include its dependencies, `gatsby-plugin-sharp` and `gatsby-transformer-sharp`:

```
# If using NPM
$ npm install --save gatsby-plugin-image gatsby-transformer-sharp \
  gatsby-plugin-sharp

# If using Yarn
$ yarn add gatsby-plugin-image gatsby-transformer-sharp gatsby-plugin-sharp
```

You'll need to add all three of these to the [plugins] section of your *gatsby-config.js* file:

```
// gatsby-config.js
module.exports = {
  plugins: [
    `gatsby-plugin-image`,
    `gatsby-plugin-sharp`,
    `gatsby-transformer-sharp`
  ],
}
```

There's one final step you need to take. Because we're starting from scratch here, you have to install `gatsby-source-filesystem` (the source plugin that will identify the images in your filesystem and provide them to the GraphQL API):

```
# If using NPM
$ npm install --save gatsby-source-filesystem

# If using Yarn
$ yarn add gatsby-source-filesystem
```

Now you can configure `gatsby-source-filesystem` in *gatsby-config.js*. Note that you'll need to provide the path leading to where the images are located in your codebase:

```
// gatsby-config.js
module.exports = {
  plugins: [
    `gatsby-plugin-image`,
    `gatsby-plugin-sharp`,
    `gatsby-transformer-sharp`,
    {
      resolve: `gatsby-source-filesystem`,
      options: {
        path: `${__dirname}/src/images`
      }
    },
  ],
}
```

As this configuration suggests, for the source plugin to detect them, you'll need to create a new directory named *images* within your *src* directory. Place a high-resolution image in this directory—preferably a large one—to test `gatsby-plugin-image`'s features. For my example image, I'm using a photograph of Pikes Peak (*https://oreil.ly/HZpQr*), the mountain that towers over my hometown of Colorado Springs, named *pikes-peak.jpg*.

### Static images with gatsby-plugin-image

The `gatsby-plugin-image` plugin ships with two components to handle image rendering: `StaticImage` and `GatsbyImage`. The `StaticImage` component is used for static images that won't change after you render them in the desired location. For dynamic images originating from an external data source such as a CMS, you'll need to use the `GatsbyImage` component (not to be confused with Gatsby 2.0's `gatsby-image` component), covered in the following section.

The `StaticImage` component can be used to refer to images in the surrounding file-system. To see how it works, change the contents of *index.js* to the following, including the import of the `StaticImage` component:

```
// src/pages/index.js
import React from "react"
import { StaticImage } from "gatsby-plugin-image"

export default function Home() {
  return (
    <StaticImage
      src="../images/pikes-peak.jpg"
      alt="Pikes Peak, known as Tava in the Ute language and Heey-otoyoo' in
      the Arapaho language"
    />
  )
}
```

You can also use the `src` prop to refer to external images at other URLs. In either case, you'll need to use a string or a local variable in the component's scope rather than a prop made available to the component, since the image is loaded at build time. When you build the Gatsby site, the `StaticImage` component will retrieve the image from the filesystem or from the external URL you specified and generate the sizes and formats that are required for a responsive image.

> Because remote images are downloaded and resized during the Gatsby build at build time, if the image is changed remotely, you will need to rebuild the site to see the image update.

The `StaticImage` component also allows configuration via props that adjust the size of the image and its layout, the type of placeholder used, and other image processing settings. Change the image component to use these prop values instead, which will ensure the image loads with a blurred placeholder and a fixed layout, such that resizing the image's container does not change the image's dimensions:

```
// src/pages/index.js
import React from "react"
import { StaticImage } from "gatsby-plugin-image"

export default function Home() {
  return (
    <StaticImage
      src="../images/pikes-peak.jpg"
      alt="Pikes Peak, known as Tava in the Ute language and Heey-otoyoo' in
      the Arapaho language"
      placeholder="blurred"
      layout="fixed"
    />
  )
}
```

Now, run `gatsby develop` to see the fully built site working in your browser. The image you provided should now be loading gracefully into your Gatsby page, as shown in Figure 7-4, and if you refresh the page, you will see the blurred placeholder gracefully give way to show the full image.

> For more information about the props that can be used to configure the `StaticImage` component and limitations for component usage, see the full API documentation (*https://oreil.ly/cbr1J*).

*Figure 7-4. The sample image, processed through* `gatsby-plugin-image`, *displaying after a blur-up effect in the Gatsby page*

### Dynamic images with gatsby-plugin-image

Dynamic images that come from external data sources or through a GraphQL query need to use the `GatsbyImage` component instead of the `StaticImage` component. In this section, we'll switch to using `gatsby-source-filesystem` and Gatsby's internal GraphQL API to write a query that will yield a responsive and optimized image. Replace the contents of *src/pages/index.js* with the following, taking care not to forget the new import of `graphql` from Gatsby:

```
// src/pages/index.js
import React from "react"
import { graphql } from "gatsby"

export default function Home() {
  return <div>Hello world!</div>
}

export const query = graphql`
  {
    file(relativePath: {
      eq: "pikes-peak.jpg"
    }) {
      childImageSharp {
        gatsbyImageData(width: 300)
      }
    }
  }
`
```

Our GraphQL query can also take additional configuration options like the ones we saw in the previous section, and you can test these in GraphiQL:

---

```
// src/pages/index.js
import React from "react"
import { graphql } from "gatsby"

export default function Home() {
  return <div>Hello world!</div>
}

export const query = graphql`
  {
    file(relativePath: {
      eq: "pikes-peak.jpg"
    }) {
      childImageSharp {
        gatsbyImageData(
          width: 300
          placeholder: BLURRED
        )
      }
    }
  }
`
```

Next, import the GatsbyImage component. Display the image using its JSX element:

```
// src/pages/index.js
import React from "react"
import { graphql } from "gatsby"
import { GatsbyImage, getImage } from "gatsby-plugin-image" ❶

export default function Home({ data }) {
  const image = getImage(data.file) ❷
  return <GatsbyImage ❸
    image={image}
    alt="Pikes Peak, known as Tava in the Ute language and Heey-otoyoo' in
     the Arapaho language"
  />
}

export const query = graphql`
  {
    file(relativePath: {
      eq: "pikes-peak.jpg"
    }) {
      childImageSharp {
        gatsbyImageData(
          width: 300
          placeholder: BLURRED
        )
      }
    }
  }
`
```

❶ Import `GatsbyImage` and `getImage`, a helper function, from `gatsby-plugin-image` as dependencies.

❷ Invoke `getImage()` to take a given `File` node and return the `gatsbyImageData` object, which is then passed to the `GatsbyImage` component.

❸ Use a `<GatsbyImage />` element to provide the image to JSX.

As illustrated in Figure 7-5, after running `gatsby develop`, you should see that the image of Pikes Peak respects the width of 300 pixels set in the GraphQL query.

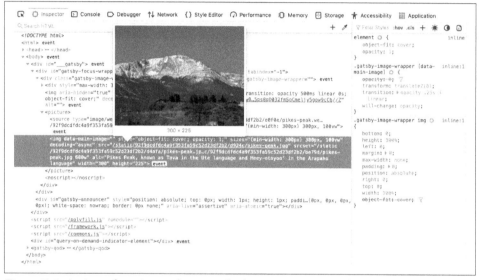

*Figure 7-5. A view of our image from inside the Inspector in Firefox, showing a width of 300 pixels in lieu of the high-resolution version of the image*

 Many external data sources are represented with source plugins in the Gatsby ecosystem that provide native support for `gatsby-plugin-image`. For more information about these, consult the `gatsby-plugin-image` documentation's section on using images from a CMS or CDN (*https://oreil.ly/KYwwI*).

## The gatsby-image Component (Gatsby 2.0)

If you're using Gatsby 2.0, the `gatsby-image` component is the typical approach to image handling, though you can use the `gatsby-plugin-image` plugin with Gatsby 2.0 as well. Because many Gatsby developers have not yet migrated to Gatsby 3.0, for completeness's sake, this section will walk through the same example as in the previous section, using this component.

---

For more information about migrating from `gatsby-image` to `gatsby-plugin-image`, consult the Gatsby documentation's migration guide for images (*https://oreil.ly/Zps7y*).

In Gatsby 2.0 (but deprecated in Gatsby 3.0), `gatsby-image` is a React component that combines the native image-processing capabilities available in Gatsby with modern image-loading techniques in order to optimize the loading of images in your Gatsby site. The `gatsby-image` component works seamlessly with Gatsby's GraphQL API and uses the plugins `gatsby-plugin-sharp` and `gatsby-transformer-sharp` to enable image transformations.

Gatsby developers should not consider the `gatsby-image` component a possible drop-in substitution for the JSX `<img />` tag, because `<img />` enables some image characteristics that are unavailable in `gatsby-image`.

## Using gatsby-image

To keep things simple, let's explore the `gatsby-image` component in a small-scale Gatsby site where we can limit complexity. To begin, clone another Gatsby "Hello World" starter:

```
$ gatsby new gtdg-ch7-gatsby-image gatsbyjs/gatsby-starter-hello-world
$ cd gtdg-ch7-gatsby-image
```

Then install the component and include its dependencies, `gatsby-plugin-sharp` and `gatsby-transformer-sharp`:

```
# If using NPM
$ npm install --save gatsby-image gatsby-transformer-sharp gatsby-plugin-sharp

# If using Yarn
$ yarn add gatsby-image gatsby-transformer-sharp gatsby-plugin-sharp
```

You'll need to add both of these plugins to your *gatsby-config.js* file:

```
// gatsby-config.js
module.exports = {
  plugins: [`gatsby-plugin-sharp`, `gatsby-transformer-sharp`],
}
```

There's one final step you need to take. Because we're starting from scratch here, you have to install `gatsby-source-filesystem` (the source plugin that will identify the images in your filesystem and provide them to the GraphQL API):

```
# If using NPM
$ npm install --save gatsby-source-filesystem
```

```
# If using Yarn
$ yarn add gatsby-source-filesystem
```

Now you can configure *gatsby-config.js*. Note that you'll need to provide the path leading to where the images are located in your codebase:

```
// gatsby-config.js
module.exports = {
  plugins: [
    `gatsby-transformer-sharp`,
    `gatsby-plugin-sharp`,
    {
      resolve: `gatsby-source-filesystem`,
      options: {
        path: `${__dirname}/src/images`
      }
    },
  ],
}
```

As this configuration suggests, for the source plugin to detect them you'll need to create a new directory named *images* within your *src* directory. Place a high-resolution image in this directory—preferably a large one—to test gatsby-image's features. For my example image, I'm using a photograph of Pikes Peak, the mountain that towers over my hometown of Colorado Springs, named *pikes-peak.jpg*.

Now that you have an image that you wish to process using the gatsby-image component, you can use gatsby-source-filesystem and Gatsby's internal GraphQL API to write the query that will yield a responsive and optimized image. The gatsby-image component comes with several ready-made GraphQL fragments that provide boilerplate templates for common use cases such as responsive, optimized images. One example GraphQL fragment available in gatsby-image is GatsbyImageSharp Fluid, which defines the image processing specifications for such a query. To test it, replace the contents of *src/pages/index.js* with the following:

```
// src/pages/index.js
import React from "react"
import { graphql } from "gatsby"

export default function Home() {
  return <div>Hello world!</div>
}

export const query = graphql`
  {
    file(relativePath: {
      eq: "pikes-peak.jpg"
    }) {
      childImageSharp {
```

```
            fluid {
                ...GatsbyImageSharpFluid
            }
        }
    }
}
```

Next, replace the rendering code with the `gatsby-image` component's `<Img>` JSX element, which displays the fragment in JSX and allows React to understand how to render the image appropriately based on your specifications:

```
// src/pages/index.js
import React from "react"
import { graphql } from "gatsby"
import Img from "gatsby-image" ❶

export default function Home({ data }) {
  return <Img ❷
    fluid={data.file.childImageSharp.fluid}
    alt="Pikes Peak, known as Tava in the Ute language and Heey-otoyoo' in
    the Arapaho language"
  />
}

export const query = graphql`
  {
    file(relativePath: {
      eq: "pikes-peak.jpg"
    }) {
      childImageSharp {
        fluid {
          ...GatsbyImageSharpFluid
        }
      }
    }
  }
`
```

❶  Import `Img` from `gatsby-image` as a dependency.

❷  Use an `<Img />` element to provide the image to JSX.

By using the `GatsbyImageSharpFluid` GraphQL fragment, we can create *fluid* images that have multiple sizes depending on the current viewport size (such as in a mobile or desktop environment). When the page begins rendering, the `gatsby-image` component "blurs up" the image so that you see a blurry preview as it loads, and it also begins lazy-loading any other images on the page that are not above the fold in the current viewport.

Run `gatsby develop` to see the fully built site working in your browser. The image you provided should now be loading gracefully into your Gatsby page, as shown in Figure 7-6, and if you refresh the page you will see the blur-up effect gracefully yield the full image.

*Figure 7-6. The sample image, processed through `gatsby-image`, displaying after a blur-up effect in the Gatsby page*

Now, try zooming in such that your viewport is less than 800 pixels in width. If you refresh the page and inspect the element, as illustrated in Figure 7-7, you'll see that rather than displaying the full high-resolution image, the browser selects an image of size 640×480 from the source set. When you resize the viewport, Gatsby automatically adjusts the image to respect your new viewport size.

> For more information about the `gatsby-image` component, consult the Gatsby documentation (*https://oreil.ly/Bx9E0*).

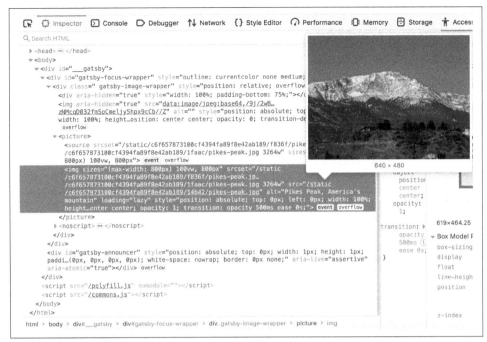

*Figure 7-7. A view of our image from inside the Inspector in Firefox, showing the smaller image size of 640×480 being used in this smaller viewport rather than the full image*

# Working with Videos

Though Gatsby lacks a single dedicated component for handling videos in Gatsby sites, videos are nonetheless an important category of assets that we as Gatsby developers need to serve through site implementations. Like images, videos can be either externally hosted through providers such as YouTube or Vimeo or self-hosted as file assets.

By far the easiest method to introduce an externally hosted video into your Gatsby site is to use an `<iframe>` element that refers to the video URL. Such an approach generally satisfies the requirements for one-off videos from services such as YouTube, Vimeo, Twitch, and others that are included in Gatsby pages and components. However, there are situations in which you may wish to create custom components that can be reused for a variety of videos. And as we saw with images in "Working with Assets" on page 191, there may be scenarios where we need to embed videos in Markdown files that provide content for our sites.

# Creating Custom Components for Hosted Videos

To display a video, we can write a custom component for hosted videos that we can then include in a JSX template.

Consider the following example of a React component for repeatable video display:

```
// src/components/video.js
import React from "react"

const Video = ({ videoUrl, videoTitle, ...props }) => (
  <div className="video">
    <iframe
      src={videoUrl}
      title={videoTitle}
      allow="accelerometer; autoplay; encrypted-media; gyroscope;
             picture-in-picture"
      frameBorder="0"
      webkitallowfullscreen="true"
      mozallowfullscreen="true"
      allowFullScreen
    />
  </div>
)

export default Video
```

With React, we can then reuse this component on any page, such as the home page of our Gatsby "Hello World" starter. Here's an example of a working video component used in such an example home page for illustration:

```
// src/pages/index.js
import React from "react"
import Video from "../components/video"

export default function Home() {
  <Video
    videoUrl="https://www.youtube.com/watch?v=BYxWtHMQ1oI"
    videoTitle="Tinashe and MAKJ's music video for Save Room for Us"
  />
}
```

Using a repeatable component like this one can accelerate your development by allowing you to more efficiently display videos in pages and components that need them. But what if you need the data in the videoUrl and videoTitle attributes to be provided programmatically, from Markdown files or through GraphQL? To accomplish that task, we'll need to bring GraphQL into the picture.

# Querying Videos from Markdown Using GraphQL

As we saw with images, sometimes a requirement of Gatsby sites is to use Markdown to create individual blog posts or articles that can later be processed into a template by Gatsby through `gatsby-source-filesystem`. For instance, consider a typical Markdown blog post that includes an embedded video in its `frontmatter` fields, like the one we created in Chapter 6:

```
---
title: "Consectetur adipiscing elit"
date: "2020-12-05"
videoUrl: https://www.youtube.com/watch?v=BYxWtHMQ1oI
videoTitle: Tinashe and MAKJ's music video for Save Room for Us
---

Donec lacinia vulputate porttitor.

Duis lacinia venenatis mi eget posuere.

- Phasellus rutrum dolor at lectus imperdiet
- At condimentum leo dapibus

Morbi fringilla tincidunt aliquam.
```

After installing `gatsby-source-filesystem` and configuring it to register these files, as shown in the previous chapter, you can begin to query the Markdown files for the information contained within the `frontmatter` fields. Assuming your source plugin is configured to register files under `${__dirname}/src`, you can update the post template we wrote in Chapter 6 so that it issues a GraphQL query that retrieves the needed information:

```
// src/templates/post.js
import React from "react"
import { graphql } from "gatsby"
import Layout from "../components/layout"
import Video from "../components/video" ❶

export default function Post({ data }) {
  const post = data.markdownRemark
  return (
    <Layout>
      <h1>{post.frontmatter.title}</h1>
      <Video ❷
        videoUrl={post.frontmatter.videoUrl}
        videoTitle={post.frontmatter.videoTitle}
      />
      <div dangerouslySetInnerHTML={{ __html: post.html }} />
    </Layout>
  )
}
```

```
export const query = graphql`
  query($slug: String!) {
    markdownRemark(
      fields: {
        slug: {
          eq: $slug
        }
      }
    ) {
      html
      frontmatter {
        date(fromNow: true)
        title
        videoUrl ❸
        videoTitle
      }
    }
  }
`
```

❶ Add an `import` statement to bring in the video component we wrote.

❷ Add the `videoUrl` and `videoTitle` fields from the Markdown `frontmatter` to the GraphQL query.

❸ Add the video component to the rendering code.

It's also possible to embed components such as this repeatable video component within your Markdown files using MDX, a format that permits the interpolation of JSX into Markdown. This is a more advanced use case; for more information on MDX, consult Chapter 13 and Gatsby's MDX documentation (*https://oreil.ly/YePtP*).

## Self-Hosting Your Own Videos

In Gatsby, it's also perfectly possible to self-host your own videos and to embed them using the HTML5 `<video>` element instead of the `<iframe>` used to embed videos from a third-party provider. Media formats can be highly complex, especially when it comes to video extensions and codecs. In many cases, video conversion software will be required to generate *.webm* and *.mp4* files that can play in a variety of settings.

The Gatsby documentation recommends the Mozilla Developer Network's page on media formats for HTML audio and video (*https://oreil.ly/QccYa*) for a primer on HTML5 video handling.

The HTML5 `<video>` element provides a means of including multiple `<source>` child elements that represent the various video file formats you need to support. When the browser loads a page containing a `<video>` element, it will run through the `<source>` videos until it finds a format that it supports by default.

It's usually optimal to import your video files from your local filesystem directly using Webpack. Suppose you have a video that you want to display on the Gatsby "Hello World" starter's home page. Here's how to do that using Webpack:

```
// src/pages/index.js
import React from "react"
import WhaleMp4 from "../videos/whalewatching-video.mp4" ❶
import WhaleWebm from "../videos/whalewatching-video.webm"

export default function Home() {
  return (
    <video controls> ❷
      <source src={WhaleMp4} type="video/mp4" />
      <source src={WhaleWebm} type="video/webm" />
      Sorry, your browser lacks support for embedded HTML5 videos.
    </video>
  )
}
```

❶ Register the available video formats with Webpack, using `import` statements.

❷ Use an HTML5 `<video>` element to embed the video.

 Gatsby has an official example codebase named "Using Video" (*https://oreil.ly/dVDhf*) that demonstrates the use of HTML5 `<video>` tags in working Gatsby code.

Remember that while hosting your own videos gives you maximum control and flexibility when it comes to managing your videos, using the HTML5 `<video>` element requires consideration for disabled users with different access needs. It is strongly recommended to include either captions for the video, a transcript (or subtitles), or an audio description for accessibility purposes.

In HTML5, the `<track>` element provides powerful capabilities for assistive content such as captions. Here's an example of the same home page, with an additional imported captions file that makes the video much more accessible:

```
// src/pages/index.js
import React from "react"
import WhaleMp4 from "../videos/whalewatching-video.mp4"
import WhaleWebm from "../videos/whalewatching-video.webm"
import WhaleCaptions from "file-loader!../videos/whalewatching-captions.vtt" ❶
```

```
export default function Home() {
  return (
    <video controls>
      <source src={WhaleMp4} type="video/mp4" />
      <source src={WhaleWebm} type="video/webm" />
      <track kind="captions" srcLang="en" src={WhaleCaptions} /> ❷
      Sorry, your browser lacks support for embedded HTML5 videos.
    </video>
  )
}
```

❶  Register the format for displaying timed text tracks with Webpack.

❷  Use an HTML5 `<track>` element to embed the captions file.

 The prefix `file-loader!` before the path leading to the captions file in this example allows Webpack to understand the *.vtt* caption file and to import it successfully as it would any other asset.

Though a comprehensive examination is well outside the scope of this book, the `<track>` element can also accept different `kind` attribute values, such as `captions`, `subtitles`, and `descriptions`, depending on the assistive content you're providing.

# Working with Fonts

When it comes to assets in Gatsby, fonts might seem a bit of an odd duck, but all typefaces that aren't natively available on users' machines must come from some font asset or set of font assets. Fonts are crucial not only for typography in CSS but also for your Gatsby site's brand identity. There are two types of fonts that we as Gatsby developers need to handle: *local fonts* available on our filesystems and *web fonts* that are hosted externally.

 Gatsby recommends limiting the use of custom fonts to solely the essentials required for performance reasons. This might mean limiting the font to a certain weight (excluding Black and using only Bold, for instance), excluding ligatures that add to the file size, or optimizing the font file to provide only the glyphs used in the website.

# Adding Local Fonts

If you already have font files in your filesystem that you wish to use for a Gatsby site, they will carry file extensions like *.ttf, .otf, .woff,* or *.woff2.* Though Gatsby has no opinion about where to place your font files, it's common to store them inside the *src/ fonts* folder to distinguish fonts from other assets.

If you are using a global stylesheet, such as for your layout component, you can use well-established CSS techniques to provide a font file to the stylesheet. One way to do this is to simply insert an `@font-face` at-rule at the start of your CSS file, as shown in the following example. You can then refer to the font name (surrounded by double quotes) when you define the `font-family` property for any subsequent selector:

```
/* src/components/layout.css */
@font-face {
  font-family: "Open Sans";
  src: url("../fonts/OpenSans-Regular-webfont.woff2") format("woff2"),
      url("../fonts/OpenSans-Regular-webfont.woff") format("woff");
}

body {
  font-family: "Open Sans", Helvetica, Arial, sans-serif;
}
```

Some developers prefer to separate the `@font-face` at-rule into a separate CSS file and use an `@import` at-rule to import the fonts into another stylesheet. This is particularly useful if you only need the fonts for particular component stylesheets or if you're accustomed to SCSS paradigms, where fonts are often separated out into a "globals" or "typography" file. In that case, you might wish to create two separate CSS files, like this:

```
/* src/css/typography.css */
@font-face {
  font-family: "Open Sans";
  src: url("../fonts/OpenSans-Regular-webfont.woff2") format("woff2"),
      url("../fonts/OpenSans-Regular-webfont.woff") format("woff");
}

/* src/components/layout.css */
@import "../css/typography.css";

body {
  font-family: "Open Sans", Helvetica, Arial, sans-serif;
}
```

This makes perfect sense if you have local font files available. But what if you need to use an externally hosted web font, such as those made available through Google Fonts, Adobe Fonts (formerly known as Typekit), or sites like Font Squirrel? Because those typefaces are composed of externally hosted font files, you'll need a different approach.

# Adding Web Fonts

When it comes to fonts that are externally hosted, it's certainly possible to simply replace the relative paths in `@font-face` at-rules with external URLs, but this can often detrimentally impact performance due to the additional request.

If you're using Google Fonts or Adobe Fonts in your Gatsby project, there are varying methods to import those fonts without harming performance.

### Adding Google Fonts

For Google Fonts, Gatsby recommends importing the web fonts into JavaScript through Fontsource, a package provider for Google Fonts in JavaScript. Each Google Fonts typeface has an equivalent package available in Fontsource. To make a Google Fonts typeface available to your Gatsby site, first execute the appropriate NPM or Yarn command to install the Fontsource package of your choice, where *font-name* is the name of your font in `kebab-case` (e.g., Open Sans becomes `open-sans`):

```
# If using NPM
$ npm install @fontsource/font-name

# If using Yarn
$ yarn add @fontsource/font-name
```

For Open Sans, the NPM installation command would be:

```
$ npm install @fontsource/open-sans
```

Then, import the package into your Gatsby site. Though Gatsby recommends importing it through the layout component (*src/components/layout.js*), as found in Gatsby's default starter, you can also import it through a page component (e.g., *src/pages/index.js*) or even *gatsby-browser.js*, which interacts with Gatsby's API for browser operations. For instance, here's how to import it in the layout component:

```
// src/components/layout.js
import "@fontsource/open-sans"
```

As is, this imported package will default to a font weight of 400 with all styles (italic, etc.) included. To select only a particular weight or style, you can modify the referenced package to target only a subset of the typeface:

```
// src/components/layout.js
// Select only weight of 600 with all styles included.
import "@fontsource/open-sans/600.css"

// Select only weight of 400 with only italic style included.
import "@fontsource/open-sans/400-italic.css"
```

This series of import statements would result in glyphs being made available in all styles for a weight of 600 and only italic for a weight of 400. Once you've imported a font into your layout component, you can then refer to the font within your layout stylesheet:

```
/* src/components/layout.css */
body {
    font-family: "Open Sans", Helvetica, Arial, sans-serif;
}
```

 For a full examination of Fontsource capabilities, which is outside the scope of this book, consult the Fontsource monorepo documentation (*https://oreil.ly/VlzsY*).

## Adding Adobe Fonts (Typekit)

For users of Adobe Fonts, Gatsby provides a handy plugin known as gatsby-plugin-web-font-loader that allows you to supply a credential to access closed fonts. First, you'll need to install the plugin:

```
# If using NPM
$ npm install --save gatsby-plugin-web-font-loader

# If using Yarn
$ yarn add gatsby-plugin-web-font-loader
```

Then you need to provide your Typekit or Adobe Fonts ID to the Gatsby configuration file, preferably through an environment variable through a library such as dotenv:

```
// gatsby-config.js
plugins: [
  {
    resolve: `gatsby-plugin-web-font-loader`,
    options: {
      typekit: {
        id: process.env.TYPEKIT_ID,
      },
    },
  },
],
```

You can then refer to the typeface name as normal in your CSS stylesheets or CSS-in-JS. For instance, in a hypothetical layout component stylesheet:

```
/* src/components/layout.css */
body {
    font-family: "Avenir", Helvetica, Arial, sans-serif;
}
```

For lesser-known services such as Fonts.com, FontSpace, and others, the `gatsby-plugin-web-font-loader` plugin offers separate options. For more information about these, consult the `gatsby-plugin-web-font-loader` (*https://oreil.ly/yYkeR*) and Web Font Loader documentation (*https://oreil.ly/3cIpY*).

# Conclusion

Assets can be complicated beasts to manage in any scenario due to their complexity and potential impact on performance, but through its general asset handling, image and video management, and font-loading capabilities, Gatsby attempts to make those challenges easier for developers on a variety of fronts. For instance, the `gatsby-plugin-image` plugin can be used to generate responsive, optimized images at a fraction of the time normally spent on such optimizations. And Gatsby provides solutions not only for local assets in the developer's filesystem, but also externally hosted assets that can benefit from its performance enhancements.

Whether you require an image, a video, a font, or some other asset, it's important to consider the ramifications of one approach over the other. For instance, while using the *static* folder is optimal for quick-and-dirty exceptions where assets should not be managed by Webpack, it removes the opportunity to leverage many of the features that Gatsby is known for. As we'll see in the next chapter, assets are critical for the kinds of data-driven features commonly requested in Gatsby implementations.

# CHAPTER 8

# Adding Data-Driven Features to Gatsby Sites

Over the course of the last several chapters, we've explored some of the most important concepts in Gatsby when it comes to working with data, whether that data consists of JSON or assets made available through GraphQL. Now it's time for us to revisit some real-world applications and use cases that are relevant to those building Gatsby sites for clients and organizations.

In Chapter 3, we focused solely on features that don't require management of data through Gatsby's internal data layer, whether because of intelligent defaults or because there is no need for GraphQL. Here, we'll concentrate on real-life applications and requirements driven by data that obligate the use of GraphQL and other aspects of Gatsby we've explored in the intervening chapters. We'll implement various features that are key for Gatsby sites dealing with data, such as site search, commenting, blog taxonomy, pagination, RSS feeds, and user authentication.

## Adding Site Search

Implementing site search can be challenging even for traditional websites, let alone more modern and dynamic sites that need to behave like interactive applications too. Any site search, whether in Gatsby or not, requires three components:

*Search index*
> The search index is a corpus of all of the data you wish to make available to a search engine, recorded in a format optimized for search use cases. Without a search index, a site search feature would need to scrape through your site looking for results every time a user wanted to find something instead of using a ready-made index.

*Search engine*

The search engine's role is to accept a search query, compare it to the search index, and return any matched documents from the search index to the user.

*Search interface*

Finally, a search interface of some sort—for our purposes, typically a React component—needs to be made available to the user so that they can input search queries and view search results.

There are two recommended approaches to adding site search to a Gatsby site, and they are shared with many other JavaScript frameworks as well:

1. Use an open source search service. Leveraging an open source search service (e.g., `elasticlunr` (*https://oreil.ly/OJOjp*), `flexsearch` (*https://oreil.ly/pMSDW*), `js-search` (*https://oreil.ly/Svnkt*)) to power site search for your Gatsby site comes with the benefit of free and offline-enabled search. But it also comes with a cost: because the entire search index needs to be made available on the client, the client bundle can explode in size, which impacts performance.

2. Use an API-driven search service. Leveraging an external search service (e.g., Elasticsearch (*https://www.elastic.co/elasticsearch*), Solr (*https://solr.apache.org*), Algolia (*https://www.algolia.com*)) can mitigate impacts on scalability, because search users don't need to retrieve the entire search index to persist on the client side. The drawback, however, is that most API-driven search services require paid hosting or a paid subscription.

In the coming sections, we'll take a look at implementing search with Algolia, an API-driven search service.

 The Gatsby documentation provides a comprehensive tutorial (*https://oreil.ly/jkNFW*) for using the open source `js-search` library with both small and medium-sized datasets and large datasets, but due to its significant length, I won't summarize its procedures here.

## Implementing Site Search with Algolia

*Algolia* is a popular API-driven site search platform that is intended for use in JavaScript applications. The free tier permits a limited number of searches per month; payment is required for more frequent searches. Because Algolia provides components out of the box, there's no need to set up your own search server. To use it on any site (not just Gatsby sites), Algolia requires developers to provide a list of pages as well as their locations and navigation scheme, and the Algolia API returns results based on a search query that is compared with an Algolia-hosted search index.

Because Algolia handles the search engine, the only two items you need to worry about as a Gatsby developer are populating the search index and building a search interface. Fortunately, the `gatsby-plugin-algolia` plugin handles automatic indexing of your Gatsby pages every time you run `gatsby build`. You can use GraphQL queries to indicate what Algolia should track: this allows you to customize which pages from your Gatsby site and what information to index.

 Algolia provides a distinct product known as DocSearch (*https://oreil.ly/R39SY*) for Gatsby and other developers who wish to offer search across documentation sites. This eliminates the need to conduct any manual indexing via web scraping.

## Configuring gatsby-plugin-algolia

Let's start from scratch with a new Gatsby blog starter, and immediately go ahead and install the Algolia plugin for Gatsby:

```
$ gatsby new gtdg-ch8-algolia gatsbyjs/gatsby-starter-blog
$ cd gtdg-ch8-algolia

# If using NPM
$ npm install --save gatsby-plugin-algolia

# If using Yarn
$ yarn add gatsby-plugin-algolia
```

Now you need to add some configuration to your *gatsby-config.js* file, which will identify your Algolia account to the `gatsby-plugin-algolia` plugin and authorize it. In the API Keys section of your Algolia dashboard, you'll find the key credentials required: an Application ID, a Search-Only API Key, and an Admin API Key. Using a library such as `dotenv`, place those into a separate *.env* file to keep them safe:

```
ALGOLIA_APP_ID=your_app_id
ALGOLIA_SEARCH_KEY=your_search_only_api_key
ALGOLIA_ADMIN_KEY=your_admin_api_key
```

The next step is to add a few options (`appI`, `apiKey`, and `queries`) to your Algolia configuration within the Gatsby configuration file, as follows:

```
// gatsby-config.js
plugins: [
  {
    resolve: `gatsby-plugin-algolia`,
    options: {
      appId: process.env.ALGOLIA_APP_ID,
      apiKey: process.env.ALGOLIA_ADMIN_KEY,
      queries: require("./src/utils/algolia-queries")
    },
```

```
      },
    ],
```

As you may have noticed, the configuration of `gatsby-plugin-algolia` requires the creation of an additional utility file located at *src/utils/algolia-queries.js*, which will contain what Algolia needs to understand how to index your Gatsby site.

## Querying Pages with GraphQL for Indexing

To instruct Algolia how to index your Gatsby content, you need to create a new file at *src/utils/algolia-queries.js* (or wherever the `queries` option in your Gatsby configuration file points). The GraphQL queries you insert into the queries file will return information that is then converted into a set of Algolia records, which are composed of key/value pairs with data needing to be indexed.

Here's an example queries file that instructs Algolia how to populate its records. Go ahead and add this to your codebase in the appropriate location (*src/utils/algolia-queries.js*):

```
// src/utils/algolia-queries.js
const escapeStringRegexp = require("escape-string-regexp")

const pagePath = `content`
const indexName = `Pages`

const pageQuery = `{
  pages: allMarkdownRemark(
    filter: {
      fileAbsolutePath: { regex: "/${escapeStringRegexp(pagePath)}/" },
    }
  ) {
    edges {
      node {
        id
        frontmatter {
          title
        }
        fields {
          slug
        }
        excerpt(pruneLength: 5000)
      }
    }
  }
}`

function pageToAlgoliaRecord({ node: { id, frontmatter, fields, ...rest } }) {
  return {
    objectID: id, ❶
    ...frontmatter,
    ...fields,
```

```
      ...rest,
    }
}

const queries = [ ❷
  {
    query: pageQuery, ❸
    transformer: ({ data }) => ( ❹
      data.pages.edges.map(pageToAlgoliaRecord)
    ),
    indexName, ❺
    settings: { attributesToSnippet: [`excerpt:20`] }, ❻
  },
]

module.exports = queries
```

❶ Each Algolia record must have a unique identifier that is provided as `objectID`. Here, we provide an identifier not only to the record, but also the `slug` (in `fields`), the `title` (in `frontmatter`), and the `excerpt`.

❷ This file's primary export is a list of queries. Each query defines a single index for Algolia, though multiple indexes are possible with Algolia.

❸ Each index must be associated with a GraphQL query that is responsible for fetching the pages and any data to be indexed.

❹ A transformer transforms the GraphQL data to an Algolia record according to logic that we write; in this case, this logic is contained in `pageToAlgoliaRecord`.

❺ Every index must have a name by which it can be identified.

❻ Finally, each query has optional settings that we can use to instruct Algolia to do custom work.

Once you've finished writing the indexing logic for Algolia, you can test the `gatsby-plugin-algolia` plugin and ensure that indexing is taking place by running `gatsby build`. Your terminal output will contain logged events that look like the following:

```
# gatsby build terminal output
success Building static HTML for pages - 7.623s - 5/5 0.56/s
Algolia: 1 queries to index
Algolia: query 0: executing query
Algolia: query 0: graphql resulted in 3 records
Algolia: query 0: splitting in 1 jobs
```

The number of records that "result" from `graphql` should match the number of pages you have in your Gatsby site. If you log into your Algolia account and check the newly created Pages index in your list of Algolia indices, you'll see your indexed content represented.

There are two things to keep in mind when troubleshooting Algolia indexing of Gatsby sites:

- If you see a GraphQL error such as `Field 'fileAbsolutePath' is not defined by type MarkdownRemarkFilterInput`, this is a sign that the plugin wasn't able to find pages in your Gatsby project. You'll need to check the GraphQL query and the path you configured for `gatsby-source-filesystem`.

- If you see an Algolia error such as `AlgoliaSearchError: Record at the position...is too big`, you've exceeded Algolia's limit of 10 KB for a single index entry.

Covering the React `InstantSearch` library (*https://oreil.ly/fDLan*), Algolia's UI framework for implementing Algolia search, is outside the scope of this book. The Algolia documentation has information about multiple indices (*https://oreil.ly/4ZK8O*), structuring data into records (*https://oreil.ly/EDQW0*), and optional query settings (*https://oreil.ly/Kj9AY*). The Gatsby documentation provides a comprehensive tutorial (*https://oreil.ly/bVuTx*) for creating a search widget or UI with these tools, but you can also use your own.

# Adding a Commenting System

Though many blogs lack commenting sections for each post, a commenting system is a common need for blogs that wish to invite engagement from readers. One of the biggest challenges of implementing a commenting system is that there are a variety of options available to choose from, each with its own trade-offs, including Commento (*https://commento.io*), Disqus (*https://oreil.ly/UGdZ9*), Facebook Comments (*https://oreil.ly/WIeYB*), FastComments (*https://fastcomments.com*), Gitalk (*https://oreil.ly/sunkA*), Staticman (*https://staticman.net*), Talkyard (*https://www.talkyard.io*), and Utterances (*https://utteranc.es*).

As with many features in Gatsby, it's also possible to create your own commenting system from scratch. For more information, consult Tania Rascia's blog post on the Gatsby blog (*https://oreil.ly/sC6Ms*).

For our purposes, due to its ease of use and high degree of adoption and maturity, we'll implement a Disqus commenting system that displays on every blog post we have. Disqus is widely used by media organizations and hobbyist bloggers alike, and it comes with a feature-rich free tier and first-class support for React. In addition, Disqus benefits from a large user base and a distinctive design that many blog readers will immediately recognize.

 Though Disqus comments are lazy-loaded so as not to block any other loading on the page, introducing Disqus also means that your site is no longer truly static, owing to the fact that Disqus dynamically injects its commenting system into the page through an `<iframe>` embed. This may be less desirable or even prohibitive for organizations that deal with compliance considerations or personally identifiable information.

Let's start with a clean slate. First, create a new Gatsby blog starter:

```
$ gatsby new gtdg-ch8-commenting gatsbyjs/gatsby-starter-blog
$ cd gtdg-ch8-commenting
```

Next, install the `disqus-react` library, which you'll need to insert Disqus comments into your Gatsby site:

```
# If using NPM
$ npm install --save disqus-react

# If using Yarn
$ yarn add disqus-react
```

If you don't already have a Disqus account, you can sign up now on the website (*https://disqus.com*). Create a Disqus site, and copy the shortname. Now you need to identify your Disqus site to Disqus in Gatsby so it can make the connection between the two. To do this, you'll need to identify your Disqus shortname as an environment variable, as follows:

```
# .env
# Provides Disqus site shortname to enable Disqus comments
GATSBY_DISQUS_SHORTNAME=myDisqusShortname
```

To make Disqus's commenting system available on every single blog post page generated by Gatsby, you need to edit the blog post template. In the blog starter, open *src/templates/blog-post.js* and add an `import` statement to the very top that imports the `DiscussionEmbed` component from `disqus-react`:

```
// src/templates/blog-post.js
import * as React from "react"
import { Link, graphql } from "gatsby"
import { DiscussionEmbed } from "disqus-react"
```

Now, just inside the `BlogPostTemplate`, add another `const` definition, this time identifying your Disqus shortname in a Disqus configuration object:

```
// src/templates/blog-post.js
const BlogPostTemplate = ({ data, location }) => {
  const post = data.markdownRemark
  const siteTitle = data.site.siteMetadata?.title || `Title`
  const { previous, next } = data

  const disqusConfig = {
    shortname: process.env.GATSBY_DISQUS_SHORTNAME,
    config: {
      identifier: post.fields.slug,
      title: post.frontmatter.title,
    },
  }
}
```

Note that in order to access the slug value, you'll need to update your GraphQL
query to acquire that value as well. Modify solely the unaliased markdownRemark portion of the GraphQL query so it looks like this:

```
// src/templates/blog-post.js
markdownRemark(id: { eq: $id }) {
  id
  excerpt(pruneLength: 160)
  html
  fields {
    slug
  }
  frontmatter {
    title
    date(formatString: "MMMM DD, YYYY")
    description
  }
}
```

The final step is to add the Disqus comments component to the section of the blog
post template where it should reside:

```
// src/templates/blog-post.js
<article
  className="blog-post"
  itemScope
  itemType="http://schema.org/Article"
>
  <header>
    <h1 itemProp="headline">{post.frontmatter.title}</h1>
    <p>{post.frontmatter.date}</p>
  </header>
  <section
    dangerouslySetInnerHTML={{ __html: post.html }}
    itemProp="articleBody"
  />
  <hr />
  <DiscussionEmbed {...disqusConfig} />
  <hr />
```

```
  <footer>
    <Bio />
  </footer>
</article>
```

# Adding Taxonomy to Blog Posts

In Chapter 6, we took a look at programmatic page creation and how to use the *gatsby-node.js* file to generate pages based on arbitrary Markdown blog posts. Now that you understand how programmatic page creation works, many of the elements in the Gatsby blog starter will make more sense.

A common need for blogs is *taxonomy*: the combination of tags and categories that enriches the blog reader's experience by letting them read more content relevant to their interests. In Gatsby, the easiest way to facilitate this is to create tag pages for your blog and insert tag links into your individual blog posts. More complex solutions exist, particularly if you're integrating with a headless CMS, but we'll focus on the Markdown use case in this section.

To kick things off, clone a new version of the Gatsby blog starter:

```
$ gatsby new gtdg-ch8-taxonomy-pagination gatsbyjs/gatsby-starter-blog
$ cd gtdg-ch8-taxonomy-pagination
```

The directory structure of this blog starter differs quite a bit from the blog we built in Chapter 6, but we can still find our Markdown posts in the *content/blog* directory.

## Adding Tags and Querying for All Tags

The first thing we need to do is add a new field to the frontmatter in our Markdown blog posts. Let's add a field called tags to *content/blog/my-second-post/index.md* with a few sample tags. Note that in Markdown, fields can be strings, numbers, or arrays; we'll use an array here to enable multiple tags:

```
---
title: My Second Post!
date: "2015-05-06T23:46:37.121Z"
tags: ["eggs", "food", "cooking"]
---

Wow! I love blogging so much already.

Did you know that "despite its name, salted duck eggs can also be made
from chicken eggs, though the taste and texture will be somewhat different,
and the egg yolk will be less rich."?
([Wikipedia Link](https://en.wikipedia.org/wiki/Salted_duck_egg))

Yeah, I didn't either.
```

Let's add a few tags to the other blog posts included with the starter as well, *hello-world* and *new-beginnings*. The following examples are truncated to show only the frontmatter section of each blog post file—the tags don't necessarily correspond to the posts' content, but we can work on that later!

```
---
title: Hello World
date: "2015-05-01T22:12:03.284Z"
description: "Hello World"
tags: ["eggs", "food", "cooking", "books"]
---


---
title: New Beginnings
date: "2015-05-28T22:40:32.169Z"
description: This is a custom description for SEO and Open Graph purposes,
rather than the default generated excerpt. Simply add a description field
to the frontmatter.
tags: ["animals", "food", "books"]
---
```

Now, once we restart the development server, we can query for those fields in Graph-iQL. Issue the following query to see your tags in a GraphQL response:

```
{
  allMarkdownRemark {
    group(field: frontmatter___tags) {
      tag: fieldValue
      totalCount
    }
  }
}
```

The response to this query is shown in Figure 8-1. As you can see, we now have a full list of the tags in our blog post, as well as the count of blog posts per tag. The group field used here causes the query to group all blog posts by the tags field before returning each tag with the number of posts in the totalCount field.

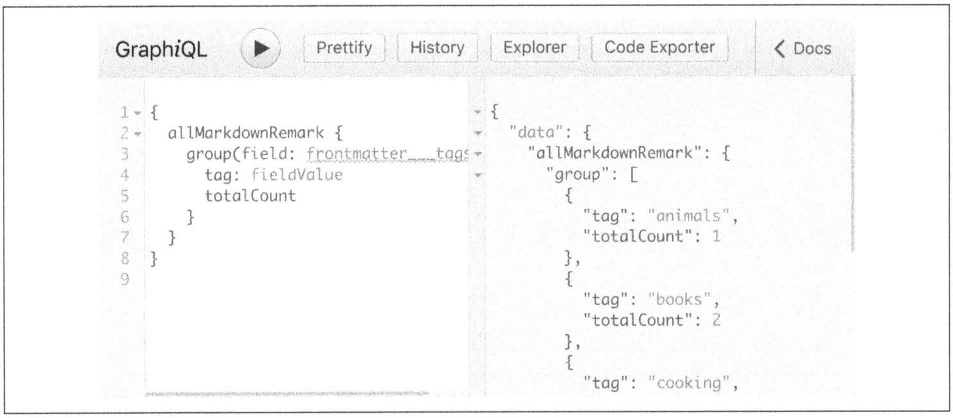

*Figure 8-1. The result of the preceding query, which returns a list of blog post tags with the total count of blog posts associated with each tag*

## Adding a Tag Page Template

Th next step is to create a tag page template (we covered template files in Chapter 6) for each individual tag and use it within `createPages` in *gatsby-node.js* to generate individual tag pages. Later, we'll build a Gatsby page that lists all of the tags together in a tag index.

Create a new file named *src/templates/tag.js* for the individual tag page template, and insert the following code:

```
// src/templates/tag.js
import React from "react"
import { Link, graphql } from "gatsby"

const Tag = ({ pageContext, data }) => {
  const { tag } = pageContext
  const { edges, totalCount } = data.allMarkdownRemark
  const tagHeader = `${totalCount} post${ ❶
    totalCount === 1 ? "" : "s"
  } tagged with "${tag}"`

  return (
    <>
      <h1>{tagHeader}</h1>
      <ul>
        {edges.map( ({node}) => { ❷
          const { slug } = node.fields
          const { title } = node.frontmatter
          return (
            <li key={slug}>
              <Link to={slug}>{title}</Link>
            </li>
          )
```

```
        })}
      </ul>
    </>
  )
}

export default Tag

export const pageQuery = graphql`
  query($tag: String) {
    allMarkdownRemark( ❸
      limit: 100,
      sort: {
        fields: [frontmatter___date],
        order: DESC
      },
      filter: {
        frontmatter: {
          tags: {
            in: [$tag]
          }
        }
      }
    ) {
      totalCount
      edges {
        node {
          fields {
            slug
          }
          frontmatter {
            title
          }
        }
      }
    }
  }
`
```

❶ Create a `tagHeader` that adds the plural suffix s when the `totalCount` field for the tag in question is greater than 1.

❷ Map each of the blog posts in your Markdown files to an unordered list item, provided that the blog post carries the tag in question.

❸ Retrieve the first 100 blog posts, sorting them in descending chronological order and filtering based on whether the blog post has the tag assigned or not.

Our work isn't quite done yet for the individual tag pages. The next thing we need to do is instruct Gatsby to use this individual tag page template to programmatically create the tag pages we need.

## Programmatic Tag Page Creation with gatsby-node.js

Now that we have a Gatsby page template for individual tag pages, we need to use the *gatsby-node.js* file and the `createPages` API to generate individual tag pages in addition to the individual blog post pages already reflected in the file. Modify the `import` statements and `exports.createPages` implementation in *gatsby-node.js* to the following code.

 Note that this example contains only the new state of the `exports.createPages` implementation of the file; for brevity, the example excludes `exports.onCreateNode` and `exports.create SchemaCustomization`.

```
// gatsby-node.js
const path = require(`path`)
const _ = require(`lodash`) ❶
const { createFilePath } = require(`gatsby-source-filesystem`)

exports.createPages = async ({ graphql, actions, reporter }) => {
  const { createPage } = actions

  // Define a template for blog post
  const blogPost = path.resolve(`./src/templates/blog-post.js`)

  // Define a template for individual tags
  const tagTemplate = path.resolve(`./src/templates/tag.js`) ❷

  // Get all markdown blog posts sorted by date
  const result = await graphql(
    `
    {
      postsRemark: allMarkdownRemark( ❸
        sort: { fields: [frontmatter___date], order: DESC }
        limit: 100
      ) {
        nodes {
          id
          fields {
            slug
          }
          frontmatter {
            tags
          }
        }
```

```
      }
      tagsGroup: allMarkdownRemark(limit: 100) { ❹
        group(field: frontmatter___tags) {
          fieldValue
        }
      }
    }
  `
)

if (result.errors) {
  reporter.panicOnBuild(
    `There was an error loading your blog posts`,
    result.errors
  )
  return
}

const posts = result.data.postsRemark.nodes ❺

// Create blog post pages, but only if there's at least one Markdown file
// found at "content/blog" (defined in gatsby-config.js).
// `context` is available in the template as a prop and as a variable in
// GraphQL.

if (posts.length > 0) {
  posts.forEach((post, index) => {
    const previousPostId = index === 0 ? null : posts[index - 1].id
    const nextPostId = index === posts.length - 1 ? null :
        posts[index + 1].id

    createPage({
      path: post.fields.slug,
      component: blogPost,
      context: {
        id: post.id,
        previousPostId,
        nextPostId,
      },
    })
  })
}

// Create individual tag pages.
const tags = result.data.tagsGroup.group ❻
if (tags.length > 0) {
  tags.forEach(tag => {
    createPage({
      path: `/tags/${_.kebabCase(tag.fieldValue)}/`,
      component: tagTemplate,
      context: {
        tag: tag.fieldValue,
```

```
      },
    })
  })
  }
}
```

**❶** Here, we add a new dependency: the `lodash` library, which contains a utility for converting strings to `kebab-case`.

**❷** We add our individual tag page template as a constant just below the blog post page template, referring to the location of the tag page template (*src/templates/ tag.js*).

**❸** Our original GraphQL query had only one instance of the `allMarkdownRemark` field. Because both blog posts and tags require us to access the `allMarkdownRe mark` field, our new GraphQL query aliases the first `allMarkdownRemark` field, which returns blog posts from Markdown files, to `postsRemark`.

**❹** The second `allMarkdownRemark` field, which returns tags from Markdown files, is aliased to `tagsGroup`. Within that `allMarkdownRemark` field, we retrieve each tag.

**❺** Because we needed to alias our original `allMarkdownRemark` field to `postsRe mark`, we need to modify the `const` definition of posts to `result.data.postsRe mark.nodes` instead of the original `result.data.allMarkdownRemark`.

**❻** Finally, our code culminates in a `forEach` loop that invokes `createPage` for each given tag. The tag template we created earlier is used to generate the new individual tag page, located at */tags/{tag}*, where *{tag}* is the tag name converted to `kebab-case`.

Note that we've passed `tag.fieldValue` into the `createPage` invocation through the `context` object. This is the value that is used in the *src/templates/tag.js* template by GraphQL to limit our search to only posts that carry that tag. If we revisit the GraphQL query in *src/templates/tag.js*, we can see that `tag.fieldValue`, found in *gatsby-node.js*, is passed in as the `$tag` query variable:

```
// src/templates/tag.js
export const pageQuery = graphql`
  query($tag: String) {
    allMarkdownRemark(
      limit: 100,
      sort: { fields: [frontmatter___date], order: DESC },
      filter: { frontmatter: { tags: { in: [$tag] }}}
    ) {
      totalCount
```

```
      edges {
        node {
          fields {
            slug
          }
          frontmatter {
            title
          }
        }
      }
    }
  }
`
```

Now that we have working individual tag pages at */tags/food*, */tags/books*, etc., as seen in Figure 8-2, we can move on to creating a tag index page that lists every tag represented in our blog.

# 3 posts tagged with "food"

- New Beginnings

- My Second Post!

- Hello World

*Figure 8-2. Our individual tag page template, now working at /tags/food and correctly displaying the three blog posts we assigned the tags to earlier*

## Adding a Tag Index Page

Our final step doesn't require us to use *gatsby-node.js*, because we'll only ever have one index of tags. For more complex taxonomies, where there is a tree of tags, you might need to use *gatsby-node.js* to create pages programmatically based on arbitrary tag groups. For our purposes, however, we'll assume there is only one group of tags that aren't associated with any higher tags in a hierarchy.

Because we don't need to do any programmatic page creation for our tag index page, we can simply create a new Gatsby page at *src/pages/tags.js*. For the tag index page, we'll want to list out all of the tags, along with the number of posts associated with each tag. Create a new page at *src/pages/tags.js* and add the following:

```
// src/pages/tags.js
import React from "react"
import { Link, graphql } from "gatsby"
import kebabCase from "lodash/kebabCase"

const TagIndex = ({
  data: {
```

```
      allMarkdownRemark: { group }
    }
}) => (
  <>
    <h1>Tags</h1>
    <ul>
      {group.map(tag => (
        <li key={tag.fieldValue}>
          <Link to={`/tags/${kebabCase(tag.fieldValue)}/`}>
            {tag.fieldValue} ({tag.totalCount})
          </Link>
        </li>
      ))}
    </ul>
  </>
)

export default TagIndex

export const pageQuery = graphql`
  {
    allMarkdownRemark(limit: 100) {
      group(field: frontmatter___tags) {
        fieldValue
        totalCount
      }
    }
  }
`
```

When we save this file, restart the development server, and navigate to */tags*, we'll see our tag index displaying properly, as illustrated in Figure 8-3. By extending our GraphQL query even further, we could enrich this tag index page with full blog posts displaying instead of only links to those content items.

*Figure 8-3. Our completed tag index page, displaying each tag along with the number of blog posts associated with it*

# Adding Pagination

*Pagination* is the act of separating a particularly long page or list of content into multiple pages to avoid overwhelming the user. Given a list of hundreds or thousands of entries, pagination can, from a single Gatsby template, display a limited number of items per page. In Gatsby, the quickest way to achieve pagination is to use the GraphQL API and the *gatsby-node.js* file.

Let's take a look at an example. Building off the work we did in the previous section on blog taxonomy, let's continue from where we left off. When you spin up a new Gatsby blog starter, a page is created at *src/pages/index.js* that represents the blog post index: a list of blog posts sorted in descending chronological order. At the moment, our blog displays three blog posts. But what if we want to paginate the blog index such that only two blog posts display per page?

## Preparing for Pagination in Page Templates

In GraphQL, we can think of pagination as a combination of `limit` and `skip` arguments. On the first page of our blog index, we'll see a limit of two blog posts with no skip. On the second page, however, we need to skip the two blog posts already displayed on the first paginated page, in addition to the standard limit of two blog posts.

The first step is to create a new file at *src/templates/blog-list.js*. This will become our blog index template that will govern each paginated blog index page:

```
// src/templates/blog-list.js
import React from "react"
import { Link, graphql } from "gatsby"

export default class BlogList extends React.Component {
  render() {
    const posts = this.props.data.allMarkdownRemark.edges
    return (
      <ul>
        {posts.map(({ node }) => {
          const title = node.frontmatter.title || node.fields.slug
          return (
            <li key={node.fields.slug}>
              <Link to={node.fields.slug}>{title}</Link>
            </li>
          )
        })}
      </ul>
    )
  }
}

export const blogListQuery = graphql`
  query blogListQuery($skip: Int!, $limit: Int!) {  ❶
```

---

```
    allMarkdownRemark(
      sort: { fields: [frontmatter___date], order: DESC }
      limit: $limit ❷
      skip: $skip
    ) {
      edges {
        node {
          fields {
            slug
          }
          frontmatter {
            title
          }
        }
      }
    }
  }
`
```

❶  Here, we provide query variables to the GraphQL query that will eventually be
   provided through the context object in *gatsby-node.js*, as we saw in the previous
   section on taxonomy.

❷  Next, we add arguments on our `allMarkdownRemark` field to add the eventual
   `limit` and `skip` values that will come from the context object in *gatsby-node.js*.

## Generating Paginated Pages with gatsby-node.js

In order to create paginated pages for our list of blog posts, with two blog posts per
page, we need to use *gatsby-node.js* to generate some new pages. Our Gatsby blog
starter already has a blog index, namely *src/pages/index.js*, but our goal here is to create a new page at the path */blog*, with further paginated pages taking the
paths */blog/2*, */blog/3*, */blog/4*, etc. Open your *gatsby-node.js* file, scroll to the end of
the `exports.createPages` section of the code, and add the following lines:

```
// gatsby-node.js
exports.createPages = async ({ graphql, actions, reporter }) => {
  // ...

  // Create paginated blog index pages.
  const postsList = result.data.postsRemark.nodes
  const postsPerPage = 2
  const numPages = Math.ceil(postsList.length / postsPerPage)
  Array.from({ length: numPages }).forEach((_, i) => {
    createPage({
      path: i === 0 ? `/blog` : `/blog/${i + 1}`,
      component: path.resolve("./src/templates/blog-list.js"),
      context: {
        limit: postsPerPage,
        skip: i * postsPerPage,
```

```
            numPages,
            currentPage: i + 1,
          },
        })
      })
    }
```

This new logic will run through all the blog posts, identifying where the cutoffs are for each pair (since we set `postsPerPage` to 2). Each page will list two blog posts, adhering to `postsPerPage`, until there are fewer than two blog posts remaining. When you run `gatsby develop` after this step, when you navigate to */blog, /blog/2, /blog/3*, etc., you'll see your list of blog posts paginated, as illustrated in Figures 8-4 and 8-5.

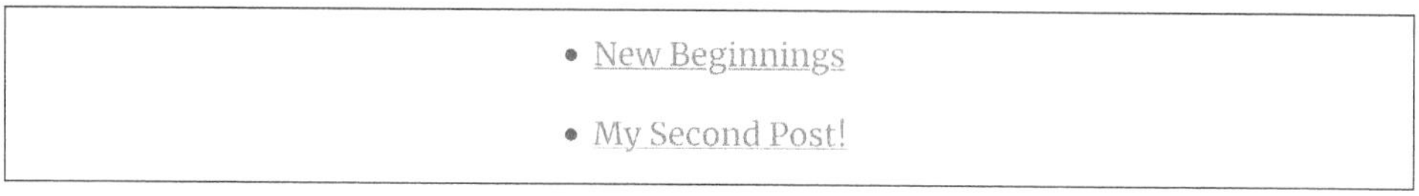

- New Beginnings
- My Second Post!

*Figure 8-4. The first page of our paginated blog index at /blog, displaying the first two blog posts in descending chronological order*

- Hello World

*Figure 8-5. The second page of our paginated blog index at /blog/2, displaying the last blog post—our blog has only three blog posts, so we have only two pages*

 For more details about how to add links to the previous or next page in the list as well as the traditional page-by-page navigation found at the bottom of paginated web pages, consult Nicky Meuleman's tutorial on pagination in Gatsby (*https://oreil.ly/F36wv*).

# Adding an RSS Feed

Another common need for Gatsby sites, especially those that regularly update content, is an *RSS feed*. This is an XML file that lists website content in a format amenable to news aggregators or feed readers, which subscribe to the feed but do not carry over any other aspects of the website. Because many Gatsby sites are blogs that update regularly, an RSS feed is another means by which to distribute your content to your readers.

# Adding an RSS Feed to a Markdown Blog

If you're building on top of the Gatsby blog starter, adding an RSS feed requires an additional plugin and some additional code in *gatsby-node.js*. To begin, let's clone a new version of the Gatsby blog starter to start from a relatively blank slate:

```
$ gatsby new gtdg-ch8-rss gatsbyjs/gatsby-starter-blog
$ cd gtdg-ch8-rss
```

Now, we need to install `gatsby-plugin-feed`, a handy plugin that can help us automate what might otherwise be a tedious task of generating an RSS feed:

```
# If using NPM
$ npm install --save gatsby-plugin-feed

# If using Yarn
$ yarn add gatsby-plugin-feed
```

The `gatsby-plugin-feed` plugin will generate a new RSS feed at */rss.xml* each time we run `gatsby build` or `npm run build`—i.e., on every production Gatsby build. We also need to add the plugin to the Gatsby configuration file, as usual. No additional options are required for the basic functionality of `gatsby-plugin-feed` in the Gatsby blog starter:

```
// gatsby-config.js
plugins: [`gatsby-plugin-feed`]
```

One of the things we need for the `gatsby-plugin-feed` plugin to work properly is a means of identifying content with unique names. For many blogs this will be a URL or a slug value. In *gatsby-node.js*, our Gatsby blog starter comes pre-equipped with the necessary logic to provide a slug value for each blog post:

```
// gatsby-node.js
exports.onCreateNode = ({ node, actions, getNode }) => {
  const { createNodeField } = actions

  if (node.internal.type === `MarkdownRemark`) {
    const value = createFilePath({ node, getNode })
    createNodeField({
      name: `slug`,
      node,
      value,
    })
  }
}
```

When you run `gatsby build`, an *rss.xml* file will be generated. And if you run `gatsby serve` afterwards, you'll be able to see your *rss.xml* file in production.

Though this solution works perfectly for Gatsby developers who are building on top of the Gatsby blog starter and using a Markdown blog, it doesn't quite fit the bill for other data sources besides Markdown or for unusual Markdown use cases. We'll see how to deal with those next.

## Adding an RSS Feed for Non-Markdown Content

Fortunately, we can use both *gatsby-config.js* and *gatsby-node.js* to customize how our RSS feed displays and how it works with the data we have, whether that means an unusual approach to a Markdown blog or a data source such as a CMS that has its own way of serving content in JSON.

One of the configuration options provided by `gatsby-plugin-feed` for *gatsby-config.js* is a `serialize` option that allows Gatsby developers to customize and rewrite the default RSS feed schema, the plugin generates. This is useful for cases in which you're retrieving content from an external source and need to rejigger it so it adheres to a different structure.

Consider the following example configuration for `gatsby-plugin-feed`, which demonstrates several options:

```
// gatsby-config.js
plugins: [
  {
    resolve: `gatsby-plugin-feed`,
    options: {
    query: ` ❶
      {
        site {
          siteMetadata {
            title
            description
            siteUrl
            site_url: siteUrl
          }
        }
      }
    `,
    feeds: [
      {
        serialize: ({ query: { site, allMarkdownRemark } }) => { ❷
          return allMarkdownRemark.edges.map(edge => {
            return Object.assign({}, edge.node.frontmatter, {
              description: edge.node.excerpt,
              date: edge.node.frontmatter.date,
              url: site.siteMetadata.siteUrl + edge.node.fields.slug,
              guid: site.siteMetadata.siteUrl + edge.node.fields.slug,
              custom_elements: [{ "content:encoded": edge.node.html }],
            })
          })
        },
        query: ` ❸
```

```
        {
          allMarkdownRemark(
            sort: { order: DESC, fields: [frontmatter___date] },
          ) {
            edges {
              node {
                excerpt
                html
                fields { slug }
                frontmatter {
                  title
                  date
                }
              }
            }
          }
        }
      `,
      output: "/rss.xml",
      title: "My Gatsby RSS Feed",
    },
  ],
  },
},
],
```

❶  The query option retrieves certain information that every RSS feed will need—in
    this case, namely the site's name (title) and the URL (siteUrl). Note that this is
    different from the GraphQL query that is used later to serialize our content into a
    distinct structure for our RSS feed.

❷  The feeds array contains one or more objects, each of which consists of a serial
    ize option and a GraphQL query string on which the serialization is based
    (query). Our example has only one, but you could potentially have multiple
    objects depending on your requirements.

❸  Finally, we provide a GraphQL query that is used by the serialize method to
    generate the desired structure for our RSS feed.

There are several other alternative configuration options that gatsby-plugin-feed
can accept in the Gatsby configuration file, as illustrated by Table 8-1.

> Additional options are available as the plugin depends on the rss
> package, which has its own itemOptions documentation (*https://
> oreil.ly/TrZ4G*).

*Table 8-1. Configuration options for* `gatsby-plugin-feed`

| Option | Type | Required? | Description |
|--------|------|-----------|-------------|
| query | String | Optional | A GraphQL query that retrieves necessary global information for the RSS feed, such as the site name (`title`) and site URL (`siteUrl`) |
| feeds | Array | Optional | An array containing options for each generated RSS feed: |

> `serialize`: A method for assigning site information or content to RSS feed fields (optional but strongly recommended to customize feed output)
>
> `query`: A GraphQL query that retrieves necessary content to populate the RSS feed (required)
>
> `output`: A path dictating the eventual location of the generated RSS feed (required)
>
> `title`: A name for the RSS feed (required)
>
> `match`: A regular expression string that dictates whether a given page will be referenced in the RSS feed or excluded (optional; e.g., `"^/blog/"`)
>
> `link`: An external RSS feed path that overrides the output option provided (optional; e.g., `https://feeds.feedburner.com/gatsby/blog`)

If you're creating an RSS feed for a podcast or podcast website, you may wish to include iTunes RSS blocks, which include formats that are incompatible with GraphQL. For more information, consult the Gatsby documentation on syntax for iTunes RSS blocks (*https://oreil.ly/sGftS*).

# Adding Authentication

Among the most important features that many websites require is *user authentication*. Whether that involves access to privileged portions of a Gatsby site or authentication into an external service, authentication is a complex and nuanced topic. Given the widening need to protect private and personally identifiable information (PII), authentication is an important skill in any Gatsby developer's toolkit.

Recently, there's been a trend for websites, including Gatsby sites, to be decoupled entirely from any server-side backend. For this reason, and because Gatsby is a front-end client as a presentation layer, a third-party service is required to perform authentication in Gatsby. This differs from many monolithic architectures, where authentication can occur as part of the same implementation.

As with site search, which we discussed in "Adding Site Search" on page 223, there are both open source options (e.g., a Node.js app driven by Passport.js or a Ruby on Rails API driven by Devise) and third-party SaaS providers for authentication (e.g., Firebase, Auth0, AWS Amplify, and Netlify Identity). As illustrated in Figure 8-6, in these implementations, a user is verified on the client—in this case, Gatsby—by an authentication provider or service. That provider or service returns an access token that allows a client to access protected or private data.

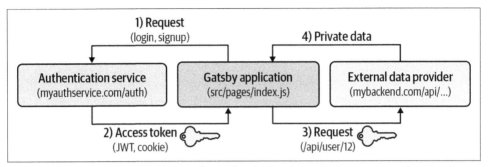

Figure 8-6. *How authentication works in Gatsby implementations—an authentication service returns a token that then grants access to some other data*

As this figure shows, the typical authentication process in Gatsby consists of the following steps:

1. Gatsby issues a request to an authentication provider or service to either register a new user or log in as that user if their account exists.

2. If the credentials provided by Gatsby in the request (such as a username/password pair) match a user in the authentication provider or service, it responds with a token (such as a JSON Web Token, or JWT) that grants the user the ability to use the token to access privileged data.

3. With the token in hand, Gatsby then issues a request to an external data source, such as an API or CMS, where privileged data is available for retrieval. The data server reads the key and allows Gatsby to access that privileged information.

4. Finally, the server sends data back to Gatsby so that it can pass that privileged information into React components.

 The approach to implement this form of authentication in Gatsby is identical to the patterns found in other React ecosystems, including Create React App.

# Preparing for Authentication

To examine how to work with all three of the elements identified in Figure 8-6, let's spin up a rudimentary Gatsby site that we can use to test authentication and manage private routes that need to handle privileged data. We'll use the "Hello World" starter:

```
$ gatsby new gtdg-ch8-authentication gatsbyjs/gatsby-starter-hello-world
$ cd gtdg-ch8-authentication
```

A typical Gatsby site with authentication will require a few links. To make this as simple as possible, we'll provide three navigation items in a navigation bar:

- Home (no authentication)
- Profile (requires authentication)
- Logout (if logged in)

For now, let's create a new component at *src/components/nav.js* with the following code and a few placeholder links:

```
// src/components/nav.js
import React from "react"
import { Link } from "gatsby"

export default function Nav() {
  return (
    <div
      style={{
        display: "flex",
        flex: "1",
        justifyContent: "space-between",
        borderBottom: "1px solid #d1c1e0",
      }}
    >
      <span>You are not logged in</span>
      <nav>
        <Link to="/">Home</Link>
        {` | `}
        <Link to="/">Profile</Link>
        {` | `}
        <Link to="/">Logout</Link>
      </nav>
    </div>
  )
}
```

We'll also add a layout component (*src/components/layout.js*) that will surround every page's content and display the navigation bar at the top of the page:

```
// src/components/layout.js
import React from "react"
import Nav from "./nav"

const Layout = ({ children }) => (
  <>
    <Nav />
    {children}
  </>
```

```
)
export default Layout
```

Finally, let's modify our home page (*src/pages/index.js*) to use the layout component:

```
// src/pages/index.js
import React from "react"

import Layout from "../components/layout"

export default function Home() {
  return (
    <Layout>
      <h1>Hello world!</h1>
    </Layout>
  )
}
```

Because there is such a wide variety of authentication services available, rather than focus on any one of them in this section, we'll create a fictional authentication provider in our Gatsby code that will handle authentication for us.

To do this, we'll create a new file at *src/services/auth.js* and insert the following code:

```
// src/services/auth.js
export const isBrowser = () => typeof window !== "undefined"

export const getUser = () =>
  isBrowser() && window.localStorage.getItem("gatsbyUser")
    ? JSON.parse(window.localStorage.getItem("gatsbyUser"))
    : {}

const setUser = user =>
  window.localStorage.setItem("gatsbyUser", JSON.stringify(user))

export const handleLogin = ({ username, password }) => {
  if (username === `ahmed` && password === `pass`) {
    return setUser({
      username: `ahmed`,
      name: `Ahmed`,
      email: `ahmed@example.com`,
    })
  }
  return false
}

export const isLoggedIn = () => {
  const user = getUser()
  return !!user.username
}

export const logout = callback => {
  setUser({})
```

```
    callback()
  }
```

In short, this rudimentary authentication service will check whether the user's username and password are available in `localStorage`, handle a login by returning that user's profile information, and finally, provide logic for login and logout operations.

## Creating Client-Only Routes

As mentioned in Chapter 3, Gatsby uses the `@reach/router` library, now part of React Router, which facilitates the ability to create routes that are available only to users who have undergone authentication. To add this functionality, we'll use the `createPage` API to detect all routes with the prefix */app/*, which will characterize restricted routes.

Because we're using Gatsby's "Hello World" starter, there isn't yet a *gatsby-node.js* file. Let's go ahead and create one, in the process implementing the `onCreatePage` method:

```
// gatsby-node.js
// Implement Gatsby's onCreatePage API, called after every page is created.
exports.onCreatePage = async ({ page, actions }) => {
  const { createPage } = actions

  // page.matchPath is a client-only key for matching pages.
  if (page.path.match(/^\/app/)) {
    page.matchPath = "/app/*"

    // Update the page.
    createPage(page)
  }
}
```

Now, to account for all of the routes prefixed with */app/*, we'll need to create a generic page (*src/pages/app.js*) that will eventually be responsible for displaying restricted content:

```
// src/pages/app.js
import React from "react"
import { Router } from "@reach/router"

import Layout from "../components/layout"
import Profile from "../components/profile"
import Login from "../components/login"

const App = () => (
  <Layout>
    <Router>
      <Profile path="/app/profile" />
      <Login path="/app/login" />
    </Router>
```

```
  </Layout>
)

export default App
```

The next things we'll need are components for each of the client-only routes: one for profiles and one for the login process. First, let's create the profile component that will eventually display privileged user data (*src/components/profile.js*):

```
// src/components/profile.js
import React from "react"

const Profile = () => (
  <>
    <h1>Your profile</h1>
    <ul>
      <li>Name: [Name placeholder]</li>
      <li>Email: [Email placeholder]</li>
    </ul>
  </>
)

export default Profile
```

And here's the login component (*src/components/login.js*), which handles unauthenticated users' login processes:

```
// src/components/login.js
import React from "react"
import { navigate } from "gatsby"
import { handleLogin, isLoggedIn } from "../services/auth"

class Login extends React.Component {
  state = { ❶
    username: ``,
    password: ``,
  }

  handleUpdate = event => { ❷
    this.setState({
      [event.target.name]: event.target.value,
    })
  }

  handleSubmit = event => { ❸
    event.preventDefault()
    handleLogin(this.state)
  }

  render() {
    if (isLoggedIn()) {
      navigate(`/app/profile`)
    }
```

```
      return (
        <>
          <h1>Log in</h1>
          <form ❹
            method="post"
            onSubmit={event => {
              this.handleSubmit(event)
              navigate(`/app/profile`)
            }}
          >
            <label>
              Username
              <input type="text" name="username" onChange={this.handleUpdate} />
            </label>
            <label>
              Password
              <input
                type="password"
                name="password"
                onChange={this.handleUpdate}
              />
            </label>
            <input type="submit" value="Log In" />
          </form>
        </>
      )
    }
  }

  export default Login
```

❶ Set up a `state` object for the user-provided username and password.

❷ Provide a handler for when form fields are updated so as to update the `state` object.

❸ Provide a handler for the submission of the form, which calls our authentication service.

❹ Render a form whose submission will trigger the `handleSubmit` method.

If you start your development server, you'll notice that access to all of these routes is currently unrestricted; nothing stops us from accessing the profile route, for instance.

# Managing Private Routes

Now, we need to perform verification of the user's privileges to access restricted content. To do that, we can create a `PrivateRoute` component that checks whether the user is logged in (`!isLoggedIn()`) and, if so, displays the restricted component containing private data:

```
// src/components/private-route.js
import React from "react"
import { navigate } from "gatsby"
import { isLoggedIn } from "../services/auth"

const PrivateRoute = ({ component: Component, location, ...rest }) => {
  if (!isLoggedIn() && location.pathname !== `/app/login`) {
    navigate("/app/login")
    return null
  }
  return <Component {...rest} />
}

export default PrivateRoute
```

Our next step is to add the private route to our `Router` in *src/pages/app.js* so it uses the `PrivateRoute` component instead:

```
// src/pages/app.js
import React from "react"
import { Router } from "@reach/router"

import Layout from "../components/layout"
import PrivateRoute from "../components/private-route"  ❶
import Profile from "../components/profile"
import Login from "../components/login"

const App = () => (
  <Layout>
    <Router>
      <PrivateRoute path="/app/profile" component={Profile} />  ❷
      <Login path="/app/login" />
    </Router>
  </Layout>
)

export default App
```

❶ Import the component.

❷ Replace the profile route with our `PrivateRoute` component.

## Providing Privileged Data to Routes

Though we now have our client-only routes in place, further refactoring is required for us to be able to view the privileged data as an authenticated user. To start, we'll need to modify the navigation bar component (*src/components/nav.js*) in order to distinguish between what's displayed to an authenticated user versus an unauthenticated user:

```
// src/components/nav.js
import React from "react"
import { Link, navigate } from "gatsby" ❶
import { getUser, isLoggedIn, logout } from "../services/auth"

export default function Nav() {
  let greetingMessage = "" ❷
  if (isLoggedIn()) {
    greetingMessage = `Hello ${getUser().name}`
  } else {
    greetingMessage = "You are not logged in"
  }
  return (
    <div
      style={{
        display: "flex",
        flex: "1",
        justifyContent: "space-between",
        borderBottom: "1px solid #d1c1e0",
      }}
    >
      <span>{greetingMessage}</span> ❸
      <nav>
        <Link to="/">Home</Link>
        {` | `}
        <Link to="/app/profile">Profile</Link> ❹
        {` | `}
        {isLoggedIn() ? ( ❺
          <a
            href="/"
            onClick={event => {
              event.preventDefault()
              logout(() => navigate(`/app/login`))
            }}
          >
            Logout
          </a>
        ) : null}
      </nav>
    </div>
  )
}
```

❶ A few additional dependencies are required: namely the `navigate` method from Gatsby and the `getUser`, `isLoggedIn`, and `logout` methods from *src/services/auth.js*.

❷ Add a new variable called `greetingMessage` to replace the string "You are not logged in." When the user is logged in, they receive a greeting message containing their username. Otherwise, they see the "You are not logged in" message.

❸ Replace the placeholder string "You are not logged in" with `greetingMessage`.

❹ Replace the placeholder link for our profile route so it points to the route */app/profile* instead.

❺ Perform another `isLoggedIn` check to verify that the user is logged in. If so, a "Logout" link will display; otherwise no link will display.

We also need to refactor our index page and our profile component to reflect these changes. Our index page will either allow the user to log in or, if already logged in, to navigate to their profile:

```
// src/pages/index.js
import React from "react"
import { Link } from "gatsby"  ❶
import { getUser, isLoggedIn } from "../services/auth"

import Layout from "../components/layout"

export default function Home() {
  return (
    <Layout>
      <h1>Hello {isLoggedIn() ? getUser().name : "world"}!</h1>
      <p>
        {isLoggedIn() ? (  ❷
          <>
            You are logged in, so check your{" "}
            <Link to="/app/profile">profile</Link>
          </>
        ) : (
          <>
            You should <Link to="/app/login">log in</Link> to see restricted
            content
          </>
        )}
      </p>
    </Layout>
  )
}
```

❶ Add the required dependencies, including Gatsby's `<Link />` component and the `getUser` and `isLoggedIn` methods from our authentication service.

❷ Provide a check of `isLoggedIn` that determines whether a user sees a link to their profile as an authenticated user or a link to log in as an unauthenticated user.

The changes we need to make to our profile component are merely to display our privileged information. When our one and only user is logged in, they'll see their account details:

```
// src/components/profile.js
import React from "react"
import { getUser } from "../services/auth" ❶

const Profile = () => (
  <>
    <h1>Your profile</h1>
    <ul>
      <li>Name: {getUser().name}</li> ❷
      <li>Email: {getUser().email}</li>
    </ul>
  </>
)
export default Profile
```

❶ Import the `getUser` method from our authentication service.

❷ Add the profile information returned by that method.

Now, when we start our development server, we can see our Gatsby site from the perspective of an unauthenticated user (Figure 8-7), a user who is logging in (Figure 8-8), and our sole user, Ahmed, after logging in (username `ahmed`, password `pass`; Figure 8-9).

Authentication is a common feature request for Gatsby developers. Gatsby has a bevy of resources available, including a simple authentication example (*https://oreil.ly/Rk0C2*), an example email application (*https://oreil.ly/gyFOH*), and the open source Gatsby store (*https://oreil.ly/ISDAS*). The Gatsby ecosystem has resources for integrations with Auth0 (*https://oreil.ly/btDN6*), Firebase (*https://oreil.ly/BrV8O*), and Netlify Identity (*https://oreil.ly/rFwJC*).

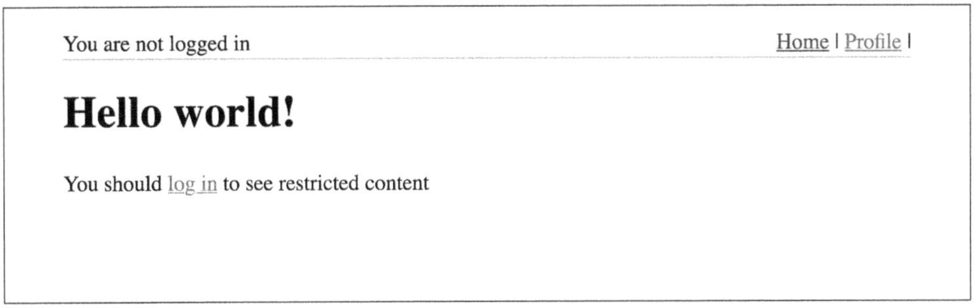

*Figure 8-7. Our authentication-enabled Gatsby site from the perspective of an unauthenticated user*

*Figure 8-8. Our authentication-enabled Gatsby site from the perspective of an unauthenticated user about to log in*

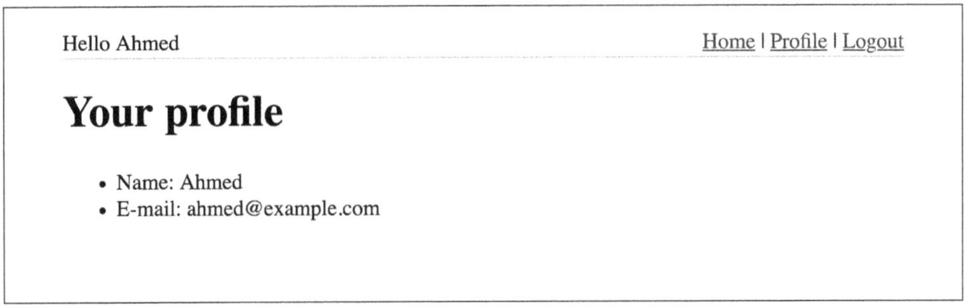

*Figure 8-9. Our authentication-enabled Gatsby site from the perspective of an authenticated user*

There you have it! Though this examination of authentication dispensed with any integration with a real-world authentication service, you can see how Gatsby operates as a bridge between a data source and an authentication service—which could be part of the same system—to serve restricted content in a graceful way without sacrificing security.

# Conclusion

Over the course of this chapter, we've explored how to implement various data-driven features in Gatsby: namely site search, commenting, blog taxonomy, pagination, RSS feeds, and user authentication. Unlike the use cases we examined in Chapter 3, these requirements obligated us to work with the Gatsby data layer, and in particular with the GraphQL API within Gatsby. In the process, we touched on many of the concepts covered in the intervening chapters, including programmatic page creation and working with Markdown.

Armed not only with the data-driven features we've inspected over the last several chapters but also the examples demonstrated in this chapter, we can now move on to some of the most important emerging elements in the Gatsby ecosystem: Gatsby themes and Gatsby recipes, both of which are important to the higher-level management of Gatsby codebases and implementations and can accelerate many of the time-consuming procedures involved in boilerplate setup and dependency management.

# PART III

# Extending Gatsby

# CHAPTER 9

# Gatsby Plugins and Starters

There are many ways to extend Gatsby sites to incorporate additional functionality or to provide kickstarters for faster development. In particular, plugins and starters are crucial for offering additional capabilities beyond the scope of what Gatsby supplies out of the box. Like Gatsby themes, which we'll cover in Chapter 10, plugins and starters can both be installed entirely from the Gatsby CLI. In addition to officially supported plugins that represent common use cases, there are many community-supported plugins and starters available on the Gatsby website. We've already seen several examples of both in this book, but we haven't yet covered how to make your own.

In this chapter, we'll explore not only how to create Gatsby plugins and starters, but also how to make them available to other interested developers by publishing them. In addition to tailor-made starters, I'll show you how to make your own source plugins, which are responsible for retrieving data from other sources, and transformer plugins, which transform data so Gatsby can work with it.

## Creating Gatsby Starters

As we covered earlier in the book, *starters* in Gatsby are boilerplate example projects that Gatsby developers can employ to spin up a new site for rapid development. So far in this book, we've covered three extremely common starters used frequently by Gatsby practitioners as foundations for new sites: gatsby-starter-hello-world, gatsby-starter-default, and gatsby-starter-blog.

There are countless other starters available in Gatsby's Starter Library (*https://oreil.ly/ FXMVf*), which Gatsby recommends developers of starters browse for inspiration and to ensure that a starter doesn't already exist that handles their specific use case. In the coming sections, we'll discuss how to initialize a starter project, enable configuration of your starter, assess performance and accessibility considerations, and finally, license, test, and release your completed starter implementation.

# Gatsby Starter Requirements

Every Gatsby starter must contain all of the files and directories listed in Table 9-1 within its source code in order to be installable as a starter.

*Table 9-1. Gatsby starter file requirements*

| File/Directory | Description |
| --- | --- |
| README.md | A file that instructs developers how to install and configure the project, as well as providing any other pertinent information such as available features, project structure, tips and advice, and how to contribute |
| package.json | A file listing all of the project's Gatsby dependencies and scripts, and any other required JavaScript dependencies |
| gatsby-config.js | A file containing configuration data and a list of additional plugins required by the starter |
| src/pages | A directory for Gatsby page components, which must include at least one JavaScript file named *index.js* |
| static | A directory containing static assets that will not be processed, such as a *favicon.ico* file |
| .gitignore | A manifest file indicating to Git which files and directories should be excluded from source control management, such as the *node_modules* directory, Gatsby *.cache* and *public* directories, and environment variable *.env* files |
| .prettierrc (optional) | An optional configuration file for Prettier, a JavaScript library for linting and formatting JavaScript for Gatsby development |
| LICENSE | A file containing a relevant license for your starter (Gatsby recommends a license file containing the BSD Zero Clause License (*https://oreil.ly/4dr4c*)) |

In addition to these requirements, there are some best practices that Gatsby starters should follow to be both discoverable and useful for developers. Your Gatsby starters should be:

*Located at a stable URL*
    Without a single, stable URL where the starter is available, such as a GitHub repository or NPM package page, developers won't be able to discover your starter or use it in their own sites.

*Open source*
    Though many developers write closed-source Gatsby plugins for their employers, for a Gatsby starter to be usable by any developer, it needs to have a permissive open source license.

*Configurable*
    The best starters are those that are optimized to accept a variety of configuration settings in its Gatsby configuration file.

*Performant*

Like Gatsby itself, Gatsby starters should endeavor to maximize their use of Gatsby's performance optimizations to keep loading times minimal.

*Web-accessible*

To provide equitable user experiences for disabled people, Gatsby starters should be evaluated not just for their performance but also for their accessibility.

Remember from our first discussion of Gatsby starters in Chapter 2 that they can be installed by executing a command adhering to the following template, where *site-name* is the name of the generated Gatsby site and *starter-url* is the location of the starter:

```
$ gatsby new site-name starter-url
```

Here's an example of a typical command to install the default starter:

```
$ gatsby new my-gatsby-site \
  https://github.com/gatsbyjs/gatsby-starter-default
```

As long as your starter is available in a publicly available source code management provider such as GitHub or GitLab, it's installable.

## Enabling Starter Configuration

Because the Gatsby configuration file is often the primary entry point for Gatsby developers upon coming across a new starter, it's important to leverage metadata in that configuration wherever possible. Some of the most essential metadata you may wish to have starter users configure includes:

*Site title*

The site title is probably the most frequently overridden configuration in a starter's configuration file.

*Author details*

Many Gatsby starters additionally allow for key information such as the site author's name, contact information, and a brief bio.

*Site description*

For SEO purposes, it's best to include a description of the site that can be used to identify it more expressively to users.

In addition, starters that connect with external data sources or third-party services may wish to derive much of this configuration from a source plugin, declared as a dependency in the Gatsby configuration file. And because starters can be reused as themes (discussed in more detail in the next chapter), including a Gatsby theme file for configuration can provide developers using your starter with even more power off the shelf. In short, starters are excellent opportunities to demonstrate to other developers how to satisfy common requirements of Gatsby.

## Starter Performance and Accessibility

Starter performance is an important consideration, particularly for developers specifically leveraging the framework for its speed. To ensure your starter adheres as closely to performance best practices as possible, it's strongly recommended to use tools such as Lighthouse or WebPageTest to assess the performance of your starter and to offer recommendations to starter users about how to deal with site performance concerns.

> Lighthouse (*https://oreil.ly/uPNGm*) and WebPageTest (*https://oreil.ly/u5NSi*) both provide documentation concerning usage and configuration.

Ensuring starters are web-accessible for people with disabilities is another issue relevant to user experience. The following best practices can help improve the overall accessibility of your starter:

*Color contrast*
> Most sites on the web lack adequate color contrast for users with low vision or colorblindness. WebAIM provides recommendations for implementing color contrast that adhere to Web Content Accessibility Guidelines (WCAG) 2 standards (*https://oreil.ly/0e7sw*).

*Keyboard focus indicators*
> Many users cannot use a mouse to navigate content and must instead use a keyboard to navigate Gatsby pages, whether due to tremors or a motor disability. WebAIM provides recommendations for keyboard accessibility adhering to WCAG 2 guidelines (*https://oreil.ly/LIAti*).

*Alternative text*
> All images and other visual media in your Gatsby starter should have alternative text available that describes the asset in words. WebAIM provides recommendations for alternative text according to WCAG 2 recommendations (*https://oreil.ly/gtmEr*).

*Semantic HTML use*
> Structuring your markup semantically is crucial for users who use alternative methods to access content. Retaining the semantic value of HTML is also important for SEO. WebAIM provides recommendations for semantic HTML (*https://oreil.ly/Cb6pq*) conforming to WCAG 2.

*Accessible forms*
> Form inputs must be labeled, and forms should be both fillable and navigable via the keyboard. WebAIM provides recommendations for accessible forms conforming to WCAG 2 (*https://oreil.ly/oFELN*).

Because the markup you manipulate in the form of JSX elements in Gatsby is typically not representative of the markup that will appear in the browser and be presented to users, it's best to test both your starter's performance and its accessibility in conditions that approximate the experience of real-world users. This means performing a production-ready build of your starter and evaluating it in context.

> For additional resources about ensuring the accessibility of your starter, consult the A11y Project (*https://oreil.ly/HqWKW*), WebAIM (*https://webaim.org*), and the Deque Systems article "Accessibility Tips in Single-Page Applications" (*https://oreil.ly/h4fx2*).

# Licensing, Testing, and Releasing Starters

Because Gatsby starters behave just like normal Gatsby projects, you can install a starter and take no further action besides executing `gatsby develop` (to spin up a local development server) or `gatsby build` (to perform a full build). If you're building your starter by executing `gatsby build`, execute `gatsby serve` to ensure your starter functions according to your vision in a production environment.

Gatsby recommends that starters contain the BSD Zero Clause License (0BSD) due to its greater permissiveness than the more commonplace MIT License, whose verbiage may make it less appealing for starters that will be used by many different developers.

> More information about the BSD Zero Clause License (*https://oreil.ly/HPBW7*), MIT License (*https://oreil.ly/dyAzz*), and other licenses is available on ChooseALicense.com (*https://chooseali cense.com*).

Once your starter is publicly available in a location such as GitHub, you can add it to the Gatsby Starter Library, where you can tag it with keywords such as `drupal` or `csv` to make it even more discoverable by the larger Gatsby community. Before you add your starter to the library, however, ensure that the `gatsby new` command works with your new starter to avoid any unexpected surprises after release.

Information about how to add your starter to the Gatsby Starter Library is available in the Community Contributions (*https://oreil.ly/eFju6*) section of the Gatsby documentation.

# Creating Gatsby Plugins

As we've seen throughout this book, *plugins* are the primary method of extending Gatsby's functionality with additional features. In technical terms, plugins are Node.js packages that are installed as dependencies and configured in the Gatsby configuration file. For developers who need a variety of capabilities, they can provide just the right mix of functionality for a powerful Gatsby site.

In the coming sections, we'll talk about how to create a plugin and make it configurable before moving on to specific types of plugins that differ in their behavior.

## Plugin Nomenclature

Gatsby plugins you create must adhere to the naming conventions of other Gatsby plugins for Gatsby to recognize them. These naming conventions are outlined in Table 9-2, where * represents a wildcard.

*Table 9-2. Gatsby plugin naming conventions*

| Convention | Example | Description |
| --- | --- | --- |
| gatsby-source-* | gatsby-source-sanity | Use source plugin nomenclature if your plugin loads data from an external data source, third-party source, or local filesystem. |
| gatsby-transformer-* | gatsby-transformer-remark | Use transformer plugin nomenclature if your plugin converts data from a particular format (e.g., YAML or CSV) into a Gatsby-manipulable JavaScript object. |
| gatsby-{plugin}-* | gatsby-remark-images | Use nested plugin nomenclature if your plugin is a dependency for an existing plugin by prefixing the plugin name with the name of the plugin it depends upon. This is required if you wish to include a plugin in the options configuration of another plugin. |
| gatsby-theme-* | gatsby-theme-blog | Use Gatsby theme nomenclature for Gatsby themes, which are treated as plugins. |
| gatsby-plugin-* | gatsby-plugin-* | Use generic plugin nomenclature for generic plugins that don't fit into any of the previous categories. |

## Initializing a New Plugin Project

Every plugin requires a *package.json* file containing metadata about the plugin. NPM also employs this file to display information about the plugin on its dedicated package page. Because all generic plugins, at their core, are JavaScript packages manipulable

by NPM, to create one you can simply initialize a new JavaScript package by executing the following commands:

```
$ gatsby new gtdg-ch9-plugin gatsbyjs/gatsby-starter-default
$ cd gtdg-ch9-plugin
$ mkdir plugins && cd plugins
$ mkdir gatsby-plugin-hello-world && cd gatsby-plugin-hello-world
$ npm init
```

The NPM CLI will then provide a series of selectable options in the terminal to store initial values that are necessary for your *package.json* file. For this example, set gatsby-plugin-hello-world as the name and *index.js* as the entry point.

As we'll see in the next section, plugins can serve as implementations of core Gatsby APIs (Gatsby Node APIs, Gatsby Browser APIs, Gatsby SSR APIs) by means of their respective files (*gatsby-node.js, gatsby-browser.js, gatsby-ssr.js*). Within the *gatsby-node.js* file inside our plugin (*plugin/gatsby-plugin-hello-world*), we can implement the createPage, createResolvers, and sourceNodes APIs, all of which manipulate (or create) a given data node in Gatsby.

The most common API that generic plugins utilize is the Gatsby Node API, which we cover in detail in Chapter 14. It facilitates operations like the following, which are common requirements of generic and other types of plugins:

- Load API keys to issue requests.
- Issue requests against APIs.
- Create Gatsby data nodes according to the API response.
- Create individual pages programmatically using created nodes.

As you can see, in addition to performing programmatic page creation through custom code in our Gatsby site's *gatsby-node.js* file, we can undertake the same processes in the context of a plugin.

 Gatsby also makes available a starter for creating plugins, gatsby-starter-plugin (*https://oreil.ly/ZxVSE*), with some information already prepopulated.

## Plugin Configuration with Options

As we've seen in various Gatsby plugins we've explored throughout this book so far, many plugins provide *configuration options* that are managed by developers to customize how they function within a Gatsby site. For source plugins, this might mean configuring the data source by providing a URL and access token. For other plugins, it might mean configuring how images are processed or how Markdown is transformed.

### Accessing and passing plugin configuration options

In the Gatsby configuration file, a typical plugin object (required so that Gatsby recognizes the plugin) contains a `resolve` string (the plugin name). Optionally, the plugin object can also contain an `options` object that exposes available configuration. Consider the following example of a "hello world" plugin, which accepts three options:

```
// gatsby-config.js
module.exports = {
  plugins: [
    {
      resolve: `gatsby-plugin-hello-world`,
      options: {
        optionA: `Hello world`,
        optionB: true,
        greeting: `Hello world`,
      }
    },
  ],
}
```

This allows Gatsby developers to provide arbitrary configuration that is then leveraged by the plugin to perform further work. A Gatsby plugin can access three Gatsby APIs from within its code:

- Gatsby Node API (*gatsby-node.js*)

- Gatsby Browser API (*gatsby-browser.js*)

- Gatsby Server-Side Rendering (SSR) API (*gatsby-ssr.js*)

Suppose that the objective of our plugin is to display a `console.log` message in the terminal containing our `greeting` option value, but only if `optionB` is `true`. We can leverage the Gatsby Node API by creating a new *gatsby-node.js* file specific to our plugin under the directory *plugins/gatsby-plugin-hello-world*:

```
// plugins/gatsby-plugin-hello-world/gatsby-node.js
exports.onPreInit = (_, pluginOptions) => {
  if (pluginOptions.optionB === true) {
    console.log(
      `Logging "${pluginOptions.greeting}" to the console`
    )
  }
}
```

Within the Gatsby Node API, the `onPreInit` API is among the first to execute when you run `gatsby develop` or `gatsby build`. We can now see how any plugin can access its configuration options through the *gatsby-config.js* file. But what kinds of options can be passed into a typical Gatsby configuration file for use by a plugin?

Fortunately, any JavaScript data type can be passed in to our Gatsby plugins as configuration options, as illustrated in Table 9-3.

Gatsby has no opinion on the name of the second argument provided in plugin code that implements the Gatsby Node, Browser, and SSR APIs. For instance, developers building Gatsby themes may wish to use `themeOptions` instead of `pluginOptions` as the argument name for readability.

*Table 9-3. Acceptable JavaScript types for Gatsby plugin configuration options*

| Data type | Example | Example plugin |
|---|---|---|
| Boolean | `true` | `gatsby-plugin-sharp` |
| String | `https://my-backend.io/graphql` | `gatsby-source-graphql` |
| Array | `['documents', 'products']` | `gatsby-source-mongodb` |
| Object | `{`<br>`    host: 'localhost',`<br>`    user: 'root',`<br>`    password: 'myPassword',`<br>`    database: 'user_records'`<br>`}` | `gatsby-source-mysql` |

Because Gatsby themes, which we cover in the next chapter, are considered by Gatsby to be a type of plugin, themes can receive configuration options from their surrounding site by exporting the contents of *gatsby-config.js* as a function rather than an object. We'll return to this in the next chapter, but suffice it to say for this discussion of configuration that plugins cannot do this.

### Validating plugin configuration with an options schema

It's one thing to allow configuration options that dictate how Gatsby plugins should customize their functionality to be passed in, but what happens when a developer provides option values that are not accepted because they are outside the scope of what the plugin can handle as an input? In other words, how do we *validate* the configuration options passed in to our plugins?

To validate plugin configuration options, we need an *options schema* against which the options can be compared. Options schemas aren't required for Gatsby plugins, but to enforce correct input and prevent any unintended outcomes, using them is a best practice. Gatsby makes available a `pluginOptionsSchema` API for defining options schemas.

To accomplish this, Gatsby uses Joi (*https://oreil.ly/hksH6*), a schema description language and validator for JavaScript. In our *gatsby-node.js* file, we create a new instance of Joi to return a `Joi.object` schema for the options we expect developers to pass in. Let's take a second look at the `gatsby-plugin-hello-world` plugin we built earlier:

```
// gatsby-config.js
module.exports = {
  plugins: [
    {
      resolve: `gatsby-plugin-hello-world`,
      options: {
        optionA: `Hello world`, // String
        optionB: true, // Boolean, optional
        greeting: `Hello world`, // String
      }
    },
  ],
}
```

Consider a scenario in which we want to ensure `optionA` and `greeting` are passed in as required options, but `optionB` is optional and not required. To accomplish this with Joi's schema definition approach, we can add our implementation of the `pluginOptionsSchema` API to *gatsby-node.js* within our plugin's directory:

```
// plugins/gatsby-plugin-hello-world/gatsby-node.js
exports.pluginOptionsSchema = ({ Joi }) => {
  return Joi.object({
    optionA: Joi.string().required().description(`Enables optionA.`),
    optionB: Joi.boolean().description(`Enables optionB.`),
    greeting: Joi.string().required().description(`Greeting logged to
        console.`),
  })
}
```

Enforcing a plugin options schema for Gatsby plugins ensures we cover all scenarios where plugin users supply unexpected input. Thanks to Joi's error handling, if a plugin user supplies options that don't adhere to the schema, upon the next execution of `gatsby develop` an error will display instructing them to correct their options accordingly. For example, consider a scenario where a plugin user passes in a Boolean instead of a string to `optionA`. The following error would appear:

```
ERROR #11331  PLUGIN

Invalid plugin options for "gatsby-plugin-hello-world":

- "optionA" must be a string
```

For comprehensive documentation about Joi, how it furnishes schemas, and how it validates data, see the Joi API documentation (*https://joi.dev/api*).

### Best practices for writing options schemas

Many of the best practices for writing options schemas come from Joi itself, but they apply to Gatsby plugins by extension. Gatsby's best practices for use of the `pluginOp tionsSchema` API include adding descriptions to options, setting default values for options, validating external access where needed, adding custom error messages where desired, and deprecating options in major version releases rather than silently deleting them from the schema. In this section, we'll cover each of these in turn.

First, be sure to *provide a description* for each plugin configuration option by using the `.description()` method to explain its rationale. A schema definition including descriptions can accelerate others' understanding of your schema and aid tooling that generates plugin options documentation based on the schema you define.

Second, it's important to *set default values* for configuration options that allow for fallbacks. For instance, in our "hello world" Gatsby plugin, we could define a default greeting value such that if the user doesn't provide a custom value, we default to a generic message. In Joi, this can be done with the `.default()` method, which will then result in the default greeting being logged in all plugin APIs when the user doesn't supply their own string value:

```
// plugins/gatsby-plugin-hello-world/gatsby-node.js
exports.pluginOptionsSchema = ({ Joi }) => {
  return Joi.object({
    optionA: Joi.string().required().description(`Enables optionA.`),
    optionB: Joi.boolean().description(`Enables optionB.`),
    greeting: Joi.string()
      .required()
      .default(`This is the default greeting.`)
      .description(`Greeting logged to console.`),
  })
}
```

Third, and particularly important for source plugins, *validate external access*. Whenever communicating with external services or third-party data sources, it's typically the case that we need to query APIs that we don't manage. Because of the risk involved in relying on external APIs, it's important to validate asynchronously the user's ability to access the API, which is possible through Joi's `.external()` method. By providing more descriptive errors earlier in the process, you can quickly communicate to users that their credentials are invalid.

For example, consider a scenario where we need to write a source plugin that consumes content from a Contentful space (i.e., a content repository). Though `gatsby-source-contentful`'s plugin options schema is much more complicated than this contrived example suggests, you can see how we can perform access checks against Contentful directly within our Joi schema definition:

```
// plugins/gatsby-source-contentful-example/gatsby-node.js
exports.pluginOptionsSchema = ({ Joi }) => {
  return Joi.object({
    accessToken: Joi.string().required(),
    spaceId: Joi.string().required(),
    // Additional Contentful options.
  }).external(async pluginOptions => {
    try {
      await contentful
        .createClient({
          space: pluginOptions.spaceId,
          accessToken: pluginOptions.accessToken,
        })
        .getSpace()
    } catch (err) {
      throw new Error(
        `Cannot access Contentful space "${pluginOptions.spaceId}" with the
        provided access token. Double-check it is correct and try again!`
      )
    }
  })
}
```

Fourth, it's a best practice in plugin options schemas to *add informative custom error messages* in cases where validation fails for a specific field. Joi includes a `.messages()` method with which plugin developers can overwrite error messages for particular error types. For instance, given a Joi error type of `any.required`, which indicates that a `.required()` invocation has failed, we could provide a custom error message for our required `optionA` value as follows:

```
// plugins/gatsby-plugin-hello-world/gatsby-node.js
exports.pluginOptionsSchema = ({ Joi }) => {
  return Joi.object({
    optionA: Joi.string()
      .required()
      .description(`Enables optionA.`)
      .messages({
        // Override the error message if .required() fails.
        "any.required": `"optionA" needs to be defined as true or false.`,
      }),
    optionB: Joi.boolean().description(`Enables optionB.`),
    greeting: Joi.string().required().description(`Greeting logged to
        console.`),
  })
}
```

Fifth, it's important to *deprecate obsolete options* once they're no longer required by your plugin in a new major version release. However, users may be confused if the new major version of your plugin lacks an option they had previously in their plugin configuration. Due to the potential for cryptic error messages that don't indicate that a plugin option is no longer present in the schema, Joi offers a `.forbidden()` method that Gatsby plugin authors should use to indicate that the option is no longer necessary. In addition, it's a best practice to include a custom error message that indicates the deprecation. Consider a scenario where we deprecate `optionA` as a plugin option:

```
// plugins/gatsby-plugin-hello-world/gatsby-node.js
exports.pluginOptionsSchema = ({ Joi }) => {
  return Joi.object({
    optionA: Joi.string()
      .required()
      .description(`Enables optionA.`)
      .forbidden()
      .messages({
        // Override the error message if .forbidden() fails.
        "any.unknown": `"optionA" is no longer supported. Use "optionB"
                       instead.`,
      }),
    optionB: Joi.boolean().description(`Enables optionB.`),
    greeting: Joi.string().required().description(`Greeting logged to
      console.`),
  })
}
```

Because Gatsby developers of any background could be making use of your plugin in their own Gatsby sites, it's important to not only document your options schema clearly but to provide an excellent developer experience that carries through version releases of your plugins. Adhering to these best practices will ensure a favorable experience for those who are eager to use the plugin you've contributed to the Gatsby ecosystem.

For a full accounting of the available error types in Joi's `.mes sages()` method, consult the Joi API documentation (*https:// oreil.ly/gq1VG*).

## Performing unit testing on options schemas

Because plugins are commonly used by a wide variety of developers, it's important to perform unit testing on the options schema to verify that it behaves as you expect. The Gatsby ecosystem offers an official package specifically for unit testing various configuration possibilities and how they validate against an options schema. To perform unit testing on your options schema, install the `gatsby-plugin-utils` package:

```
# If using NPM
$ npm install --dev gatsby-plugin-utils

# If using Yarn
$ yarn add --dev gatsby-plugin-utils
```

The --dev flag will ensure this developer-facing tooling is not included as a user-facing dependency. Now, within the plugin directory you can create a new directory, _tests_, containing a *gatsby-node.js* file that will perform your unit tests against the Gatsby Node API.

To write a unit test, you can use the testPluginOptionsSchema function available in the gatsby-plugin-utils package together with a test runner like Jest (*https://jestjs.io*) (see Chapter 11 for more on Jest). This function consists of two parameters: the plugin's Joi schema definition and an example options object to test with. It returns an object containing an isValid Boolean set to true or false based on the test's success, in addition to an errors array that contains any error messages thrown as the validation fails. Here's an example of how we can apply unit testing to our recently created Gatsby plugin using Jest:

```
// plugins/gatsby-plugin-hello-world/__tests__/gatsby-node.js
import { testPluginOptionsSchema } from "gatsby-plugin-utils"
import { pluginOptionsSchema } from "../gatsby-node"

describe(`pluginOptionsSchema`, () => {
  it(`should invalidate incorrect options`, async () => {
    const options = {
      optionA: undefined, // Should be a string
      optionB: `I am a string`, // Should be a Boolean
      greeting: 3.14159, // Should be a string
    }
    const { isValid, errors } = await testPluginOptionsSchema(
      pluginOptionsSchema,
      options
    )

    expect(isValid).toBe(false)
    expect(errors).toEqual([
      `"optionA" is required`,
      `"optionB" must be a string`,
      `"greeting" must be a string`,
    ])
  })

  it(`should validate correct options`, async () => {
    const options = {
      optionA: false,
      optionB: `12345`,
      greeting: `Hello world`,
    }
```

```
    const { isValid, errors } = await testPluginOptionsSchema(
      pluginOptionsSchema,
      options
    )

    expect(isValid).toBe(true)
    expect(errors).toEqual([])
  })
})
```

Performing unit testing on options schemas is always a best practice, especially when your plugin will be used by the Gatsby community and developers who seek robust, well-tested plugins to depend on in their implementations.

 For more information about Jest, consult the Jest documentation (*https://jestjs.io*).

Now that we've covered options schemas and plugin configuration, which are concepts that apply to every Gatsby plugin, we can turn our attention to the initial steps required to create each and every plugin, regardless of type. In "Publishing and Maintaining Plugins" on page 308, we'll explore how to release and maintain Gatsby plugins for community use.

## Interacting with Gatsby Lifecycle APIs

Let's take a look at an example using the Gatsby plugin we created earlier. In the following example *gatsby-node.js* file, our plugin implements the `sourceNodes` lifecycle API as a function. To avoid complexity, we've hardcoded the data we need as opposed to performing a request:

```
// plugins/gatsby-plugin-hello-world/gatsby-node.js
exports.sourceNodes = ({ actions, createNodeId, createContentDigest }) => {
  const nodeData = {
    title: "Sample Node",
    description: "Here is a sample node!",
  }
  const newNode = {
    ...nodeData,
    id: createNodeId("SampleNode-testid"), ❶
    internal: {
      type: "SampleNode",
      contentDigest: createContentDigest(nodeData), ❷
    },
  }
  actions.createNode(newNode)
}
```

❶ Create a new node entitled "Sample Node" based on the `title` parameter.

❷ If this process works, a new top-level field, `allSampleNode`, will be made available in our GraphQL schema and by extension our GraphQL API internal to Gatsby once we restart the development server.

As you can see, this plugin implements the `sourceNodes` API to create a new node as functionality beyond what Gatsby core offers. Over the course of creating plugins, you'll interact with a variety of Gatsby Node APIs like `sourceNodes` to realize the functionality your plugins provide.

# Creating Source Plugins

As we saw in Chapter 5, source plugins are Gatsby plugins that have to do with sourcing data from an external database, a third-party service, or a local filesystem. In this section, we'll walk through how to create a rudimentary source plugin that consumes an API.

Source plugins retrieve data from remote sources or local filesystems and expose them through Gatsby's GraphQL API as nodes. In the process, source plugins are therefore responsible for translating remote or local data into a format that Gatsby, and by extension Gatsby developers, can understand. Remember that there are no limitations to populating your Gatsby site with data from multiple source plugins, including multiple source plugins of the same type.

## Initializing Projects for Source Plugin Development

If there isn't a source plugin that matches your use case or fulfills your requirements, it's time to consider creating one of your own, which you can optionally distribute to the wider Gatsby community and by contributing it to the plugin ecosystem. In this walkthrough, we'll use an example API to keep things as simple as possible and create a source plugin whose goal is to provide content for a blog.

To demonstrate as many of the available features in source plugins as possible, our source plugin will:

- Issue requests to an API.
- Convert response data into Gatsby nodes.
- Connect certain nodes to enable relationships between blog post authors and blog posts.
- Accept plugin configuration options.

- Optimize images recorded as URLs so we can process them with `gatsby-image` (or, if building a Gatsby v3 plugin, `gatsby-plugin-image`).

To start, let's use Gatsby's "Hello World" starter to spin up a new example website:

```
$ gatsby new gtdg-ch9-example-site gatsbyjs/gatsby-starter-hello-world
```

Because our Gatsby site will depend on our source plugin, we need to create a separate Gatsby project for the source plugin. Fortunately, Gatsby provides a plugin starter to quickly spin up a new plugin project:

```
$ gatsby new gtdg-ch9-source-plugin gatsbyjs/gatsby-starter-plugin
```

Now, you should have two directories at the same level named gtdg-ch9-example-site and *gtdg-ch9-source-plugin*.

Though we could create our source plugin directly within the plugins directory of the Gatsby site we just created, maintaining it as a separate project makes releasing later on easier, in addition to benefiting from separate source control management. Remember that directly adding plugin code to your plugins directory makes it a local plugin.

If you open the *gtdg-ch9-source-plugin* directory, you'll see the following files represented. This is the typical structure of an initial source plugin project:

```
/gtdg-ch9-source-plugin
├── .gitignore
├── gatsby-browser.js
├── gatsby-node.js
├── gatsby-ssr.js
├── index.js
├── LICENSE
├── package.json
├── package-lock.json
└── README.md
```

Most of our modifications to this plugin starter will be located in the *gatsby-node.js* file, as that is where we leverage the Gatsby Node API to populate our GraphQL API with the data we retrieve. The *gatsby-node.js* file allows us to customize and extend the default Gatsby build process at various points.

## Installing the Source Plugin

In order to test that our source plugin is working as intended, we need to install it into our example Gatsby site, given that we didn't introduce it as a local plugin earlier. Because Gatsby recognizes only those plugins identified within the *gatsby-config.js* file, we need to include it there in our example site. Our plugin is not intended for public use yet, so we'll use the `require.resolve()` method, which is used for plugins located elsewhere in the filesystem, to add it:

```
// gtdg-ch9-example-site/gatsby-config.js
module.exports = {
  plugins: [
    {
      resolve: require.resolve(`../gtdg-ch9-source-plugin`),
    },
  ],
}
```

 For more information about referring to local plugins that aren't yet installable because they're still under development, consult the Gatsby documentation on creating local plugins (*https://oreil.ly/ wFYv9*). You can include a plugin by using require.resolve() and a filepath, or by using npm link or yarn link to reference the package.

Now, when we run gatsby develop within the *gtdg-ch9-example-site* directory, we can see our new plugin represented within the terminal output as Gatsby loads plugins found in the Gatsby configuration file. Note that because we have not modified any code within the plugin itself, especially the *package.json* file, it still carries the name gatsby-starter-plugin:

```
$ gatsby develop
success open and validate gatsby-configs - 0.032s
success load plugins - 0.076s
Loaded gatsby-starter-plugin
success onPreInit - 0.017s
```

This output is printed to the terminal thanks to the prepopulated contents of the *gatsby-node.js* file in our source plugin, which contains the following onPreInit function:

```
// gtdg-ch9-source-plugin/gatsby-node.js
exports.onPreInit = () => console.log("Loaded gatsby-starter-plugin")
```

Now that we can confirm our plugin is appearing as expected in the gatsby develop terminal output, we can start getting our hands dirty with the plugin code itself.

## Creating GraphQL Nodes

Before we turn our attention to the actual querying process that results in the retrieval of data from an external source, let's use some hardcoded data within our file to populate some initial nodes in Gatsby's GraphQL API. To do this, we need to invoke the createNode Gatsby function within the sourceNodes API in the plugin's *gatsby-node.js* file, just as we did for programmatic page creation. Replace the contents of *gatsby-node.js* with the following code:

```
// gtdg-ch9-source-plugin/gatsby-node.js
const POST_NODE_TYPE = `Post`

exports.sourceNodes = async ({ ❶
  actions,
  createContentDigest,
  createNodeId,
  getNodesByType,
}) => {
  const { createNode } = actions

  const data = {
    posts: [
      { id: 1, description: `My first post!` },
      { id: 2, description: `Post number two!` },
    ],
  }

  // Recurse through data and create Gatsby nodes.
  data.posts.forEach(post =>
    createNode({ ❷
      ...post,
      id: createNodeId(`${POST_NODE_TYPE}-${post.id}`),
      parent: null,
      children: [],
      internal: { ❸
        type: POST_NODE_TYPE,
        content: JSON.stringify(post),
        contentDigest: createContentDigest(post),
      },
    })
  )

  return
}
```

❶  We implement the Gatsby sourceNodes API, one of Gatsby's Node APIs run during the build process, and extract certain Gatsby utilities that make it easy for us to create nodes, such as createContentDigest and createNodeId.

❷  We store our hardcoded data as an array and recurse our way through it, invoking the createNode method for each individual post represented in the array.

❸  We provide certain required fields, such as a node identifier and a content digest, which includes the entirety of the content (in this case, the value of post). Gatsby uses these to track nodes whose content has changed.

If you've been following along with this example, you can now run gatsby develop and point your browser to *https://localhost:8000/___graphql* to test our GraphQL API in GraphiQL. Issue the following query:

```
{
  allPost {
    edges {
      node {
        id
        description
      }
    }
  }
}
```

You'll receive a response that consists of our hardcoded data, as illustrated in Figure 9-1.

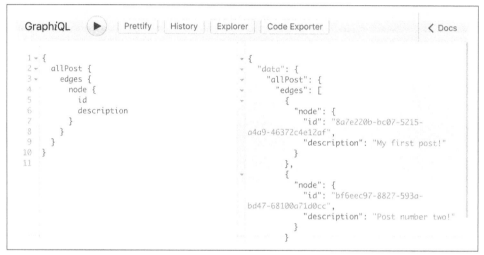

*Figure 9-1. The result of our* `allPost` *query containing the two hard-coded blog posts represented in our custom source plugin*

Unfortunately, we're not quite done, as the data represented in the GraphQL API's response is static and hardcoded. In other words, it doesn't reflect the sort of dynamic, evolving data we often need to query from APIs in the wild. But now that the source plugin logic to make those posts available to the GraphQL API is working as intended, we can narrow our focus to solely the querying process.

## Querying and Sourcing Remote Data

Because there are so many approaches to querying data from external providers, including not just distinct API specifications but also distinct request clients, it's far outside the scope of this book to cover the full range of libraries available (like `http.get`, `axios`, and `node-fetch`, all of which are built into Node.js).

In this walkthrough, we'll use a GraphQL client, which enables our source plugin to query the external API. Optionally, our source plugin could also use subscriptions to preemptively update the data in the site when the data present in the API changes. To provide a query mechanism, we'll use an Apollo client, which we'll need to install into our source plugin project along with the other dependencies. Remember, you can retrieve your data however you see fit using the APIs and libraries most appropriate for your requirements.

To follow along, within the *gtdg-ch9-source-plugin* directory, execute the following command:

```
$ npm install apollo-cache-inmemory apollo-client apollo-link \
    apollo-link-http apollo-link-ws apollo-utilities graphql graphql-tag \
    node-fetch ws subscriptions-transport-ws
```

If you open your source plugin's *package.json* file, you'll see a dependencies section at the end of the file that lists all of the packages you just installed.

### Configuring an Apollo client to retrieve data

Now, let's reopen that *gatsby-node.js* file within our in-progress source plugin to begin integrating our upstream GraphQL API into our project so that we can use our Apollo client as a means to query authentic, not just hardcoded, data. First, we'll need to import the dependencies we just introduced. We do this at the start of the file, before the first const statement:

```
// gtdg-ch9-source-plugin/gatsby-node.js
const { ApolloClient } = require("apollo-client")
const { InMemoryCache } = require("apollo-cache-inmemory")
const { split } = require("apollo-link")
const { HttpLink } = require("apollo-link-http")
const { WebSocketLink } = require("apollo-link-ws")
const { getMainDefinition } = require("apollo-utilities")
const fetch = require("node-fetch")
const gql = require("graphql-tag")
const WebSocket = require("ws")

const POST_NODE_TYPE = `Post`

exports.sourceNodes = async ({
// ...
```

The next step in our process is to add code that will configure our Apollo client to subscribe to data in the upstream GraphQL API. This code comes before we write a sourceNodes function and after we define the POST_NODE_TYPE constant, such that our plugin's *gatsby-node.js* file now appears as follows:

```
// gtdg-ch9-source-plugin/gatsby-node.js
const { ApolloClient } = require("apollo-client")
const { InMemoryCache } = require("apollo-cache-inmemory")
```

```
const { split } = require("apollo-link")
const { HttpLink } = require("apollo-link-http")
const { WebSocketLink } = require("apollo-link-ws")
const { getMainDefinition } = require("apollo-utilities")
const fetch = require("node-fetch")
const gql = require("graphql-tag")
const WebSocket = require("ws")

const POST_NODE_TYPE = `Post`

const client = new ApolloClient({
  link: split(
    ({ query }) => {
      const definition = getMainDefinition(query)
      return (
        definition.kind === "OperationDefinition" &&
        definition.operation === "subscription"
      )
    },
    new WebSocketLink({
      uri: `ws://localhost:4000`,
      // or `ws://gatsby-source-plugin-api.glitch.me/`
      options: {
        reconnect: true,
      },
      webSocketImpl: WebSocket,
    }),
    new HttpLink({
      uri: "http://localhost:4000",
      // or `https://gatsby-source-plugin-api.glitch.me/`
      fetch,
    })
  ),
  cache: new InMemoryCache(),
})

exports.sourceNodes = async ({
// ...
```

We'll run through the entire file at the end of the process step by step, but for now, the most important thing to understand from the preceding sample code is that we've made available an Apollo client, a type of request client for GraphQL APIs. This Apollo client allows us to invoke query methods to retrieve data from the configured data source. This example demonstrates both local and deployed versions of the upstream GraphQL API.

For more information about the Apollo packages we installed to make our client work, consult the Apollo documentation (*https:// oreil.ly/N6vBl*). Apollo is just one approach to querying data sources, and it's a best practice to leverage what works most optimally for your requirements.

## Querying data from the API

Now that we have our Apollo client configured in adherence with our requirements, we can issue queries on behalf of Gatsby to retrieve the information we need. Our next step is to replace the hardcoded information within our sourceNodes function by defining a GraphQL query and passing it to the Apollo client.

Replace the following section of code:

```
// gtdg-ch9-source-plugin/gatsby-node.js
exports.sourceNodes = async ({
  actions,
  createContentDigest,
  createNodeId,
  getNodesByType,
}) => {
  const { createNode } = actions

  const data = {
    posts: [
      { id: 1, description: `My first post!` },
      { id: 2, description: `Post number two!` },
    ],
  }
}
```

with the code shown here—in the process, we'll retrieve the other information we need for each post from the API:

```
// gtdg-ch9-source-plugin/gatsby-node.js
exports.sourceNodes = async ({
  actions,
  createContentDigest,
  createNodeId,
  getNodesByType,
}) => {
  const { createNode } = actions

  const { data } = await client.query({
    query: gql`
      query {
        posts {
          id
          description
          slug
          imgUrl
          imgAlt
```

```
        author {
          id
          name
        }
      }
      authors {
        id
        name
      }
    }
  `,
})
```

Before we move forward, let's take stock of the current state of the *gatsby-node.js* file in preparation for introducing another node to represent authors from the API. It should contain the following:

```
// gtdg-ch9-source-plugin/gatsby-node.js
const { ApolloClient } = require("apollo-client")
const { InMemoryCache } = require("apollo-cache-inmemory")
const { split } = require("apollo-link")
const { HttpLink } = require("apollo-link-http")
const { WebSocketLink } = require("apollo-link-ws")
const { getMainDefinition } = require("apollo-utilities")
const fetch = require("node-fetch")
const gql = require("graphql-tag")
const WebSocket = require("ws")

const POST_NODE_TYPE = `Post`

const client = new ApolloClient({ ❶
  link: split(
    ({ query }) => {
      const definition = getMainDefinition(query)
      return (
        definition.kind === "OperationDefinition" &&
        definition.operation === "subscription"
      )
    },
    new WebSocketLink({
      uri: `ws://gatsby-source-plugin-api.glitch.me/`,
      options: {
        reconnect: true,
      },
      webSocketImpl: WebSocket,
    }),
    new HttpLink({
      uri: `https://gatsby-source-plugin-api.glitch.me/`,
      fetch,
    })
  ),
  cache: new InMemoryCache(),
```

```
})

exports.sourceNodes = async ({
  actions,
  createContentDigest,
  createNodeId,
  getNodesByType,
}) => {
  const { createNode } = actions

  const { data } = await client.query({ ❷
    query: gql`
      query {
        posts {
          id
          description
          slug
          imgUrl
          imgAlt
          author {
            id
            name
          }
        }
        authors {
          id
          name
        }
      }
    `,
  })

  // Recurse through data and create Gatsby nodes.
  data.posts.forEach(post =>
    createNode({ ❸
      ...post,
      id: createNodeId(`${POST_NODE_TYPE}-${post.id}`),
      parent: null,
      children: [],
      internal: {
        type: POST_NODE_TYPE,
        content: JSON.stringify(post),
        contentDigest: createContentDigest(post),
      },
    })
  )

  return
}
```

❶ Here we configure a new Apollo client, thanks to the availability of the Apollo dependencies we installed earlier.

❷ We define a new GraphQL query that is used by the Apollo client to issue a request against the upstream GraphQL API our Gatsby site relies on.

❸ We create Gatsby nodes by recursing through the API response and extracting the information we need to populate each individual node.

Now, let's account for the authors, which need to be represented as nodes in their own right within Gatsby:

```
// gtdg-ch9-source-plugin/gatsby-node.js
const { ApolloClient } = require("apollo-client")
const { InMemoryCache } = require("apollo-cache-inmemory")
const { split } = require("apollo-link")
const { HttpLink } = require("apollo-link-http")
const { WebSocketLink } = require("apollo-link-ws")
const { getMainDefinition } = require("apollo-utilities")
const fetch = require("node-fetch")
const gql = require("graphql-tag")
const WebSocket = require("ws")

const POST_NODE_TYPE = `Post`
const AUTHOR_NODE_TYPE = `Author`  ❶

const client = new ApolloClient({
  link: split(
    ({ query }) => {
      const definition = getMainDefinition(query)
      return (
        definition.kind === "OperationDefinition" &&
        definition.operation === "subscription"
      )
    },
    new WebSocketLink({
      uri: `ws://gatsby-source-plugin-api.glitch.me/`,
      options: {
        reconnect: true,
      },
      webSocketImpl: WebSocket,
    }),
    new HttpLink({
      uri: `https://gatsby-source-plugin-api.glitch.me/`,
      fetch,
    })
  ),
  cache: new InMemoryCache(),
})

exports.sourceNodes = async ({
```

```
    actions,
    createContentDigest,
    createNodeId,
    getNodesByType,
}) => {
  const { createNode } = actions

  const { data } = await client.query({
    query: gql`
      query {
        posts {
          id
          description
          slug
          imgUrl
          imgAlt
          author {
            id
            name
          }
        }
        authors {
          id
          name
        }
      }
    `,
  })

  // Recurse through data and create Gatsby nodes.
  data.posts.forEach(post =>
    createNode({
      ...post,
      id: createNodeId(`${POST_NODE_TYPE}-${post.id}`),
      parent: null,
      children: [],
      internal: {
        type: POST_NODE_TYPE,
        content: JSON.stringify(post),
        contentDigest: createContentDigest(post),
      },
    })
  )
  data.authors.forEach(author =>
    createNode({ ❷
      ...author,
      id: createNodeId(`${AUTHOR_NODE_TYPE}-${author.id}`),
      parent: null,
      children: [],
      internal: {
        type: AUTHOR_NODE_TYPE,
        content: JSON.stringify(author),
```

```
            contentDigest: createContentDigest(author),
        },
    })
  )

  return
}
```

❶ First, we add another constant representing the type name of the `Author` nodes. This should remain consistent across the site, just like the type name of the `Post` nodes.

❷ Second, we include a recursive handler for author nodes that runs through each individual author retrieved from the API and generates a new Gatsby node for each one.

We can test this again by issuing the following query in GraphiQL after running `gatsby develop` on our example site and navigating to *https://localhost:8000/____graphql*:

```
{
  allPost {
    edges {
      node {
        id
        description
        imgUrl
      }
    }
  }
  allAuthor {
    edges {
      node {
        id
        name
      }
    }
  }
}
```

The result of our GraphQL query is illustrated in Figure 9-2.

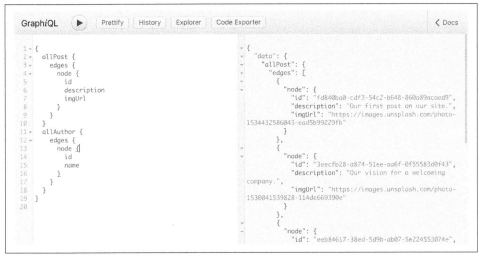

*Figure 9-2. The result of our GraphQL query after introducing handling for* `Author` *nodes in addition to* `Post` *nodes*

## Optimizing remote images and creating remote File nodes

A common requirement of Gatsby sites is to retrieve image URLs from an external resource before optimizing those remote images for use in Gatsby by means of the `gatsby-image` component. In our scenario, as you can see in Figure 9-2, each post in the upstream API is accompanied by an `imgUrl` field containing an Unsplash image URL. With source plugins, we can preemptively retrieve the images we need and optimize them to prevent any impact on performance due to fetching remote images.

To optimize images based on their remote URLs, we need to add `File` nodes to Gatsby to represent each of the remote images. Then, we need to install the required plugins to both find the images and provide needed data for the `gatsby-image` component. Let's start by installing one source plugin we know we'll need from the get-go into our custom source plugin:

```
$ npm install gatsby-source-filesystem
```

Note that our in-progress source plugin has `gatsby-source-filesystem` as a dependency. It's perfectly appropriate to have plugins, even source plugins, depend on one another in hierarchically complex ways. Next, we need to implement another Gatsby API, `onCreateNode`. For each node created in Gatsby, we want to check if it was a post and, if so, create a file based on the `imgUrl` field therein.

To do this, we need to first add the Gatsby helper we need to create the `File` node, namely `createRemoteFileNode`, within our dependency imports at the top of the file:

```
// gtdg-ch9-source-plugin/gatsby-node.js
const { ApolloClient } = require("apollo-client")
```

```
const { InMemoryCache } = require("apollo-cache-inmemory")
const { split } = require("apollo-link")
const { HttpLink } = require("apollo-link-http")
const { WebSocketLink } = require("apollo-link-ws")
const { getMainDefinition } = require("apollo-utilities")
const fetch = require("node-fetch")
const gql = require("graphql-tag")
const WebSocket = require("ws")
const { createRemoteFileNode } = require(`gatsby-source-filesystem`)
```

Then we'll export a new onCreateNode function at the bottom of the file and invoke the createRemoteFileNode helper inside for each creation of a Post node:

```
// gtdg-ch9-source-plugin/gatsby-node.js
exports.onCreateNode = async ({
  node, // i.e. the just-created node
  actions: { createNode },
  createNodeId,
  getCache,
}) => {
  if (node.internal.type === POST_NODE_TYPE) { ❶
    const fileNode = await createRemoteFileNode({ ❷
      // The remote image URL for which to generate a node.
      url: node.imgUrl,
      parentNodeId: node.id,
      createNode,
      createNodeId,
      getCache,
    })

    if (fileNode) {
      node.remoteImage___NODE = fileNode.id ❸
    }
  }
}
```

❶ Each time we create a node with createNode, we check if the node is a Post.

❷ If it is, then we create a remote node, which returns a fileNode.

❸ We define the new File node's id value as a field named remoteImage___NODE.

In Gatsby, this last step establishes a clear relationship between this field and the File node, thus allowing File node fields to be queried via this relationship from the Post node. In Gatsby parlance, this is known as *inference*. If we were to exclude the ___NODE suffix, which establishes the relationship with the Post nodes, we would solely be able to retrieve the identifier of remoteImage through the following query:

```
{
  allPost {
    edges {
```

```
      node {
        remoteImage
        # Returns a UUID.
      }
    }
  }
}
```

But that's not very helpful when we need information from the `File` node to which the identifier found in the `Post` node refers. Adding the `___NODE` suffix to establish the needed relationship across different node types enables us to query the related node's internals as well:

```
{
  allPost {
    edges {
      node {
        remoteImage {
          id
          relativePath
        }
      }
    }
  }
}
```

The final state of our source plugin's *gatsby-node.js* file is as follows:

```
// gtdg-ch9-source-plugin/gatsby-node.js
const { ApolloClient } = require("apollo-client")
const { InMemoryCache } = require("apollo-cache-inmemory")
const { split } = require("apollo-link")
const { HttpLink } = require("apollo-link-http")
const { WebSocketLink } = require("apollo-link-ws")
const { getMainDefinition } = require("apollo-utilities")
const fetch = require("node-fetch")
const gql = require("graphql-tag")
const WebSocket = require("ws")
const { createRemoteFileNode } = require(`gatsby-source-filesystem`)

const POST_NODE_TYPE = `Post`
const AUTHOR_NODE_TYPE = `Author`

const client = new ApolloClient({
  link: split(
    ({ query }) => {
      const definition = getMainDefinition(query)
      return (
        definition.kind === "OperationDefinition" &&
        definition.operation === "subscription"
      )
    },
    new WebSocketLink({
```

```
        uri: `ws://gatsby-source-plugin-api.glitch.me/`,
        options: {
          reconnect: true,
        },
        webSocketImpl: WebSocket,
      }),
      new HttpLink({
        uri: `https://gatsby-source-plugin-api.glitch.me/`,
        fetch,
      })
  ),
  cache: new InMemoryCache(),
})

exports.sourceNodes = async ({
  actions,
  createContentDigest,
  createNodeId,
  getNodesByType,
}) => {
  const { createNode } = actions

  const { data } = await client.query({
    query: gql`
      query {
        posts {
          id
          description
          slug
          imgUrl
          imgAlt
          author {
            id
            name
          }
        }
        authors {
          id
          name
        }
      }
    `,
  })

  // Recurse through data and create Gatsby nodes.
  data.posts.forEach(post =>
    createNode({
      ...post,
      id: createNodeId(`${POST_NODE_TYPE}-${post.id}`),
      parent: null,
      children: [],
      internal: {
```

```
        type: POST_NODE_TYPE,
        content: JSON.stringify(post),
        contentDigest: createContentDigest(post),
      },
    })
  )

  data.authors.forEach(author =>
    createNode({
      ...author,
      id: createNodeId(`${AUTHOR_NODE_TYPE}-${author.id}`),
      parent: null,
      children: [],
      internal: {
        type: AUTHOR_NODE_TYPE,
        content: JSON.stringify(author),
        contentDigest: createContentDigest(author),
      },
    })
  )

  return
}

exports.onCreateNode = async ({
  node, // i.e. the just-created node
  actions: { createNode },
  createNodeId,
  getCache,
}) => {
  if (node.internal.type === POST_NODE_TYPE) {
    const fileNode = await createRemoteFileNode({
      // The remote image URL for which to generate a node.
      url: node.imgUrl,
      parentNodeId: node.id,
      createNode,
      createNodeId,
      getCache,
    })
    if (fileNode) {
      node.remoteImage___NODE = fileNode.id
    }
  }
}
```

We now have local image files generated from the remote image URLs, and we've established the association between our images and posts. But we still haven't done anything with the transformer plugins we need to make these images available for use with the gatsby-image component.

We cover schema customization in Gatsby at length in Chapter 13. If you'd like an early look at Gatsby's schema customization APIs, you can also consult the Gatsby documentation on the subject (*https://oreil.ly/ag86r*).

### Transforming File nodes with Sharp plugins

As we saw in our examination of the `gatsby-image` component in Chapter 7, Sharp plugins are what make the optimization of Gatsby v2 images possible during build-time compilation. We can leverage those same plugins to apply optimizations to the images we now have available in our filesystem. Because these transformations occur at build time, we need to install Sharp dependencies in the example site (i.e., within the *gtdg-ch9-example-site* directory), unless we plan to package them with the source plugin. Execute the following command to install the required dependencies:

```
$ npm install gatsby-plugin-sharp gatsby-transformer-sharp
```

Then, add both plugins to the Gatsby configuration file:

```
// gatsby-config.js
module.exports = {
  plugins: [
    {
      resolve: require.resolve(`../gtdg-ch9-source-plugin`),
    },
    `gatsby-plugin-sharp`,
    `gatsby-transformer-sharp`,
  ],
}
```

Now that we've installed the Sharp plugins, we know that they'll execute after the source plugin has populated our GraphQL API. In the process, the Sharp plugins will transform each `File` node into an optimized image set and incorporate fields for the optimized images within the `childImageSharp` field. The `gatsby-transformer-sharp` plugin seeks out `File` nodes with appropriate image extensions (like *.jpg* and *.png*), creates the optimized versions, and generates the GraphQL fields on our behalf.

Now, when we start up the development server, we'll be able to access those optimized images through GraphiQL with the following query, whose response is illustrated in Figure 9-3:

```
{
  allPost {
    edges {
      node {
        remoteImage {
          childImageSharp {
            id
```

```
              }
            }
          }
        }
      }
    }
  }
```

```
GraphiQL  ▶  Prettify  History  Explorer  Code Exporter        ‹ Docs

 1 ▾ {                                      ▾ {
 2 ▾   allPost {                            ▾   "data": {
 3 ▾     edges {                            ▾     "allPost": {
 4 ▾       node {                                   "edges": [
 5 ▾         remoteImage {                  ▾         {
 6             childImageSharp {            ▾           "node": {
 7               id                         ▾             "remoteImage": {
 8             }                                           "childImageSharp": {
 9           }                                               "id": "2ca9529f-
10         }                                   87db-5203-8275-42c8e683594a"
11       }                                                 }
12     }                                                 }
13   }                                                 },
14                                                     {
                                            ▾           "node": {
                                            ▾             "remoteImage": {
                                                          "childImageSharp": {
```

*Figure 9-3. The response for the preceding query, showing the individual Sharp-optimized images now available as part of each* `Post` *node*

## Establishing Foreign Key Relationships

We've successfully established relationships between two nodes that have interrelated information, namely our `Post` and `File` nodes, through the `___NODE` suffix in our *gatsby-node.js* file. But we also need to draw similar referential relationships between `Post` and `Author` nodes so that we can generate author pages listing the blog posts they've contributed. In order to link those two nodes together, we need to establish a *foreign key relationship*.

The quickest way to establish such a relationship is to customize the GraphQL schema to account for the association between the `Post` and `Author` types. Through an implementation of the `createSchemaCustomization` API, you can define how a node's data structures look and, in the process, link a node to other nodes to establish a relationship.

Add the following `createSchemaCustomization` function to the bottom of the source plugin's *gatsby-node.js* file:

```
// gtdg-ch9-source-plugin/gatsby-node.js
exports.createSchemaCustomization = ({ actions }) => {
  const { createTypes } = actions
  createTypes(`
```

```
    type Post implements Node {
      id: ID!
      slug: String!
      description: String!
      imgUrl: String!
      imgAlt: String!
      # Create relationships between Post and File nodes
      # for optimized images.
      remoteImage: File @link ❶
      # Create relationships between Post and Author nodes.
      author: Author @link(from: "author.name" by: "name") ❷
    }
    type Author implements Node {
      id: ID!
      name: String!
    }`
  )
}
```

❶ We ask Gatsby to find a `remoteImage` field within `Post` nodes and link that field
to a `File` node using the identifier in the `File` node.

❷ We create an `Author` node type by instructing Gatsby to link together
`author.name` on the `Post` node and `name` on an arbitrary `Author` node in the
`Author` type. As you can see, we can use this `name` field or any arbitrary field to
link these node types together, as opposed to an `id`.

Because we've now established the relationship between `Post` nodes and `File` nodes
at the schema level rather than upon node creation, which is more brittle, we can
remove the ___NODE suffix from the *gatsby-node.js* file and rely instead on this schema
customization. Here is the complete version of our source plugin's *gatsby-node.js* file:

```
// gtdg-ch9-source-plugin/gatsby-node.js
const { ApolloClient } = require("apollo-client")
const { InMemoryCache } = require("apollo-cache-inmemory")
const { split } = require("apollo-link")
const { HttpLink } = require("apollo-link-http")
const { WebSocketLink } = require("apollo-link-ws")
const { getMainDefinition } = require("apollo-utilities")
const fetch = require("node-fetch")
const gql = require("graphql-tag")
const WebSocket = require("ws")
const { createRemoteFileNode } = require(`gatsby-source-filesystem`)

const POST_NODE_TYPE = `Post`
const AUTHOR_NODE_TYPE = `Author`

const client = new ApolloClient({
  link: split(
    ({ query }) => {
```

```
      const definition = getMainDefinition(query)
      return (
        definition.kind === "OperationDefinition" &&
        definition.operation === "subscription"
      )
    },
    new WebSocketLink({
      uri: `ws://gatsby-source-plugin-api.glitch.me/`,
      options: {
        reconnect: true,
      },
      webSocketImpl: WebSocket,
    }),
    new HttpLink({
      uri: `https://gatsby-source-plugin-api.glitch.me/`,
      fetch,
    })
  ),
  cache: new InMemoryCache(),
})

exports.sourceNodes = async ({
  actions,
  createContentDigest,
  createNodeId,
  getNodesByType,
}) => {
  const { createNode } = actions

  const { data } = await client.query({
    query: gql`
      query {
        posts {
          id
          description
          slug
          imgUrl
          imgAlt
          author {
            id
            name
          }
        }
        authors {
          id
          name
        }
      }
    `,
  })

  // Recurse through data and create Gatsby nodes.
```

```
    data.posts.forEach(post =>
      createNode({
        ...post,
        id: createNodeId(`${POST_NODE_TYPE}-${post.id}`),
        parent: null,
        children: [],
        internal: {
          type: POST_NODE_TYPE,
          content: JSON.stringify(post),
          contentDigest: createContentDigest(post),
        },
      })
    )

    data.authors.forEach(author =>
      createNode({
        ...author,
        id: createNodeId(`${AUTHOR_NODE_TYPE}-${author.id}`),
        parent: null,
        children: [],
        internal: {
          type: AUTHOR_NODE_TYPE,
          content: JSON.stringify(author),
          contentDigest: createContentDigest(author),
        },
      })
    )

    return
}

exports.onCreateNode = async ({
  node, // i.e. the just-created node
  actions: { createNode },
  createNodeId,
  getCache,
}) => {
  if (node.internal.type === POST_NODE_TYPE) {
    const fileNode = await createRemoteFileNode({
      // The remote image URL for which to generate a node.
      url: node.imgUrl,
      parentNodeId: node.id,
      createNode,
      createNodeId,
      getCache,
    })
    if (fileNode) {
      node.remoteImage = fileNode.id  ❶
    }
  }
}
```

```
exports.createSchemaCustomization = ({ actions }) => { ❷
  const { createTypes } = actions
  createTypes(`
    type Post implements Node {
      id: ID!
      slug: String!
      description: String!
      imgUrl: String!
      imgAlt: String!
      # Create relationships between Post and File nodes
      # for optimized images.
      remoteImage: File @link
      # Create relationships between Post and Author nodes.
      author: Author @link(from: "author.name" by: "name")
    }
    type Author implements Node {
      id: ID!
      name: String!
    }`
  )
}
```

❶ Remove the aforementioned suffix.

❷ Add schema customization.

Now, thanks to these foreign key relationships, we can issue the following query in GraphiQL to get a post's author and a post's remote image as part of the allPost query as opposed to in separate queries:

```
{
  allPost {
    edges {
      node {
        id
        author {
          name
        }
        remoteImage {
          id
        }
      }
    }
  }
}
```

The result of this query is shown in Figure 9-4.

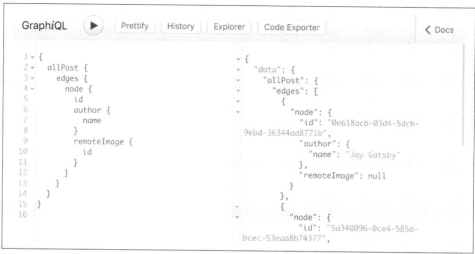

*Figure 9-4. The result of the preceding query in GraphiQL, demonstrating the ability to query related types in a single allPost query*

Now, you can use these GraphQL queries in conjunction with page and component queries to populate your pages with the necessary information, including data from the external GraphQL API as well as optimized versions of the remote Unsplash images. A typical page query for a blog's home page might look something like this:

```
{
  allPost {
    edges {
      node {
        id
        slug
        description
        imgAlt
        author {
          id
          name
        }
        remoteImage {
          id
          childImageSharp {
            id
            fluid {
              ...GatsbyImageSharpFluid
            }
          }
        }
      }
    }
  }
}
```

## Using Plugin Options to Allow Customization

In "Creating Gatsby Plugins" on page 266, I introduced the concept of plugin options to allow plugin users to customize the plugin configuration according to their needs. Source plugins also need to be configured, including information such as the arbitrary URL at which an external API or database is located.

Consider a scenario where our source plugin requires some additional option (say, optionC). To account for this, we can add an option to *gatsby-config.js* to pass the value in to the source plugin:

```
// gtdg-ch9-example-site/gatsby-config.js
module.exports = {
  plugins: [
    {
      resolve: require.resolve(`../gtdg-ch9-source-plugin`),
      options: {
        optionC: true,
      },
    },
    `gatsby-plugin-sharp`,
    `gatsby-transformer-sharp`,
  ],
}
```

Within our source plugin, to handle the plugin option appropriately, we can either introduce an options schema with validation or use it within the files we use to hook into Gatsby APIs, like our implementation of the sourceNodes API in *gatsby-node.js*:

```
// gtdg-ch9-source-plugin/gatsby-node.js
exports.sourceNodes = async ({
  actions,
  createContentDigest,
  createNodeId,
  getNodesByType
}, pluginOptions) => {
  const { createNode, touchNode, deleteNode } = actions
  console.log(pluginOptions.optionC) // true
}
```

Fortunately, plugin options work the same way across the board, whether you're building a generic, source, or transformer plugin.

> Enabling GraphQL subscriptions on your Apollo client is well outside the scope of this book, but the Gatsby documentation provides an exhaustive tutorial for proactively updating data with subscriptions (*https://oreil.ly/SzmAA*) as part of a longer walkthrough that covers the same material as this source plugin overview.

# Creating Transformer Plugins

*Transformer plugins* comprise the other class of plugins that operate on Gatsby's data layer. The most logical way to think about the relationship between source plugins and transformer plugins is as follows: if source plugins populate nodes with external data, then transformer plugins transform that data into new output nodes or new node fields in the same node.

Many Gatsby sites require both source and transformer plugins to function properly, as it's often the case that the data we receive from an external source isn't ready for use within the Gatsby GraphQL API. Due to this loose coupling between source and transformer plugins, it's eminently possible to create arbitrary but highly complex data transformation pipelines in the Gatsby context.

> For a comprehensive walkthrough of an end-to-end transformer plugin implementation process, consult the Gatsby documentation's how-to guide on creating a Remark transformer plugin (*https://oreil.ly/23qPX*).

## Reviewing an Example: gatsby-transformer-yaml

Just like other types of plugins, transformer plugins are typical NPM packages, containing a *package.json* file enumerating dependencies as well as a *gatsby-node.js* file where we can implement Gatsby Node APIs. One example of a transformer plugin that is common in the Gatsby community is `gatsby-transformer-yaml`, which accepts YAML nodes (e.g., a *.yml* file of media type `text/yaml`) and outputs JavaScript objects that represent the YAML data structure.

Let's work through a very rudimentary example of transformer plugins using the YAML-to-JavaScript example use case. To avoid the complexity of source plugins entirely, we'll use `gatsby-source-filesystem` to account for our untransformed YAML files as `File` nodes rather than an external service. Each YAML file looks like the following:

```
# src/data/sample.yml
- name: Toni Morrison
  description: Author of The Bluest Eye, Song of Solomon, and Beloved
- name: Alice Walker
  description: Author of The Color Purple, Meridian, and >>>
The Third Life of George Copeland
```

Given a collection of YAML files that resemble this one in structure, how can we transform these into JavaScript objects that Gatsby can understand and manipulate?

## Ensuring Needed Data Is Sourced

Because transformer plugins often work in tandem with source plugins, let's first make sure our `gatsby-source-filesystem` plugin is pulling appropriately from the local filesystem. If all of our YAML files are located in *src/data/* within our Gatsby site, we can execute the following to install `gatsby-source-filesystem`:

```
$ npm install gatsby-source-filesystem
```

In our Gatsby configuration file, we identify the relevant directory containing the YAML files to the source plugin:

```
// gatsby-config.js
module.exports = {
  plugins: [
    {
      resolve: `gatsby-source-filesystem`,
      options: {
        path: `./src/data/`,
      },
    },
  ],
}
```

As we know from our previous experiences with the `gatsby-source-filesystem` plugin, each of these files will then be exposed in the GraphQL API as `File` nodes and therefore can be queried as follows:

```
{
  allFile {
    edges {
      node {
        internal {
          type
          mediaType
          description
          owner
        }
      }
    }
  }
}
```

Once the sourcing process is complete, we now have a collection of `File` nodes that represent our YAML files. But Gatsby still cannot work with the data contained inside.

## Transforming Nodes

Just like with source plugins, we need to leverage Gatsby's Node APIs to conduct the needed data transformation within *gatsby-node.js*. We'll make use of the onCreate Node API, which is a lifecycle API traversed upon each `File` node's creation, to conduct the transformation for us and make the information available to GraphQL.

To start, we need to install several dependencies, including `js-yaml` and `lodash`:

```
$ npm install js-yaml lodash
```

To keep things simple, we'll write the plugin directly in the site's logic before extracting it out as a plugin later. Within the site's *gatsby-node.js* file, we'll add the following:

```
// gatsby-node.js
const jsYaml = require(`js-yaml`) ❶

exports.onCreateNode = async ({ node, loadNodeContent }) => { ❷
  function transformObject(object, id, type) { ❸
    const yamlNode = {
      ...object,
      id,
      children: [],
      parent: null,
      internal: {
        contentDigest: createContentDigest(object),
        type,
      },
    }
    createNode(yamlNode)
  }

  // Only handle nodes of mediaType `text/yaml`.
  if (node.internal.mediaType !== `text/yaml`) {
    return
  }
  const content = await loadNodeContent(node)
  const parsedContent = jsYaml.load(content) ❹
}
```

❶  Import the `js-yaml` library as a dependency. This will perform the conversion of YAML to JavaScript objects on our behalf.

❷  Implement the onCreateNode API to detect whether a `File` node is a YAML file.

❸  This is a transformation function that will serve as a helper function to parse the YAML files into Gatsby nodes that match their structure, creating a new `yaml` Node with each recursion.

❹ If the `File` node is a YAML file, perform the transformation by invoking `js-yaml.load()`.

## Establishing the Transformer Relationship

Next, we need to create the relationship between the parent `File` node and the child nodes (transformed YAML content) by using the `createParentChildLink` function. If we don't do this, Gatsby has no clue which transformed YAML nodes are associated with which `File` nodes sourced from the filesystem. The transformer relationship will center on the parent `File` node's id value, which we add to each `yamlNode` to forge the connection:

```
// gatsby-node.js
const jsYaml = require(`js-yaml`)

exports.onCreateNode = async ({ node, loadNodeContent }) => {
  function transformObject(object, id, type) {
    const yamlNode = {
      ...object,
      id,
      children: [],
      parent: node.id,  ❶
      internal: {
        contentDigest: createContentDigest(object),
        type,
      },
    }
    createNode(yamlNode)
    createParentChildLink({  ❷
      parent: node,
      child: yamlNode,
    })
  }

  // Only handle nodes of mediaType `text/yaml`.
  if (node.internal.mediaType !== `text/yaml`) {
    return
  }
  const content = await loadNodeContent(node)
  const parsedContent = jsYaml.load(content)
}
```

❶ Identify the parent of each transformed YAML object as the `File` node it was transformed from.

❷ Establish a link between the parent `File` node and the child transformed YAML node.

For other examples of transformation relationships, consult the source code for the `gatsby-transformer-remark` plugin (*https:// oreil.ly/ndXcF*) and the `gatsby-transformer-sharp` plugin (*https:// oreil.ly/LcF9w*).

## Creating New Nodes from Derived Data and Querying

Our final step is to generate new nodes based on the transformed data by iterating through each transformed YAML object within the `onCreateNode` function and invoking our transformation helper function where needed. We'll modify our *gatsby-node.js* file to look like the following:

```
// gatsby-node.js
const jsYaml = require(`js-yaml`)
const _ = require(`lodash`) ❶

exports.onCreateNode = async ({
  node,
  actions, ❷
  loadNodeContent,
  createNodeId,
  createContentDigest,
}) => {
  function transformObject(object, id, type) {
    const yamlNode = {
      ...object,
      id,
      children: [],
      parent: node.id,
      internal: {
        contentDigest: createContentDigest(object),
        type,
      },
    }
    createNode(yamlNode)
    createParentChildLink({
      parent: node,
      child: yamlNode,
    })
  }

  const { createNode, createParentChildLink } = actions ❸

  // Only handle nodes of mediaType `text/yaml`.
  if (node.internal.mediaType !== `text/yaml`) {
    return
  }
  const content = await loadNodeContent(node)
  const parsedContent = jsYaml.load(content)
```

```
    parsedContent.forEach( (object, i) => {  ❹
      transformObject(
        object,
        object.id ? object.id : createNodeId(`${node.id} [${i}] >>> YAML`),
        _.upperFirst(_.camelCase(`${node.name} Yaml`))
      )
    })
  }
```

❶  Import lodash as a dependency for its casing helper functions.

❷  Pull additional elements that we'll need later from the onCreateNode API, includ-
    ing actions, createNodeId, and createContentDigest.

❸  Extract the createNode and createParentChildLink functions from actions.

❹  Iterate through our transformed YAML objects to populate new nodes with
    them.

Now, we can query for our YAML directly within the Gatsby GraphQL API as
follows:

```
{
  allSampleYaml {
    edges {
      node {
        id
        name
        description
      }
    }
  }
}
```

 Transformations from one format to another can be time-
consuming and computationally expensive. To avoid having to
repeat the entire process for each build and avoid some of the
latency, we can employ Gatsby's global cache. For more information, consult the Gatsby documentation page about using the
Gatsby cache in transformer plugins (*https://oreil.ly/VImK5*).

# Publishing and Maintaining Plugins

Once you've created a plugin, whatever its type, it's time to consider releasing it to the Gatsby community so others can benefit from it. Of course, there is nothing stopping you from keeping your plugin private and using it locally, and many organizations leveraging Gatsby do just that with proprietary, closed-source plugins. However, given that Gatsby is an open source framework, it's in the best interests of the community and ecosystem to consider publishing and maintaining your plugin.

> The NPM documentation contains a guide to contributing packages to the NPM registry (*https://oreil.ly/jMqiT*), and the Gatsby documentation provides guides for required files in plugins (*https://oreil.ly/t7ZEj*) and a README template for contributing plugins to the community (*https://oreil.ly/BwXBP*).

## Submitting Plugins to the Gatsby Plugin Library

One of the easiest ways to ensure your plugin reaches a wider audience is to submit it to the Gatsby Plugin Library (*https://oreil.ly/Ye1Rx*), a public resource for Gatsby users seeking plugins that satisfy different requirements. Follow these steps to ensure your plugin is included:

1. Publish a package to the NPM registry.
2. Include any required files within your plugin repository—usually *package.json* and a Gatsby API file such as *gatsby-node.js*.
3. Add a `keywords` field to your plugin's *package.json* file, containing at minimum `gatsby` and `gatsby-plugin`. If your plugin is a theme (see the next chapter), also add `gatsby-theme`.
4. Add documentation for your plugin, including at minimum a README file.

Once Gatsby's official Algolia account reindexes all Gatsby plugins meant to be represented in the Plugin Library, you'll be able to find your plugin there and share the link with your team or others.

> If referring to an image for your plugin, be sure to use an absolute URL rather than a relative URL, as the information is used in various locations.

# Maintaining Plugins

Maintaining a plugin for the long haul can be difficult work. Open source maintenance is often a thankless job that is poorly compensated, if at all. Nonetheless, longterm maintenance is a core responsibility of plugin authors. Once the development work is complete, it's time to consider how to handle issues like security vulnerabilities, semantic versioning, and dependency updates that don't break Gatsby sites.

### Handling plugin patches and improvements

Gatsby, like many other JavaScript ecosystems, recommends semantic versioning to manage your releases. Though a full overview of semantic versioning is well outside the scope of this book, it's best to adhere to some best practices. The first public release of a plugin is often assigned version 0.1.0 or 1.0.0, the latter of which is generally reserved for the first stable release of a package.

When bugs are fixed or minor issues resolved, that generally results in a *patch release* (from 0.1.0 to 0.1.1 or 1.0.0 to 1.0.1). If you've added or modified features in the plugin, that is broadly considered grounds for a *minor release* (from 0.1.0 to 0.2.0 or 1.0.0 to 1.1.0). Finally, *major releases* are reserved for changes that break the API or disrupt backward compatibility.

> For more information about semantic versioning, consult *Semantic Versioning 2.0.0 (https://semver.org)*.

### Writing a README and documentation

The README file in your plugin repository should also be very clear about major version releases so your plugin users don't get confused. If you lack a separate documentation site, the README is your primary opportunity to give plugin users the rationales for changes to your plugin, working examples, and an account of how major version releases evolve the project.

Gatsby recommends performing spring cleaning of your plugin repository every so often to clear out older versions that are no longer needed. In the vast majority of cases, only the last few versions are required.

### Managing dependency versions

The Gatsby documentation recommends two distinct tools for verifying and managing dependency versions. In JavaScript ecosystems, dependency management can be particularly difficult, but projects like Version Lens (*https://oreil.ly/wBpxF*) for Visual

Studio Code and the `npm-check-updates` CLI (*https://oreil.ly/eoWTe*) offer useful introspection and automated management capabilities.

While Version Lens provides a tool to update dependencies directly from within your *package.json* file in your development tool, namely by displaying the latest version number available for a given package, using `npm-check-updates` offers a more active means of determining if any dependencies are obsolete. To use `npm-check-updates`, install the package and then execute the `ncu` command:

```
$ npm install -g npm-check-updates
$ ncu -u
```

Remember that the primary motivation for releasing a plugin to the community is to benefit those users in the community who need it. As such, it may also be a good idea to provide user support and example codebases for potential users. Gatsby, for instance, uses Discord as its primary conduit for community support. The more resources you have available for your users, the more likely they are to adopt your plugin and perhaps even contribute to it on their own time.

> For more information about dependency version management, consult the Version Lens documentation (*https://oreil.ly/AvsRy*) and `npm-check-updates` documentation (*https://oreil.ly/b4UUF*), respectively.

# Conclusion

Plugins are the primary way to extend functionality for any Gatsby site, while starters offer foundations on which other Gatsby developers can build. Generic, source, and transformer plugins serve as essential entry points for Gatsby developers looking to customize or add functionality. In addition, plugin options and options schemas undergird the configuration system in Gatsby, allowing for arbitrary settings to be enabled and disabled on a per-plugin basis.

Though source plugins are responsible for retrieving data and transformer plugins for converting data, the two classes of plugins share much more in common than it may seem. Plugin options work precisely the same way across both, as do the release and maintenance processes. This brings us to our next subject, Gatsby themes, which are a special type of plugin with some unusual quirks and features.

# CHAPTER 10

# Gatsby Themes

In the previous chapter, we looked at two ways to extend Gatsby functionality with plugins and starters. But these aren't the only means to extend Gatsby sites. *Themes* are a subset of Gatsby plugins that provide additional functionality through a distinct Gatsby configuration file. Because themes can encompass not only aesthetic differences but also additions to features like data sourcing and interface code, the name is a bit of a misnomer. One useful way to think of a Gatsby theme is as a Gatsby site that has its own configuration and can be installed into another Gatsby site.

In this chapter, we'll first look at themes in the context of the larger Gatsby ecosystem by comparing them to other ecosystem elements like plugins and starters. Then, we'll cover how to use a Gatsby theme in an existing site before directing our attention to how to create Gatsby themes from scratch. Finally, we'll end this chapter with an examination of two concepts that make themes in Gatsby unique: shadowing and composition.

## Gatsby Themes in Context

A theme in Gatsby is a special kind of plugin that contains its own *gatsby-config.js* and is responsible for providing prebuilt functionality, data sourced from external sources, and UI code. To create a Gatsby theme, all of the baseline default configuration (shared functionality, data sourcing, design elements, etc.) is abstracted out of a Gatsby site and converted into an installable package.

Since they behave just like other Gatsby plugins, themes can be provided through a registry (such as NPM), and other Gatsby sites that leverage a theme can manage it as just another dependency in the *package.json* file. While these characteristics distinguish themes from plugins and starters, it can sometimes be difficult for Gatsby developers to determine when it's appropriate to use a plugin, starter, or theme. Let's take a closer look at the differences.

## Differences from Plugins and Starters

In terms of maintenance, plugins and themes differ considerably from starters in that they can be released and updated as normal packages. Because starters are often immediately updated and diverge considerably from the source once installed, it's much more challenging to synchronize changes once they've begun to deviate in development. In fact, this limitation of starters was one of the primary motivators for offering themes in the first place. As such, themes are more flexible than starters. But what are the similarities and differences between plugins and themes?

When it comes to configuration, plugins and themes are similar in that both provide configuration options so that their consumers can apply arbitrary settings to them, to an extent much more powerful than with starters (which largely allow you to set only the name of the directory into which they will be installed and are configurable through only direct modification of code). Plugins and themes both enable *shadowing*, which allows Gatsby sites that use them to override a specific file with their own homegrown version of it, thus offering different behavior.

The most important difference between a plugin and a theme is that whereas a plugin is leveraged on its own in a Gatsby site, themes are capable of abstracting the functionality provided by multiple plugins into a single theme. In short, themes provide collections of plugins in addition to custom components. This means that you can install a single theme to access functionality across multiple plugins, whereas without themes, you would need to install plugins individually. While custom components in plugins are intended for use as is in a Gatsby site, custom components in themes are intended for use through shadowing, so that their functionality can be overridden and customized.

 The Gatsby documentation contains a page that comprehensively accounts for the differences between plugins, starters, and themes (*https://oreil.ly/GjgmU*) and a flowchart for developers choosing between them.

## Deciding Between Using and Creating a Theme

Before we turn to the actual usage and creation of themes, it's important to be able to make an educated decision about whether to leverage a preexisting theme that exists in the wider Gatsby ecosystem or to create a new theme from scratch. That decision making should include the following considerations:

- Consider using an existing theme if:

  — You already have an existing Gatsby site with considerable divergence from any available Gatsby starter, making it impossible to restore such a state.

  — You wish to rely on the theme's versioning and release management instead of rolling your own.

  — You plan to leverage multiple features on your site, but no starter exists in the wild with the right blend of functionality (use multiple themes instead).

- Consider creating a new theme if:

  — You plan to reuse similar features as a bundle of functionality repeated across and depended on by multiple Gatsby sites.

  — You wish to share your new Gatsby functionality with others.

# Using Gatsby Themes

If you've made the decision to use an existing Gatsby theme rather than creating one from scratch, you have a few options. You can either create a new site based on a theme, use a theme in an existing Gatsby site you've already implemented, or use multiple Gatsby themes in that site. We'll cover each of these approaches in turn in this section.

## Starting a New Site from a Theme

The fastest way to use an existing theme to spin up a new Gatsby site is to leverage a starter that is associated with the theme. For example, `gatsby-starter-blog-theme`, a Gatsby starter, is a theme starter for the `gatsby-theme-blog` theme. As opposed to a regular Gatsby starter, which we've seen multiple times throughout this book, a *theme starter* creates a new site that both installs and configures one or multiple Gatsby themes.

Creating a new Gatsby site based on a Gatsby theme starter involves precisely the same process as installing any other starter. For instance, to install the Gatsby blog theme starter, execute the following command:

```
$ gatsby new gtdg-ch10-using-themes gatsbyjs/gatsby-starter-blog-theme
```

Let's take a quick look at what happens inside the site after executing this command. First, as with any Gatsby site created from a starter, you'll see that some information is already prepopulated for you in the Gatsby configuration file:

```
// gatsby-config.js
module.exports = {
  plugins: [
    {
      resolve: "gatsby-theme-blog",
```

```
      options: {},
    },
  ],
  // Customize your site metadata:
  siteMetadata: {
    title: "My Blog Title",
    author: "My Name",
    description: "My site description...",
    siteUrl: "https://www.gatsbyjs.com/",
    social: [
      {
        name: "twitter",
        url: "https://twitter.com/gatsbyjs",
      },
      {
        name: "github",
        url: "https://github.com/gatsbyjs",
      },
    ],
  },
}
```

In addition, when you use the theme starter to create a new Gatsby blog, it will auto-matically scaffold example blog posts for use with your site, such as the one located at */content/posts/hello-world/index.mdx*:

```
---
title: Hello, world!
path: /hello-world
---
I'm an example post!
```

Now, when you run `gatsby develop`, you'll see a fully fledged blog in your local development server, which will update normally as you modify files in the codebase and save them. And whenever you need to update the theme to a new version due to a new release, you can do so by updating `gatsby-theme-blog`'s entry to that version in *package.json* (for example, changing ^3.0.0 to ^4.0.0 when that version is released):

```
// package.json
{
  "name": "gatsby-starter-blog-theme",
  "private": true,
  "version": "0.0.1",
  "scripts": {
    "develop": "gatsby develop",
    "start": "gatsby develop",
    "build": "gatsby build",
    "clean": "gatsby clean"
  },
  "license": "0BSD",
  "dependencies": {
```

```
    "gatsby": "^3.8.1",
    "gatsby-theme-blog": "^3.0.0",
    "react": "^17.0.2",
    "react-dom": "^17.0.2",
    "theme-ui": "0.7.3"
  }
}
```

and running the following to fetch the desired version:

```
$ npm install gatsby-theme-blog
```

 Though this section covered only gatsby-theme-blog and gatsby-starter-theme-blog, all Gatsby theme starters function this same way.

# Using a Theme in an Existing Site

As you saw in the previous section, while it's perfectly feasible to spin up a new Gatsby site based on a theme thanks to theme starters, it's often the case that you already have a Gatsby implementation in progress that can't benefit from a theme starter. In this scenario, you'll need to install a theme into a preexisting Gatsby site.

Fortunately, since Gatsby themes, like plugins, are simply Node.js packages at their core, you can use the normal approach to install dependencies to add the theme by executing the following in the root of your Gatsby site:

```
$ npm install gatsby-theme-blog
```

Just like plugins, Gatsby themes can also accept theme options for configuration. When you add gatsby-theme-blog to your *gatsby-config.js* file, for instance, you can configure under which base directory the blog posts are represented by passing in a basePath option, as seen in this example:

```
// gatsby-config.js
module.exports = {
  plugins: [
    {
      resolve: `gatsby-theme-blog`,
      options: {
        // basePath defaults to `/`.
        basePath: `/blog`,
      },
    },
  ],
}
```

Though `gatsby-theme-blog` is an example of a *public theme*, which is available on registries like NPM, it's perfectly appropriate to create *private themes* that remain proprietary and closed-source. NPM (*https://oreil.ly/AeGZD*) and the GitHub Package Registry (*https://oreil.ly/cy9wJ*) allow hosting of private themes.

## Using Multiple Gatsby Themes

One of the characteristics of Gatsby themes that makes them unique is their *composability*. Though theme composition is a topic deserving of its own examination, for now it's enough to know that the fact that Gatsby themes are composable means that you can install multiple themes in a single Gatsby site in much the same way you can install an arbitrary number of plugins.

One example of this in the Gatsby ecosystem is the `gatsby-starter-theme` project, which consists of two Gatsby themes composed together: `gatsby-theme-blog`, which we've already seen in this chapter, and `gatsby-theme-notes`, which is for bite-sized pieces of content that aren't blog posts in their own right. Creating a new site based on `gatsby-starter-theme`, which you can do with the following command, outputs a *gatsby-config.js* file with two prepopulated themes:

```
$ gatsby new gtdg-ch10-using-multiple-themes gatsbyjs/gatsby-starter-theme
```

In the following Gatsby configuration file, for example, `gatsby-theme-blog` is configured with its default settings, while `gatsby-theme-notes` accepts two theme options:

```
// gatsby-config.js
module.exports = {
  siteMetadata: {
    title: `Shadowed Site Title`,
  },
  plugins: [
    {
      resolve: `gatsby-theme-notes`,
      options: {
        mdx: true,
        basePath: `/notes`,
      },
    },
    // with gatsby-plugin-theme-ui, the last theme in the config
    // will override the theme-ui context from other themes
    { resolve: `gatsby-theme-blog` },
  ],
}
```

According to the theme options configured here, a blog will be available at the root URL (/), and notes will be available from */notes*.

For a comprehensive end-to-end tutorial that demonstrates how to use multiple themes together in a working Gatsby site, consult the Gatsby documentation (*https://oreil.ly/w6qy6*).

# Creating Gatsby Themes

It's often the case that no existing theme in the Gatsby ecosystem quite satisfies your requirements. If you're implementing multiple Gatsby sites that share a certain modicum of functionality based on a theme, it may be a good idea to write your own theme. In this section, we'll examine how to create new themes using Gatsby's theme workspace starter. We'll also look at common conventions for Gatsby themes, and how to convert starters into themes.

## Creating New Themes

Because Gatsby has a vested interest in the community contributing themes back into the ecosystem, it provides an official starter for creating themes from scratch known as `gatsby-starter-theme-workspace`. This starter can be used to scaffold a new theme alongside a site that you can use to try out the theme:

```
$ gatsby new gtdg-ch10-creating-themes gatsbyjs/gatsby-starter-theme-workspace
```

When you change directories into the codebase, you'll find a directory structure that looks like this, with an example site living alongside the theme directory:

```
.
├── example
│   ├── src
│   │   └── pages
│   │       └── index.js
│   ├── gatsby-config.js
│   ├── package.json
│   └── README.md
├── gatsby-theme-minimal
│   ├── gatsby-config.js
│   ├── index.js
│   ├── package.json
│   └── README.md
├── .gitignore
├── package.json
└── README.md
```

The Gatsby theme workspace starter produces two Yarn workspaces in order to ease the process of theme development. Leveraging Yarn workspaces allows Gatsby to manage two or more packages within a single directory (in this case our root folder). This means that we can maintain multiple themes and example sites within a single unified project, all while still enabling dependency updates to new versions, as Yarn continues to track the dependencies.

 You can also develop your theme as a local theme, using the same mechanism we used earlier to leverage local plugins. This would allow you to use techniques like yarn link and npm link, though Gatsby recommends using Yarn workspaces instead. For more information about the motivations behind using Yarn workspaces, consult the article "Setting Up Yarn Workspaces for Theme Development" (*https://oreil.ly/AJM07*) on the Gatsby blog.

To familiarize ourselves with this unusually structured codebase, let's inspect a few key elements: namely the *package.json* file, the */gatsby-theme-minimal* directory, and the */example* directory.

First let's take a look at *package.json*, in the root of the new project:

```
// gtdg-ch10-creating-themes/package.json
{
  "name": "gatsby-starter-theme-workspace",
  "private": true,
  "version": "0.0.1",
  "main": "index.js",
  "license": "MIT",
  "scripts": {
    "build": "yarn workspace example build"
  },
  "workspaces": ["gatsby-theme-minimal", "example"]
}
```

There are two things to notice here:

1. The build script leverages Yarn workspaces to build only the example site.

2. We have a new workspaces array that accounts for the example site and the in-progress scaffolded theme.

The */gatsby-theme-minimal* directory is where we'll be doing the bulk of our theme development, and inside we find three files besides *README.md*:

- *gatsby-config.js* is another Gatsby configuration file that represents the configuration for our theme, not for the project in general.

- *index.js* is the entry point for our theme; since all themes are technically plugins, Gatsby requires this entry point, even if it is empty, so it can treat the theme like a plugin.

- *package.json* lists the dependencies for our theme when installed by theme users and should include Gatsby as a peer dependency.

Finally, the /*example* directory contains a fully fledged Gatsby site that both installs and leverages the theme from its local directory, thus helping us avoid the back-and-forth friction of dependency management while we're developing a theme. Inside, we find two salient items besides *README.md* and *package.json*:

- *gatsby-config.js* is yet another Gatsby configuration file that represents the configuration for our example site (such as plugins extraneous to our theme), not for the theme or project in general.
- The /*src* directory contains the source code for any Gatsby pages (and added components), just like in a normally functioning independent Gatsby site.

 For a comprehensive end-to-end tutorial on creating themes, consult the Egghead course on authoring Gatsby themes (*https://oreil.ly/bNDfw*) and its accompanying walkthrough in the Gatsby documentation (*https://oreil.ly/go7KS*).

# Gatsby Theme Conventions

Because Gatsby themes are relative newcomers to the Gatsby ecosystem, having only emerged in the last several years as of this writing, theme conventions are still solidifying. Nonetheless, there are certain best practices that all Gatsby themes should follow to ensure their proper usage. In this section, we'll cover naming conventions, separation of concerns, theme customization, and semantic versioning for Gatsby themes.

### Nomenclature and required directories

Without exception, the name of every Gatsby theme must begin with the prefix `gatsby-theme-`. This is to ensure that Gatsby can effectively identify theme packages when it performs build-time compilation.

As we saw from the example of `gatsby-theme-blog`, some themes are responsible for scaffolding directories to give guidance to theme users and to house certain important information. It's often the case that we need to prepare some required directories that will be leveraged by other plugins or that scaffold a required folder, such as the *src/pages* directory. We can use the `onPreBootstrap` lifecycle hook to initialize required directories so builds don't fail.

In this example, we create a *gatsby-node.js* file to indicate to Gatsby that for the theme to function properly, we need two directories (Gatsby's usual *src/pages* directory as well as a *posts* directory):

```
// gatsby-theme-minimal/gatsby-node.js
exports.onPreBootstrap = ({ store, reporter }) => {
```

```
    const { program } = store.getState()
    const dirs = [
      path.join(program.directory, "posts"),
      path.join(program.directory, "src/pages"),
    ]
    dirs.forEach(dir => {
      if (!fs.existsSync(dir)) {
        reporter.log(`Creating the ${dir} directory`)
        mkdirp.sync(dir)
      }
    })
  }
```

Using Gatsby lifecycle hooks within *gatsby-node.js* can help you avoid some of the common pitfalls that occur when others try to use your Gatsby theme, especially missing directories that are required for use by the theme. Naming your theme according to Gatsby conventions is also essential for the proper functioning of your theme in arbitrary Gatsby sites.

### Separating data queries from rendering components

Up until now, most of the example Gatsby pages that we've seen have co-located data queries and data rendering in the same file to make it easier to connect the dots between a data query and the renderer that handles the response data. Many developers prefer to formalize a *separation of concerns* that distinguishes between components of code that are responsible for querying data and others that perform rendering.

In Gatsby themes, separating data queries into independent components distinct from those handling rendering is often preferable to the co-location common in Gatsby pages. This is due to the fact that Gatsby themes often provide code components that are intended to be shadowed (i.e., overridden).

Without a clean separation between data query code and rendering code, a theme user would need to understand both how to issue page queries and how to perform JSX rendering. When those components are separated into distinct files, it becomes much easier for theme consumers to override individual JSX components (e.g., Blog PostList or UserCard) without having to rewrite the page query or StaticQuery providing the data.

If you need to separate out page queries so they can be overridden, you can use a typical Gatsby template file to perform the necessary data collection and then provide that data to a separate component—here, a JSX component known as <BlogPost List /> (*src/components/blog-post-list.js*):

```
// example/src/templates/blog-post-list.js
import React from "react"
import { graphql } from "gatsby"
```

```
import PostList from "../components/blog-post-list"

export default function MyPostsList(props) {
  return <BlogPostList posts={props.allMdx.edges} />
}

export const query = graphql`
  query {
    allMdx(
      sort: {
        order: DESC,
        fields: [frontmatter___date]
      }
      filter: {
        frontmatter: {
          draft: {
            ne: true
          }
        }
      }
    ) {
      edges {
        node {
          id
          frontmatter {
            title
            path
            date(formatString: "MMMM DD, YYYY")
          }
        }
      }
    }
  }
`
```

If you need to separate out static queries from a non-page component so they can be overridden, you can use the layout component to pass the response data from the data query to smaller rendering components as React props. In the following example, our layout component issues a static query to fetch site metadata, which is then used to populate smaller components within the layout:

```
// example/src/components/layout.js
import React from "react"
import { useStaticQuery, graphql } from "gatsby"

import Header from "../header.js"

const Layout = ({ children }) => {
  const {
    site: { siteMetadata },
  } = useStaticQuery(
    graphql`
```

```
        query {
          site {
            siteMetadata {
              title
            }
          }
        }
      `
    )

    const { title } = siteMetadata

    return (
      <>
        <Header title={title} />
        <main>{children}</main>
      </>
    )
  }
```

```
export default Layout
```

Whether you perform data querying from the standpoint of a page component (with typical page queries) or a non-page component (with static queries), it's important to allow theme users who wish to override functionality to shadow either the data querying or the rendering mechanism rather than struggling with a component that does both. This is one way that themes differ from normal page queries: they are intended to be readable by other developers, not just ourselves or our immediate developer teams.

### Providing data customization in themes

Data queries and response data are typical places where theme users may wish to override the default data in place. For instance, consider one of the most common queries issued by Gatsby: a query to fetch site metadata such as the site title and description. A theme can provide a default query that pulls from metadata the user set in the *gatsby-config.js* file of the site that is using the theme.

Gatsby themes allow the use of hooks to issue arbitrary static queries at any point in other code throughout the Gatsby site. For instance, here's an example of a hook, use SiteMetadata, that issues a static query (which doesn't need a particular component type as it can be executed anywhere) to fetch the required information from the surrounding site's Gatsby configuration file:

```
// gatsby-theme-minimal/src/hooks/use-site-metadata.js
import { graphql, useStaticQuery } from "gatsby"

export default function useSiteMetadata() {
  const data = useStaticQuery(graphql`
    {
```

```
      site {
        siteMetadata {
          title
          social {
            twitter
            github
            instagram
          }
        }
      }
    }
  `)

  return data.site.siteMetadata
}
```

This hook can then be used in the context of other components within the theme, such as a shared header component that can also be accessed within the Gatsby site. Because we've used a static query, this hook could feasibly be used anywhere in our theme and on any site that has the theme installed:

```
// gatsby-theme-minimal/src/components/header.js
import React from "react"
import { Link } from "gatsby"

import useSiteMetadata from "../hooks/use-site-metadata"

export default function Header() {
  const { title, social } = useSiteMetadata()
  return (
    <header>
      <Link to="/">{title}</Link>
      <nav>
        <a href={`https://twitter.com/${social.twitter}`}>Twitter</a>
        <a href={`https://github.com/${social.github}`}>GitHub</a>
        <a href={`https://instagram.com/${social.instagram}`}>Instagram</a>
      </nav>
    </header>
  )
}
```

When we run gatsby develop in the *example* folder, we can see the installed theme functioning correctly. These sorts of hooks can be used to override and provide defaults for a variety of data querying needs, allowing you to separate concerns between the data queries that drive your site as a whole and the unique rendering mechanisms you provide for the data you need.

### Releasing and versioning Gatsby themes

Releasing themes works precisely the same way as releasing a plugin (see Chapter 9), so I won't repeat the instructions to publish to the Gatsby Plugin Library and the

NPM package registry in this section. Because themes, like plugins, are typically intended for use by other Gatsby developers rather than strictly for private use, the same best practices in terms of semantic versioning also apply.

Gatsby outlines several best practices for semantic versioning in themes that account for various changes you may need to make as you evolve your theme, such as removing queries that certain sites may depend on. As we saw in the previous chapter, in semantic versioning there are three types of releases. These are summarized here with information relevant for themes:

- *Patch* (0.0.x) releases are bug fixes that are backward-compatible, so no breaking changes are made. Public APIs should remain unaffected. For themes, a patch release might entail fixing a bug in a component, adding error handling or default values, or upgrading upstream dependencies to their latest minor and patch versions.

- *Minor* (0.x.0) releases introduce new features that remain backward-compatible, so no changes break existing theme users' sites. In minor versions, existing public APIs should remain unaffected. For themes, a minor release might entail adding new pages or queries, adding new theme configuration options, rendering additional data, adding new props to a component, or adding a new MDX shortcode.

- *Major* (x.0.0) releases include any new bug fixes or features that are not backward-compatible, meaning these changes will break Gatsby sites using the theme. In major version releases, a migration path or guide should be provided in order to upgrade the theme to the latest version. For themes, a major version release might include changing a filename (which requires updates to any files that shadow that file), removing or modifying props accepted by a component, modifying queries, removing theme configuration options or modifying how they work, removing attributes in schema definitions, removing default data, or changing plugins or plugin configuration.

 For a more detailed overview of semantic versioning in Gatsby themes, consult the semantic versioning section (*https://oreil.ly/ PMRgp*) of the guide to Gatsby theme conventions and *Semantic Versioning 2.0.0 (https://semver.org)*.

## Converting Starters into Themes

Earlier, we explored how to build themes from scratch using the Gatsby theme workspace starter. But this isn't the only way to create a new theme; Gatsby developers can also convert starters into working Gatsby themes. In fact, the Gatsby documentation pinpoints this conversion path from starters to themes as one of the major motivations for how themes were designed in the first place.

Recall that a starter is a sample Gatsby boilerplate that, once modified, loses all tether to its original source. Meanwhile, a theme is a type of plugin that can be updated and modified according to version updates and modifications made by theme users. In many cases, you may wish to convert a starter into a theme to allow the theme user to receive updates to code that cannot be handled by starters as a rule.

In other words, modifying a starter immediately forces the developer to track all of their changes, whereas shadowing a theme means overriding defaults that are updated as new theme versions are released.

The first step to convert a starter is to modify your *package.json* file so that it represents the typical characteristics expected of a theme. To ensure Gatsby itself and other developers who choose to use your theme are able to discover it, follow these steps:

1. Modify the name to match Gatsby naming conventions. Recall that whereas Gatsby starter names are prefixed with `gatsby-starter-`, Gatsby theme names begin with `gatsby-theme-`. For instance, if your starter is named `gatsby-starter-hello-world`, you can change it in *package.json* to `gatsby-theme-hello-world`. If you plan to release your theme publicly as a registered package, ensure the namespace you plan to occupy is unused.

2. Include required development dependencies. Because themes are packages in their own right but cannot be used in isolation from a Gatsby site, it's important to clarify to users of your package that there are certain required dependencies. Every theme should include `gatsby`, `react`, and `react-dom` as `peerDependencies`, as in the following example:

```
// package.json
{
  "name": "gatsby-theme-blog",
  // ...
  "peerDependencies": {
    "gatsby": "^3.0.0",
    "react": "^17.0.0",
    "react-dom": "^17.0.0"
  },
}
```

3. Create an *index.js* file at the project root. Every JavaScript package must include an *index.js* file, even if it's empty, to be executable as JavaScript. This is a limitation of Node.js, as Node.js seeks an *index.js* file first and foremost when Gatsby resolves the theme dependency. You could also provide an alternative file for the `main` key, as seen here:

```
// package.json
{
  "name": "gatsby-theme-blog",
  "version": "3.0.0",
```

```
  "description": "A Gatsby theme for miscellaneous blogging with a >>>
  dark/light mode",
    "main": "other-alternative-file.js",
  }
```

The second step is handling path resolution. Starters and themes differ in one fundamental way: whereas starters are composed of executable Gatsby code, themes converted from starters are no longer automatically executed whenever a Gatsby CLI command is run, as all of the logic is now housed in a dependency. Because the Gatsby CLI looks for pages to build within the site and not in dependencies, you may encounter errors after following the preceding steps for unresolved paths.

To ensure that the paths represented in your starter are created whenever Gatsby builds a site based on your new theme, you can enforce the creation of those required paths using the `createPage` function in *gatsby-node.js*, as follows:

```
// gatsby-theme-minimal/gatsby-node.js
const createArticles = (createPage, createRedirect, edges) => {
  edges.forEach(({ node }, i) => {
    // Additional logic goes here.

    createPage({
      path: pagePath,
      component: require.resolve(`./src/templates/article.js`),
      context: {
        id: node.id,
        prev,
        next,
      },
    })
  })
}
```

If you had this code in your starter's *gatsby-node.js* file, it would simply look for the template found in the site's *src/templates/article.js* rather than the location you intend: *node_modules/gatsby-theme-minimal/src/templates/post.js*. To avoid this issue, you use `require.resolve` to point to a local template rather than `path.resolve`, which would have Gatsby seek the template in the surrounding site instead.

Pay close attention to where these paths need to switch their resolution, now that you have two places where paths need to be represented properly: your surrounding Gatsby site and your theme dependency. Another common place where `path.resolve` invocations may need to be substituted with `require.resolve` is in your theme's *gatsby-config.js* file.

# Theme Shadowing

As I've alluded to a few times in this chapter, Gatsby themes are particularly compelling not just as extensions of existing Gatsby functionality, but also for their flexibility. As we've seen, *theme composition* permits multiple Gatsby themes to be arbitrarily installed into a single Gatsby site. *Theme shadowing*, meanwhile, allows end users of Gatsby themes to replace any file in the *src* directory with their own overriding implementation instead.

In this section, we'll cover how theme shadowing works and its various forms. In the process, we'll look at several real-world examples to understand how theme shadowing adds considerable value to the relatively new concept of Gatsby themes.

Gatsby themes allow you to shadow any file that is handled by Webpack for bundling. This means theme users can override not only individual JavaScript or TypeScript files but also JSON and YAML files as well as CSS stylesheets that are imported into the site. For instance, consider a scenario where we have a theme that provides an article component for content articles. Theme shadowing allows us to override that article component with our own desired logic.

To demonstrate this, let's walk though one of Gatsby's official themes, `gatsby-theme-blog`, which is also a wonderful reference for theme developers.

Because Gatsby themes are relatively new entrants to the Gatsby developer experience, Gatsby recommends working with more "monolithic" themes before decomposing them into composable themes. For more information about theme composition and shared global layouts, consult the theme composition page in the Gatsby documentation (*https://oreil.ly/Be7hl*).

## Theme Shadowing in gatsby-theme-blog

To begin, let's create a new site based on the Gatsby blog theme starter, which will automatically set up what we need:

```
$ gatsby new gtdg-ch10-theme-shadowing gatsbyjs/gatsby-starter-blog-theme
```

Once you've installed the starter, change directories into the scaffolded site. You'll encounter an internal directory structure that looks like the following:

```
gtdg-ch10-theme-shadowing
├── content
│   ├── assets
│   │   └── avatar.png
│   └── posts
│       ├── hello-world
│       │   └── index.js
│       └── my-second-post.mdx
├── src
│   └── gatsby-theme-blog
│       ├── components
│       │   └── bio-content.js
│       └── gatsby-plugin-theme-ui
│           └── index.js
├── .gitignore
├── .prettierrc
├── gatsby-config.js
├── LICENSE
├── package-lock.json
├── package.json
└── README.md
```

As you can see, in our *src* directory, we have a *gatsby-theme-blog* directory containing just a few files, namely *bio-content.js* and *colors.js*. These are files that *shadow*, or override, the identically named files found in the theme plugin itself. If you were to open the *node_modules* directory containing the installed theme, you would see the unshadowed versions of those files as well as other shadowable files from the theme.

Open *src/gatsby-theme-blog/components/bio-content.js*, where you'll find the following code:

```
// src/gatsby-theme-blog/components/bio-content.js
import React from "react"
import { Themed } from "theme-ui"
```

```
/**
 * Change the content to add your own bio
 */

export default function Bio() {
  return (
    <>
      This is where <Themed.a href="http://example.com/">your name</Themed.a>
      {` `}
      goes.
      <br />
      Or whatever, you make the rules.
    </>
  )
}
```

With this *bio-content.js* component shadowing the *bio-content.js* component in our installed plugin, we can now rewrite the file to our heart's content to provide the specific bio we want to provide instead. This will override the logic in the upstream theme's file and apply the custom logic we've written in the shadowed component. As you can see, any JavaScript component within a theme can be shadowed. But what about other files, like files provided by a theme's dependency rather than the theme itself?

## Shadowing Other Files

The `gatsby-theme-blog` theme incidentally installs the `gatsby-plugin-theme-ui` plugin, which provides a variety of CSS styles to the theme. This plugin includes a preset, `gatsby-theme-ui-preset`, which is used by the `gatsby-theme-blog` theme. To shadow a file from a plugin that a theme depends on, we can use much the same approach as before.

Within the *src* directory, the directory *gatsby-plugin-theme-ui* contains shadowed files that will override the installed `gatsby-plugin-theme-ui` dependency's files. For instance, to override the *index.js* file in the installed plugin within our site, we can create a shadow file, *index.js*, and pass in overriding information. Here's an example:

```
// src/gatsby-plugin-theme-ui/index.js
const darkBlue = `#007acc`
// const lightBlue = `#66E0FF`
const blueGray = `#282c35`

const theme = {
  colors: {
    text: blueGray,
    primary: darkBlue,
    heading: blueGray,
  },
```

```
}

export default theme
```

Gatsby will combine these values with those already found in `gatsby-theme-ui-preset` to produce a synthesized version of the *index.js* file and style values. Whenever these values conflict with those found in the installed plugin, your shadowed files will take precedence.

Remember that any source file handled by Webpack, regardless of extension, can be shadowed to override the upstream theme. Consider, for example, a situation in which you have a theme (let's call it `gatsby-theme-layout`) that provides a CSS stylesheet such as *components/layout.css*. Gatsby developers can create a new folder within their site (*src/gatsby-theme-layout*) to provide files that shadow the theme's CSS:

```
/* src/gatsby-theme-layout/components/layout.css */
body {
    background-color: rebeccapurple;
}
```

This would then override the entirety of the CSS stylesheet in the upstream theme with the new shadow CSS stylesheet.

> Gatsby can intelligently guess what extension the component or file that needs to be imported carries when it comes to JavaScript and TypeScript. For instance, if you import a TypeScript file such as *src/components/article.tsx* as shown here, Gatsby can infer that *article.tsx* is the correct component:
>
> ```
> import Article from "./article"
> ```
>
> This is particularly useful in theme shadowing, because you can write an *article.js* component that shadows an *article.tsx* TypeScript component without running into transpilation issues.

## Extending Shadowed Files

Theme shadowing doesn't just allow you to override entire files, like we've seen up to this point. After all, one of the issues with the CSS override example from the previous section is that you may not want such a small stylesheet to override every single line of CSS in the upstream file. Instead of overriding theme files, sometimes we need to *extend* those theme files through theme shadowing.

The primary method of extending shadowed files is to import the component you intend to shadow and then render it, in the process providing any additional information you want to include. Consider the following example adapted from the Gatsby documentation, which depicts a bio component that needs to pull from a theme's components and extend them into a shadow component with extended functionality:

```
// src/gatsby-theme-blog/components/bio.js
import React from "react"
import { Avatar, MediaObject, Icon } from "gatsby-theme-blog"

export default function Bio({ name, bio, avatar, twitterUrl, githubUrl }) {
  return (
    <MediaObject>
      <Avatar {...avatar} />
      <div>
        <h3>{name}</h3>
        <p>{bio}</p>
        <a href={twitterUrl}>
          <Icon name="twitter" />
        </a>
        <a href={githubUrl}>
          <Icon name="github" />
        </a>
      </div>
    </MediaObject>
  )
}
```

In this example, all of the code within the `<MediaObject />` component allows us to add to the theme's default rendering of that component. If we didn't extend the component in this way, we would instead need to copy the entire component from the upstream theme as a separate component in our site.

 The previous example imports the components from the theme dependency, but you can also write more efficient code by importing the shadowed component into another component by referring to it directly, like this:

```
import {
  Author
} from "gatsby-theme-blog/src/components/bio"
```

Though theme shadowing is an effective way to use themes for more robust architectures in Gatsby, there's always a risk of shadowing too much. As a best practice, if you're finding that you're overriding or extending a large number of files in the upstream theme, it might be a good idea to consider a fork of the theme instead and create a distinct theme. Gatsby officially supports this model by providing "core" themes, like `gatsby-theme-blog-core`, a dependency for `gatsby-theme-blog`, that can serve as foundations for forks of `gatsby-theme-blog` or new themes.

For more information about leveraging shadowed components with distinct prop APIs in React, consult the Gatsby documentation (*https://oreil.ly/m52zP*). The documentation also contains a guide on how theme shadowing and theme composition operate under the hood (*https://oreil.ly/0wQvZ*).

# Conclusion

Though themes differ from plugins and starters in many significant ways, they are useful for a variety of use cases, particularly to allow for packaged portions of functionality repeated across multiple sites to be managed gracefully as a single dependency. Though many Gatsby users will use Gatsby themes to override aesthetic elements to their heart's content, others will override data queries or other functionality to more richly customize their sites with prefabricated code.

Gatsby themes also introduce two new concepts to our vocabulary: composition and shadowing. Theme composition is compelling because it allows us to combine arbitrary themes in a single Gatsby site. Meanwhile, theme shadowing is what allows us to override the files in individual themes to extend our sites with custom code.

Though themes are relatively new to the Gatsby ecosystem, they portend a new era of Gatsby development. And while this chapter concludes our examination of extending Gatsby, we will next turn to how to ensure Gatsby is ready for the real world through debugging and testing.

# PART IV

# Production Gatsby

# CHAPTER 11

# Debugging and Testing Gatsby

Once your Gatsby implementation is complete, you'll often find that you need to troubleshoot some issues before you can deploy your site to production. In Gatsby, it's possible to do test-driven development (TDD) by writing unit tests in Jest (*https://jestjs.io/*) and performing tests on various aspects of the development experience.

Even with a robust test architecture, however, sometimes Gatsby sites fail for obscure reasons and require a deeper level of troubleshooting and debugging. Fortunately, the Gatsby ecosystem provides a variety of tools for testing your sites ahead of time to help you avoid problems and debug them when issues arise. Before your site can go into production, it's essential to ensure that it functions the way you intend.

In this chapter, we'll cover testing strategies, including unit testing and component-level testing, and debugging tactics, including for static builds, server-side rendering issues, and other issues that arise during development.

 Sometimes during development, it will be useful to spin up a local development server that provides local HTTPS support. For more information, consult the Gatsby documentation's guide to local HTTPS (*https://oreil.ly/4Q6xm*).

## Testing Gatsby

Gatsby enables *unit testing*—testing that evaluates atomic units of functionality—with limited additional setup through Jest. The Jest framework can be used on its own for *snapshot testing*—testing that compares visual states of the application to track regressions in the user experience—and in conjunction with other libraries for unit testing of React components and components containing GraphQL queries.

But these aren't the only kinds of testing that can be performed on Gatsby sites. The field of testing in web development has seen an explosion of innovation in recent years, with other techniques like *visual regression testing* (evaluating differences due to changes in visual application behavior) and *end-to-end testing* (evaluating whether an application functions correctly from beginning to end) made available by emerging ecosystems. In this section, we'll cover how to unit-test with Jest and perform other types of testing with other tools.

It's also possible to use Google Analytics (*https://oreil.ly/8pb52*) in conjunction with Netlify (*https://www.netlify.com*) to perform *A/B* or *split testing* (evaluating two different online states of an application to compare them against each other) on a Gatsby site, a procedure that is well beyond the scope of this book. Consult the A/B testing guide in the Gatsby documentation for a walkthrough (*https://oreil.ly/11qr2*).

## Unit Testing with Jest

Unit testing refers to the concept of testing and evaluating the quality of each unit of functionality made available by an implementation—in this case, a Gatsby site. Though Gatsby doesn't offer a unit testing framework out of the box for efficiency reasons, Gatsby developers can use Jest to power unit testing with a minimal amount of overhead. However, because Gatsby's build process is slightly unusual when it comes to the sort of JavaScript that Jest deals with, standard Jest implementations need some adjustment to work properly with Gatsby sites.

An exhaustive introduction to unit testing and Jest is beyond the scope of this brief overview, but you can consult the Jest documentation for more information (*https://oreil.ly/NtVKj*), as well as the Using Jest example (*https://oreil.ly/8eedr*) provided by Gatsby for an example using `@testing-library/react` (*https://oreil.ly/QFr2A*). If you're using Emotion or Styled Components to power CSS-in-JS for your Gatsby site, consult the Gatsby documentation's guide to testing CSS-in-JS with Jest (*https://oreil.ly/FuDnA*) and the `jest-styled-components` documentation (*https://oreil.ly/4lJY8*).

### Configuring Jest

Let's walk through a typical Jest test suite built for a Gatsby site. This will demonstrate a standard configuration of Jest that integrates seamlessly with Gatsby's build process. To begin, we'll spin up a new version of the Gatsby blog starter:

```
$ gatsby new gtdg-ch11-unit-testing gatsbyjs/gatsby-starter-blog
$ cd gtdg-ch11-unit-testing
```

Jest requires us to install several dependencies. We need to install `babel-jest` and `babel-preset-gatsby` in order to ensure that the Babel presets Jest will use match those that are found in our Gatsby site, since Gatsby uses its own unique Babel configuration (this is particularly important if you have an unusual Babel preset that was customized beyond Gatsby's own preset and needs to be accounted for in your unit testing):

```
$ npm install --save-dev jest babel-jest react-test-renderer \
  babel-preset-gatsby identity-obj-proxy
```

In the same directory as our *gatsby-config.js* file (i.e., in the root of the Gatsby project), we'll add a *jest.config.js* file that contains some defaults and also instructs Jest to use the `babel-jest` package:

```
// jest.config.js
module.exports = {
  transform: {  ❶
    "^.+\\.jsx?$": `<rootDir>/jest-preprocess.js`,
  },
  moduleNameMapper: {  ❷
    ".+\\.(css|styl|less|sass|scss)$": `identity-obj-proxy`,
    ".+\\.(jpg|jpeg|png|gif|eot|otf|webp|svg|ttf|woff|woff2|mp4|webm >>>
|wav|mp3|m4a|aac|oga)$": `<rootDir>/__mocks__/file-mock.js`,
  },
  testPathIgnorePatterns: [  ❸
    `node_modules`,
    `\\.cache`,
    `<rootDir>.*/public`
  ],
  transformIgnorePatterns: [`node_modules/(?!(gatsby)/)`],  ❹
  globals: {  ❺
    __PATH_PREFIX__: ``,
  },
  testURL: `http://localhost`,  ❻
  setupFiles: [`<rootDir>/loadershim.js`],  ❼
}
```

❶ The `transform` object instructs Jest to transform all files with the *.js* or *.jsx* extension using a *jest-preprocess.js* file, which Jest expects to encounter in the project root. Let's go ahead and add this file now to tell Jest that it should use Gatsby's Babel preset when setting up this transformer:

```
// jest-preprocess.js
const babelOptions = {
  presets: ["babel-preset-gatsby"],
}

module.exports = require("babel-jest")
                  .default
                  .createTransformer(babelOptions)
```

❷ The `moduleNameMapper` object indicates to Jest how it should handle imports, much like Webpack rules. Because Jest is incapable of handling static file imports as mocks (dummy modules that don't do anything), we need to manually create mocks that represent assets. For stylesheets such as *layout.css*, we'll use the `identity-obj-proxy` package to handle this for us. For all other assets, however, we'll need to create a directory in the project root named *__mocks__* and add a manual mock named *file-mock.js*:

```
// __mocks__/file-mock.js
module.exports = "test-file-stub"
```

❸ The `testPathIgnorePatterns` array tells Jest which directories to ignore—in this case, the *node_modules*, *.cache*, and *public* directories, which aren't things we need to unit-test.

❹ The `transformIgnorePatterns` array is important, and may differ from other Jest implementations you are familiar with. Because the Gatsby framework by default includes ES6 code that remains untranspiled as a rule, we need to indicate to Jest that files containing code not meant to be transpiled shouldn't be transformed by instructing Jest to ignore the Gatsby module. Otherwise, we'll encounter an error that looks like this:

```
/my-app/node_modules/gatsby/cache-dir/gatsby-browser-entry.js:1
({"Object.<anonymous>":function(module,exports,require, >>>
__dirname,__filename,global,jest){import React from "react"
                                  ^^^^^^
SyntaxError: Unexpected token import
```

❺ The `globals` object defines the `__PATH_PREFIX__` string, which Gatsby sets itself and might be required by some components.

❻ The `testURL` string identifies a valid URL rather than the default of `about:blank`, which doesn't work with `localStorage` (an issue resolved in Jest 23.5.0 and later).

❼ The `setupFiles` array permits us to enumerate files that should be included before tests are run. `setupFiles` cannot accept a function, so we'll need to create another file, *loadershim.js*, in the project root containing the following code:

```
// loadershim.js
global.___loader = {
  enqueue: jest.fn()
}
```

If you need to modify your Babel configuration, perform those modifications in the *jest-preprocess.js* file. See Chapter 14 and consult the Gatsby Babel configuration guide for more information (*https://oreil.ly/BO5vl*).

Before we proceed to writing and running unit tests in Jest for Gatsby, one final step that may be useful is to create a mock for the Gatsby module itself in the *__mocks__* directory under the filename *gatsby.js*. If you're using native Gatsby exports like `Link` or `graphql`, this will help you avoid errors down the road by ensuring they're not absent:

```
// __mocks__/gatsby.js
const React = require("react")
const gatsby = jest.requireActual("gatsby")

module.exports = {
  ...gatsby,
  graphql: jest.fn(),
  Link: jest.fn().mockImplementation(
    // These props cannot be used on `a` elements
    ({
      activeClassName,
      activeStyle,
      getProps,
      innerRef,
      partiallyActive,
      ref,
      replace,
      to,
      ...rest
    }) =>
      React.createElement("a", {
        ...rest,
        href: to,
      })
  ),
  StaticQuery: jest.fn(),
  useStaticQuery: jest.fn(),
}
```

Mocking ensures Jest tests won't hang when they come across the `graphql` function, `Link` component, and `StaticQuery` component in your Gatsby code.

If you're using TypeScript to write your Gatsby site, your Jest configuration will require additional dependencies to handle typings, different transformer configuration approaches, and, if you're using `tsconfig` paths, other settings that are accounted for in the Jest with TypeScript section of the Gatsby documentation (*https://oreil.ly/9HHYw*).

## Writing unit tests

Though a comprehensive accounting of writing Jest tests is outside the scope of this chapter, let's write a rudimentary unit test that checks to make sure that our Gatsby blog starter correctly renders the expected <Bio /> component (*src/components/bio.js*) that is found in the starter.

First, we need to create a new directory within the same directory as our components (*src/components*) named __tests__. As an alternative, you can place the test file alongside the component in the same directory, with the extension *.spec.js* or *.test.js* (a matter of personal preference, since Jest correctly interprets both). In the following example, we place the test file named *bio.js* in *src/components/__tests__*:

```
// src/components/__tests__/bio.js
import React from "react"
import renderer from "react-test-renderer"

import Bio from "../bio"

describe("Bio", () => {
  it("renders correctly", () => {
    const tree = renderer
      .create(<Bio />)
      .toJSON()
    expect(tree).toMatchSnapshot()
  })
})
```

This test will employ `react-test-renderer` to render the component, which we import into the test file. Thereafter, it will create a snapshot of the component that reflects its initial state on the first test run. Any future test runs will compare the resulting snapshots with the initial snapshot, allowing for quick detection of deltas that have generated regressions.

You can also use these unit tests in Jest to test components that accept props, such as the header component:

```
// src/components/__tests__/header.js
import React from "react"
import renderer from "react-test-renderer"

import Header from "../header"

describe("Header", () => {
  it("renders correctly", () => {
    const tree = renderer
      .create(<Header siteTitle="Default Starter" />)
      .toJSON()
    expect(tree).toMatchSnapshot()
  })
})
```

Writing unit tests will ensure that your code stays pristine and doesn't introduce any regressions in functionality. But now that you know how to author unit tests in Jest, how can you run them?

### Running unit tests

If you inspect the *package.json* file that is generated by the Gatsby blog starter, you'll find that there's already an NPM script available known as `test`—but it simply outputs an error message, as you can see in the following example:

```
// package.json
  "scripts": {
    "build": "gatsby build",
    "develop": "gatsby develop",
    "format": "prettier --write \"**/*.{js,jsx,ts,tsx,json,md}\"",
    "start": "npm run develop",
    "serve": "gatsby serve",
    "clean": "gatsby clean",
    "test": "echo \"Write tests! -> https://gatsby.dev/unit-testing\" >>>
&& exit 1"
  }
```

To ensure that this NPM script instead runs Jest unit tests that you've created, you need to modify the string associated with the `test` key to `jest`, as follows:

```
// package.json
  "scripts": {
    "build": "gatsby build",
    "develop": "gatsby develop",
    "format": "prettier --write \"**/*.{js,jsx,ts,tsx,json,md}\"",
    "start": "npm run develop",
    "serve": "gatsby serve",
    "clean": "gatsby clean",
    "test": "jest"
  }
```

Now, you can run all your Jest unit tests by executing the following command in your terminal:

```
$ npm test
```

To run unit tests together with a flag that enables a watch mode, which tracks changes to files and runs another regimen of unit tests when changes are detected in those files, use this command:

```
$ npm test -- --watch
```

When you run a round of unit tests successfully, you will see a notice in your terminal about snapshots being created, and alongside your *__tests__* directory, a *__snapshots__* directory will appear containing JSON representations of each component you tested (in our case, the `<Bio />` and `<Header />` components).

To have a convenient means of comparing snapshots against one another, you can check your __snapshots__ directory into your source repository so you don't publish any new code changes without verifying that the snapshots match the intended result. An additional advantage of tracking your snapshots in source control is that you have a record of how your units of functionality have evolved over time.

To update the initial snapshot so new changes aren't considered regressions, you can run another round of tests and instruct Jest to update the original snapshot to the new state:

```
$ npm test -- -u
```

Though these unit tests are powerful for verifying that your snapshots match the expected rendered output, what about situations in which you need to do more involved checking to ensure that the DOM of your components matches the rendered output? For this, you can use a tool such as `@testing-library/react`, which enables you to write both unit and integration tests for React components (which all Gatsby components are, in the end).

 If you're using a continuous integration (CI) system that runs tests for you, like CircleCI or Travis, those systems typically require snapshots to be checked into source control.

## Testing React Components

The `@testing-library/react` library includes several helpers on top of `react-dom` and `react-dom/test-utils` to aid in ensuring that whenever the implementation (though not the functionality) of your component evolves, your tests won't break. If you followed the steps in the previous section to install and configure Jest, you can pick up right here. Otherwise, check to ensure that you have Jest installed and configured correctly for your Gatsby site.

First, you'll need to install several additional development dependencies (`devDependencies`):

```
$ npm install --save-dev @testing-library/react @testing-library/jest-dom
```

At the root of your project, in the same directory as *package.json* and *gatsby-config.js*, create a new file named *setup-test-env.js* containing the following import:

```
// setup-test-env.js
import "@testing-library/jest-dom/extend-expect"
```

Because this JavaScript file is executed every time Jest runs a test, you don't need to add this `import` statement to every single test file. Now, you need to make Jest aware of this file and indicate its location. If your *jest.config.js* file is in the same state it was in at the end of the previous section, all you need to do is add a new key, `setupFile sAfterEnv`, to the `module.exports` object and identify the file you just created:

```
// jest.config.js
module.exports = {
  // Other Jest configuration.
  setupFiles: [`<rootDir>/loadershim.js`],
  setupFilesAfterEnv: ["<rootDir>/setup-test-env.js"],
}
```

Now, you can write tests that use `@testing-library/react` instead of `react-test-renderer`, and you have access to a much richer range of methods to use to introspect the rendered DOM elements and ensure they match your snapshots. Here is one example of a rudimentary test that ensures our `<Bio />` component contains a particular string as opposed to the child elements it comes with by default in the unmodified Gatsby blog starter:

```
// src/components/__tests__/bio.js
import React from "react"
import { render } from "@testing-library/react"

const Bio = () => (
  <div className="bio" data-testid="main-bio">
    Hello! This is my bio!
  </div>
)

test("Displays the correct title", () => {
  const { getByTestId } = render(<Bio />)
  // The next line describes our assertion.
  expect(getByTestId("main-bio"))
    .toHaveTextContent("Hello! This is my bio!")
})
```

We've covered unit tests at a high level in this section, but that doesn't mean unit testing is the only type of testing you should be concerned with. For small-scale testing, unit tests do the trick, but sometimes it's important to have a more holistic view of the visual design of your components as well as a sense of how your site performs end-to-end across multiple pages. We'll turn our attention to these two types of tests next.

Gatsby pages and components containing GraphQL queries require special handling, covered in the Gatsby documentation's guide to testing components with GraphQL (*https://oreil.ly/otksm*). For additional information, consult the documentation for `@testing-library/react` (*https://oreil.ly/nqO9G*) and custom Jest matchers in `@testing-library/jest-dom` (*https://oreil.ly/lQqBU*).

# Visual Testing with Storybook

Though unit testing is powerful for situations where you need to maintain functional parity over time, sometimes a visual testing approach can be even more fruitful for maintaining a high-quality Gatsby implementation. One tool that has become popular for visual inspection and testing of JavaScript components is *Storybook*, a development environment for UI components that allows developers to see their components across various states and understand what components they can leverage and what props they accept.

To install and configure Storybook, the quickest way to get started is to use the npx command, which comes packaged with NPM. NPX, used to execute packages (as opposed to the NPM installer), is useful because it will scaffold a directory structure with default configuration already in place to maximize productivity. Execute the following command in the root of your project:

```
$ npx -p @storybook/cli sb init
```

 If you're using a version of NPM older than 5.2.0, because NPX is a newer addition to NPM, you will need to run the following instead:

```
$ npm install -g @storybook/cli
$ sb init
```

Though Storybook will scaffold a fully constructed set of directories and files within them in the *.storybook* directory, Gatsby requires some adjustments to Storybook's default configuration. If you open *.storybook/main.js*, you'll find this configuration:

```
// .storybook/main.js
module.exports = {
  stories: [
    "../src/**/*.stories.mdx",
    "../src/**/*.stories.@(js|jsx|ts|tsx)"
  ],
  addons: ["@storybook/addon-actions", "@storybook/addon-links"],
}
```

You'll need to extend this Storybook configuration to embrace Gatsby's own ES6 code that remains untranspiled, similarly to how we configured Jest to do so in "Testing Gatsby" on page 335. Change your Storybook configuration to the following, adding webpackFinal after the lines in the previous example, as follows:

```
// .storybook/main.js
module.exports = {
  stories: [
    "../src/**/*.stories.mdx",
    "../src/**/*.stories.@(js|jsx|ts|tsx)"
  ],
  addons: ["@storybook/addon-actions", "@storybook/addon-links"], >>>
```

```
webpackFinal: async config => {
    config.module.rules[0].exclude = [/node_modules\/(?!(gatsby)\/)/]
    config.module.rules[0].use[0].loader = require.resolve("babel-loader")
    config.module.rules[0].use[0].options.presets = [
      require.resolve("@babel/preset-react"),
      require.resolve("@babel/preset-env"),
    ]
    config.module.rules[0].use[0].options.plugins = [
      require.resolve("@babel/plugin-proposal-class-properties"),
      require.resolve("babel-plugin-remove-graphql-queries"),
    ]
    config.resolve.mainFields = ["browser", "module", "main"]
    return config
  },
}
```

These lines configure Webpack to handle the Gatsby module correctly and to ensure that Storybook uses Gatsby's ES6 entry point (which prepopulates dependencies) rather than the default CommonJS entry point (which executes dependencies on demand). Now, you need to provide a configuration file that will add certain global parameters and Storybook decorators to ensure Storybook works with Gatsby. Replace the contents of the file named *preview.js* in the *.storybook* directory with the following code:

```
// .storybook/preview.js
import { action } from "@storybook/addon-actions"

// This prevents Gatsby Link from triggering errors in Storybook.
global.___loader = {
  enqueue: () => {},
  hovering: () => {},
}

// This global variable prevents the "__BASE_PATH__ is not defined" error
// inside Storybook.
global.__BASE_PATH__ = "/"

// Navigating through a Gatsby app using gatsby-link or any other
// gatsby component will use the `___navigate` method. In Storybook
// it makes more sense to log an action than doing an actual navigate.
// Check out the actions addon docs for more info:
// https://github.com/storybookjs/storybook/tree/master/addons/actions.

window.___navigate = pathname => {
  action("NavigateTo:")(pathname)
}

export const parameters = {
  actions: { argTypesRegex: "^on[A-Z].*" },
  controls: {
    matchers: {
      color: /(background|color)$/i,
```

```
      date: /Date$/,
    },
  },
}
```

With both of these configuration files in place, you can now write Storybook stories. Storybook will seek any files with a *.stories.js* extension and load them automatically in your Storybook interface for you. For Gatsby components, these stories can live alongside the components in the same directory. But for Gatsby pages, since Gatsby restricts what JavaScript files are permitted in the *src/pages* directory, you'll need to create a *__stories__* directory in the *src* directory.

A full walkthrough of Storybook is outside the scope of this book, but as an example adapted from the Gatsby documentation, here's a Storybook *story*, which in Storybook parlance describes a rendered component that is displayed in the Storybook interface:

```
// src/components/bio.stories.js
import React from "react"

export default {
  title: "Bio",
}

export const bioStory = () => (
  <div style={{ padding: "1rem", backgroundColor: "#ccc" }}>
    <h1 style={{ color: "blue" }}>Hello world and Storybook!</h1>
  </div>
)
```

 For a comprehensive introduction to Storybook, consult the Storybook documentation (*https://storybook.js.org*) and Mathspy's Gatsby starter (*https://oreil.ly/uGKgk*) containing both Jest and Storybook. The Gatsby documentation (*https://oreil.ly/Opdhj*) also has information about how to work with Storybook 4 and Type-Script implementations.

## End-to-End Testing with Cypress

Visual testing and unit testing both permit small-scale observation of how quality changes over time across individual Gatsby components and pages. However, there are often situations where, as a Gatsby developer, it will be desirable to perform *end-to-end* (e2e) testing that involves not only single pages and components but navigating through an entire Gatsby site with multiple pages and components involved in one test.

This is particularly important for accessibility testing when it comes to accessible client-side routing, as an e2e test can reveal when navigating between pages isn't working properly due to a missing Reach route change or other issue. Though there are multiple systems commonly used for e2e testing, Cypress is a common choice.

Because e2e testing typically requires a second parallel server to be running alongside Gatsby's local development server, you'll want to use the `start-server-and-test` library to manage both in parallel. Add the following to your development dependencies (`devDependencies`):

```
$ npm install --save-dev cypress start-server-and-test \
  @testing-library/cypress
```

Cypress comes with the ability to configure certain global settings. Do that now by creating a new *cypress.json* file in your project root:

```
// cypress.json
{
  "baseUrl": "http://localhost:8000/"
}
```

This `baseUrl` configuration will ensure that every URL that Cypress visits or issues a request to will be prefixed with the correct domain for our Gatsby development server. Next, you need to add Cypress scripts to our *package.json* to ensure you can run Cypress tests from the terminal:

```
// package.json
{
  "scripts": {
    "develop": "gatsby develop",
    "test:jest": "jest",
    "cy:open": "cypress open",
    "test:e2e": "start-server-and-test develop http://localhost:8000 cy:open"
  }
}
```

If you're using Cypress in the context of a CI provider like CircleCI or Travis, you will need to use the `cypress run` command instead of `cypress open`:

```
"cy:run": "cypress run",
```

To kick off a Cypress test, execute the following after installing other dependencies required for Cypress (*https://oreil.ly/U16mW*):

```
$ npm run test:e2e
```

 To distinguish between Jest unit tests and end-to-end Cypress tests, you may want to consider changing the `npm run test` command to `npm run test:jest`. This will avoid any possible confusion with an `npm run test:e2e` command for Cypress.

You'll see a new directory named *cypress* created within the root of your project.

If you're running your Gatsby development server with HTTPS enabled (i.e., gatsby develop --https), you will need to indicate to start-server-and-test that it needs to disable SSL certificate checks, because these will cause Cypress to hang. In your *package.json*, your test:e2e command should be changed to the following to include an environment variable that disables certificate checks:

```
"test:e2e": "START_SERVER_AND_TEST_INSECURE=1
start-server-and-test develop
http://localhost:8000 cy:open"
```

One of the most common use cases for end-to-end testing with Cypress is accessibility testing, which requires a library such as Axe. Though building in automated accessibility testing is a best practice for Gatsby sites, it's also a best practice to perform at least some manual accessibility testing lest something fall through the cracks.

You can install those additional Axe dependencies now:

```
$ npm install --save-dev cypress-axe axe-core
```

Because you already ran Cypress once, you can open the already created *cypress/support/index.js* file and import the additional dependencies you now need, including @testing-library/cypress:

```
// cypress/support/index.js
import "./commands"
import "cypress-axe"
import "@testing-library/cypress/add-commands"
```

Though Cypress will look for tests within the *cypress/integration* directory by default, accessibility tests that visit multiple pages are considered end-to-end tests and should be placed in a new *cypress/e2e* directory as a best practice. In this case, you'll need to configure an integrationFolder in your Cypress configuration as follows:

```
// cypress.json
{
  "baseUrl": "http://localhost:8000/",
  "integrationFolder": "cypress/e2e"
}
```

To finish our exploration of Cypress end-to-end testing, let's create a rudimentary test that checks for the absence of accessibility violations on the initial load of the home page of our example Gatsby site, which in this chapter is our Gatsby blog starter. Create a new file in the *cypress/e2e* directory named *accessibility.test.js* with the following contents:

```
// cypress/e2e/accessibility.test.js
/// <reference types="Cypress" /> ❶

describe("Accessibility tests", () => {
  beforeEach(() => {
    cy.visit("/").get("main").injectAxe() ❷
  })
  it("Has no detectable accessibility violations on load", () => {
    cy.checkA11y() ❸
  })
  it("Navigates to blog post and checks for accessibility violations", () => {
    cy.findByText(/new beginnings/i) ❹
      .click()
      .checkA11y()
  })
})
```

❶  This comment facilitates autocompletion if you're using certain IDEs (such as those with IntelliSense).

❷  As the cy.visit() method suggests, Cypress visits the home page of your Gatsby site and waits until the page load is complete. The subsequent chained methods find the <main> HTML element (using cy.get(), as Gatsby may "finish" loading too quickly), where the Axe accessibility testing API is injected and made available.

❸  The cy.checkA11y() method performs a check for any accessibility errors on the home page.

❹  The cy.findByText() method finds the first blog post displayed in the Gatsby blog starter and navigates to it, performing another check for accessibility errors on that page.

You can extend this end-to-end accessibility test by working through some additional assertions using the should method to check whether a given link has text legible to screen readers and has an href attribute, as is expected of all links:

```
// cypress/e2e/accessibility.test.js
describe("Accessibility tests", () => {
  // Previous assertions.
  it("Focuses on the header link and asserts its attributes", () => {
    cy.findAllByText("Gatsby Starter Blog").focus()
    cy.focused()
      .should("have.text", "Gatsby Starter Blog")
      .should("have.attr", "href", "/")
  })
})
```

A full examination of Cypress and Axe is beyond the scope of this brief introduction to end-to-end testing, but Cypress offers a getting started guide (*https://oreil.ly/xgaKJ*), core concepts page (*https://oreil.ly/6L7Xq*), and API reference (*https://oreil.ly/odi9U*). In addition, Gatsby provides a Cypress example (*https://oreil.ly/eEbJj*) and a guide to customizing Axe options (*https://oreil.ly/3xyKK*). For more information about Axe, see the Axe documentation (*https://www.deque.com/axe*).

# Debugging Gatsby

Like other development frameworks, Gatsby isn't free of bugs, whether they are attributable to developer error or something upstream in the framework. At various points in the Gatsby development experience, you might run into unexpected problems with static builds, rendering, the build process itself, the Gatsby cache, or asynchronous lifecycle methods. Gatsby also offers a performance tracing tool that you can use to identify areas of your site that require more optimization.

The official Gatsby documentation tracks a range of frequent issues that developers encounter during Gatsby development and common troubleshooting solutions to resolve them (*https://oreil.ly/8lzuv*).

## Debugging Static Builds

Because Gatsby's static build process ultimately generates a series of HTML files that maximize the speed at which Gatsby sites load in the browser, some issues can be difficult to diagnose. In many cases, issues surrounding static builds involve inaccessible globals or Webpack bundling issues. The Gatsby documentation outlines four specific cases that are common in Gatsby sites:

1. *Undefined browser globals.* Because JavaScript can be executed on the server side or the client side, if your code references the window or document object, those objects may be unavailable except when the Gatsby site is loaded in a browser. During the build process, you may run into errors such as window is not defined, as it is undefined before the site reaches the browser. There are two ways to handle this:

    a. If your code requires the use of the window or document object in the browser, perform a check to ensure window or document is defined so that the code within the check is executed only in the browser, as follows:

    ```
    if (typeof window !== `undefined`) {
      // Your window-reliant code here.
    }
    ```

b. If the offending code with references to the `window` or `document` object is within the `render` function of a React component, you'll need to relocate that code into a `componentDidMount` lifecycle method in React or, if you're using React hooks, into a `useEffect` hook implementation to prevent its execution outside the browser.

2. *Improperly exported pages.* Because Gatsby automatically generates pages based on the contents of the *pages* directory, you must ensure that all files within that directory are exporting either a React component or a string. Otherwise, Gatsby's automatic page generation will fail.

3. *Collision of `import` and `require` in a single file.* In Webpack 4, the bundler no longer permits the use of both `import` and `require` statements within the same file. Instead, Gatsby recommends using only `import` statements within Gatsby files, including *gatsby-ssr.js* and *gatsby-browser.js*.

4. *Improper hydration.* Gatsby allows for client-side functionality to proceed by hydrating rendered HTML with React. If this hydration doesn't happen correctly, you will run into inconsistencies between the results of the `gatsby develop` and `gatsby build` commands. If you discover inconsistencies between the build results, it's likely that some logic in *gatsby-ssr.js* or *gatsby-browser.js* is causing a mismatch between the HTML generated by the server and that understood by the client.

---

## Avoiding Issues with the Window Object

One edge case not enumerated in this list relates to NPM modules that are used as dependencies in Gatsby sites and refer to the `window` object. Because these are upstream dependencies, if you report the issue and request a check on the `window` object it may take some time before the maintainer responds. To avoid hacking into the module itself, which compromises dependency management, in *gatsby-node.js* you can customize your Webpack configuration such that during server-side rendering, the module is replaced with an empty dummy module:

```
// gatsby-node.js
exports.onCreateWebpackConfig = ({
  stage, loaders, actions
}) => {
  if (stage === "build-html") {
    actions.setWebpackConfig({
      module: {
        rules: [
          {
            test: /module-without-window-defined-check/,
            use: loaders.null(),
          },
```

```
            ],
          },
        })
    }
  }
```

An alternative to this approach is to use the loadable-components package (*https://oreil.ly/kEpil*), which allows developers to use code splitting to force a module to dynamically load only in the browser and not during server-side rendering.

## Debugging the Build Process

Because both the gatsby build and gatsby develop scripts are technically Node.js applications at their core, you can debug issues that occur within the execution of those scripts using commonly available standard approaches and tools for Node.js application development. Using Node.js debugging tools can be useful for situations where you need to identify a problem area in a *gatsby-node.js* file or another file that influences the build process or instantiation of the local development server.

For Gatsby developers familiar with debugging JavaScript in the browser, the console object is available with a console.log() method to print any values that need verification or introspection to the browser console during execution:

```
console.log(anObject)
```

Because the console object is also built into Node.js, you can add an invocation of console.log() to any executed code in your *gatsby-node.js* file or any other file—including Gatsby pages and components—to print the variable's value into the terminal output, just like in the browser console. Consider the following example from gatsby-source-filesystem, in which we print the args variable to the Node.js console in the terminal:

```
// gatsby-node.js
const { createFilePath } = require("gatsby-source-filesystem")

exports.onCreateNode = args => {
  console.log(args)
  const { actions, node } = args
  if (node.internal.type === "MarkdownRemark") {
    const { createNodeField } = actions

    const value = createFilePath({ node, getNode })
    createNodeField({
      name: `slug`,
      node,
      value,
    })
  }
}
```

Observe the difference between `console.log()` statements that are executed at build time and can be seen in the terminal, like in the *gatsby-node.js* file, and those statements that are executed on the client side, whose results will display in the browser console instead of the terminal.

 If you use VS Code Debugger or Chrome DevTools for Node during the development process, these tools can help you perform similar debugging to that which you can do in a browser by connecting a debugger, even including the use of breakpoints. Consult the Gatsby documentation (*https://oreil.ly/W6mun*) for in-depth guides to debugging Node.js with both VS Code Debugger and Chrome DevTools for Node.

## Debugging Server-Side Rendering Issues

Gatsby performs server-side rendering as part of its build process to facilitate faster page loads on the browser. Hooking into this rendering process involves creating or modifying the *gatsby-ssr.js* file. One of the server-side rendering APIs commonly leveraged during the build process is the `replaceRenderer` API, which can be used to customize or otherwise adjust the ways in which Gatsby renders out the contents of your site in static form. The most common use cases for this API generally involve the use of Redux, Styled Components, or other CSS-in-JS libraries that need to influence the markup rendered on the server side.

The `replaceRenderer` API is employed by various Gatsby plugins in the ecosystem to extend Gatsby so it supports these libraries, or any custom code that needs to modify how Gatsby generates its initial HTML output for the browser. This logic is executed solely during the build process (i.e., when `gatsby build` is executed), not during local development (`gatsby develop`). Sometimes, when multiple plugins require usage of the `replaceRenderer` API through their respective *gatsby-ssr.js* files, conflicts can occur between them.

If multiple plugins are simultaneously using the API at the same time, during the build process you'll encounter an error that looks like the following, where `default-site-plugin` represents the local Gatsby site's *gatsby-ssr.js* file, not the plugin's:

```
warning replaceRenderer API found in these plugins:
warning gatsby-plugin-one, default-site-plugin
warning This might be an error, see: https://www.gatsbyjs.com/docs/debugging-
replace-renderer-api/
warning Duplicate replaceRenderer found, skipping gatsby-ssr.js for plugin:
gatsby-plugin-one
```

The easiest way to correct an issue with conflicting *gatsby-ssr.js* files is to identify the offending `replaceRenderer` API code in the plugin's *gatsby-ssr.js* file and copy it into your Gatsby site's own *gatsby-ssr.js* file. This needs to happen because only the *gatsby-*

*ssr.js* file for the site being built will be executed during the build process, which accepts only a single *gatsby-ssr.js* file.

 For a common real-world example of how to copy the replaceRen derer API code in a plugin's *gatsby-ssr.js* file into the Gatsby site's native *gatsby-ssr.js* file, consult the example involving Redux and Styled Components in the Gatsby documentation (*https://oreil.ly/ xrseG*).

## Debugging Cache Issues

Gatsby contains its own internal cache that is used to accelerate plugin handling, and especially the data sourcing process. Sometimes the Gatsby cache can fail, manifesting in strange and perhaps silent errors involving stale content, where the most up-to-date content doesn't display despite an upstream content update, and recent modifications to plugin code that don't appear to execute.

Gatsby uses a *.cache* directory to cache certain elements of the Gatsby site. Starting with Gatsby v2.1.1, the gatsby clean command is available to clear out the Gatsby cache and ensure the most recent versions of your plugin code and content are represented in your site:

```
$ gatsby clean
```

Prior to v2.1.1, an NPM script was required in the site's *package.json* file, as follows:

```
// package.json
{
  "scripts": {
    "clean": "rm -rf .cache"
  }
}
```

To run this NPM script for v2.1.0 and earlier, execute:

```
$ npm run clean
```

## Debugging Asynchronous Lifecycle Methods

For Gatsby developers who are used to previous paradigms of JavaScript programming, the introduction of specific syntax for asynchronicity into JavaScript may be a rude awakening. As of Node.js v8, Node.js can natively handle the async and await keywords, which are used to identify functions that should be treated asynchronously but are written as if they were synchronous. The async and await keywords are particularly useful for situations where consecutive Promises were chained together in older JavaScript, which often led to confusing and hard-to-read code.

Within Gatsby, certain lifecycle methods, like `createPages` in Gatsby's Node APIs, are presumed by the framework to be asynchronous. This means it is generally assumed that a value may not immediately be available upon the execution of the `createPages` logic. Methods like `createPages` will eventually resolve to a value (or not resolve, throwing an error) represented by a `Promise`. In asynchronous JavaScript with `Promises`, we wait for the `Promise` to resolve to a usable value, and in Gatsby's case, the lifecycle method in question (such as `createPages`) is considered complete once the `Promise` resolves.

Gatsby's Node APIs handle a great deal of asynchronous logic, such as requests for data from external sources, invocations of `graphql`, and more. For this reason, Gatsby developers may encounter difficult-to-debug errors when writing logic in *gatsby-node.js* that does not correctly return `Promises`. The resolutions of these promises may occur after the lifecycle method is considered by Gatsby to be complete, thus returning a value that was expected but now is never used.

When writing logic in *gatsby-node.js*, pay close attention to whether a method is expected to be asynchronous or not. For instance, in the following example, not including the `await` keyword shown ahead of the invocation of `graphql` would result in absent data, since `createPages` will not wait for the value representing the result of `graphql` to be returned:

```
// gatsby-node.js
exports.createPages = async function ({ actions, graphql }) {
  await graphql(`
    {
      allMarkdownRemark {
        edges {
          node {
            fields {
              slug
            }
          }
        }
      }
    }
  `).then(res => {
    res.data.allMarkdownRemark.edges.forEach(edge => {
      const slug = edge.node.fields.slug
      actions.createPage({
        path: slug,
        component: require.resolve(`./src/templates/article.js`),
        context: {
          slug
        },
      })
    })
  })
```

```
  })
}
```

There are also scenarios where it is necessary to wait for a series of unconnected Promises to resolve before proceeding. In JavaScript, the `Promise.all()` method encapsulates multiple asynchronous actions, such as a data fetch (e.g., `fetch().then()`) that represents a `Promise` but needs to query multiple APIs or data sources. Consider the following example, in which we retrieve data from multiple APIs:

```
// gatsby-node.js
const fetch = require("node-fetch")

exports.createPages = async function ({ actions, graphql }) {
  const [siteAData, siteBData] = await Promise.all([
    fetch("https://site-a.com/api/articles").then(res => res.json()),
    fetch("https://site-b.com/api/products").then(res => res.json()),
  ])

  // Further logic with actions.createPage.
}
```

Because one of the `fetch` operations may conclude before the other, we need to ensure that Gatsby awaits the resolution of all `Promises` contained therein before proceeding and marking the `createPages` lifecycle method as complete.

# Conclusion

Getting a Gatsby site ready to go live in production isn't just a matter of putting the finishing touches on implementation. During the development process, it's often the case that small bugs or larger issues creep into code that can stymie even the best-planned development cycle. For this reason, Gatsby provides a robust set of tools for testing Gatsby sites during implementation and debugging issues as they arise.

Fortunately, many of the practices we've outlined in this chapter are foundational to JavaScript or Node.js in addition to Gatsby itself, but that doesn't mean that developers building Gatsby sites should give testing and debugging short shrift on the journey to a live Gatsby site. The tools and techniques covered in this chapter will serve you particularly well as we move on to our next topic, deploying Gatsby sites, where it's a bit less permissible for things to go wrong—especially when building for customers.

# CHAPTER 12

# Deploying Gatsby

Once you've done the work to spruce up your codebase (through best practices for testing and debugging your Gatsby site), it's time to push your site into production so your users can begin to interact with your Gatsby implementation. Because it's an SSG at its core, there are several aspects of Gatsby that require some unique approaches to handling deployments and managing environments. Unlike other JavaScript technologies like React or Angular, Gatsby requires a serverless approach to hosting infrastructure that may be unfamiliar.

In this chapter, we'll start with a comprehensive introduction to how Gatsby handles environment variables, a subject we've touched on many times throughout this book but have not accorded its own full coverage. Then we'll explore how to handle unusual hosting requirements such as assets hosted elsewhere and Gatsby sites located on paths other than domain roots. Finally, we'll examine some of the most commonly used hosting infrastructure providers for Gatsby builds and deployments (Netlify, Vercel, Gatsby Cloud, and others), which each have independent and compelling advantages for developers working in their ecosystems.

## Environment Variables

Gatsby developers can use environment variables to provide values that need to be distinct across development environments. They are most commonly used to obfuscate certain information that may be sensitive and should not be exposed to others.

Some environments require different information to customize behavior in those environments. Others, for security reasons, need to ensure certain sensitive credentials like access tokens and configuration values aren't exposed to the public. Regardless of their use, the environment variables we have in our local development environment need to be provided to the production environment, or other hosted environments, in a private and secure way.

There are two types of environment variables that are commonly used by Gatsby developers in their implementations:

*Project environment variables*
> These are environment variables that dictate behavior in disparate environments and need to be defined in particular places, (such as a local development environment or remote production environment), in order to pass critical values to the site in each respective environment.

*Operating system–level environment variables*
> We've seen a few examples throughout this book of OS-level environment variables, which accompany command-line executions as part of a build or deployment command. In Node.js, for instance, it's common to prefix commands with definitions of environment variables where those environment variables need to be introduced as arguments, as we'll see in the next section.

Both of these types of variables require special handling by Gatsby, which provides two environments out of the box in its framework. Though Gatsby can support additional environments, these two are the most commonly required:

*Development environment*
> Gatsby considers any situation in which you run the `gatsby develop` command to be the development environment for its purposes.

*Production environment*
> Running `gatsby build` or `gatsby serve` locally or in a hosted solution instantiates a production environment in Gatsby terms.

The two types of environment variables are only accessible for use during build-time compilation, when Node.js is running. Because no environment variable is exposed at runtime (since Gatsby is fundamentally an SSG), Gatsby needs to retrieve those environment variables and embed them into the client-side JavaScript bundle that it produces. In Gatsby's internals, this is handled by the `DefinePlugin` plugin in Webpack.

Upon their availability in Gatsby's client-side code, both project and OS-level environment variables can be accessed through the `process.env` global variable in Node.js. Because these environment variables are embedded only during build-time compilation, updating them requires you to restart the development server, or to perform a site rebuild, for the modifications to take effect.

It's possible in Gatsby to set up additional environments with a bit of additional work, such as arbitrary staging and test environments for needs such as quality assurance (QA). For more information, consult the Gatsby documentation's guide to creating additional environments (*https://oreil.ly/7TwWO*), with a real-world example involving Gatsby's Google Analytics plugin.

# Defining Environment Variables

Environment variables in Gatsby can be placed:

- In client-side JavaScript through environment configuration files, as we've seen in previous chapters
- In server-side Node.js implementations via infrastructure providers like Netlify, operating systems, or command-line executions of NPM scripts

Let's take a closer look at client-side environment variables and server-side environment variables in turn.

### Client-side environment variables

With regard to environment variables that need to be available in the client-side JavaScript bundle generated by Gatsby, it's a best practice to create an environment configuration file, which carries the prefix *.env* and usually an extension that identifies the environment in question. For a development environment, this takes the form *.env.development*, whereas for a production environment, the form is *.env.production*. These files need to be defined in your project root and can contain arbitrary project environment variables that apply to your project:

```
# .env.development
MY_ENV_VAR_FOR_DEV=foo

# .env.production
MY_ENV_VAR_FOR_PROD=bar
```

In Gatsby, OS-level environment variables carry the prefix `GATSBY_`. These will become available in the client-side browser-ready bundle Gatsby creates on your behalf:

```
# .env.development
GATSBY_DEV_ENV_VAR=foo

# .env.production
GATSBY_PROD_ENV_VAR=bar
```

## Server-side environment variables

Unlike other implementations that leverage universal JavaScript, Gatsby performs all compilation at build time, which means that only those scripts executed during the build will provide environment variables on the server side. More specifically, Gatsby runs a few Node.js scripts in succession during the build-time compilation process, including the logic found in *gatsby-config.js* and *gatsby-node.js*.

Because Node.js has access to OS-level environment variables while it is executing, environment variables can be added:

- By adding them before NPM scripts in the command line
- By providing them to an infrastructure provider
- Within the operating system itself

In a Linux terminal (or on macOS), you can add an environment variable to an arbitrary NPM script as follows:

```
$ MY_ENV_VAR=bar npm run develop
```

Unlike client-side project environment variables exposed to the browser as part of Gatsby's creation of a client bundle, server-side environment variables will not be automatically detected when Node.js scripts are executed. Thus, it's strongly recommended that you use the `dotenv` library to introspect the available *.env.\** files and include those values in the NPM scripts' execution. Since `dotenv` is already a defined dependency in Gatsby's *package.json* file, you don't need to install it separately and can instead require it in your *gatsby-config.js* or *gatsby-node.js* file as follows:

```
// gatsby-node.js
require("dotenv").config({
  path: `.env.${process.env.NODE_ENV}`,
})
```

These values are now available through `process.env`, a global variable injected into Node.js upon its execution, as we saw in the previous section with client-side environment variables.

 Gatsby developers leveraging Windows operating systems for development need to undertake a slightly different approach (*https://oreil.ly/sYBLD*) for server-side OS-level environment variables included in a terminal command.

## Using Environment Variables

It's a best practice not to commit environment configuration files to source control providers unless there is absolute certainty no sensitive credentials are contained inside.

Many Gatsby developers utilize local environment configuration files to manage that sensitive information outside of source control, while simultaneously providing environment variables to continuous deployment (CD) providers in the infrastructure provider's own interface.

To illustrate this, consider an example in which you need to consume two different versions of an API as a data source, one that exposes "development" data and the other exposing "production" data. Your environment configuration files might contain an API access token shared across both API environments, but the APIs are referred to distinctly:

```
# .env.development
GATSBY_BASE_URL=https://dev.my-api-host.com/api
API_ACCESS_TOKEN=da62e848ded24f69b246312456b55a66

# .env.production
GATSBY_BASE_URL=https://live.my-api-host.com/api
API_ACCESS_TOKEN=da62e848ded24f69b246312456b55a66
```

When you need to refer to the API URL again in your code anywhere in your Gatsby site, including in Gatsby pages and components, you can do so as follows:

```
// src/pages/index.js
<img src={`${process.env.GATSBY_BASE_URL}/hero.jpg`} alt="Hero image" />
```

There are certain reserved environment variables that Gatsby does not permit you to override, as they're used internally to optimize Gatsby builds: attempting to set NODE_ENV or PUBLIC_DIR yourself will result in errors.

Any environment variable prefixed with GATSBY_ will automatically be embedded as process.env.GATSBY\_\* in compiled JavaScript, which means that the variable will be available within the context of the browser without being unintentionally exposed elsewhere. For all other environment variables without the GATSBY_ prefix, your Gatsby site can access values such as API_ACCESS_TOKEN on the server side (i.e., Node.js) via the process.env variable, just as when configuring source plugin options:

```
// gatsby-config.js
plugins: [
  {
    resolve: `gatsby-source-contentful`,
```

```
    options: {
      spaceId: `mySpaceId`,
      accessToken: process.env.CONTENTFUL_ACCESS_TOKEN,
    },
  },
],
```

 An environment variable named ENABLE_GATSBY_REFRESH_END
POINT is commonly used by Gatsby developers to permit sourced
data to be refreshed from an external source while running the
Gatsby local development server (gatsby develop). More information can be found in the Gatsby documentation's guide to
refreshing content (*https://oreil.ly/NJxnq*). In addition, Gatsby
makes available build variables (*https://oreil.ly/OZcqE*) (e.g.,
CI=true) for more advanced CD configuration.

# Using Path and Asset Prefixes

The vast majority of Gatsby sites are hosted at the root of their domain (e.g., *exam-
ple.com/*), and their assets are usually located in some directory within that domain
(e.g., *example.com/img* or *example.com/css*). However, there are certain scenarios in
which Gatsby developers prefer to host their Gatsby sites at a different location than
the domain root, as well as situations where external assets outside the domain need
to be used.

In this section, we'll cover both of these conditions in detail. Deploying a Gatsby site
to a location other than the domain root requires the use of *path prefixes* in Gatsby
site configuration, while employing assets from a different domain requires developers to use *asset prefixes* to identify where those files are located.

## Path Prefixes

Sometimes, Gatsby developers need to implement sites that fit into an existing path
system on a domain that houses other sites. For instance, you may have a Gatsby site
that coexists with other Gatsby sites and needs to be under a particular path (say,
*example.com/gatsby-site*). As a matter of fact, some hosting providers—notably Git-
Hub Pages—obligate the use of an internal path rather than the domain root (e.g.,
*example.github.io/gatsby-site*), unless a custom domain is used.

Without a path prefix, the site itself and any assets that are located within the site's
internal directory structure will fail upon deployment. All paths on the site, and all
paths to site assets, require a path prefix in this scenario.

To configure a path prefix, add a pathPrefix key to your *gatsby-config.js* file, as
follows:

```
// gatsby-config.js
module.exports = {
  pathPrefix: `/gatsby-site`,
}
```

For instance, if you have a Gatsby blog that needs to be located under the path prefix /blog after the domain, you can enforce that distinction in your Gatsby configuration file:

```
// gatsby-config.js
module.exports = {
  pathPrefix: `/blog`,
}
```

Whenever you perform a Gatsby build or serve your Gatsby site through a server, you must also pass the `--prefix-paths` flag in order to ensure that your path prefix value is accounted for during the build process. Note that this is also the case when using hosting providers that ask developers to provide a build command in deployment configuration.

To build your Gatsby site with the path prefix, execute the following:

```
$ gatsby build --prefix-paths
```

To serve the site, execute the following:

```
$ gatsby serve --prefix-paths
```

Without this flag, even if you configure the path prefix within your Gatsby configuration file, the build process will ignore your `pathPrefix` value and build the site assuming that you wish to situate it in the domain root.

> The Gatsby `<Link />` component respects path prefixes and will ensure that path prefixes are accounted for during the build process. This means that you never need to include the path prefix when you add a path to the `to` prop of the component. Gatsby's `navigate` helper also respects path prefixes. For more information, consult the Gatsby documentation's guide to in-app linking with path prefixes (*https://oreil.ly/0txUI*). Where you do need to construct paths manually because neither of these solutions works for your use case, you can use the `withPrefix` helper provided by Gatsby to manually add the path prefix (*https://oreil.ly/6cXpV*).

# Asset Prefixes

The end result of a Gatsby build is a collection of HTML files representing the Gatsby site and assets such as images, videos, JavaScript files, and CSS files. Today, it's common practice for Gatsby developers to deploy the Gatsby-generated static HTML to a domain root but to leverage a different domain, such as a CDN, for other assets.

Introduced in Gatsby v2.4.0, asset prefixes allow you to enforce this distinction in your Gatsby builds by setting a prefix for assets that need to be hosted elsewhere, whether due to limitations of the infrastructure or corporate hosting policies. As with path prefixes, adding asset prefixes to your Gatsby site is a matter of including them in your *gatsby-config.js* file, as follows:

```
// gatsby-config.js
module.exports = {
  assetPrefix: `https://cdn.example-cdn.com`,
}
```

Likewise, to ensure your asset prefixes are taken into account during the build process, whenever you perform a build or a serve of a Gatsby site you must include the `--prefix-paths` flag:

```
$ gatsby build --prefix-paths
$ gatsby serve --prefix-paths
```

Note that if you have path prefixes set in addition to asset prefixes, both of these will be respected upon the execution of the command.

One of the biggest benefits of asset prefixes is the fact that script embeds and references to stylesheets, images, and other assets will come prepopulated with the correctly prefixed paths. For instance, a JavaScript file known as *main.js* will appear in your generated static HTML like this:

```
<!-- Gatsby HTML -->
<script src="https://cdn.example-cdn.com/main.js"></script>
```

However, asset prefixes also require an additional step: unless you deploy the assets referred to in your static HTML to your CDN of choice or other domain, your Gatsby site will be making references to nonexistent files. Gatsby recommends two approaches as best practices for ensuring your assets are available on a CDN or other domain when the static HTML is presented to an end user: using an `onPostBuild` API hook in *gatsby-node.js* or using custom scripts in your *package.json* file.

To ensure the contents of your *public/* folder, which houses all JavaScript files, CSS stylesheets, and other Gatsby-managed assets, are uploaded to the correct location using the `onPostBuild` API hook, add the following to your *gatsby-node.js* file:

```
// gatsby-node.js
const assetsDir = `public`

exports.onPostBuild = async function onPostBuild() {
  // Take the public directory and place its contents somewhere (e.g. a CDN).
}
```

Another option is to add a script to your *package.json* file. Many providers and CDN services offer a CLI that can be used to upload the assets in your *public/* folder, like in the following example that demonstrates a file sync to an Amazon S3 bucket:

```
// package.json
{
  "scripts": {
    "build": "gatsby build --prefix-paths",
    "postbuild": "aws s3 sync public s3://myAwsBucket"
  }
}
```

Path and asset prefixes are powerful tools that enable the deployment of Gatsby sites and their assets to arbitrary locations and are particularly useful in more advanced hosting use cases that require differentiated configuration. In the next section, we direct our attention to individual hosting services and their use.

 There are some additional considerations when using asset prefixes, such as their interaction with path prefixes and the `gatsby-plugin-offline` plugin, which are accounted for in the Gatsby documentation (*https://oreil.ly/8Xhjo*).

# Deploying to Hosting Services

Once you've configured your deployment, whether that means populating environment variables or customizing path and asset prefixes, it's time to deploy your Gatsby site to an infrastructure provider. There are a variety of hosting solutions for Gatsby sites that run the gamut from static site hosting companies such as Netlify (*https://www.netlify.com*), Vercel (*https://vercel.com*), and Gatsby Cloud (*https://oreil.ly/KftNP*) to broader hosting platforms that offer Jamstack-catered services like Azure (*https://oreil.ly/5p1qi*) and Amazon Web Services (*https://aws.amazon.com*), and even solutions like GitHub Pages that act as hosted services for static files.

Because these platforms are both extensive in their own right and constantly evolving, it would be impossible to cover them comprehensively in this book. In the coming sections, we'll take a quick look at some of the most popular solutions that are available at the time of writing and introduce some of the considerations you will want to think over as you use these services. To make an educated decision about which infrastructure best suits your needs, I recommend that you visit these services' sites and perform your own due diligence.

## Netlify

As of this writing, Netlify is one of the most popular solutions among Gatsby developers (including this author) seeking a convenient hosting platform for Gatsby sites. Netlify performs continuous deployments triggered by interactions with source control providers such as GitHub, GitLab, and Bitbucket, and it provides a slew of other features, including a global CDN, full domain name system (DNS) support, automated TLS support for HTTPS, and more.

Netlify offers two ways to host Gatsby sites on its platform, the easiest being through a Git repository. The other approach is to upload your generated Gatsby site in the form of a folder generated as the Gatsby build result.

 This section covers only the use of Gatsby with a Git repository. The Gatsby documentation offers a guide to uploading Gatsby site folders to Netlify (*https://oreil.ly/knKfl*).

With the use of Git repositories, Netlify allows Gatsby developers to roll back builds by reversing Git commits that trigger Gatsby builds in Netlify. Whenever new code is pushed to a Git repository that is integrated with Netlify, the platform will automatically create a new build of your Gatsby site, whether the codebase is housed in a public or private code repository. Many Gatsby developers prefer this approach as it obviates the need to manually manage builds and upload build results.

When you log in to Netlify, you'll see a "New site from Git" button that will guide you through a wizard to select a source control provider and the code repository in which your Gatsby site is managed. Netlify will then display the following configuration options for your Netlify site:

- *Branch to deploy.* You can customize which branch Netlify should monitor for new code pushes that ought to trigger new Gatsby builds. By default, Netlify selects the master or main branch.

- *Build command.* This is the command that Netlify will execute to complete a build; it defaults to npm run build. Note that for cases where you need to account for path prefixes or asset prefixes, customizing this may be necessary.

- *Publish directory.* Gatsby, by default, provides its build results in a *public* directory. In Netlify the default is also *public*, but it allows developers to choose an arbitrary folder in their codebase that houses the build result.

- *Advanced build settings.* This is where Netlify users can configure other arbitrary settings for Gatsby site builds. For instance, if you need to set environment variable values that are normally only available in the local development environment, you can do so here.

Once you click the "Deploy site" button, Netlify will automatically kick off a build and deploy process to generate a new Gatsby build hosted in Netlify. The Deploys tab will display options such as "Deploy log," which allows you to view the build log as the build proceeds, and a new live site URL will be generated, at which you can view the production version of your Netlify site.

For more information about hosting Gatsby sites on Netlify, consult the Gatsby documentation, which includes custom domain setup information (*https://oreil.ly/ekHkV*), and the Netlify documentation, which provides a step-by-step guide to setting up Gatsby on Netlify (*https://oreil.ly/WSP7u*).

# Vercel

Like Netlify, Vercel (formerly known as Zeit) offers a cloud platform for static sites like Gatsby sites and a trigger-based mechanism from Git providers to conduct continuous deployment. Vercel's offerings include autoscaling, a global edge network, asset compression, cache invalidation, and a zero-configuration developer experience.

Like Netlify, Vercel is most powerful when integrated directly with a Git repository using Vercel's native Import Flow after connecting the integration to GitHub, GitLab, or Bitbucket. Each code push will trigger a new build and deployment that can be arbitrarily specified to occur only on specific branches or all branches. These will generate what Vercel calls *preview deployments*, and all modifications made to the `master` or `main` branch will facilitate *production deployments*. Vercel also offers custom domain support via the account holder's Domain Settings page.

For more information about hosting Gatsby sites on Vercel, consult the Gatsby documentation's guide to Gatsby on Vercel (*https://oreil.ly/DHEL4*), or Vercel's example Gatsby codebase (*https://oreil.ly/27N3l*), official guide to hosting Gatsby on Vercel (*https://oreil.ly/pYRYE*), and documentation pages on Vercel deployments (*https://vercel.com/docs*) and Vercel custom domains (*https://oreil.ly/YwrzE*).

# Gatsby Cloud

Gatsby Cloud is a platform provided by Gatsby (the company), which was cofounded by Gatsby creator Kyle Mathews and Sam Bhagwat in 2019. Gatsby Cloud's primary value proposition is the expertise of the Gatsby core team and tools catering directly to the Gatsby framework. As of this writing, Gatsby Cloud offers the following features:

- *Quick Connect.* Gatsby Cloud's developer onboarding process facilitates rapid integration of a CMS, a prepopulated content model, and a Gatsby starter that is already connected to the source data through its wizard.

- *Real-time preview.* Gatsby Cloud provides content teams with the ability to preview content changes and code changes within the context of a Gatsby site using temporary URLs that are shareable across collaborative teams. Gatsby Cloud also offers a mechanism to hot-reload previews based on incoming webhook notifications from configured CMSs.

- *Builds.* Gatsby Cloud provides a fast build service and offers deployments to CDN solutions and hosting providers like Netlify and Vercel.
- *Hosting.* As of 2021, Gatsby Cloud provides a hosting service for Gatsby sites that includes a free TLS certificate supporting HTTPS.
- *Reports.* Gatsby Cloud offers off-the-shelf support for automated Lighthouse reports that suggest improvements in performance and accessibility, giving developers optimization opportunities outside of manual Lighthouse reports during development.

Gatsby Cloud provides integrations with the following CMSs as well as POST endpoints for CMSs that support webhooks for features such as real-time preview:

- Automatic CMS integration: Contentful, Cosmic, DatoCMS, Sanity
- Manual CMS integration: Contentstack, Drupal, Strapi, WordPress

Gatsby Cloud also provides integrations with the following hosting providers:

- Netlify
- Amazon S3
- Firebase
- Google Cloud Storage
- Fastly

 For more information about Gatsby Cloud, consult the Gatsby Cloud documentation (*https://oreil.ly/0D7Bq*). The Gatsby guide to deploying to Gatsby Cloud (*https://oreil.ly/oxRR5*) provides instructions to set up a new Gatsby site, import an existing Gatsby site, and set up hosting on Gatsby Cloud.

# AWS Amplify

AWS Amplify is a service provided by Amazon Web Services (AWS) that offers a client library, a command-line toolchain, and an AWS Console for continuous deployment and static site hosting. With the Amplify CLI, Gatsby developers can provision full-stack implementations that account for in-app authentication, data storage, serverless GraphQL and REST APIs, web analytics, Lambda functions, and more. The Amplify Console grants access to both single-page application and static site hosting, as well as features such as continuous deployment, globally available CDNs, custom domains with HTTPS, feature branch deployments, and site-level password protection.

To use AWS Amplify, you need to create an AWS account and have a Gatsby site ready for import.

There is a Gatsby Auth starter with AWS Amplify (*https://oreil.ly/ FYo7c*) available as an example of a Gatsby site optimized for use with this service.

Once you log in to the AWS Amplify Console, click "Get started" under the Deploy heading, which will take you to a wizard where you can connect a branch from your code repository managed by GitHub, GitLab, Bitbucket, or AWS CodeCommit. This allows AWS Amplify to perform continuous deployment. AWS Amplify will then pre-populate some default build settings, including environment variables.

After you click "Save and deploy," the AWS Amplify Console will trigger a new build and deployment and make your build artifacts available at a URL that ends in *.amplifyapp.com*. Once this process is complete, AWS Amplify will also display screenshots of your Gatsby site on various devices.

For more information about AWS Amplify, consult the Gatsby documentation's guide to Gatsby on AWS Amplify (*https://oreil.ly/ WabQy*), the Gatsby blog post on publishing Gatsby sites to AWS Amplify (*https://oreil.ly/goWh4*), and the livestream by Jason Lengstorf and Nader Dabit on building and deploying Gatsby sites with AWS Amplify (*https://youtu.be/i9HG8CV-_dQ*).

# Azure

Azure is Microsoft's native hosting platform, with a variety of services including serverless features and static website hosting through Azure Static Web Apps. The Azure Static Web Apps service also includes support for a built-in CDN, authentication, continuous deployment, and HTTPS. In order to utilize Azure as your static site host, your Gatsby site needs to be available in a source repository.

After signing in to Azure, search for the Static Web Apps service, select it, and click Add to add a new static site. Then, configure your new Azure application and link it to your source repository by entering the required project details (your Azure subscription and an Azure resource group) and Static Web Apps configuration (name and region) before authenticating with your source control provider. Identify the source repository and the code branch.

Azure will then bring you to a build configuration wizard, which will allow you to specify the following build settings:

- *App location.* This can be left blank if your Gatsby project is located at the root of your source repository. If the repository includes both frontend and backend code in separate directories, identify only the Gatsby site's directory.

- *API location.* This can be left blank or filled in with the location of a backend API; the default value is `api`.

- *App artifact location.* This field should be filled in with the directory containing the build artifacts generated by each Azure build, such as *public*, which is Gatsby's default public directory.

Once your application is created in Azure, the Static Web Apps service will initiate a deployment for you automatically, after which you can view your site. With the Git-Hub Action Azure creates on your behalf in the GitHub repository, Azure will notify you once the deployment is ready for review. This process takes several minutes.

 For more information about hosting Gatsby on Azure, consult the Gatsby documentation's guide to using Gatsby with Azure (*https://oreil.ly/xtKAc*) as well as the Azure Static Web Apps documentation (*https://oreil.ly/0kq5G*), which includes information about using custom domains (*https://oreil.ly/YTGWG*), a walkthrough (*https://oreil.ly/Mrxjk*) and quickstart (*https://oreil.ly/SBbJ9*) guide for Gatsby, and information about routing (*https://oreil.ly/sh5EH*) and authentication (*https://oreil.ly/5cDgn*).

# Amazon S3

For Gatsby developers who desire deeper interaction with their deployments, Amazon S3 is a lower-level alternative to AWS Amplify. An object storage provider offered by AWS, Amazon S3 also provides an integration with Amazon CloudFront, a global CDN. Once you have an account with access to the AWS Console, you can install the AWS CLI (*https://aws.amazon.com/cli*) and configure it to authenticate into your account with your AWS key and secret:

```
$ pip install awscli
$ aws configure
```

The most direct way to deploy your Gatsby site to S3 is to use the Gatsby S3 plugin, which provides configuration options for your S3 bucket:

```
$ npm install gatsby-plugin-s3
```

Configure your newly installed plugin in *gatsby-config.js* with information about your S3 bucket:

```
// gatsby-config.js
plugins: [
  {
    resolve: `gatsby-plugin-s3`,
    options: {
      bucketName: "my-s3-bucket-name",
    },
  },
]
```

Then, add a deploy script to your Gatsby site's *package.json* file by providing a deploy command using the Gatsby S3 plugin:

```
// package.json
"scripts": {
  "deploy": "gatsby-plugin-s3 deploy"
}
```

Once you've configured the plugin and this NPM script, you can execute the following chained commands to deploy the site to your S3 bucket:

```
$ npm run build && npm run deploy
```

 For more information about hosting Gatsby on S3, consult the Gatsby documentation's guide to using Gatsby with S3 (*https://oreil.ly/7W3oW*), which includes information about using environment variables and setting up CloudFront. Also consult the S3 documentation (*https://aws.amazon.com/s3*).

# Heroku

Heroku, now part of Salesforce, is a common hosting solution for both single-page JavaScript applications and static sites. The Heroku CLI offers rich interactions with Heroku's build and deployment capabilities, as well as a variety of other features for continuous integration and continuous deployment.

If you're using the Heroku CLI (*https://oreil.ly/rBdK5*), the quickest way to set up builds and deployments of your Gatsby site is to set Heroku's Node.js (`heroku/nodejs`) and Static (`heroku-buildpack-static`) "buildpacks" in your Gatsby project root:

```
$ heroku buildpacks:set heroku/nodejs
$ heroku buildpacks:add https://github.com/heroku/heroku-buildpack-static.git
```

To enable integration with Heroku's Platform API, you can also optionally include the buildpacks in Heroku's *app.json* manifest:

```
// app.json
{
  "buildpacks": [
    {
```

```
        "url": "heroku/nodejs"
      },
      {
        "url": "https://github.com/heroku/heroku-buildpack-static"
      }
    ]
  }
```

In either scenario, Heroku will detect the NPM build script within your Gatsby site's *package.json* file and automatically execute it, as long as your *package.json* file defines the script as follows:

```
// package.json
{
  "scripts": {
    "build": "gatsby build"
  }
}
```

For the Heroku Static buildpack to understand where the build result of your Gatsby site will be located, you also need to configure the path to your generated static assets, which is the *public* directory in typical Gatsby sites. Create a *static.json* manifest in your Gatsby project root and provide the options Heroku needs:

```
// static.json
{
  "root": "public/",
  "headers": {
    "/**": {
      "Cache-Control": "public, max-age=0, must-revalidate"
    },
    "/**.css": {
      "Cache-Control": "public, max-age=31536000, immutable"
    },
    "/**.js": {
      "Cache-Control": "public, max-age=31536000, immutable"
    },
    "/static/**": {
      "Cache-Control": "public, max-age=31536000, immutable"
    },
    "/icons/*.png": {
      "Cache-Control": "public, max-age=31536000, immutable"
    }
  },
  "https_only": true,
  "error_page": "404.html"
}
```

This *static.json* manifest for the Heroku Static buildpack also identifies certain caching configuration options optimized for your Gatsby site.

For more information about Gatsby on Heroku, consult Gatsby's guide to hosting Gatsby on Heroku (*https://oreil.ly/GFnwS*), the `heroku-buildpack-static` documentation (*https://oreil.ly/vEASY*), and the Heroku Platform API documentation (*https://oreil.ly/RgB8L*).

# Firebase

Firebase, now part of Google, is a developer-oriented hosting platform that, like Heroku, offers a CLI for developers who wish to perform infrastructure operations through the terminal. Firebase enables deployment of both dynamic web applications and static sites to a global CDN. Before getting started with this service, users wishing to deploy Gatsby sites need to have a Firebase account and a Firebase project in that account.

To deploy your Gatsby site as a Firebase project, install the Firebase CLI by executing the following command:

```
$ npm install -g firebase-tools
```

Firebase allows you to use the command line to authenticate into your account and to list the available Firebase projects:

```
$ firebase login
$ firebase projects:list
```

Change directories into your Gatsby project root, if you aren't in that folder already, and initialize a new Firebase project:

```
$ firebase init
```

The Firebase CLI will then walk you through a process to select the Firebase services to install and to identify a Firebase project in your account to associate with the Gatsby site. It's recommended to choose the Firebase Hosting option. The Firebase CLI will also prompt you to identify a public directory, which defaults to *public*, the same as Gatsby's own default.

Like Heroku, Firebase creates a manifest file (*firebase.json*) you should edit to provide cache configuration. The Gatsby documentation recommends this approach to Firebase manifests unless you have more advanced caching requirements:

```
// firebase.json
{
  "hosting": {
    "public": "public",
    "ignore": ["firebase.json", "**/.*", "**/node_modules/**"],
    "headers": [
      {
        "source": "**/*",
        "headers": [
```

```
          {
            "key": "cache-control",
            "value": "public, max-age=0, must-revalidate"
          }
        ]
      },
      {
        "source": "static/**",
        "headers": [
          {
            "key": "cache-control",
            "value": "public, max-age=31536000, immutable"
          }
        ]
      },
      {
        "source": "**/*.@(css|js)",
        "headers": [
          {
            "key": "cache-control",
            "value": "public, max-age=31536000, immutable"
          }
        ]
      },
      {
        "source": "sw.js",
        "headers": [
          {
            "key": "cache-control",
            "value": "public, max-age=0, must-revalidate"
          }
        ]
      },
      {
        "source": "page-data/**",
        "headers": [
          {
            "key": "cache-control",
            "value": "public, max-age=0, must-revalidate"
          }
        ]
      }
    ]
  }
}
```

Upon saving this manifest, you can perform a Gatsby build to generate the contents of the *public* directory:

```
$ gatsby build
```

Then, deploy your site to Firebase by executing the following command, after which your website will be available from a domain ending in *.firebaseapp.com* or *.web.app*:

```
$ firebase deploy
```

Each time you update your Gatsby site, be sure to rebuild your site and redeploy.

 For more information about hosting Gatsby on Firebase, consult the Firebase documentation (*https://oreil.ly/o79j4*), the Firebase CLI reference (*https://oreil.ly/mEO3n*), Firebase's quickstart guide (*https://oreil.ly/Bajym*), and Firebase's guide to using custom domains (*https://oreil.ly/4NQcj*).

# GitHub Pages

Though GitHub Pages isn't a typical hosting platform, its ease of use means it's a popular solution for Gatsby developers who want to host their websites directly through their GitHub repositories. There are three different options for Gatsby developers who have selected GitHub Pages for deployment:

- Use a path that corresponds to the GitHub account name and repository name, such as *github-user.github.io/repository-name* or *github-user.github.io/docs*.
- Use a *github.io* subdomain that corresponds to the GitHub account or organization name, such as *github-user.github.io/*.
- Use the subdomain solution, but configured to leverage a custom domain.

 If your Gatsby repository on GitHub is private or internal to your GitHub account or organization, any published Gatsby site will expose any information in the Gatsby build to the general public, so ensure that your repository is devoid of any sensitive data before publishing your site to GitHub Pages.

GitHub Pages can be configured through GitHub itself and the gh-pages NPM package. First, navigate to your Gatsby site's repository on GitHub and select Settings under your repository name. Navigate to the GitHub Pages page, where you can choose a branch such as master or main if you plan to publish your Gatsby site to a *github.io* subdomain. You can also select gh-pages, which you'll need to create if it isn't represented among your branches, to publish to a path such as *github-user.github.io/custom-path*.

Within your Gatsby project root, install the gh-pages NPM package into your development dependencies:

```
$ npm install --save-dev gh-pages
```

To deploy your Gatsby site to a path such as *github-user.github.io/repository-name*, you'll need to modify your *gatsby-config.js* file to account for the path prefix and your *package.json* file to include the path prefix in Gatsby builds. In this scenario, be sure your GitHub Pages branch is set to `gh-pages`. In *gatsby-config.js*:

```
// gatsby-config.js
module.exports = {
  pathPrefix: "/{repository-name}",
}
```

In package.json:

```
// package.json
{
  "scripts": {
    "deploy": "gatsby build --prefix-paths && gh-pages -d public"
  }
}
```

Then, to deploy, you can execute the following command, which will execute the Gatsby build and publish the *public* directory to GitHub Pages:

```
$ npm run deploy
```

To deploy your Gatsby site to the *github-user.github.io/* subdomain without a path prefix, the site needs to be up to date with your desired production state on the `main` or `master` branch, or whichever branch is your repository's default branch. In this scenario, there is no need to configure a path prefix or include it with the Gatsby build command. The deploy script in your *package.json* should instead be defined as follows:

```
// package.json
{
  "scripts": {
    "deploy": "gatsby build && gh-pages -d public -b master"
  }
}
```

Once you run the following command, your Gatsby site will be published to the subdomain rather than an internal path:

```
$ npm run deploy
```

 For more information about hosting Gatsby on GitHub Pages, consult the Gatsby documentation's guide to using Gatsby with GitHub Pages (*https://oreil.ly/iLuYY*), which contains information on using a custom domain, and deploying from a continuous integration (CI) service. Also consult the GitHub Pages documentation (*https://pages.github.com*) for more usage information.

# Conclusion

When you've finished building your Gatsby site and have ensured no issues remain that block release, it's important to give careful thought to deployment. You'll want to facilitate the optimal deployment infrastructure for your site, both now and in the future. Thanks to environment variables, path prefixes, and asset prefixes, Gatsby provides a variety of mechanisms to protect your site from prying eyes and to deploy it and its assets flexibly.

In addition, various infrastructure providers offer compelling cases for using their services to deploy your Gatsby site. Though we didn't venture too deeply into the inner workings of any of these services, you should have a good idea of the options available—and the number of available hosting solutions for Gatsby sites will only continue to grow. Having covered some of the most important concerns for placing your Gatsby site in the hands of your users, in the next two chapters we'll delve into some advanced concepts in Gatsby and how it works on the inside to conclude our journey through the Gatsby framework.

# PART V

# Advanced Gatsby

# CHAPTER 13

# Advanced Topics in Gatsby

In the previous chapters, we've examined some of the most important beginning and intermediate use cases when developing Gatsby sites. But there are also many features available in Gatsby for more advanced use cases. For example, as a Gatsby developer, you may wish to automate certain tasks during Gatsby site setup, customize the GraphQL schema emitted by Gatsby's schema generation process, configure how Gatsby bundles sites, add components to Markdown files managed in Gatsby, or optimize your site's performance beyond Gatsby's defaults.

In this wide-ranging chapter, we'll cover some advanced use cases and features that go well beyond Gatsby's default capabilities that are available from starters. We'll explore creating Gatsby recipes, an example of infrastructure as code (IaC); adding components to Markdown using the MDX library; customizing Gatsby's GraphQL schema and bundling process; and optimizing performance using Gatsby's cache layer and other techniques relevant to both development and production use cases.

## Creating Recipes

In this section we'll explore *recipes* in Gatsby, which are configuration files or scripts that Gatsby ingests to generate predefined and consistent environments across development and production with minimal overhead. We'll also discuss the concept of IaC and how to automate common Gatsby site operations.

### Infrastructure as Code

IaC involves the notion of managing discrete environments (such as development, testing, and production) through configuration files and scripts that ensure consistency across your site builds. Differences between environments, such as differing

Node.js versions, are a common but often subtle source of problems for developers. IaC is intended to minimize this sort of "drift."

In Gatsby, configuration files describe the resources required by your project, including the dependencies and specific versions relied on by your Gatsby site. In addition, many Gatsby developers leverage plugins and themes that also need to be handled with cross-environment consistency. Because configuration files can be managed through source control, like other source files in Gatsby projects, we can use them to instantiate consistent environments every time we need to. This reduces the risk of errors caused as environments drift and provides a shared foundation for automated tasks.

## Automating Site Operations with Recipes

Because Gatsby recipes are a relatively new feature, introduced late in the Gatsby 2.0 release cycle, you may need to upgrade to the latest version of Gatsby to access recipe features:

```
$ npm install -g gatsby-cli@latest
$ npm install gatsby@latest
```

Then, run the following command in the root of an existing Gatsby project to access the list of available recipes:

```
$ gatsby recipes
```

You'll see output in your terminal that looks like the following and allows you to select from a variety of available recipes:

```
Select a recipe to run
>>Add a custom ESLint config
  Add Jest
  Add Gatsby Image
  Add Gatsby Theme Blog
  Add Gatsby Theme Blog Core
  Add Gatsby Theme Notes
  Add persistent layout component with gatsby-plugin-layout
  Add Theme UI
  Add Chakra UI
  Add Emotion
  Add support for MDX Pages
  Add support for MDX Pages with images
  Add Styled Components
  Add Tailwind
  Add Sass
  Add TypeScript
  Add Cypress testing
  Add animated page transition support
```

When you select one of these recipes and hit the Return key, your Gatsby site will automatically be equipped with the features it provides, set up on your behalf by

Gatsby. Recipes are written using Markdown and MDX, which we explore further in the next section. This means that recipes are not only easy to write, but also familiar to Gatsby developers across your team who have experience with MDX. As an example, here is the recipe to set up Styled Components, which is one of the options in the preceding list:

```
# Setup Styled Components

[Styled Components](https://styled-components.com/) is visual primitives for
the component age.
Use the best bits of ES6 and CSS to style your apps without stress

---

Install necessary NPM packages

<NPMPackage name="gatsby-plugin-styled-components" />
<NPMPackage name="styled-components" />
<NPMPackage name="babel-plugin-styled-components" />

---

Install the Styled Components plugin in gatsby-config.js

<GatsbyPlugin name="gatsby-plugin-styled-components" />

---

Sweet, now it's ready to go.

Let's also write out an example page you can use to play
with Styled Components.

<File
  path="src/pages/styled-components-example.js"
  content="https://gist.githubusercontent.com/KyleAMathews/ >>>
34541b87c4194ba2290eedbe8a0b1fe0/raw/ >>>
dba4d3ffecb5f2a3a36e0e017387185a9835c685/styled-components-example.js"
/>

---

Read more about Styled Components on the official docs site:

https://styled-components.com/
```

If there isn't a recipe in this list that suits your needs, you can author your own or use one contributed to the ecosystem by the Gatsby community. To run a local Gatsby recipe located on your machine, execute the following command:

```
$ gatsby recipes ./my-local-recipe.mdx
```

To run a remote recipe, such as one contributed by the community, you'd execute a command like the following:

```
$ gatsby recipes https://my-recipes-host.com/remote-recipe.mdx
```

Now that we've introduced the concept of recipes, let's dig into those strange JSX elements you may have noticed in the Styled Components example, like `<NPMPackage>` and `<File>`. In the next section, we'll explore MDX, a means of adding JSX components directly into your Markdown files (and a technology that can be leveraged for much more than Gatsby recipes!).

 For more information about Gatsby recipes, consult the Gatsby documentation's guide to IaC (*https://oreil.ly/KnA5k*) as well as the Gatsby recipes announcement (*https://oreil.ly/gnUrs*) and documentation on developing recipes (*https://oreil.ly/W68ho*).

# Adding Components to Markdown with MDX

In the previous section, we saw that Gatsby recipes are written with JSX elements interpolated into Markdown files. But what are these elements, and how is it possible to write JSX elements directly within Markdown? The answer lies in MDX.

MDX is an extension to the Markdown format that allows Markdown and JSX users to interpolate JSX elements into Markdown documents, making it possible to add React components into Gatsby blog posts and pages. Markdown already has certain HTML elements available out of the box and supports inline HTML—but MDX takes this a step further by allowing developers to insert JSX directly into their Markdown documents.

## Getting Started with MDX

Consider the following example Markdown document (say, *src/blog/blog-post.md*):

```
# Hello MDX!

Here is a [link](https://example.com).

<figure class="figure">
  <object data="figure.svg" type="image/svg+xml"></object>
  <figcaption>An illustration of MDX in Markdown.</figcaption>
</figure>
```

We can write a `Figure` component based on this in JSX, such as the following:

```
// src/components/figure.jsx
import React from "react"

export const Figure = props => {
```

```
    return (
      <figure className="chart">
        <object data={props.data} type="image/svg+xml"></object>
        <figcaption>{props.caption}</figcaption>
      </figure>
    )
}
```

Now, we can insert this `Figure` component into the same Markdown document, *src/blog/blog-post.md*, using MDX:

```
import { Figure } from './components/Figure';

# Hello MDX!

Here is a [link](https://example.com).

<Figure data="figure.svg" caption="An illustration of MDX in Markdown." />
```

The Gatsby ecosystem makes available a starter, `gatsby-starter-mdx-basic`, to add MDX support instantly to a new Gatsby site. To spin up a new Gatsby site using this starter, execute the following command:

```
$ gatsby new gtdg-ch13-mdx gatsbyjs/gatsby-starter-mdx-basic
```

It's also possible to leverage MDX within an existing Gatsby site by adding certain dependencies, by executing the following command. Remember that sourcing data in Gatsby sites from Markdown files also requires `gatsby-source-filesystem`, which we install here as well:

```
$ npm install gatsby-plugin-mdx @mdx-js/mdx @mdx-js/react \
  gatsby-source-filesystem
```

Then, add the `gatsby-plugin-mdx` plugin to *gatsby-config.js*:

```
module.exports = {
  plugins: [
    // ....
    `gatsby-plugin-mdx`,
  ],
}
```

To set relevant configuration options for your requirements, add an `options` object:

```
module.exports = {
  plugins: [
    // ....
    {
      resolve: `gatsby-plugin-mdx`,
      options: {
        // Options for gatsby-plugin-mdx
      }
    }
```

```
    ],
  }
```

Table 13-1 outlines the relevant configuration options.

*Table 13-1. Configuration options for `gatsby-plugin-mdx`*

| Key | Default | Description |
| --- | --- | --- |
| `extensions` | `[".mdx"]` | Configure the file extensions that `gatsby-plugin-mdx` will process. |
| `defaultLayouts` | `{}` | Set the layout components for MDX source types. |
| `gatsbyRemarkPlugins` | `[]` | Use Gatsby-specific plugins for Remark (a Markdown processor). |
| `remarkPlugins` | `[]` | Specify Remark (a Markdown processor) plugins. |
| `rehypePlugins` | `[]` | Specify Rehype (an HTML processor) plugins. |
| `mediaTypes` | `["text/mark down", "text/x-markdown"]` | Determine which media types are processed by MDX. |
| `shouldBlockNodeFrom Transformation` | `(node) => false` | Disable MDX transformation for nodes where this function returns `true`. |
| `commonmark` | `false` | Use CommonMark (a Markdown specification). |

 For more information about MDX, consult the MDX website (*https://mdxjs.com*) and the MDX plugin documentation for Gatsby (*https://oreil.ly/JX1Yu*). For more information about performing migrations from Remark (*https://remark.js.org*) (a Markdown processor) to MDX, consult the Gatsby documentation's guide to migrating Remark to MDX (*https://oreil.ly/Qi8B9*).

# Creating MDX Pages

Once you have `gatsby-plugin-mdx` available, either through Gatsby's own MDX starter or by installing it into an existing Gatsby site, any MDX files located within Gatsby's *src/pages* directory will automatically be converted into pages. For instance, if you create a page *src/pages/about.mdx*, Gatsby renders it at *my-site.com/about*.

You can use frontmatter in Markdown to define certain fields that will be available in Gatsby's GraphQL API as well through the `allMdx` root field. For example, suppose you have an MDX file with the following frontmatter:

```
---
title: Hello MDX!
date: 2021-04-19
---

# Hello MDX!
```

You can query for this frontmatter material by issuing the following GraphQL query either in GraphiQL or any in other file in your Gatsby site that supports GraphQL queries:

```
query {
  allMdx {
    edges {
      node {
        frontmatter {
          title
          date(formatString: "MMMM DD, YYYY")
        }
      }
    }
  }
}
```

If your Markdown document is located in your *src/pages* directory and not programmatically generated, you can also export the query directly within the document itself, if you wish to have your GraphQL query and Markdown located in the same file:

```
---
title: Hello MDX!
date: 2021-04-19
---

import { graphql } from "gatsby"

# Hello MDX!

export const pageQuery = graphql`
  query {
    allMdx {
      edges {
        node {
          frontmatter {
            title
            date(formatString: "MMMM DD, YYYY")
          }
        }
      }
    }
  }
`
```

In MDX files, frontmatter must precede `import` statements referring to outside React components.

MDX also makes available frontmatter within your MDX file itself, meaning you can reference frontmatter fields within JSX elements from inside the MDX document, as follows:

```
---
title: Hello MDX!
date: 2021-04-19
---

# Hello MDX!

<ul>
  <li>Title: {props.pageContext.frontmatter.title}</li>
  <li>Date: {props.pageContext.frontmatter.date}</li>
</ul>
```

## Importing Components into MDX Files

As we saw previously, we can import arbitrary React components into our Markdown documents, such as the Figure component we wrote earlier in this section:

```
---
title: Hello MDX!
date: 2021-04-19
---

import { Figure } from './components/figure';

# Hello MDX!

<ul>
  <li>Title: {props.pageContext.frontmatter.title}</li>
  <li>Date: {props.pageContext.frontmatter.date}</li>
</ul>

<Figure data="figure.svg" caption="An illustration of MDX in Markdown." />
```

Components used in MDX files can also be universally leveraged across a Gatsby site as shortcodes, thanks to the MDXProvider component. To make the Figure component available to all your MDX files, for instance, you could add the following inside your layout component:

```
// src/components/layout.js
import React from "react"
import { MDXProvider } from "@mdx-js/react"
import { Figure } from "./figure"

const shortcodes = { Figure }

export default function Layout({ children }) {
  return (
    <MDXProvider components={shortcodes}>{children}</MDXProvider>
```

```
  )
}
```

Any MDX components that are passed into `MDXProvider` as the `components` prop will
be available to any MDX documents that are rendered by the provider. This means
you no longer need to import the components manually within your MDX files:

```
---
title: Hello MDX!
date: 2021-04-19
---

# Hello MDX!

<ul>
  <li>Title: {props.pageContext.frontmatter.title}</li>
  <li>Date: {props.pageContext.frontmatter.date}</li>
</ul>

<Figure data="figure.svg" caption="An illustration of MDX in Markdown." />
```

> It's also possible to use JavaScript exports directly within MDX files
> for other purposes, like exporting page metadata or defining a lay-
> out. For more information on these use cases, consult the Gatsby
> documentation's section on using JavaScript exports in MDX
> (*https://oreil.ly/Rd60G*). The documentation also contains informa-
> tion on lazy-loading components in MDX files (*https://oreil.ly/*
> *4jng5*) for performance reasons.

## Customizing Markdown Components

It's possible to substitute each HTML element that MDX renders with a custom
implementation as an alternative. This enables Gatsby developers to leverage a set of
design system (collections of repeatable design patterns in code) components when
rendering MDX files. For example, the following layout component substitutes certain elements, like <h1>, with React components that we've defined.

Table 13-2 lists all of the components that can be customized using the `MDXProvider`
component.

```
// src/components/layout.js
import { MDXProvider } from "@mdx-js/react"
import * as DesignSystem from "your-design-system"

export default function Layout({ children }) {
  return (
    <MDXProvider
      components={{
        // Map HTML element tag to React component
        h1: DesignSystem.H1,
```

```
      h2: DesignSystem.H2,
      h3: DesignSystem.H3,
      // Or define component inline
      p: props => <p {...props} style={{ color: "rebeccapurple" }} />,
    }}
  >
    {children}
  </MDXProvider>
)
}
```

*Table 13-2. Components customizable through `MDXProvider`*

| Element | Name | Markdown syntax |
|---|---|---|
| p | Paragraph | (Two carriage returns) |
| h1 | Heading 1 | # |
| h2 | Heading 2 | ## |
| h3 | Heading 3 | ### |
| h4 | Heading 4 | #### |
| h5 | Heading 5 | ##### |
| h6 | Heading 6 | ###### |
| thematicBreak | Thematic break | *** |
| blockquote | Blockquote | |
| ul | Unordered list | *, -, or + |
| ol | Ordered list | 1. |
| li | List item | *, -, or + |
| table | Table | `--- |
| tr | Table row | `This |
| td/th | Table cell | \| |
| pre | Pre | ```js console.log()``` |
| code | Code | `console.log()` |
| em | Emphasis | _emphasis_ |
| strong | Strong | **strong** |
| delete | Delete | ~~strikethrough~~ |
| code | Inline code | `console.log()` |
| hr | Break | --- |
| a | Link | https://mdxjs.com or [MDX](https://mdxjs.com) |
| img | Image | ![alt](https://mdx-logo.now.sh) |

MDX is one element of Gatsby's ecosystem that can accelerate the development of Gatsby sites by enabling the interpolation of arbitrary components into Markdown documents. This introduces much greater flexibility for content authors working in

Markdown who have a working knowledge of HTML as well. In the next section, we turn our attention to schema customization, another of Gatsby's advanced features.

 The `gatsby-plugin-mdx` plugin is compatible with all of Gatsby's Remark plugins, including `gatsby-remark-images`. For more information about using Remark plugins with MDX, consult the Gatsby documentation's guide to MDX plugins (*https://oreil.ly/ OmEso*).

# Schema Customization

During the build lifecycle, which we cover in detail in the final chapter of this book, Gatsby generates a GraphQL schema that enables Gatsby developers to query data from a variety of external or internal sources. This step takes place automatically during the Gatsby bootstrap.

However, there are often scenarios where some schema customization is required in order to adjust the shape of data returned by queries, or to enrich the query layer with additional functionality. In this section, we walk through Gatsby's Schema Customization API, which allows us to customize the schema so it adheres to our needs.

## Explicitly Defining Data Types

In many Gatsby sites, we need to merge data from disparate sources and schemas into a synthesized GraphQL API that can be consumed from any Gatsby component. Standardizing discrete formats into a single schema supports long-term maintenance and a more efficient developer experience. Schema customization allows us to combine distinct data types into a cohesive schema—in fact, this is what Gatsby does through its source plugins when developers query data from multiple sources through the API.

Source and transformer plugins provide a means for Gatsby to recognize disparate data types. But these plugins in and of themselves don't necessarily reformat the data entering GraphQL according to specifications we as Gatsby developers set. Take, for example, the following three documents, which represent a blog article, a list of authors of blog articles, and a list of translators of blog articles.

The first file is an example blog article formatted in Markdown, located at *src/data/ article-1.md*:

```
---
title: Article one
date: 2020-04-19
author: james.baldwin@expat-journal.net
translations:
  - English
```

```
---

# Lorem ipsum

Dolor sit amet.
```

The second file is a JSON list of authors that includes the author of this article:

```
// src/data/author.json
[
  {
    "name": "Baldwin",
    "firstName": "James",
    "email": "james.baldwin@expat-journal.net",
    "created": "2018-09-02"
  },
  {
    "name": "Toklas",
    "firstName": "Alice",
    "email": "alice.toklas@expat-journal.net",
    "created": "2016-03-23"
  }
]
```

The third file is a JSON list of translators, none of whom is referenced in the article:

```
// src/data/translator.json
[
  {
    "name": "wa Goro",
    "firstName": "Wangui",
    "email": "wangui.wagoro@translation-society.org",
    "multipleLanguages": true
  }
]
```

As we've seen in previous chapters, we can immediately begin querying the data contained in these files by leveraging the gatsby-source-filesystem source plugin in conjunction with the gatsby-transformer-remark (Markdown) and gatsby-transformer-json (JSON) transformer plugins:

```
module.exports = {
  plugins: [
    {
      resolve: `gatsby-source-filesystem`,
      options: {
        name: `src`,
        path: `${__dirname}/src/data/`,
      },
    },
    `gatsby-transformer-remark`,
    `gatsby-transformer-json`,
```

```
    ],
  }
```

Using these plugins out of the box and configured to pull from these directories results in a Node for each of these items of, respectively, type MarkdownRemark (Markdown), AuthorJson (JSON), and TranslatorJson (JSON).

## The Node interface and automatic type inference

In Gatsby's GraphQL schema, these three data types (MarkdownRemark, AuthorJson, and TranslatorJson) are each represented using the Node interface, which defines the GraphQL fields mutually shared by Node objects that are generated by source and transformer plugins (namely id, parent, children, and several internal fields such as type). Written in GraphQL's Schema Definition Language (SDL), the Node interface is defined as follows:

```
interface Node {
  id: ID!
  parent: Node!
  children: [Node!]!
  internal: Internal!
}

type Internal {
  type: String!
}
```

The types that are created by source and transformer plugins, like gatsby-source-filesystem, gatsby-transformer-remark, and gatsby-transformer-json, are implementations of this Node interface. For instance, the Node type TranslatorJson will be defined in the GraphQL schema as follows:

```
type TranslatorJson implements Node {
  id: ID!
  parent: Node!
  children: [Node!]!
  internal: Internal!
  name: String
  firstName: String
  email: String
  multipleLanguages: Boolean
}
```

Fields whose value types end with an exclamation point represent nullability, indicating whether a field value can be null or not; they must have a non-null value.

Gatsby performs inference to determine the field types (i.e., String, Boolean, etc.)—it inspects the contents of every field and validates its type to translate each data shape into meaningful type definitions. Gatsby is usually quite adept at this process of automatic type inference, though it consumes significant resources in doing so and has trouble deciding between types if multiple types (e.g., String and Date) are represented in a particular field. One potential consequence of this approach is that if data sources change the way they expose data, automatic type inference suddenly fails.

### Creating explicit type definitions

For this reason, it can often be preferable to create type definitions manually, explicitly defining types so that Gatsby can validate the field and inform you if there is malformed data, such as an invalid Date. Through the createSchemaCustomization Node API, Gatsby provides a means for developers to supply the GraphQL schema with explicit type definitions in *gatsby-node.js* using the createTypes action, which accepts as inputs type definitions written in GraphQL's SDL:

```
// gatsby-node.js
exports.createSchemaCustomization = ({ actions }) => {
  const { createTypes } = actions
  const typeDefs = `
    type AuthorJson implements Node {
      created: Date
    }
  `
  createTypes(typeDefs)
}
```

Thanks to Gatsby's automatic type inference capability, there is no need for us to also provide explicit type definitions for the other field types, unless we wish to. Nevertheless, there are situations where providing an unabridged type definition may be preferable, in the process opting out of Gatsby's automatic type inference. This is especially the case for larger Gatsby sites working with substantial amounts of data where type inference begins to detrimentally impact performance.

The @dontInfer type directive in Gatsby can be used to opt out of automatic type inference for a field, but the catch is that you must provide all type definitions explicitly for that field to be made available for querying via the GraphQL API. For example, opting out of automatic type inference for the AuthorJson type would mean that we would need to provide a full type definition:

```
// gatsby-node.js
exports.createSchemaCustomization = ({ actions }) => {
  const { createTypes } = actions
  const typeDefs = `
    type AuthorJson implements Node @dontInfer {
      name: String!
```

```
          firstName: String!
          email: String!
          created: Date
      }
      `
    createTypes(typeDefs)
  }
```

Note that Gatsby's internal Node interface fields (id, parent, children, internal) are automatically created by Gatsby and don't require inclusion in the unabridged type definition.

 There are several extensions available in GraphQL type definitions that can be used to specify the media types that are acceptable and child relations that need to be established with a parent type. For more information about these, consult the Gatsby documentation's sections on defining media types and child relations (*https://oreil.ly/MEuZe*).

### Handling nested types

GraphQL fields can handle scalar values—namely String, Date, ID, Int, Float, Boolean, and JSON—but fields can also contain complex values in the form of objects. To handle these nested fields, we need to provide an explicit type definition for the nested type. For instance, we may wish to ensure that each MarkdownRemark (Markdown document) Node contains a frontmatter field known as frontmatter .translations that *itself* is a list of strings:

```
// gatsby-node.js
exports.createSchemaCustomization = ({ actions }) => {
  const { createTypes } = actions
  const typeDefs = `
    type MarkdownRemark implements Node {
      frontmatter: Frontmatter
    }
    type Frontmatter {
      translations: [String!]!
    }
    `
  createTypes(typeDefs)
}
```

Note that because we are specifying the Frontmatter type for the first time using this createTypes action, we cannot simply supply a bare Frontmatter definition without accounting for it in the overarching MarkdownRemark type—without that, GraphQL will have no awareness of the Frontmatter field. For this reason, Gatsby recommends as a best practice beginning from the standpoint of the types generated by source and transformer plugins when writing type definitions.

Though GraphQL's SDL provides a sufficiently concise way to author type definitions that customize the schema, the `create Types` action also allows for type definitions that use Gatsby Type Builders (*https://oreil.ly/dxUkT*), which can offer more leeway than SDL syntax and result in less verbosity than direct implementations of `graphql-js`. For more information about foreign key fields, default field values, and available extensions and directives, consult the Gatsby documentation's sections on foreign key fields (*https://oreil.ly/rK1Y5*), extensions and directives (*https://oreil.ly/y6EqQ*), setting default field values (*https://oreil.ly/pSaQ4*), and creating custom extensions (*https://oreil.ly/vdKJ1*).

## Implementing the createResolvers API

In the course of schema customization, sometimes type definitions are insufficient for requirements in Gatsby sites. For example, the GraphQL SDL and Gatsby Type Builders can handle the vast majority of use cases when it comes to adding type definitions, but more granularity is occasionally necessary in the form of custom resolvers, which allow us to specify how fields should be resolved in the GraphQL schema. This is done through implementations of the `createResolvers` Node API:

```
// gatsby-node.js
exports.createResolvers = ({ createResolvers }) => {
  const resolvers = {
    Frontmatter: {
      author: {
        resolve(source, args, context, info) {
          return context.nodeModel.getNodeById({
            id: source.author,
            type: "AuthorJson",
          })
        },
      },
    },
  }
  createResolvers(resolvers)
}
```

Implementations of the `createResolvers` API enable Gatsby developers to extend types with new fields without overriding the field type. Since the `createResolvers` function is executed near the end of the schema generation process, modification of an existing field type would require the regeneration of input types (`field`, `sort`, etc.), which would be an expensive operation. For this reason, specifying field types is best handled in implementations of the `createTypes` action, unless you have more advanced requirements.

While implementing the `createResolvers` API, Gatsby permits access to the internal data store and Gatsby's own query capabilities through the `context.nodeModel` object that is made available in each resolver. In this manner, Gatsby developers can directly access nodes by their identifiers by invoking `getNodeById` and `getNodesByIds`, whereas all nodes can be retrieved through `getAllNodes`. You can also issue arbitrary queries from within resolver function logic through `runQuery`, which allows for `fil` `ter` and `sort` query arguments.

For example, the following `createResolvers` implementation extends the `Author` `Json` type with a field that lists all recent articles written by a particular author:

```
// gatsby-node.js
exports.createResolvers = ({ createResolvers }) => {
  const resolvers = {
    AuthorJson: {
      recentPosts: {
        type: ["MarkdownRemark"],
        resolve(source, args, context, info) {
          return context.nodeModel.runQuery({
            query: {
              filter: {
                frontmatter: {
                  author: { eq: source.email },
                  date: { gt: "2019-01-01" },
                },
              },
            },
            type: "MarkdownRemark",
            firstOnly: false,
          })
        },
      },
    },
  }
  createResolvers(resolvers)
}
```

If invoking `runQuery` from within the API implementation to sort results of the query, note that `sort.fields` and `sort.order` are both `GraphQLList` fields. Meanwhile, nested fields within `sort.fields` are accessed through dot notation rather than triple underscores, as we've seen in previous examples:

```
// gatsby-node.js
// ...
return context.nodeModel.runQuery({
  query: {
    sort: {
      fields: ["frontmatter.date"],
      order: ["DESC"],
    },
  },
  type: "MarkdownRemark",
```

```
})
// ...
```

 A powerful feature available in the createResolvers API that is beyond the scope of this overview of schema customization is custom query fields. For more information about these, consult the Gatsby documentation (*https://oreil.ly/dyvOo*).

## Creating Custom Interfaces and Unions

One final common use case for schema customization in Gatsby involves creating custom interfaces and unions across multiple types through GraphQL's abstract types. For instance, we could issue two queries for allAuthorJson and allTranslatorJson and then merge these by writing Gatsby code, but GraphQL can give us these types out of the box as a merged list.

Because both the AuthorJson and TranslatorJson types have most of their fields in common, we can create an interface that merges these two together:

```
// gatsby-node.js
exports.createSchemaCustomization = ({ actions }) => {
  const { createTypes } = actions
  const typeDefs = `
    interface Creator {
      name: String!
      firstName: String!
      email: String!
    }
    type AuthorJson implements Node & Creator {
      name: String!
      firstName: String!
      email: String!
      created: Date
    }
    type TranslatorJson implements Node & Creator {
      name: String!
      firstName: String!
      email: String!
      multipleLanguages: Boolean
    }
  `

  createTypes(typeDefs)
}
```

In addition, we can implement the createResolvers API to facilitate a new type for us, allCreator, which makes our merged list available:

```
// gatsby-node.js
exports.createResolvers = ({ createResolvers }) => {
  const resolvers = {
```

```
    Query: {
      allCreator: {
        type: ["Creator"],
        resolve(source, args, context, info) {
          return context.nodeModel.getAllNodes({ type: "Creator" })
        },
      },
    },
  }
  createResolvers(resolvers)
}
```

Now, we can access the fields for both `AuthorJson` and `TranslatorJson` and acquire the authors' and translators' email addresses as follows:

```
export const query = graphql`
  {
    allCreator {
      ... on AuthorJson {
        email
      }
      ... on TranslatorJson {
        email
      }
    }
  }
  `
```

As of Gatsby 3.0, it's possible to use interface inheritance in schema customization to achieve the same result as seen in the preceding example. Using the `implements` keyword we can inherit from the `Node` interface, which will mean that the interface will behave like a normal top-level type that implements that interface, like `allAuthorJson`. This means we no longer need a resolver in Gatsby 3.0 implementations, because Gatsby will automatically add the requisite root query fields on our behalf:

```
// gatsby-node.js
exports.createSchemaCustomization = ({ actions }) => {
  const { createTypes } = actions
  const typeDefs = `
    interface Creator implements Node {
      id: ID!
      name: String!
      firstName: String!
      email: String!
    }

    type AuthorJson implements Node & Creator {
      name: String!
      firstName: String!
      email: String!
      created: Date
    }
```

```
    type TranslatorJson implements Node & Creator {
      name: String!
      firstName: String!
      email: String!
      multipleLanguages: Boolean
    }
  `

  createTypes(typeDefs)
}
```

 In Gatsby, every type that implements an interface that can be queried must also implement the Node interface.

This also means we only need to use fragments (discussed in Chapter 4) in the query for those fields that are not shared between both types:

```
export const query = graphql`
  {
    allCreator {
      nodes {
        name
        firstName
        email
        __typeName
        ... on AuthorJson {
          created
        }
        ... on TranslatorJson {
          multipleLanguages
        }
        ... on Node {
          parent {
            id
          }
        }
      }
    }
  }
`
```

Schema customization in Gatsby also allows you to provide customizations that extend third-party GraphQL types that may have been supplied by remote sources, such as through the `gatsby-source-graphql` source plugin, by implementing the `createR esolvers` API. For more information about this, consult the Gatsby documentation's section on extending third-party types (*https://oreil.ly/TsyIS*).

# Custom Gatsby Configuration

Over the course of developing a Gatsby site, sometimes additional customization is needed to suit particular needs when it comes to how Gatsby performs a build and yields bundles for consumption. In this section, we examine custom approaches to Gatsby configuration outside of schema customization—we'll look at using Babel, Webpack, Gatsby's *html.js* file, and ESLint, as well as proxying API requests.

## Babel

Gatsby leverages Babel to provide support for both older browsers and modern Java-Script development paradigms. By default, Gatsby's Babel configuration guarantees support for the previous two versions of commonly used browsers, Internet Explorer 9+, and any other browser having more than 1% market share.

Babel in Gatsby automatically transpiles all JavaScript to ensure that all written code (including polyfills, alternative code for earlier browsers without support for certain features that are automatically added during the Gatsby build process) functions properly in older browsers. Gatsby provides a default *.babelrc* configuration file that supports compatibility for the vast majority of Gatsby sites. To customize this configuration file to your unique requirements, first install `babel-preset-gatsby`:

```
$ npm install --save-dev babel-preset-gatsby
```

Then, create a new overriding *.babelrc* configuration file in your Gatsby project root to include additional plugins, presets, and other settings. For example, passing the `targets` option object containing a `browsers` key with an array of specified browsers will override Gatsby's default supported browsers according to your configuration:

```
// .babelrc
{
  "plugins": [
    ["@babel/plugin-proposal-decorators", { "legacy": true }]
  ],
  "presets": [
    [
      "babel-preset-gatsby",
      {
        "targets": {
```

```
          "browsers": [">0.25%", "not dead"]
        }
      }
    ]
  ]
}
```

From this point forward, you can also copy certain default settings from the `babel-preset-gatsby` preset (*https://oreil.ly/9TFOd*) and override them as needed.

 For more information about which browsers are supported by Gatsby and other means to adjust this list, consult the Gatsby documentation's guide to browser support (*https://oreil.ly/YIO2N*).

## Babel Plugin Macros

Gatsby also permits the use of *Babel macros* to apply compile-time code transformations that can be more flexible than Babel plugins. Rather than including them in the *.babelrc* configuration file, we insert Babel plugin macros into the working code of the files we write. Babel macros have two key advantages:

- There is no uncertainty about where particular nonstandard or noncompliant syntax is originating from, as macros are explicitly imported in the places they are used.

- There is no need for configuration files, as macros are included in code directly on only an as-needed basis.

Because Babel plugin macros run only at compile time, like Babel plugins themselves, they are unavailable in the publicly distributed JavaScript bundle. Therefore, these macros have no impact other than the transformations they are responsible for.

Like Babel plugins, many macros are available in the JavaScript ecosystem as packages. The convention for community macros is to suffix the name of the macro, typically a description of its function, with `.macro`. For example, `preval.macro` is a macro that forces the preevaluation of the code it is responsible for. We can install this macro into our development dependencies as follows:

```
$ npm install --save-dev preval.macro
```

We can then import the macro and use it with a template literal tag to perform certain logic. For example, the following code:

```
import preval from "preval.macro"
const y = preval`module.exports = 2`
```

will yield this transformed code in the resulting project build:

```
const y = 2
```

 For more information about Babel macros, consult the Babel plugin macros documentation (*https://oreil.ly/ZV5o4*). The `awesome-babel-macros` repository (*https://oreil.ly/Y6P11*) also contains useful information about macros and macro development.

# Webpack

As a Gatsby developer, you should attempt a custom Webpack configuration only if the default Webpack configuration built into Gatsby does not support your requirements *and* there is no Gatsby plugin available in the ecosystem that meets your needs. For those cases, Gatsby provides a Node API known as `onCreateWebpackConfig` that can be implemented in *gatsby-node.js* to adjust the default Gatsby Webpack configuration.

When Gatsby generates its own Webpack configuration during the build lifecycle, it will use the `webpack-merge` library (*https://oreil.ly/VgjOJ*) to combine the two configurations together appropriately. We'll dig into the details of how Gatsby performs Webpack builds in the final chapter of this book, but for now one of the most important concepts to understand about Webpack use in Gatsby is that distinct builds are generated based on each build type or stage, of which four exist:

`develop`
: This stage occurs when you execute the `gatsby develop` command, and the Webpack configuration includes settings for hot reloading and in-page CSS injection to aid development.

`develop-html`
: This is identical to the previous stage but is responsible for rendering the HTML component, which represents the outermost component of a Gatsby site (see also the next section).

`build-javascript`
: This stage is responsible for the production JavaScript and CSS build, including the creation of route-specific JavaScript bundles and common Webpack chunks for JavaScript and CSS assets.

`build-html`
: This stage represents the production build that yields static HTML pages.

For an example of customizing Webpack configuration using the `onCreateWebpackConfig` API, consider the following code that incorporates the `less-loader` plugin for LESS stylesheet files requiring compilation:

```
// gatsby-node.js
exports.onCreateWebpackConfig = ({
  stage,
  rules,
  loaders,
  plugins,
  actions,
}) => {
  actions.setWebpackConfig({
    module: {
      rules: [
        {
          test: /\.less$/,
          use: [
            // You don't need to add the matching ExtractText plugin
            // because Gatsby already includes it and makes sure it's only
            // run at the appropriate stages, e.g. not in development
            loaders.miniCssExtract(),
            loaders.css({ importLoaders: 1 }),
            // The postcss loader comes with some nice defaults
            // including autoprefixer for our configured browsers
            loaders.postcss(),
            `less-loader`,
          ],
        },
      ],
    },
    plugins: [
      plugins.define({
        __DEVELOPMENT__: stage === `develop` || stage === `develop-html`,
      }),
    ],
  })
}
```

Another common use case, particularly for repetitive references to components in `import` statements, is to set the Webpack configuration to permit absolute imports in order to avoid specifying paths each and every time you import the components. For instance, consider the following example API implementation in *gatsby-node.js*:

```
// gatsby-node.js
exports.onCreateWebpackConfig = ({ stage, actions }) => {
  actions.setWebpackConfig({
    resolve: {
      modules: [path.resolve(__dirname, "src"), "node_modules"],
    },
  })
}
```

Instead of writing the following in Gatsby components:

```
import Footer from '../../components/footer'
```

you can write the following after adjusting the Webpack configuration accordingly:

```
import Footer from 'components/footer'
```

For more information about other advanced use cases involving the customization of Gatsby's default Webpack configuration, consult the Gatsby documentation (*https://oreil.ly/F07HX*) on importing non-Webpack tools using Yarn and modifying the Babel loader.

## Customizing html.js

Gatsby uses a React component to render <head>, <footer>, and other elements that lie outside the core application destined for the browser. For the vast majority of Gatsby sites, the *html.js* file that comes packaged with Gatsby suits most requirements, but some situations call for additional customization. To customize your site's default *html.js*, execute the following in the root of your Gatsby project:

```
$ gatsby build
$ cp .cache/default-html.js src/html.js
```

This creates an *html.js* file that overrides Gatsby's own.

Customization of the *html.js* file is recommended by Gatsby only when the appropriate Gatsby Server-Side Rendering APIs implemented in *gatsby-ssr.js* are not sufficient for your needs. Before performing this customization, consider implementing the onRenderBody (*https://oreil.ly/sOocW*) or onPreRenderHTML APIs (*https://oreil.ly/FB9hR*) instead. Plugin authors should explore using setPostBodyComponents.

Certain props found within the *html.js* file are required for Gatsby to perform rendering correctly. These are:

- headComponents
- preBodyComponents
- body
- postBodyComponents

Within the *html.js* file, you may need to add custom JavaScript that executes entirely outside Gatsby's purview, to avoid Gatsby's own JavaScript processing. To insert custom JavaScript, use React's dangerouslySetInnerHTML attribute as follows:

```
// src/html.js
<script
  dangerouslySetInnerHTML={{
```

```
  __html: `
    var name = 'world';
    console.log('Hello ' + name);
  `,
}}
/>
```

 If you encounter an error such as the following, your *html.js* file lacks a required target container in which Gatsby can perform certain actions:

```
Uncaught Error: _registerComponent(...):
Target container is not a DOM element.
```

To resolve this error, insert a `<div>` element with an `id` attribute of `___gatsby`, such as the following:

```
<div
  key={`body`}
  id="___gatsby"
  dangerouslySetInnerHTML={{ __html: this.props.body
}}
/>
```

# ESLint

ESLint is a powerful open source utility for JavaScript aimed at detecting malformed syntax using a type of static analysis known as *code linting*. Due to JavaScript's loosely typed and dynamic nature, the language is prone to syntax errors committed by developers. ESLint allows developers to run tests across their code without executing the logic.

As with Webpack, Gatsby provides a built-in ESLint configuration, and these settings should be suitable for the vast majority of Gatsby sites. However, there may be scenarios where you need to customize the ESLint configuration to adhere to certain other requirements. To do this, first replicate the configuration that is built into Gatsby by installing necessary dependencies into your development dependencies:

```
$ npm install --save-dev eslint-config-react-app
```

Then, create a configuration file for ESLint within your Gatsby project root as follows:

```
$ touch .eslintrc.js
```

 When there is no ESLint configuration file available, Gatsby instead adds a rudimentary ESLint loader implicitly that is responsible for piping feedback from the ESLint checker into the terminal or console. This is done through the built-in `eslint-loader` utility.

Add the following initial configuration to your ESLint configuration file, after which you'll be able to include any additional presets, plugins, and linting rules required for your unique needs:

```
// .eslintrc.js
module.exports = {
  globals: {
    __PATH_PREFIX__: true,
  },
  extends: `react-app`,
}
```

 If you create an empty ESLint configuration file devoid of any data, this will disable ESLint for your Gatsby site, because Gatsby will assume your configuration file should override its own built-in ESLint configuration.

## Proxying API Requests

The final portion of this section deals with proxying API requests, which involves customizing the Gatsby configuration file. Many Gatsby developers employ an architectural approach that involves hosting the backend server implementation and frontend React application from the same host and port, which can lead to issues when sourcing data for presentation in Gatsby, as some source plugins expect distinct hostnames or ports.

To mitigate this problem, Gatsby's development server can be instructed through configuration to proxy any unknown incoming requests to the API server during development with the proxy field in *gatsby-config.js*. The proxy field accepts a single object or an array of objects, as the following example demonstrates:

```
// gatsby-config.js
module.exports = {
  proxy: [
    {
      prefix: "/api",
      url: "https://dev-my-site.com",
    },
    {
      prefix: "/api2",
      url: "https://dev2-my-site.com",
    },
  ],
}
```

When performing data retrieval in development, Gatsby's development server recognizes that rather than being a request for a static asset, the request is for API data. As such, Gatsby will then proxy the API request to the designated fallback as set in the

Gatsby configuration file. For instance, a request to */api/articles* will be proxied to *https://dev-my-site.com/api/articles*.

> The proxy configuration in Gatsby takes effect only in the development server and has no effect in production. For more information about advanced proxying use cases like adding middleware with the `developMiddleware` option and self-signed certificates, consult the Gatsby documentation's guide to advanced proxying (*https://oreil.ly/35HAZ*).

# Performance Optimization

The topic of performance is a broad one, and this book cannot possibly do it justice. But fortunately, Gatsby includes many performance enhancements that ensure a high-performing Gatsby site with little to no additional work. For instance, Gatsby comes prepackaged with common modern paradigms for performant websites such as link prefetching, code splitting, and other techniques.

For developers working on large-scale Gatsby sites, performance optimization is a fundamental consideration that can have outsized impacts on the success of the site in the long run. In this section, we cover caching best practices, progressive web app functionality, offline support, profiling, performance tracing, and conditional page builds, all of which concern Gatsby's performance across the stack.

> Two common developer tools to analyze performance are Lighthouse, which provides performance auditing for Gatsby sites in the browser, and Guess.js, which uses machine learning to predict which pages a user will navigate to from the current page, preloading only those resources accordingly. For more information, consult the Gatsby documentation's guides to auditing with Lighthouse (*https://oreil.ly/aOaxL*) and optimizing with Guess.js (*https://oreil.ly/gRYj1*).

## Caching Gatsby Sites

One of the foundational best practices for Gatsby static sites is to perform proper HTTP caching, which enables browsers to optimally cache resources from a given website such that the user experiences a near-instantaneous load. The Gatsby documentation outlines several types of resources in the *public* directory that should be cached (or not) according to a particular set of configurations:

*HTML*

HTML files should not be cached by the browser, because each Gatsby rebuild updates the contents of static HTML files that Gatsby generates. Browsers should be set to verify on each request whether a newer version of the HTML file needs to be downloaded.

*Page data*

Gatsby recommends excluding the JSON files located in the *public/page-data* directory from browser caching, because these files are also entirely updated on each rebuild and, in fact, can be updated without a rebuild taking place. Therefore, browsers should be set to verify on each request whether new page data is available for download.

*App data*

The *app-data.json* file includes the build hash for the most recent deployment of the Gatsby site and thus ought to share the same `cache-control` header as *page-data.json*, so that the version of application data loaded in the browser remains in sync with the current Gatsby deployment.

*Static files*

Files in the *static* directory are designed to be cached in perpetuity. Gatsby generates paths for each file in this directory that are associated with the contents of the file, such that filepaths change when the file contents evolve.

*JavaScript and CSS assets*

Any JavaScript and CSS assets that are handled by Webpack should be cached in perpetuity as well, as they are unchanging unless their file contents change. The only exception to this best practice is the */sw.js* file, which is generated by the `gatsby-plugin-offline` plugin (see ""Adding Offline Support with Service Workers" on page 411").

Table 13-3 outlines the `cache-control` headers that should be set for each of these asset types when caching Gatsby sites.

*Table 13-3. Appropriate `cache-control` headers for different Gatsby asset types*

| Asset type | Header |
|---|---|
| HTML | `cache-control: public, max-age=0, must-revalidate` |
| Page data | |
| App data | |
| Static files | `cache-control: public, max-age=31536000, immutable` |
| JavaScript and CSS assets | |
| */sw.js* | `cache-control: public, max-age=0, must-revalidate` |

The `gatsby-plugin-netlify` and `gatsby-plugin-s3` plugins have automated caching headers enabled for their respective infrastructures.

The following cache header can also be used for HTML, page data, and app data, because no-cache enables a cache to deliver cached content so long as it validates the freshness of the cache first:

```
cache-control: public, no-cache
```

## Adding a Progressive Web App Manifest File

Progressive web apps (PWAs) are websites that can run in the browser but also leverage certain functionality to provide native application–like advantages. For those Gatsby developers who wish to enable their Gatsby sites as PWAs, the most important step is to add a manifest file, *manifest.webmanifest*, that indicates PWA compatibility.

The gatsby-plugin-manifest plugin can create a manifest file on your behalf. To install the plugin, execute the following commands and ensure a favicon is available at *src/images/icon.png*:

```
$ gatsby new gtdg-ch13-pwa gatsbyjs/gatsby-starter-default
$ npm install gatsby-plugin-manifest
```

Then, add the plugin to the plugins array in your Gatsby configuration file, as follows:

```
// gatsby-config.js
{
  plugins: [
    {
      resolve: `gatsby-plugin-manifest`,
      options: {
        name: "GatsbyJS",
        short_name: "GatsbyJS",
        start_url: "/",
        background_color: "#6b37bf",
        theme_color: "#6b37bf",
        // Enables "Add to Homescreen" prompt and disables browser UI
        // (including back button)
        display: "standalone",
        icon: "src/images/icon.png", // Relative to the root of the site.
        // An optional attribute which provides support for CORS check.
        // Without this attribute, it will skip CORS for manifest.
        // Any invalid keyword or empty string defaults to `anonymous`.
        crossOrigin: `use-credentials`,
      },
    },
  ]
}
```

Whenever you perform another build of your Gatsby site, a *manifest.webmanifest* file will automatically be generated for your PWA-enabled site.

---

For more information about PWA functionality in Gatsby, consult the Gatsby documentation's guide to PWAs (*https://oreil.ly/6t4Rq*) and the `gatsby-plugin-manifest` plugin documentation (*https://oreil.ly/2JQQM*). See also Google's PWA overview (*https://oreil.ly/vAgtZ*).

## Adding Offline Support with Service Workers

Adding offline support with service workers is another way to improve performance, particularly because service worker usage is a PWA requirement. The `gatsby-plugin-offline` plugin automates the process of transforming a Gatsby site into an offline-first implementation that is resistant to inconsistent network conditions with the help of a service worker.

*Service workers*, in short, are scripts executed in the background by browsers that are distinct from logic run in the web page itself. In spotty network conditions, service workers can provide a better user experience in addition to supporting common features such as push notifications and synchronization of assets in the background.

To install the `gatsby-plugin-offline` plugin, execute the following command:

```
$ npm install gatsby-plugin-offline
```

Then, add the plugin to your Gatsby configuration file:

```
// gatsby-config.js
{
  plugins: [
    {
      resolve: `gatsby-plugin-manifest`,
      options: {
        // ...
      }
    },
    `gatsby-plugin-offline`,
  ],
}
```

Service workers in Gatsby are available only on production-built Gatsby sites (i.e., on `gatsby build`).

To render a custom message in the browser once your service worker discovers updated content, you can implement one of Gatsby's Browser APIs, `onServiceWorker UpdateReady`, in *gatsby-browser.js*. The following code block illustrates an example implementation, displaying a confirmation prompt requesting the user to approve a refresh of the page:

```
// gatsby-browser.js
export const onServiceWorkerUpdateReady = () => {
  const answer = window.confirm(
    `A new version of this application is available. ` +
    `Refresh to update?`
  )

  if (answer === true) {
    window.location.reload()
  }
}
```

If you need to add a custom service worker to Gatsby, for example to support a requirement unsupported by the `gatsby-plugin-offline` plugin, add a file to the *static* directory named *sw.js* (per service worker convention) and implement the `registerServiceWorker` API in *gatsby-browser.js* as follows:

```
// gatsby-browser.js
export const registerServiceWorker = () => true
```

To remove the service worker entirely from your built Gatsby site, use the Gatsby ecosystem plugin `gatsby-plugin-remove-serviceworker`.

 For more information about removing a service worker, consult the documentation for the `gatsby-plugin-offline` plugin (*https:// oreil.ly/i4NS1*). For more information about service workers in general, consult the documentation provided by Google (*https:// oreil.ly/Ln9mH*) and the Mozilla Developer Network (*https:// oreil.ly/CcO5w*).

## Profiling with React Profiler

As of React 16.5, React now includes support for profiling, which is a means of capturing information with timings that assist Gatsby developers in pinpointing performance issues within a given Gatsby site. Users of React Developer Tools can access a Profiler tab to diagnose issues, and Gatsby automatically enables profiling in development, though development profiling does not match performance in production.

To enable profiling for a given production Gatsby build, execute the following command:

```
$ gatsby build --profile
```

The profiler should be included in a Gatsby build only when necessary for performance profiling, as it adds some computational and memory overhead to a Gatsby application. Though the Profiler tab will display overarching profiling results, you may wish to customize React's profiler further to enable greater introspection into the performance of your React components.

For example, you can write a profiler component for a given "slow" component as follows:

```
import * as React from "react"
import { Profiler } from "react"

export const MyComponent = props => (
  // See https://reactjs.org/docs/profiler.html#onrender-callback
  // for onRender parameters
  <Profiler id={props.someUniqueId} onRender={capturePageMetrics}>
    <SlowComponent />
  </Profiler>
)
```

To profile Gatsby page performance, implement the `wrapPageElement` API in *gatsby-browser.js*, as demonstrated in the following example:

```
// gatsby-browser.js
import * as React from "react"
import { Profiler } from "react"

export const wrapPageElement = ({ element, props }) => (
  <Profiler id={props.someUniqueId} onRender={capturePageMetrics}>
    {element}
  </Profiler>
)
```

> For more information about the React profiler, consult the introductory blog post (*https://oreil.ly/nvA2K*) and the React profiler (*https://oreil.ly/XPivh*)documentation.

## Performance Tracing for Gatsby Builds

Profiling can give you a significant amount of information about the React side of the equation, but performance tracing to see what takes the longest during Gatsby builds is important as well. Gatsby provides performance tracing capabilities compatible with the OpenTracing (*https://opentracing.io*) standard that can be viewed in an introspection tool such as Zipkin (*https://zipkin.io*), Jaeger (*https://www.jaegertracing.io*), or Honeycomb (*https://www.honeycomb.io/tracing*).

The instrumentation in Gatsby's code is done through OpenTracing, an implementation-agnostic tracing API that requires an integrated OpenTracing-compatible library. Gatsby also offers additional tracing capabilities for GraphQL resolvers, which may have a detrimental impact on performance. As such, this is disabled by default, but it can be enabled using the `--graphql-tracing` flag as follows when kicking off a build:

```
$ gatsby build --graphql-tracing
```

Once you've added an OpenTracing-compatible library to the dependencies in your *package.json* file through a package installation, you will need to configure the library to set fields such as the tracing backend's URL and the frequency with which spans should be delivered to that tracing backend, as well as the service name for recording. OpenTracing configuration files consist of two function exports:

create

> This function creates and returns a tracer compatible with OpenTracing and is invoked when the build initializes.

stop

> This function is invoked when the build concludes. Any cleanup that the tracer needs to perform should occur at this point, including clearing any remaining span queues and delivering them to the backend.

Once you have your OpenTracing configuration file in place, you can execute a build for tracing with the following command, optionally including `--graphql-tracing`:

```
$ gatsby build --open-tracing-config-file
```

 Coverage of tracing using Jaeger and Zipkin in Gatsby is beyond the scope of this book, but you can find out more in the Gatsby documentation (*https://oreil.ly/OgqL1*). For more information about custom-built tracing, consult the Gatsby documentation's guide to adding your own tracing (*https://oreil.ly/Hkf79*). In addition, Gatsby recommends certain workarounds when scalability issues arise, such as out-of-memory errors or extremely slow builds. For more information about these, consult the documentation's guide to scaling issues (*https://oreil.ly/Fseyi*).

## Conditional Page Builds

One of the key differences between Gatsby v2 and Gatsby v3 is the new stability of conditional page builds, also known as incremental builds. In Gatsby v2, this experimental functionality was made available by enabling the `GATSBY_EXPERIMEN TAL_PAGE_BUILD_ON_DATA_CHANGES` environment variable. The core capability of conditional page builds is the ability to regenerate only those static HTML files that need to be rerendered (thus requiring the *.cache* and *public* directories from the previous build to remain in place).

To accomplish this, Gatsby tracks certain inputs that influence the generation of HTML files, including the page template being utilized by the given page, the result of each page's page query, the results of any static queries used by a page template, and any frontend source code (especially implementations of Gatsby's Browser and SSR APIs). When these remain unchanged from the previous build based on the contents of the *.cache* and *public* directories, previous HTML files that were generated in prior builds can be reused untouched.

 For more information about how to use conditional page builds, and especially one key change that obligates developers to avoid direct filesystem calls in *gatsby-ssr.js*, consult the relevant sectionin the release notes for Gatsby 3.0 (*https://oreil.ly/MguXZ*) .

# Conclusion

In this chapter, we covered a slew of advanced topics that ran the gamut from IaC with Gatsby recipes and schema customization to expert configuration and performance optimization. Though Gatsby comes equipped with many defaults that suit the vast majority of Gatsby sites, sometimes developers require more flexibility to handle more nuanced requirements or to extend existing capabilities with features like MDX. In addition, using Gatsby in production can lead to other required actions on the part of the developer to reconcile drift between environments and optimize performance for real-world conditions.

This chapter concludes our overview of how developers can leverage Gatsby for a wide variety of site development needs. But our exploration of Gatsby isn't yet at a close. In the last and final chapter of this book, we'll take a quick look behind the scenes and dig into the nuts and bolts of what makes Gatsby tick, including topics such as schema generation, page creation, query extraction and execution, writing out pages, and bundling everything together for the journey to the browser.

# CHAPTER 14

# Gatsby Internals

Throughout this book, we've taken a tour through the compelling set of features available to developers building Gatsby sites. And in the previous chapter, we explored advanced topics in Gatsby for expert-level use cases that go well beyond its out-of-the-box capabilities. But what about those who are interested in contributing to Gatsby, extending it, or learning about its inner workings?

In this chapter, we'll take a look at some of the nuts and bolts of how Gatsby functions. This will help you gain a deeper understanding of the framework, and become a better debugger when things go awry. Having a decent grasp of the internals can be helpful not only for developing your own contributions to Gatsby, but also to have an idiomatic sense of what is happening when APIs or plugins are invoked, during each stage of the Gatsby build lifecycle, and when Gatsby performs bundling to generate a high-performing static site ready for the browser.

 At the time this chapter was written, Gatsby 3.0 had only recently been released. For this reason, it covers only Gatsby 2.0, is based on the Gatsby documentation's guide to Gatsby 2.0 internals, and is not up to date for Gatsby 3.0, which was released in March 2021. For a high-level overview of the Gatsby build process with examples taken from the Gatsby CLI's terminal output during a typical build, consult the Gatsby documentation's overview of the Gatsby build process (*https://oreil.ly/1eE2s*).

## APIs and Plugins in Gatsby

When you invoke an API or plugin within Gatsby itself or in a plugin you've provided to the implementation, what does Gatsby do on the inside? In this section, we'll take a brief tour through the major phases of API and plugin execution in Gatsby from the standpoint of *gatsby-node.js*. An understanding of what portions of Gatsby are the most complex and computationally expensive will aid you in future debugging.

> This section focuses solely on the Gatsby Node APIs and associated plugins. It does not cover the functioning of the Gatsby Browser or SSR APIs, which allow developers to adjust how Gatsby behaves in the browser and during server-side rendering, respectively. For a summary of some of the most important terminology that you'll encounter in a discussion of Gatsby's internals, consult the documentation's guide to terminology used in Gatsby's source code (*https://oreil.ly/iNH2f*).

## Loading Configured Plugins

Among the very first steps performed in Gatsby's bootstrap is loading all the plugins configured in *gatsby-config.js*, as well as internal Gatsby plugins that come with the core framework. Gatsby saves these loaded plugins to Redux using the `flattened Plugins` namespace. In Redux, each plugin has the fields listed in Table 14-1.

> For more information about how Gatsby leverages Redux for data storage, consult the Gatsby documentation's guide to data storage in Redux (*https://oreil.ly/zfEW0*).

*Table 14-1. Redux fields for loaded and configured plugins*

| Field | Description |
|---|---|
| `resolve` | The absolute path to the plugin's directory |
| `id` | A concatenated string consisting of `Plugin` and a space followed by the name of the plugin; e.g., `Plugin my-plugin` |
| `name` | The name of the plugin; e.g., `my-plugin` |
| `version` | The version according to the plugin definition in *package.json*; if the plugin is a local plugin, one is generated from the file's hash |
| `pluginOptions` | The plugin options as configured in *gatsby-config.js* |
| `nodeAPIs` | The list of Gatsby Node APIs implemented by the plugin, e.g., [ `sourceNodes`, `onCreateNode` ...] |
| `browserAPIs` | The list of Gatsby Browser APIs implemented by the plugin |
| `ssrAPIs` | The list of Gatsby SSR APIs implemented by the plugin |

To view the Gatsby codebase itself, you can look at the GitHub repository (*https://oreil.ly/1UAPn*), clone the Gatsby framework, or open *node_modules/gatsby* in any existing Gatsby project. The logic governing this portion of the Gatsby bootstrap can be found in the Gatsby framework within the *src/bootstrap/load-plugins* directory, where *validate.js* performs a lookup from each of the Gatsby APIs implemented by the plugins and saves the lookup result to Redux under `api-to-plugins`.

## The apiRunInstance Object

Because some API calls in Gatsby can take longer to finish than others, every time an API is invoked, the Gatsby bootstrap creates an object called `apiRunInstance` to track the call. This object contains the fields listed in Table 14-2.

*Table 14-2. Fields in the apiRunInstance object*

| Field | Description |
| --- | --- |
| `id` | A unique identifier generated based on the type of API invoked |
| `api` | The API being invoked; e.g., `onCreateNode` |
| `args` | Any arguments passed to `api-runner-node`; e.g., an individual Node object |
| `pluginSource` | An optional name assigned to the plugin that originated the invocation |
| `resolve` | The `Promise` resolve callback to be invoked when the API has concluded its execution |
| `startTime` | The timestamp at which the API invocation was initialized |
| `span` | An OpenTracing span for build tracing |
| `traceId` | An optional argument provided to the object if the API invocation will lead to other API invocations |

> For more information about the usage of `traceId` to await downstream API calls occurring due to the ongoing API invocation resulting in other calls to APIs, consult the Gatsby documentation (*https://oreil.ly/hJ9A1*).

## Executing Plugins and Injecting Arguments

Once the previous step is complete, the Gatsby bootstrap filters the `flattenedPlugins` namespace in Redux to yield only the plugins that implement the Gatsby API that needs to be executed. For each successive plugin it encounters, Gatsby will require its *gatsby-node.js* file and invoke its exported function that implements one of the Gatsby Node APIs. For instance, if the API invoked is `sourceNodes`, Gatsby will execute `gatsbyNode['sourceNodes'](...apiCallArgs)`.

Once invoked, each API implementation is provided with a range of Gatsby actions and other functions and objects as arguments. Each of these arguments is created whenever a plugin is executed for a designated API, which permits Gatsby to rebind actions with default information for that plugin where necessary. Every action in Gatsby accepts three arguments, as follows:

- The core piece of information required by the action; for instance, a `Node` object for the `createNode` API

- The plugin invoking this action; for instance, `my-plugin`, which `createNode` uses to designate an owner for the new `Node` object

- An object with several miscellaneous action options, such as `traceId` and `parent Span` for build tracing

Passing along the full set of plugin options and action options on each and every action invocation would be unrelentingly slow for developers implementing sites or plugins. Because Gatsby is already aware of the plugin as well as `traceId` and `parent Span` when referring to the API, the bootstrap *rebinds* injected Gatsby actions so that those arguments are already available. This is done by `doubleBind` in *src/utils/api-runner-node.js*.

Each plugin is executed within a `map-series_Promise` (*https://oreil.ly/wqXxk*), thus permitting them to be run concurrently for performance. After all plugins have been executed, Gatsby removes them from `apisRunningById` and fires an `API_RUN NING_QUEUE_EMPTY` event, which results in the re-creation of any unfinished pages and the queries inside. Once this step is complete, the results are returned, allowing the bootstrap to proceed.

Now that we've covered how the Gatsby bootstrap handles each individual API and plugin it comes across, let's zoom in on the build lifecycle, which is the process Gatsby undertakes for each build. To explore this, we'll dive deeper into some of the APIs that we discussed in this section.

# The Gatsby Build Lifecycle

The Gatsby build lifecycle consists of a series of steps, many of which will be recognizable from the overviews of some of these APIs in previous chapters. After nodes are sourced and created, a schema is generated to facilitate GraphQL queries in Gatsby pages and components. Thereafter, the queries are executed to create the pages that form the eventual static site that results. In this section, we'll cover each of the lifecycle events in succession.

> For more information about the internal data bridge, an internal Gatsby plugin that is used to create nodes representing pages, plugins, and site configuration for arbitrary introspection (access of data structures that represent those assets, such as in `gatsby-plugin-sitemap`), consult the guide to the internal data bridge in the Gatsby documentation (*https://oreil.ly/8kfhp*).

# Node Creation

The `createNode` API, one of the Gatsby Node APIs, is responsible for creating nodes, which can take the form of any object. Within Redux, which Gatsby leverages to manage state, nodes are stored under the `nodes` namespace. The `nodes` namespace carries state in the form of a map of `Node` identifiers to `Node` objects.

Node creation happens first and foremost in the `sourceNodes` bootstrap stage, and all nodes created during `sourceNodes` execution are top-level nodes that lack a parent. To indicate this, source plugins set each node's `parent` field to `null`.

 For more information about node tracking, which Gatsby uses to track relationships between a node's object values (i.e., not children) and its identifier, consult the documentation (*https://oreil.ly/ CuQqC*).

## Establishing parent and child relationships

Many nodes have a relationship to a parent node or child node that establishes a dependency between the two. Gatsby's build process provides several approaches to create these relationships, which isn't straightforward due to the fact that all nodes are considered top-level objects in the Redux `nodes` namespace. For this reason, each node's `children` field consists of an array of node identifiers, each pointing to a node at the same level in that Redux namespace, as seen in the following example:

```
{
    `id1`: { type: `File`, children: [`id2`, `id3`], ...other_fields },
    `id2`: { type: `markdownRemark`, ...other_fields },
    `id3`: { type: `postsJson`, ...other_fields }
}
```

In Gatsby, all children are stored within a single collection having parent references.

Certain child nodes need to have their relationships to their parent explicitly defined. This is most often the case when nodes are transformed from other nodes through `onCreateNode` implementations, thereby establishing a relationship between the untransformed parent node and the transformed child node (or a previously transformed parent node in the case of consecutive transformations). For instance, transformer plugins often implement `onCreateNode` to create a child node, as we saw in Chapter 9, invoking `createParentChildLink` in the process. This function call pushes the transformed child node's identifier to the parent's `children` collection and commits it to Redux.

This unfortunately doesn't automatically facilitate the creation of a parent field on the child node. Plugin authors, such as those writing transformer plugins, who wish to permit access to child nodes' parents within the context of GraphQL queries need to explicitly write `childNode.parent: `parent.id`` when creating the child node.

The definition of child nodes as node identifiers within the top level of the Redux `nodes` namespace also drives what is known as *foreign key references*, which are used in GraphQL to access child nodes from the standpoint of the parent node. The names of foreign key fields accessing these foreign keys are suffixed with ___NODE. When Gatsby runs the GraphQL queries for pages and components, it adopts that value as an identifier and searches the Redux `nodes` namespace for the matching node. We'll come back to this process when we turn to schema generation.

For more information about how Gatsby handles plain objects as nodes during the node creation phase, consult the documentation (*https://oreil.ly/whaAx*).

### Handling stale nodes

Each time you run the `gatsby build` command, because Gatsby is fundamentally an SSG, there is always a nonzero chance that some node in the Redux `nodes` namespace will no longer be available because it's been removed from the upstream data source. The Gatsby build lifecycle needs to be aware of this event in order to handle all nodes appropriately.

In addition to the Redux `nodes` namespace, there is a `nodesTouched` namespace that catalogues whether a particular node identifier has been touched by Gatsby during the node creation phase. This process occurs whenever nodes are created or when the `touchNode` function is called in the Gatsby API. Any nodes that haven't been touched by the end of the node sourcing phase are deleted from the `nodes` namespace by identifying the delta between the `nodesTouched` and `nodes` Redux namespaces (as seen in *src/utils/source-nodes.ts*).

When a plugin using `source-nodes` runs again, it will re-create nodes (and therefore touch them). In certain scenarios, such as with some transformer plugins, a node may not actually change, though the node needs to be maintained for the build. For these cases, `touchNode` must be invoked explicitly by the plugin.

When you develop a Gatsby site, nodes are considered to be immutable unless those modifications are directly persisted to Gatsby's Redux implementation through a Gatsby action. If you change a `Node` object directly without making Redux aware of the change, other areas of the Gatsby framework won't be aware either. For this reason, always ensure that whenever you implement a Gatsby API such as `onCreateNode` you call a function such as `createNodeField`, which will add the updated field to the node's `node.fields` object and persist the new state to Redux. This way, later logic in the plugin will execute properly based on this new state of the node in later build stages.

 For more information about build caching in Gatsby, for instance during the creation of nodes by source and transformer plugins, consult the guide to build caching in the Gatsby documentation (*https://oreil.ly/EFZjX*).

## Schema Generation

After the nodes in your Gatsby site have been sourced from upstream data sources and transformed where necessary through plugins and their implementations of Gatsby APIs, it's time for Gatsby to generate the schema underlying the GraphQL API driving data in your Gatsby implementation. Schema generation involves several steps.

Gatsby's GraphQL schema differs considerably from many other GraphQL schemas in the wild because it synthesizes plugin- and user-defined schema information together with data inferred from the way the sourced and transformed nodes are themselves structured. The former process involves creating a schema based on data presented to Gatsby, whereas the latter process, schema inference, involves inferring a schema based on how nodes are shaped.

Both developers and plugin authors in Gatsby have the ability to define the schema themselves through a process known as *schema customization*, which we covered in the previous chapter. Typically, every node receives a certain type in GraphQL based on the way its `node.internal.type` field is defined. For example, when you leverage Gatsby's schema customization API to explicitly define the GraphQL type, all types that implement Gatsby's `Node` interface will in turn become resources of type `Node` in GraphQL, in the process having their root-level fields defined in the GraphQL schema as well.

In Gatsby, schema generation is a process that leverages the `graphql-compose` library, which is a toolkit used by many GraphQL API creators to generate schemas programmatically. For more information about this library, consult the `graphql-compose` documentation (*https://graphql-compose.github.io*).

## Schema Inference

Each time a node is created, yielding a newly sourced or transformed node, Gatsby generates *inference metadata* that can be merged with other metadata such that it's possible to define a schema for the new node that is as specific as possible to its structure. Thanks to inference metadata, Gatsby can also understand if there are any conflicts in the data and display a warning to the user. The process by which Gatsby adds to the schema it creates based on this metadata is known as *schema inference*.

To do this, Gatsby creates a `GraphQLObjectType`, or `gqlType`, for each unique `node.internal.type` field value that is encountered during the node sourcing phase. In Gatsby, each `gqlType` is an object that defines both the type name and each of the fields contained therein, which are provided by the `createNodeFields` function in Gatsby's internal *src/schema/build-node-types.js* file.

Each `gqlType` object is created before its fields are inferred, allowing for fields to be introduced later when their types are created. This is achieved in Gatsby through the use of lazy functions in the same *build-node-types.js* file.

Once the `gqlType` is created, Gatsby can begin to infer fields. The first thing it does is generate an `exampleValue`, which is the result of merging together all the fields from all the nodes of that `gqlType`. As such, this `exampleValue` variable will house all prospective field names and their values, allowing Gatsby to infer each field's type. This logic occurs in the `getExampleValues` function in *src/schema/data-tree-utils.js*.

There are three types of fields that Gatsby makes available in each node it creates by inferring the type's fields based on the `exampleValue`:

1. Fields on the created `Node` object
2. Child and parent relationship fields
3. Fields created by `setFieldsOnGraphQLNodeType`

Let's take a look at the first two of these. The third type of inferred field, created by plugins that implement the `setFieldsOnGraphQLNodeType` API, requires those plugins to return full GraphQL field declarations, including type and resolver functions.

## Inferring fields on the created Node object

Fields that are directly created on the node, meaning fields that are provided through source and transformer plugins (e.g., `relativePath`, `size`, and `accessTime` in nodes of type `File`), are typically queried through the GraphQL API in a query similar to the following:

```
node {
  relativePath,
  extension,
  size,
  accessTime
}
```

These fields are created using the `inferObjectStructureFromNodes` function in *src/schema/infer-graphql-type.js*. Based on what kind of object the function is dealing with as it encounters new objects, it can encompass one of the following three subcategories of fields provided on the created `Node` object:

- A field provided through a mapping in *gatsby-config.js*
- A field having a value provided through a foreign key reference (ending in ___NODE)
- A plain object or value (such as a string) that is passed in

First, for *fields provided through mappings* in *gatsby-config.js*, if the object field being sent for GraphQL type generation is configured in a custom manner in the Gatsby configuration file, it requires special handling. For instance, a typical mapping might look like the following, where we're mapping a linked type, `AuthorYaml`, to the `MarkdownRemark` type so that we make the `AuthorYaml.name` field available in `MarkdownRemark` as `MarkdownRemark.frontmatter.author`:

```
// gatsby-config.js
mapping: {
  "MarkdownRemark.frontmatter.author": `AuthorYaml.name`,
}
```

In this situation, the field generation is handled by the `inferFromMapping` function in *src/schema/infer-graphql-type.js*. When invoked, the function finds the type to which the identified field is mapped (`AuthorYaml`), which is known as the `linkedType`. If a field to link by (`linkedField`, in this scenario `name`) is not provided to the function, it defaults to `id`.

Then, Gatsby declares a new GraphQL field whose type is `AuthorYaml` (which is searched for within the existing list of `gqlTypes`). Thereafter, the GraphQL field resolver will acquire the value for the given node (in this example, the `author` string that should be mapped into the identified field) and conduct a search through all the nodes until it finds one with a matching type and matching field value (i.e., the correct `AuthorYaml.name`).

Second, for *foreign key references*, the suffix \_\_\_`NODE` indicates that the value of the field is an `id` that represents another node present in the Redux store. In this scenario, the `inferFromFieldName` function in *src/schema/infer-graphql-type.js* handles the field inference. In this process, which is quite similar to the field mapping process described previously, Gatsby deletes \_\_\_`NODE` from the field name (converting `author__NODE` into `author`, for instance). Then it searches for the `linkedNode` that the `id` represents in the Redux store (the `exampleValue` for `author`, which is an `id`). Upon identifying the correct node through this foreign key, Gatsby acquires the type in the `gqlTypes` list via the `internal.type` value. In addition, Gatsby will accept a `linkedField` value that adheres to the format `nodeFieldName__NODE__linked FieldName` (e.g., `author__NODE__name` can be provided instead of `id`).

Then, Gatsby returns a new GraphQL field sharing the same type as that represented by the foreign key. The GraphQL field resolver sifts through all the available Redux nodes until it encounters one with the same `id`. If the foreign key value is instead an array of `id`s, then Gatsby will return a `GraphQLUnionType`; i.e., a union of all linked types represented in the array.

Third, for *plain objects or value fields*, the `inferGraphQLType` function in *src/schema/infer-graphql-types.js* is the default handler. In this scenario, Gatsby creates a GraphQL field object whose type it infers directly by using `typeof` in JavaScript. For instance, `typeof(value) === 'string'` would result in the type `GraphQLString`. As the `graphql-js` library handles this automatically for Gatsby, there is no need for additional resolvers.

However, if the value provided is an object or an array requiring introspection, Gatsby uses `inferObjectStructureFromNodes` to recurse through the structure and create new GraphQL fields. Gatsby also creates custom GraphQL types for `File` (*src/schema/types/type-file.js*) and `Date` (*src/schema/types/type-date.js*): if the value looks like it could be a filename or a date, then Gatsby will return the correct custom type.

 For more information about how `File` types are inferred, consult the Gatsby documentation's schema inference section on `File` types (*https://oreil.ly/a7jKm*).

### Inferring child and parent fields

In this section, we'll examine the schema inference Gatsby undertakes to define child fields that have a relationship to their parent field. Consider the example of the `File` type, for which many transformer plugins exist that convert a file's contents into a format legible to Gatsby's data layer. When transformer plugins implement `onCreate` `Node` for each `File` node, this implementation produces `File` child nodes that carry their own type (e.g., `markdownRemark` or `postsJson`).

When Gatsby infers the schema for these child fields, it stores the nodes in Redux by identifying them through `ids` in each parent's `children` field. Then, Gatsby stores those child nodes in Redux as full nodes in their own right. For instance, a `File` node having two children will be stored in the Redux `nodes` namespace as follows:

```
{
  `id1`: { type: `File`, children: [`id2`, `id3`], ...other_fields },
  `id2`: { type: `markdownRemark`, ...other_fields },
  `id3`: { type: `postsJson`, ...other_fields }
}
```

Gatsby doesn't store a distinct collection of each child node type. Instead, it stores in Redux a single collection containing all of the children together. One key advantage of this approach is that Gatsby can create a `File.children` field in GraphQL that returns all children irrespective of type. However, one important disadvantage is that creating fields such as `File.childMarkdownRemark` and `File.childrenPostsJson` becomes a more complex process, since no collection of each child node type is available. Gatsby also offers the ability to query a node for its `child` or `children`, depending on whether the parent node references one or multiple children of that type.

In Gatsby, upon defining the parent `File` `gqlType`, the `createNodeFields` API will iterate over each unique type of its children and create their respective fields. For example, given a child type named `markdownRemark`, of which there is only one child node per parent `File`, Gatsby will create the field `childMarkdownRemark`. To facilitate queries on `File.childMarkdownRemark`, we need to write a custom child resolver:

```
resolve(node, args, context, info)
```

This `resolve` function will be invoked whenever we are executing queries for each page, like the following query:

```
query {
  file( relativePath { eq: "blog/my-blog-post.md" } ) {
    childMarkdownRemark { html }
  }
}
```

To resolve the `File.childMarkdownRemark` field, Gatsby will, for each parent `File` node it resolves, filter over each of its children until it encounters one of type `mark` `downRemark`, which is then returned from the resolver function. Because that `children` value is a collection of identifiers, Gatsby searches for the node by `id` in the Redux `nodes` namespace as well.

Before leaving the `resolve` function's logic, because Gatsby may be executing this query from within a page, whenever the node changes we need to ensure that the page is rerendered accordingly. As such, when changes in the node are detected, the resolver function calls the `createPageDependency` function, passing the node identifier and the page: a field available in the `context` object within the `resolve` function's signature.

Finally, once a node is created and designated a child of some parent node, that fact is noted in the child's `parent` field, whose value is the parent's identifier. Then, the GraphQL resolver for this field searches for that parent by that `id` in Redux and returns it. In the process, it also adds a page dependency through `createPageDepend ency` to record that the page on which the query is present has a dependency on the parent node.

 For more information about how Gatsby handles plain objects or value fields that represent filepaths (such as references to JSON files on disk), consult the Gatsby documentation's guide to schema inference for file types (*https://oreil.ly/FE7S8*).

## Schema Root Fields and Utility Types

In this section, we'll discuss another key step in the Gatsby build lifecycle and the enablement of GraphQL queries: the creation of *schema root fields*. In Gatsby, schema root fields are considered the "entry point" of any GraphQL query, also sometimes known as a top-level field. For each `Node` type created during the process of schema generation, Gatsby generates two schema root fields. However, third-party schemas and implementations of the `createResolvers` API are free to create additional fields.

The root fields generated by Gatsby are leveraged to retrieve either a single item of a certain `Node` type or a collection of items of that type. For example, for a given type `BlogArticle`, Gatsby will create on your behalf a `blogArticle` (singular) and an `all BlogArticle` (plural) root field. While these root fields are perfectly usable without arguments, both accept parameters that allow you to manipulate the returned data through filters, sorts, and pagination. Because these parameters depend on the given `Node` type, Gatsby generates *utility types* to support them, which are types that enable pagination, sort, and filter operations and are used in the root fields accordingly.

### Plural root fields

Plural root fields accept four arguments: `filter`, `sort`, `skip`, and `limit`. The `filter` argument permits filtering based on node field values, and `sort` reorders the result. Meanwhile, the `skip` and `limit` arguments offset the result by the number of `skip` nodes and restrict it to the number of `limit` items. In GraphQL, plural root fields return a `Connection` type for the given type name (e.g., `BlogArticleConnection` for `allBlogArticle`).

Here is an example of a plural root field query, which retrieves multiple nodes of type `blogArticle` with two arguments that filter and sort the incoming data:

```
{
  allBlogArticle(
    filter: { date: { lt: "2020-01-01" } }
    sort: { fields: [date], order: ASC }
  ) {
    nodes {
      id
    }
  }
}
```

### Singular root fields

Singular root fields also accept the `filter` parameter, but the filter is spread directly into arguments rather than as a distinct key. As such, filter parameters are passed to the singular root field directly and return the resulting object directly. If no parameters are passed, a random node of that type, if it exists, is returned. Because this random node is explicitly undefined, there is no guarantee of stability of that node across individual builds and rebuilds. If there is no node available to return, `null` is returned.

Here is an example of a singular root field query, which retrieves a single node of type `blogArticle` by identifying a field and its desired value:

```
{
  blogArticle(id: { slug: "graphql-is-the-best" }) {
    id
  }
}
```

### Pagination types

As we saw earlier in this section, when a group of nodes is returned in response to a plural root field query, the type returned is `Connection`, which represents a common pattern in GraphQL. The term *connection* refers to an abstraction that operates over paginated resources. When you query a connection in GraphQL, Gatsby returns a subset of the resulting data based on defined `skip` and `limit` parameters, but you can also perform additional operations on the collection, such as grouping or distinction, as seen in the last two rows the following table (Table 14-3).

*Table 14-3. Available additional operations on `Connection` types*

| Field | Description |
|---|---|
| edges | An edge is the actual Node object combined with additional metadata indicating its location in the paginated page; edges is a list of these objects. The edge object contains node, the actual object, and next and prev objects to retrieve the objects representing adjacent pages. |
| nodes | A flat list of Node objects. |
| pageInfo | Contains additional pagination metadata. |
| pageInfo.totalCount | The number of all nodes that match the filter prior to pagination (also available as total Count). |
| pageInfo.currentPage | The index of the current page (starting with 1). |
| pageInfo.hasNext Page, pageInfo.hasPre viousPage | Whether a previous or next page is available based on the current paginated page. |
| pageInfo.itemCount | The number of items on the current page. |
| perPage | The requested number of items on each page. |
| pageCount | The total number of pages. |
| distinct(field) | Prints distinct values for a given field. |
| group(field) | Returns values grouped by a given field. |

> For more information about the `Connection` convention in GraphQL, consult the Relay documentation's page on the connection model (*https://oreil.ly/i6WRv*).

### Filter types

For each `Node` type, a filter input type is created in GraphQL. Gatsby provides prefabricated "operator types" for each scalar (e.g., `StringQueryOperatorType`) that carry keys as possible operators (such as `eq` and `ne`) and values as appropriate values for them. Thereafter, Gatsby inspects each field in the type and runs approximately the following algorithm:

- If the field is a scalar:
  - Retrieve a corresponding operator type for that scalar.
  - Replace the field with that operator type.
- If the field is not a scalar:
  - Recurse through the nested type's fields and then assign the resulting input object type to the field.

Here's an example of the resulting types for a given `Node` type:

```
input StringQueryOperatorInput {
  eq: String
  ne: String
  in: [String]
  nin: [String]
  regex: String
  glob: String
}

input BlogFilterInput {
  title: StringQueryOperatorInput
  comments: CommentFilterInput
  # and so forth
}
```

 For more information about how Gatsby enables query filters within GraphQL queries, including discussion of the historic use of Sift, the `elemMatch` query filter, and performance considerations, consult the Gatsby documentation's guide to query filters (*https://oreil.ly/o9Bc8*).

### Sort types

For sort operations, given a field, GraphQL creates an enum of all fields (which accounts for up to three levels of nested fields) for a particular type, such as the following:

```
enum BlogFieldsEnum {
  id
  title
  date
  parent___id
  # and so forth
}
```

This field is then combined with another enum containing an order (ASC for ascending or DESC for descending) into a sort input type:

```
input BlogSortInput {
  fields: [BlogFieldsEnum]
  order: [SortOrderEnum] = [ASC]
}
```

# Page Creation

Once schema generation is complete, including schema inference and the provision of all schema root fields, utility types, and query filters, the next step in the Gatsby build lifecycle is *page creation*, which is conducted by invoking the `createPage` action. There are three primary side effects in Gatsby when a page is created.

First, the `pages` namespace, which is a map of each page's `path` to a `Page` object, is updated in Redux. The pages reducer (*src/redux/reducer/pages.ts*) is responsible for updating this each time a `CREATE_PAGE` action is executed, and it creates a foreign key reference to the plugin responsible for creating the page by adding a `pluginCrea tor___NODE` field.

Second, the `components` namespace, which is a map of each `componentPath` (a file with a React component) to a `Component` object (the `Page` object but containing an empty query string), is updated in Redux. This query string will be set during query extraction, which is covered in the next section.

Finally, the `onCreatePage` API is executed. Every time a page is created, plugins can implement the `onCreatePage` API to perform certain tasks such as creating `SitePage` nodes or acting as a handler for plugins that manage paths, like `gatsby-plugin-create-client-paths` and `gatsby-plugin-remove-trailing-slashes`.

## Query Extraction and Execution

After the `createPages` API executes, the next step in the Gatsby build lifecycle is for Gatsby to extract and execute the queries that declare data requirements for each page and component present in the Gatsby files. In Gatsby, GraphQL queries are defined as tagged `graphql` expressions. These expressions can be:

- Exported in page files
- Utilized in the context of the `StaticQuery` component
- Employed in a `useStaticQuery` hook in React code

These are all uses that we have seen previously. In addition, plugins can also supply arbitrary fragments that can be used in queries.

In this section, we'll examine the query extraction and execution process and how Gatsby furnishes the data that makes up each component and template. Note, however, that this discussion does not cover queries designated in implementations of Gatsby's Node APIs, which are usually intended for programmatic page creation and operate differently.

The majority of the source code in the Gatsby project that performs query extraction and execution is found in the *src/query* directory within the Gatsby repository (*https://oreil.ly/iz3AR*).

## Query extraction

The first step in the process is query extraction, which involves the extraction and validation of all GraphQL queries found in Gatsby pages, components, and templates. At this point in the build process, Gatsby has finished creating all the nodes in the associated Redux namespace, inferred a schema from those nodes, and completed page creation. Next, it needs to extract and compile every GraphQL query present in your source files. In the Gatsby source code, the entry point to this step in the process is `extractQueries` in *src/query/query-watcher.js*, which compiles each GraphQL query by invoking the logic in *src/query/query-compiler.js*.

> For a diagram illustrating the flow involved in query compilation, consult the Gatsby documentation's guide to query extraction (*https://oreil.ly/IShdu*). For more information about the libraries involved in this step, consult the Babel and Relay documentation for `babylon-traverse` (*https://oreil.ly/jRZmD*) and `relay-compiler` (*https://oreil.ly/sChLJ*), respectively.

The query compiler's first step is to utilize `babylon-traverse`, a Babel library, to load every JavaScript file available in the Gatsby site that contains a GraphQL query, yielding an abstract syntax tree (AST; a tree representation of source code) of results that are passed to the `relay-compiler` library. The query compilation process thus achieves two important goals:

- It lets Gatsby know if there are any malformed or invalid queries, which are immediately reported to the user.
- It constructs a tree of queries and fragments depended on by the queries and outputs an optimized query string containing all the relevant fragments.

Once this step is complete, Gatsby will have access to a map of filepaths (namely of site files containing queries) to individual query objects, each of which contains the raw optimized query text from query compilation. Each query object will also house other metadata, such as the component's path and the relevant page's `jsonName`, allowing it to connect the dots between the component and the page on which it will render.

> For more information about how Gatsby establishes dependencies between pages and nodes during this stage, consult the Gatsby documentation's guide to page → node dependency tracking (*https://oreil.ly/LkMsY*).

Next, Gatsby executes the `handleQuery` function in *src/query/query-watcher.js*. If the query being handled is a `StaticQuery`, Gatsby invokes `replaceStaticQuery` to store it in the `staticQueryComponents` namespace, which maps each component's path to an object containing the raw GraphQL query and other items. In the process, Gatsby also removes the component's `jsonName` from the `components` Redux namespace.

On the other hand, if the query is a non-`StaticQuery`, Gatsby will update the relevant component's `query` in the Redux `components` namespace by calling the `replaceCompo nentQuery` action. The final step, once Gatsby has saved each query under its purview to Redux, is to queue the queries for execution. Because query execution is primarily handled by *src/query/page-query-runner.ts*, Gatsby invokes `queueQueryForPathname` while passing the component's path as a parameter.

For diagrams illustrating the flows involved in storing queries in Redux and queuing queries for execution, consult the query extraction guide in the Gatsby documentation (*https://oreil.ly/SuWer*).

### Query execution

The second step in the query extraction and execution process is the actual execution of the queries to enable data delivery. In the Gatsby bootstrap, queries are executed by Gatsby invoking the `createQueryRunningActivity` function in *src/query/index.js*. The other two files involved in the query execution process are *queue.ts* and *query-runner.ts*, both located in the same Gatsby source directory.

For a diagram illustrating the flow involved in this step, consult the Gatsby documentation's guide to on query execution (*https://oreil.ly/HA3wA*).

The first thing Gatsby needs to do to properly execute queries is select which queries need to be executed in the first place—a stage complicated by the fact that it also needs to support the `gatsby develop` process. For this reason, it isn't simply a matter of executing the queries as they were enqueued at the end of the extraction step. The `runQueries` function is responsible for this logic.

First, all queries are identified that were enqueued after having been extracted by *src/query/query-watcher.js*. Then, Gatsby proceeds to catalogue those queries that lack node dependencies: namely, queries whose component paths are not listed in `compo nentDataDependencies`. During schema generation, each type resolver records dependencies between pages whose queries are being executed and successfully resolved nodes of that type. As such, if a component is listed in the `components`

Redux namespace but is unavailable in `componentDataDependencies`, the query has not yet been executed and requires execution. This logic is found in `findIdsWithout DataDependencies`.

As we know from spinning up a local development server using the `gatsby develop` command, each time a node is created or updated, the node must be dynamically updated—or, internally speaking, added to the `enqueuedDirtyActions` collection. As queries are executed, Gatsby searches for all nodes within this collection in order to map them to those pages that depend on them. Pages depending on dirty nodes (nodes that have gone stale and need updating) have queries that must be executed. This third step in the query execution process also concerns dirty connections that depend on a node's type. If the node is dirty, Gatsby designates all connections of that type dirty as well. This logic is found in `popNodeQueries`.

Now that Gatsby has an authoritative list of all queries requiring execution at its disposal, it will queue them for actual execution, kicking off the step by invoking the `runQueriesForPathnames` function. For each individual page or static query, Gatsby creates a new query job, an example of which is shown here:

```
{
  id: // Page path, or static query hash
  hash: // Only for static queries
  jsonName: // jsonName of static query or page
  query: // Raw query text
  componentPath: // Path to file where query is declared
  isPage: // true if not static query
  context: {
    path: // If staticQuery, is jsonName of component
    // Page object. Not for static queries
    ...page
    // Not for static queries
    ...page.context
  }
}
```

Each individual query job contains all of the information it needs to execute the query and encode dependencies between pages and nodes therein. The query job is enqueued in *src/query/query-queue.js*, which uses the `better-queue` library to facilitate parallel query execution. Because Gatsby has dependencies only between pages and nodes, not queries themselves, parallel query execution is possible. Each time an item surfaces from the queue, Gatsby invokes *query-runner.ts* to execute the query, which involves the following three parameters passed to the `graphql-js` library:

1. The Gatsby schema that was inferred during schema generation

2. The raw query text, acquired from the query job's contents

3. The context, available in the query job, containing the page's `path` and other elements for dependencies between pages and nodes

Thereafter, the `graphql-js` library will parse and execute the top-level query, invoking the resolvers defined during the schema generation process to query over all nodes of that type in the Redux store. Afterwards, the result is passed through the inner portions of the query, upon which each type's resolver is called. In some cases, these resolver invocations will use custom plugin field resolvers. Because this step may generate artifacts such as manipulated images, the query execution step of the Gatsby bootstrap is often the most time-consuming. Once this step is complete, the query result is returned.

Finally, as queries are removed from the queue and executed, their results are saved to Redux, and by extension the disk, for later consumption. This process includes conversion of the query result to pure JSON and saving it to its associated `dataPath` (relative to *public/static/d*), including the `jsonName` and hash of the result. For static queries, rather than employing the page's `jsonName`, Gatsby utilizes the hash of the query. Once this process is complete, Gatsby stores a mapping of the page to the query result in Redux for later retrieval using the `json-data-paths` reducer in Redux.

For more information about how Gatsby handles normal queries and static queries differently in query extraction and query execution, consult the documentation's guide to Gatsby's internal handling of static versus normal queries (*https://oreil.ly/hf1OA*).

# Writing Out Pages

Among the final bootstrap phases before Gatsby hands off the site to Webpack for bundling and code optimization is the process of writing out pages. Because Webpack has no awareness of Gatsby source code or Redux stores and operates on only files in Gatsby's *.cache* directory, Gatsby needs to create JavaScript files for behavior and JSON files for data that the Webpack configuration set out by Gatsby can accept.

For a diagram illustrating the flow of this bootstrap stage, consult the Gatsby documentation's guide to writing out pages (*https://oreil.ly/CU1gs*).

In the process of writing out pages, primary logic is found in *src/internal-plugins/query-runner/pages-writer.js*, and the files that are generated by this file in the *.cache* directory are *pages.json*, *sync-requires.js*, *async-requires.js*, and *data.json*. In this section, we'll walk through each of these files one by one.

### The pages.json file

The *pages.json* file represents a list of `Page` objects that are generated from the Redux `pages` namespace, accounting for the `componentChunkName`, `jsonName`, `path`, and `matchPath` for each respective `Page` object. These `Page` objects are ordered such that those pages having a `matchPath` precede those that lack one, in order to support the work of *cache-dir/find-page.js* in selecting pages based on regular expressions prior to attempting explicit paths.

Example output for a given `Page` object appears as follows:

```
{
    componentChunkName: "component---src-blog-2-js",
    jsonName: "blog-c06",
    path: "/blog",
},
// more pages
```

The *pages.json* file is created only when the `gatsby develop` command is executed; otherwise, during Gatsby builds, *data.json* is used and includes page information and other important data.

### The sync-requires.js file

The *sync-requires.js* file is a dynamically created JavaScript file that exports individual Gatsby components, generated by iterating over the Redux `components` namespace. In these exports, the keys represent the `componentChunk` name (e.g., *component---src-blog-2-js*), and values represent expressions requiring the component (e.g., `require("/home/site/src/blog/2.js")`), to yield a result like the following:

```
exports.components = {
    "component---src--blog-2-js": require("/home/site/src/blog/2.js"),
    // more components
}
```

This file is employed during the execution of *static-entry.js* to map each component's `componentChunkName` to its respective component implementation. Because *production-app.js* (covered in "Bundling Gatsby" on page 439) performs code splitting, it needs to use *async-requires.js* instead.

### The async-requires.js file

Like *sync-requires.js*, *async-requires.js* is dynamically created by Gatsby, but its motivation differs in that it is intended to be leveraged for code splitting by Webpack. Instead of utilizing `require` to include components by path, this file employs the `import` keyword together with `webpackChunkName` hints to connect the dots between a given listed `componentChunkName` and the resulting file. Because `components` is a function, it can be lazily initialized.

The *async-requires.js* file also exports a `data` function importing *data.json*, the final file covered in this section. The following code snippet illustrates an example of a generated *async-requires.js* file:

```
exports.components = {
  "component---src-blog-2-js": () =>
    import(
      "/home/site/src/blog/2.js"
      /* webpackChunkName: "component---src-blog-2-js" */
    ),
  // more components
}

exports.data = () => import("/home/site/.cache/data.json")
```

While *sync-requires.js* is leveraged by Gatsby during static page HTML generation, the *async-requires.js* file is instead used during the JavaScript application bundling process.

### The data.json file

The *data.json* file contains a complete manifest of the *pages.json* file as well as the Redux `jsonDataPaths` object that was created at the conclusion of the query execution process. It is lazily imported by *async-requires.js*, which is leveraged by *production-app.js* to load the available JSON results for a page. In addition, the *data.json* file is used during page HTML generation for two purposes:

1. The *static-entry.js* file creates a Webpack bundle (*page-renderer.js*), which is used to generate the HTML for a given path and requires *data.json* to search pages for the associated page.

2. The *data.json* file is also used to derive the `jsonName` for a page from an associated `Page` object in order to construct a resource path for the JSON result by searching for it within `data.json.dataPaths[jsonName]`.

The following example illustrates a sample generation of *data.json*:

```
{
  pages: [
    {
      "componentChunkName": "component---src-blog-2-js",
      "jsonName": "blog-2-c06",
      "path": "/blog/2"
    },
    // more pages
  ],

  // jsonName -> dataPath
  dataPaths: {
    "blog-2-c06":"952/path---blog-2-c06-meTS6Okzenz0aDEeI6epU4DPJuE",
```

```
    // more pages
}
```

# Bundling Gatsby

Once the page writing process is complete and the Gatsby bootstrap has concluded, we have a full Gatsby site ready for bundling. In this stage, Gatsby renders all finished pages into HTML through server-side rendering. Moreover, it needs to build a browser-ready JavaScript runtime that will allow for dynamic page interactions after the static HTML has loaded on the client. In this section, we'll take a look at the final steps Gatsby undertakes to ready our site for the browser.

Gatsby utilizes the Webpack bundler to generate the final browser-ready bundle for our Gatsby site. All the files required by Webpack are located in the Gatsby site's *.cache* directory, which starts out empty upon initializing a new project and is filled up by Gatsby over the course of the build.

Upon the kickoff of a build, Gatsby copies all the files located in *gatsby/cache-dir* into the *.cache* directory, including essential files like *static-entry.js* and *production-app.js*, which we cover in the next section. All the files needed to run in the browser or to generate the HTML result are included as part of *cache-dir*. Gatsby also places all the pages that were written out in the previous stage in the *.cache* directory, as Webpack remains entirely unaware of Redux.

 For more information about how Gatsby generates the initial HTML page for a Gatsby site before initializing the client-side bundle, consult the documentation's guide to page HTML generation (*https://oreil.ly/dHrKP*).

## Generating the JavaScript Bundle

First, let's walk through how Gatsby generates the JavaScript runtime that performs rehydration after the initial HTML is loaded, and all client-side work thereafter (such as the instantaneous loading of subsequent pages). There are several files involved in the process.

The entry point is the *build-javascript.ts* file in Gatsby (located in the *src/commands* directory), which dynamically generates a Webpack configuration by invoking *src/ utils/webpack.config.js*. Depending on which stage is being handled (build-javascript, build-html, develop, or develop-html), this can result in significantly different configurations. For example, consider the Webpack configuration generated for the build-javascript stage, reproduced here with comments:

```
{
  entry: {
```

```
    app: `.cache/production-app`
  },
  output: {
    // e.g. app-2e49587d85e03a033f58.js
    filename: `[name]-[contenthash].js`,
    // e.g. component---src-blog-2-js-cebc3ae7596cbb5b0951.js
    chunkFilename: `[name]-[contenthash].js`,
    path: `/public`,
    publicPath: `/`
  },
  target: `web`,
  devtool: `source-map`,
  mode: `production`,
  node: {
    ___filename: true
  },
  optimization: {
    runtimeChunk: {
      // e.g. webpack-runtime-e402cdceeae5fad2aa61.js
      name: `webpack-runtime`
    },
    splitChunks: {
      chunks: `all`,
      cacheGroups: {
        // disable webpack's default cacheGroup
        default: false,
        // disable webpack's default vendor cacheGroup
        vendors: false,
        // Create a framework bundle that contains React libraries
        // They hardly change so we bundle them together
        framework: {},
        // Big modules that are over 160kb are moved to their own file to
        // optimize browser parsing & execution
        lib: {},
        // All libraries that are used on all pages are moved into a common
        // chunk
        commons: {},
        // When a module is used more than once we create a shared bundle to
        // save user's bandwidth
        shared: {},
        // All CSS is bundled into one stylesheet
        styles: {}
      },
      // Keep maximum initial requests to 25
      maxInitialRequests: 25,
      // A chunk should be at least 20kb before using splitChunks
      minSize: 20000
    },
    minimizers: [
      // Minify javascript using Terser (https://terser.org/)
      plugins.minifyJs(),
      // Minify CSS by using cssnano (https://cssnano.co/)
```

```
      plugins.minifyCss(),
    ]
  }
  plugins: [
    // A custom webpack plugin that implements logic to write out
    // chunk-map.json and webpack.stats.json
    plugins.extractStats(),
  ]
}
```

The `splitChunks` portion of this Webpack configuration, which removes loaders, rules, and other output, is the most important part, because it contributes to how code splitting occurs in Gatsby and how the most optimized bundle is generated. Gatsby tries to create generated JavaScript files that are as granular as possible ("granular chunks") by deduplicating all modules. Once Webpack is finished compiling the bundle, it ends up with a few different bundles, which are accounted for in Table 14-4.

*Table 14-4. Bundles generated by Webpack upon completion of the `build-javascript` stage*

| Filename | Description |
| --- | --- |
| *app-[contenthash].js* | This bundle is produced from production-app.js and is configured in webpack.config.js. |
| *webpack-runtime-[contenthash].js* | This bundle contains `webpack-runtime` as a separate bundle (configured in the optimization section) and is usually required with the app bundle. |
| *framework-[contenthash].js* | This bundle contains React and as a separate bundle improves cache hit rate, because the React library is seldom updated as frequently. |
| *commons-[contenthash].js* | Libraries used on every Gatsby page are bundled into this file so that they are downloaded only once. |
| *component---[name]-[contenthash].js* | This represents a separate bundle for each page to enable code splitting. |

## The production-app.js file

The *production-app.js* file is the entry point to Webpack. It yields the *app-[contenthash].js* file, which is responsible for all navigation and page loading subsequent to the loading of the initial HTML in the browser. On first load, the HTML loads immediately; it includes a CDATA section (*https://oreil.ly/BrJVi*) (indicating a portion of unescaped text) that injects page information into the `window` object such that it's available in JavaScript straight away. In this example output, we have just refreshed the browser on a Gatsby site's */blog/3* page:

```
<![
  CDATA[ */
    window.page={
      "path": "/blog/3.js",
      "componentChunkName": "component---src-blog-3-js",
      "jsonName": "blog-3-995"
    };
```

```
    window.dataPath="621/path---blog-3-995-a74-dwfQIanOJGe2gi27a9CLKHjamc";
  */ ]
]>
```

Thereafter, the application, `webpack-runtime`, component, shared libraries, and data JSON bundles are loaded through `<link>` and `<script>` elements, upon which the *production-app.js* code initializes.

The very first thing the application does in the browser is execute the `onClientEntry` browser API, which enables plugins to perform any important operations prior to any other page-loading logic (e.g., rehydration performed by `gatsby-plugin-glamor`). The browser API executor differs considerably from `api-runner-node`, which runs Node APIs. *api-runner-browser.js* iterates through the site's browser plugins that have been registered and executes them one by one (after retrieving the plugins list from *./cache/api-runner-browser-plugins.js*, generated early in the Gatsby bootstrap).

Second, the bundle executes `hydrate`, a ReactDOM function that behaves the same way as `render`, with the exception that rather than generating an entirely new DOM tree and inserting it into the document, `hydrate` expects a ReactDOM tree to be present on the page already sharing precisely the same structure. Upon identifying the matching tree, it traverses the tree to attach required event listeners to "enliven" the React DOM. This hydration process operates on the `<div id="___gatsby">...</div>` element found in *cache-dir/default-html.js*.

Third, the *production-app.js* file uses `@reach/router` to replace the existing DOM with a `RouteHandler` component that utilizes `PageRenderer` to create the page to which the user has just navigated and load the page resources for that path. However, on first load, the page resources for the given path will already be available in the page's initial HTML thanks to the `<link rel="preload" ... />` element. These resources include the imported component, which Gatsby leverages to generate the page component by executing `React.createElement()`. Then, the element is presented to the `RouteHandler` for `@reach/router` to execute rendering.

Prior to rehydration, Gatsby begins the process of loading background resources ahead of time—namely, page resources that will be required once the user begins to navigate through links and other elements on the page. This loading of page resources occurs in *cache-dir/loader.js*, whose main function is `getResourcesForPathname`. This function accepts a path, discovers the associated page, and imports the component module's JSON query results. Access to that information is furnished by *async-requires.js*, which includes a list of every page on the Gatsby site and each associated `dataPath`. The `fetchPageResourcesMap` function is responsible for retrieving that file, which happens upon the first invocation of `getResourcesForPathname`.

To provide global state, Gatsby attaches state variables to the `window` object such that they can be used by plugins, such as `window.___loader`, `window.___emitter`, `window.___chunkMapping`, `window.___push`, `window.___replace`, and `window.___navigate`. For more information about these, consult the Gatsby documentation's guide to `window` variables (*https://oreil.ly/7TtmQ*).

# Enabling Code Splitting and Prefetching

In Gatsby, code splitting leverages a Webpack feature known as *dynamic splitting* in two cases:

- To split imported files into separate bundles if Webpack encounters an `import` function call
- To include them in the original bundle if the module in question is loaded through `require`

However, Webpack leaves the rest of the question of what modules to split up to Gatsby and the site developer.

When you load pages in the browser, there is no need to load all the scripts and stylesheets required by the other pages in the site, except when you need to prefetch them to enable instantaneous navigation. The final work Gatsby does during the bundling process is to ensure that the right JavaScript is in the correct places for Webpack to perform the appropriate code splitting.

For more information about how Gatsby performs fetching and caching of resources in both Gatsby core and `gatsby-plugin-offline`, consult the documentation's guide to resource handling and service workers (*https://oreil.ly/tMSox*).

### Splitting into and naming chunks

During Gatsby's bootstrap phase that concludes with fully written pages, the *.cache/async-requires.js* file is output. This file exports a `components` object that contains a mapping of `ComponentChunkNames` to functions that are responsible for importing each component's file on disk. This may look something like the following:

```
exports.components = {
  "component--src-blog-js": () =>
    import(
      "/home/site/src/blog.js"
      /* webpackChunkName: "component---src-blog-js" */
    ),
  // more components
}
```

As we saw in the previous section, the entry point to Webpack (*production-app.js*) needs this *async-requires.js* file to enable dynamic import of page component files. Webpack will subsequently perform dynamic splitting to generate distinct chunks for each of those imported files. One of the file's exports also includes a `data` function that dynamically imports the *data.json* file, which is also code-split.

Once it has indicated where Webpack should split code, Gatsby can customize the nomenclature of those files on disk. It modifies the filenames by using the `chunkFile name` configuration in the Webpack configuration's `output` section, set by Gatsby in *webpack.config.js* by default as *[name]-[contenthash].js*. In this naming, *[contenthash]* represents a hash of the contents of the chunk that was originally code-split. *[name]*, meanwhile, originates from the `webpackChunkName` seen in the preceding example.

 For an introduction to Webpack `chunkGroups` and chunks and their use in Gatsby, consult the Gatsby documentation's primer on `chunkGroups` and chunks (*https://oreil.ly/d25Nq*).

### Mapping chunks to chunk assets

To generate the mappings required for client-side navigation and future instantaneous loads, Gatsby needs to create:

- `<link>` and `<script>` elements that correspond to the Gatsby runtime chunk
- The relevant page chunk for the given page (e.g., with a content hash, *component--src-blog-js-2e49587d85e03a033f58.js*)

At this point, however, Gatsby is aware of only the `componentChunkName`, not the generated filename that it needs to reference in the page's static HTML.

Webpack provides a mechanism to generate these mappings in the form of a compilation hook (`done`). Gatsby registers for this compilation hook to acquire a `stats` data structure containing all chunk groups. Each of these chunk groups represents the `com ponentChunkName` and includes a list of the chunks on which it depends. Using a custom Webpack plugin of its own known as `GatsbyWebpackStatsExtractor`, Gatsby writes the chunk data to a file in the *public* directory named *webpack.stats.json*. This chunk information looks like the following:

```
// public/webpack.stats.json
{
  "assetsByChunkName": {
    "app": [
      "webpack-runtime-e402cdceeae5fad2aa61.js",
      "app-2e49587d85e03a033f58.js"
    ],
```

```
    "component---src-blog-2-js": [
      "0.f8e7f9e53550f997bc53.css",
      "0-d55d2d6645e11739b63c.js",
      "1.93002d5bafe5ca491b1a.css",
      "1-4c94a37dc2061cb7beb9.js",
      "component---src-blog-2-js-cebc3ae7596cbb5b0951.js"
    ]
  }
}
```

The *webpack.stats.json* file maps chunk groups (i.e., componentChunkName items) to the chunk asset names on which they depend. In addition, Gatsby's custom Webpack configuration also generates a *chunk-map.json* file that maps each chunk group to the core chunk for the component, yielding a single component chunk for JavaScript and CSS assets within each individual chunk group, like the following:

```
// public/chunk-map.json
{
  "app":["/app-2e49587d85e03a033f58.js"],
  "component---src-blog-2-js": [
    "/component---src-blog-2-js-cebc3ae7596cbb5b0951.css",
    "/component---src-blog-2-js-860f9fbc5c3881586b5d.js"
  ]
}
```

### Referencing chunks in current page HTML

These two files, *webpack.stats.json* and *chunk-map.json*, are then loaded by *static-entry.js* to search for chunk assets matching individual componentChunkName values during the construction of <link> and <script> elements for the current page and the prefetching of chunks for later navigation. Let's inspect each of these in turn.

First, after generating the HTML for the currently active page, *static-entry.js* creates the necessary <link> elements in the head of the current page and <script> elements just before the terminal </body> tag, both of which refer to the JavaScript runtime and client-side JavaScript relevant to that page. The Gatsby runtime bundle, named app, acquires all chunk asset files for pages and components by searching across assetsByChunkName items using componentChunkName. Gatsby then merges these two chunk asset arrays together, and each chunk is referred to in a <link> element as follows:

```
<link
  as="script"
  rel="preload"
  key="app-2e49587d85e03a033f58.js"
  href="/app-2e49587d85e03a033f58.js"
/>
```

The `rel` attribute instructs the browser to begin downloading this resource at a high priority due to the fact that it is likely to be referenced later in the document. At the end of the HTML body, in the case of JavaScript assets, Gatsby inserts the `<script>` element referencing the preloaded asset:

```
<script
  key="app-2e49587d85e03a033f58.js"
  src="app-2e49587d85e03a033f58.js"
  async
/>
```

In the case of a CSS asset, the CSS is injected directly into the HTML head inline:

```
<style
  data-href="/1.93002d5bafe5ca491b1a.css"
  dangerouslySetInnerHTML="...contents of public/1.93002d5bafe5ca491b1a.css"
/>
```

### Referencing chunks to be prefetched

The previous section accounts for how chunks handled by Webpack are referenced in the page HTML for the current page. But what about subsequent navigation to other pages, which need to be able to load any required JavaScript or CSS assets instantaneously? When the current page has finished loading, Gatsby's work isn't done; it proceeds down the page to find any links that will benefit from prefetching.

 For an introduction to this concept, consult the Mozilla Developer Network's guide to prefetching (*https://oreil.ly/oheyG*).

When Gatsby's browser runtime encounters a `<link rel="prefetch" href="..." />` element, it begins to download the resource at a low priority, and solely when all resources required for the currently active page are done loading. At this point in the book, we come full circle to one of the first concepts introduced: the `<Link />` component. Once the `<Link />` component's `componentDidMount` callback is called, Gatsby automatically enqueues the destination path into the *production-app.js* file's loader for prefetching.

Gatsby is now aware of the target page for each link to be prefetched as well as the `componentChunkName` and `jsonName` associated with it, but it still needs to know which chunk group is required for the component. To resolve this, the *static-entry.js* file requires the *chunk-map.json* file, which it injects it directly into the CDATA section of the HTML page for the current page under `window.___chunkMapping` so any *production-app.js* code can reference it, as follows:

```
<![
  CDATA[ */
    window.___chunkMapping={
      "app":[
        "/app-2e49587d85e03a033f58.js"
      ],
      "component---src-blog-2-js": [
        "/component---src-blog-2-js-cebc3ae7596cbb5b0951.css",
        "/component---src-blog-2-js-860f9fbc5c3881586b5d.js"
      ]
    }
  */ ]
]>
```

Thanks to this information, the *production-app.js* loader can now derive the full component asset path and dynamically generate a `<link rel="prefetch" ... />` element in *prefetch.js*, thereupon injecting it into the DOM for the browser to handle appropriately. This is how Gatsby enables one of its most compelling features: instantaneous navigation between its pages.

> Prefetching can be disabled by implementing the `disableCorePre fetching` browser API in Gatsby and returning `true`.

# Conclusion

In this whirlwind tour of Gatsby's internals, we walked through some of the most compelling layers of Gatsby's multifaceted build lifecycle and bundling process. Though it would require a separate book in its own right to comprehensively cover how Gatsby works under the hood, in this chapter we examined the most important considerations, including key steps in Gatsby's bootstrap, key concepts in Gatsby's use of Webpack, and how Gatsby performs code splitting and prefetching.

This final chapter was intended to offer you, as a Gatsby developer, insight into the internals of how Gatsby works its magic as an SSG for the modern web. Gatsby is evolving all the time and rapidly changing as innovations continue to take shape. One of the most enriching ways you can be a part of that progress is to contribute back to the open source project. Hopefully, this walkthrough has given you a glimpse into some of the areas where the framework can benefit from your contributions and your own invaluable insights!

# The Gatsby CLI

The Gatsby CLI is the primary means of setting up, developing, and running a Gatsby application, including within a local development server and performing production builds.

## Gatsby Cheat Sheet

First, install the global executable:

```
$ npm install -g gatsby-cli
```

Execute **gatsby --help** for a full list of available commands and options.

## Common CLI Commands

Here's a quick rundown of the commands you'll use most often, covered in more detail in "Gatsby CLI Commands" on page 452:

gatsby new *my-gatsby-site-name*
: Create a new local Gatsby site using the default starter.

gatsby develop
: Start the Gatsby development server, optionally with the flags -H and --host.

Set the host. Defaults to localhost: -p, --port.

Set the port. Defaults to 8000: -o, --open.

Open the site in the default browser: -S, --https.

Use HTTPS.

```
gatsby build
```
Compile your application and prepare it for deployment, optionally with the flag `--prefix-paths`.

Build the site with link paths prefixed (after setting `pathPrefix` in *gatsby-config.js*): `--no-uglify`.

Build the site without uglifying JavaScript bundles (for debugging): `--open-tracing-config-file`.

Enable use of an OpenTracing-compatible configuration file.

```
gatsby serve
```
Serve the production build for testing, optionally with the flags -H and `--host`.

Set host. Defaults to `localhost`: -p, `--port`.

Set port. Defaults to `9000`: -o, `--open`.

Open the site in the default browser: `--prefix-paths`.

Serve the site with link paths prefixed (if built with `pathPrefix` as set in *gatsby-config.js*).

```
gatsby info
```
Get helpful environment information that is useful for reporting issues at *https://github.com/gatsbyjs/gatsby/issues*. This command takes one optional argument: -C, `--clipboard`.

Automatically copy environment information to the clipboard.

```
gatsby clean
```
Delete Gatsby's *.cache* and *public* directories.

## Quick Start Commands

Create a new Gatsby site using the blog starter as follows:

```
$ gatsby new my-gatsby-blog-name \
  https://github.com/gatsbyjs/gatsby-starter-blog
```

Change directories into your new site's directory and start it:

```
$ cd my-gatsby-blog-name
$ gatsby develop
```

Your site is now running at *https://localhost:8000*, and you can experiment with querying your data at *https://localhost:8000/___graphql*. See more information in the Gatsby tutorial (*https://gatsby.dev/tutorial*).

See all the *Gatsby starters in the documentation (https://gatsby.dev/starters)*.

## Helpful File Definitions

Each of these files should be found at the root of your Gatsby project:

*gatsby-config.js*
Configure options for a Gatsby site, with metadata for the project title, description, plugins, etc.

*gatsby-node.js*
Implement Gatsby's Node.js APIs to customize and extend default settings influencing the build process.

*gatsby-browser.js*
Customize and extend default settings influencing the browser, using Gatsby's Browser APIs.

*gatsby-ssr.js*
Use Gatsby's Server-Side Rendering (SSR) APIs to customize default settings influencing server-side rendering.

You can find more information at *https://gatsby.dev/projects*.

## Top Documentation Pages

Table A-1 provides a quick reference to the most commonly used Gatsby documentation pages.

*Table A-1. Commonly used Gatsby documentation pages*

| Documentation page | Shortlink |
|---|---|
| Gatsby documentation | *https://gatsby.dev/docs* |
| Gatsby on GitHub | *https://github.com/gatsbyjs/gatsby* |
| Gatsby tutorial | *https://gatsby.dev/tutorial* |
| Gatsby Quick Start (for intermediate and advanced developers) | *https://gatsby.dev/quick-start* |
| Gatsby Starter Library | *https://gatsby.dev/starters* |
| Gatsby Plugin Library | *https://gatsbyjs.com/plugins* |
| Gatsby How-to Guides | *https://gatsby.dev/recipes* |
| Importing assets | *https://gatsby.dev/image* |
| Gatsby Node APIs | *https://gatsby.dev/api* |
| GraphQL Concepts | *https://gatsby.dev/graphql* |
| Deploying and Hosting | *https://gatsby.dev/deploy* |
| Gatsby Link API | *https://gatsby.dev/link* |
| Querying Data in Components Using Static Query | *https://gatsby.dev/static-query* |
| How to Contribute | *https://gatsby.dev/contribute* |

# Gatsby CLI Commands

The following is a comprehensive list of the commands available in the Gatsby CLI.

## new

The gatsby new command without any arguments will run an interactive shell that will ask a series of questions and create a Gatsby site on your behalf:

```
$ gatsby new

What would you like to name the folder where your site will be created?
my-gatsby-site

Will you be using a CMS? (single choice)
  No (or I'll add it later)
  -
  WordPress
  Contentful
  Sanity
  DatoCMS
  Shopify

Would you like to install a styling system? (single choice)
  No (or I'll add it later)
  -
  CSS Modules/PostCSS
  styled-components
  Emotion
  Sass
  Theme UI

Would you like to install additional features with other plugins? (multiple choice)
  ○ Add the Google Analytics tracking script
  ○ Add responsive images
  ○ Add page meta tags with React Helmet
  ○ Add an automatic sitemap
  ○ Enable offline functionality
  ○ Generate a manifest file
  ○ Add Markdown support (without MDX)
  ○ Add Markdown and MDX support
```

Alternatively, you can create a Gatsby site based on a starter by providing one or two arguments, which will not prompt you to configure a custom setup:

```
$ gatsby new [site-name [starter-url]]
```

The gatsby new command accepts two arguments:

*site-name*

The Gatsby site name, which will also became the name of the created project directory

*starter-url*

A Gatsby starter URL or local filepath; defaults to `gatsby-starter-default`

The *site-name* argument can consist of only alphanumeric characters. Specifying `.`, `./`, or using a space in the name will trigger an error.

# develop

After installing a Gatsby site, you can navigate to the root directory of your project and launch a local development server by running:

```
$ gatsby develop
```

The `gatsby develop` command accepts the options listed in Table A-2.

*Table A-2. gatsby develop options*

| Option | Description |
| --- | --- |
| `-H, --host` | Set host. Defaults to `localhost`. |
| `-p, --port` | Set port. Defaults to `env.PORT` or 8000. |
| `-o, --open` | Open the site in the system's default browser. |
| `-S, --https` | Use HTTPS. |
| `--inspect` | Open a port for debugging. |

For more information about how to set up a local HTTPS development server, consult the Gatsby documentation's guide to using local HTTPS (*https://oreil.ly/spuoF*).

You can also use the `gatsby develop` command to preview changes on other devices by using the host option to permit access to the development environment on other devices sharing the same network. To do this, execute:

```
$ gatsby develop -H 0.0.0.0
```

The terminal will track changes as normal but will also print a URL that you can navigate to on another device (such as a phone or tablet) to see those changes, as long as that client is located on the same network:

You can now view gatsbyjs.com in the browser.

```
Local:          http://0.0.0.0:8000/
On Your Network:  http://192.168.0.212:8000/
```

In this scenario, you can still access the local development server as usual, meaning you can access it through *https://localhost:8000* or the URL provided next to "On Your Network."

# build

To compile your Gatsby application and ready it for deployment, execute the following in the root of your Gatsby project:

```
$ gatsby build
```

The gatsby build command accepts the options listed in Table A-3.

*Table A-3. gatsby build options*

| Option | Description |
| --- | --- |
| --prefix-paths | Build the site with all link paths prefixed (after setting pathPrefix in your Gatsby configuration). |
| --no-uglify | Build the site without uglifying JavaScript bundles (for debugging purposes). |
| --profile | Build the site with React profiling. |
| --open-tracing-config-file | Enable use of an OpenTracing-compatible tracer configuration file. |
| --graphql-tracing | Enable tracing of every graphql resolver (may impact performance). |
| --no-color, --no-colors | Disable color-coded terminal output. |

In addition to the --no-color/--no-colors option, the Gatsby CLI also respects the configured NO_COLOR environment variable, if present.

Beyond these build options, you can also provide optional build environment variables that govern how a build runs for more advanced configurations. For instance, providing CI=true as an environment variable will tailor the build output for dumb terminals.

For more information about build environment variables (*https://oreil.ly/JI4T5*) and dumb terminals (*https://oreil.ly/Xpjvo*), consult the respective guides in the Gatsby documentation.

## serve

To serve the production build of your Gatsby site for testing purposes, execute the following in the root of your Gatsby project:

```
$ gatsby serve
```

The `gatsby serve` command accepts the options listed in Table A-4.

*Table A-4. gatsby serve options*

| Option | Description |
| --- | --- |
| -H, --host | Set the host. Defaults to `localhost`. |
| -p, --port | Set the port. Defaults to `9000`. |
| -o, --open | Open the site in the system's default browser. |
| --prefix-paths | Serve the site with paths prefixed (if built with `pathPrefix` configured in Gatsby configuration). |

## info

To receive helpful environment information that is required when reporting an issue in the Gatsby issue queue, execute the following command in your Gatsby project root:

```
$ gatsby info
```

The `gatsby info` command accepts the option listed in Table A-5.

*Table A-5. gatsby info options*

| Option | Description |
| --- | --- |
| -C, --clipboard | Automatically copy environment information to the system clipboard. |

## clean

To delete the Gatsby cache (*.cache*) and *public* directories, execute the following in your Gatsby project root:

```
$ gatsby clean
```

The `gatsby clean` command is useful when your project appears to have unresolvable issues, such as content not refreshing. Some of the issues this command may resolve include problems with:

- Stale data (e.g., a file or resource is not appearing)
- GraphQL (e.g., a GraphQL resource that should be present is absent)
- Dependencies (e.g., an invalid package version or unresolved console errors)
- Plugins (e.g., local plugin updates do not take effect)

## plugin

To be shown documentation about using and creating Gatsby plugins, execute the following command:

```
$ gatsby plugin docs
```

## repl

To acquire a Node.js REPL (interactive shell) with the context of your Gatsby environment, execute this command:

```
$ gatsby repl
```

 For more information about using the Node.js REPL, consult the Gatsby documentation's page on the Gatsby REPL (*https://oreil.ly/F4ihD*).

Gatsby will prompt you thereafter to type in commands and explore the site data. Once it shows the following output:

```
gatsby >
```

you can execute any of the commands listed here:

- babelrc
- components
- dataPaths
- getNodes()
- nodes
- pages
- schema
- siteConfig
- staticQueries

# Gatsby Component APIs

This appendix provides a comprehensive account of the APIs for Gatsby's built-in <Link /> and image components.

## <Link />

The Gatsby <Link /> component is used in Gatsby applications to power linking between internal pages generated by Gatsby and to enable preloading of resources on other pages such that when the link is clicked, the change is instantaneous.

 The Gatsby <Link /> component should be used only for internal (not external) links. For more information about how to handle situations in which a link's internal or external target is uncertain, consult the Gatsby documentation's guide to relative links (*https:// oreil.ly/x1t4H*).

When the <Link /> component is visible within the browser viewport, Gatsby uses an IntersectionObserver to perform a low-priority fetch. When an onMouseOver event on the <Link /> component occurs, this triggers a high-priority fetch as it is likely the user is about to navigate to that resource.

At its core, the <Link /> component is a wrapper around the Link component provided by @reach/router with Gatsby-specific enhancements, and all props provided are also passed to @reach/router's Link component.

Gatsby uses the `withPrefix` helper function (*https://oreil.ly/4y1gj*) to construct pathnames that respect configured path prefixes in uses of the `<Link />` component or the `navigate` function (see "navigate" on page 462).

# `<Link />` Usage

You should use the `<Link />` component as a replacement for HTML `<a>` tags that represent links between pages in the same Gatsby site. However, you should still use HTML `<a>` tags for all links that reference pages that are external to Gatsby, as seen in the following example:

```
import React from "react"
import { Link } from "gatsby"

const Page = () => (
  <div>
    <p>
      Check out my <Link to="/blog">blog</Link>!
    </p>
    <p>
      {/* Note that external links still use `a` tags. */}
      Follow me on <a href="https://twitter.com/gatsbyjs">Twitter</a>!
    </p>
  </div>
)
```

For an Egghead.io video tutorial demonstrating this example, see "Why and How to Use Gatsby's Link Component" by Jason Lengstorf (*https://oreil.ly/5JKNr*).

# Active Styles for `<Link />`

To apply an active state to a Gatsby `<Link />` component that indicates it is representative of the page the user is currently viewing, you can use one of two props:

- `activeStyle`, which is a style object that will be applied only when the current link item is active
- `activeClassName`, which is a class name that will be added only when the current item is active

This is illustrated in the following example:

```
import React from "react"
import { Link } from "gatsby"
```

```
const SiteNavigation = () => (
  <nav>
    <Link
      to="/"
      {/* This assumes the `active` class is defined in your CSS */}
      activeClassName="active"
    >
      Home
    </Link>
    <Link
      to="/about/"
      activeStyle={{ color: "red" }}
    >
      About
    </Link>
  </nav>
)
```

 For an Egghead.io video tutorial demonstrating this, see "Add Custom Styles to the Active Link Using Gatsby's Link Component"by Jason Lengstorf (*https://oreil.ly/8ZCx5*).

Sometimes, you may need to indicate a `<Link />` as active even if its path only partially matches the current URL. By default, the `activeStyle` and `activeClassName` props will be set on a given `<Link />` component only if there is an exact match between the path and the current URL. However, you may need to represent multilevel or other menus where, say, a `<Link />` component pointing to *blog* also needs to be active for *blog/lorem-ipsum*.

In this case, use the `partiallyActive` prop to indicate that a partial match rather than an exact match should use the given `activeStyle` or `activeClassName` prop. This is illustrated in the following example:

```
import React from "react"
import { Link } from "gatsby"

const Header = <>
  <Link
    to="/articles/"
    activeStyle={{ color: "red" }}
    partiallyActive={true}
  >
    Articles
  </Link>
</>;
```

The `partiallyActive` prop is available on only the Gatsby `<Link />` component as of Gatsby 2.1.31.

## Working with Props in `<Link />`

There are three ways that Gatsby allows you to work with props in the context of the `<Link />` component:

- The `getProps` prop is useful for advanced styling.
- The `state` prop allows you to pass state as props to the linked page.
- The `replace` prop allows you to modify the Back button's behavior.

The `getProps` prop can be used on any `<Link />` component and will yield an object that contains the following props:

- `isCurrent`, which is set to `true` if the `location.pathname` is identical to the `<Link />` component's to prop value
- `isPartiallyCurrent`, which is set to `true` if the `location.pathname` begins with the `<Link />` component's to prop value
- `href`, which is the value of the to prop
- `location`, which represents the page's `location` object

For more information about the `getProps` prop, consult @reach/router's documentation on its Link API (*https://oreil.ly/TRyfr*).

The `state` prop is used when you wish to pass data from the source page to the destination page of a `<Link />` component. This is done by passing a `state` prop to the `<Link />` component, or during an invocation of the `navigate` helper function. The destination page will have a `location` prop containing a nested `state` object whose structure represents the passed data.

Consult the following example from the Gatsby documentation:

```
const PhotoFeedItem = ({ id }) => (
  <div>
    <Link
      to={`/photos/${id}`}
      state={{ fromFeed: true }}
    >
      View Photo
    </Link>
  </div>
)

const Photo = ({ location, photoId }) => {
  if (location.state.fromFeed) {
    return <FromFeedPhoto id={photoId} />
  } else {
    return <Photo id={photoId} />
  }
}
```

 For more information about the `state` prop, consult the Egghead.io tutorial video, "Include Information About State in Navigation with Gatsby's Link Component" by Jason Lengstorf (*https://oreil.ly/Rn9wv*).

The `replace` prop is used to modify the Back button's behavior. In one of the most common cases, you can use it to ensure that the current page, which may be a page you do not want the user to be able to navigate back to using the Back button (such as a confirmation page), is not saved in the browser history. You can use the `replace` prop to substitute the current page's URL in the browser history with the destination of the `<Link />`, as seen in the following example:

```
import React from "react"
import { Link } from "gatsby"

const AreYouSureLink = () => (
  <Link
    to="/confirmation/"
    replace
  >
    Yes, I'm sure
  </Link>
)
```

For more information about the `replace` prop, consult the Egghead.io tutorial video, "Replace Navigation History Items with Gatsby's Link Component" by Jason Lengstorf (*https://oreil.ly/nSIdY*).

## navigate

In many situations, you need to enforce navigation to pages programmatically, by navigating to a different page on the user's behalf. In these cases, instead of the `<Link />` component, you need the `navigate` helper function.

The `navigate` function was formerly named `navigateTo`. The former name was deprecated in Gatsby v2 and has been removed as of Gatsby v3.

To conduct programmatic navigation, Gatsby provides a `navigate` helper function as an export that accepts `to` and `options` arguments, as seen in Table B-1.

*Table B-1. Arguments accepted by the navigate function*

| Argument | Required | Description |
|---|---|---|
| to | Required | The page to navigate to (e.g., /blog/), written as a pathname, not a full URL |
| options.state | Optional | An object containing values that will be available in the location.state object in the target page's props |
| options.replace | Optional | A Boolean value that, if set to true, replaces the current URL in the browser history |

The `navigate` function operates the same way as a clicked `<Link />` component by default in Gatsby.

The following example demonstrates the use of the `navigate` function with a `state` prop:

```
import React from "react"
import { navigate } from "gatsby"

const Form = () => (
  <form
    onSubmit={event => {
      event.preventDefault()

      const formValues = getFormValues()

      navigate(
        "/form-submitted/",
        {
```

```
        state: { formValues },
      }
    )
  }}
>
  {/* Form input elements */}
</form>
)
```

And this example demonstrates the use of the `navigate` function with a `replace` prop:

```
import React from "react"
import { navigate } from "gatsby"

const Form = () => (
  <form
    onSubmit={event => {
      event.preventDefault()

      navigate(
        "/form-submitted/",
        { replace: true }
      )
    }}
  >
    {/* Form input elements */}
  </form>
)
```

For more information about the `navigate` function, consult the Egghead.io tutorial video, "Navigate to a New Page Programmatically in Gatsby" by Jason Lengstorf (*https://oreil.ly/RHkNT*).

# gatsby-plugin-image

The Gatsby Image plugin includes two components to display responsive images in your site, one for static images and the other for dynamic images:

`StaticImage`
> Use this if the image is the same every time the component is used (e.g., a site logo or index page hero image).

`GatsbyImage`
> Use this if the image is passed in to the component as a prop, or otherwise changes (e.g., a blog post hero image or author avatar).

We'll look at these in turn in the following sections, but first, Table B-2 lists the shared props that can be passed to both components. These props are all optional, with the exception of `alt`.

*Table B-2. Props accepted by the `StaticImage` and `GatsbyImage` components*

| Prop | Type | Default | Description |
|---|---|---|---|
| `alt` (required) | `string` | | Alternative text, passed to the `<img>` tag. Required for accessibility. |
| `as` | `ElementType` | `"div"` | The HTML element used for the outer wrapper. |
| `loading` | `"eager"` or `"lazy"` | `"lazy"` | Loading behavior for the image. You should set this to `"eager"` for above-the-fold images to ensure they start loading before React hydration. |
| `className` | `string` | | The CSS class applied to the outer wrapper. |
| `imgClassName` | `string` | | The CSS class applied to the `<img>` element. |
| `style` | `CSSProperties` | | Inline styles applied to the outer wrapper. |
| `imgStyle` | `CSSProperties` | | Inline styles applied to the `<img>` element. |
| `backgroundColor` | `string` | `transparent` | The background color applied to the wrapper. |
| `objectFit` | `object-fit prop erty` | `cover` | Resizing behavior for the image within its container. |
| `objectPosition` | `object-position property` | `50% 50%` | The position of the image within its container. |

A comprehensive list of all options available to the Image plugin can be found in the Gatsby documentation (*https://oreil.ly/8zLkM*).

# StaticImage

The `StaticImage` component can take all the image options described in "Image Options" on page 466 as props, as well as all the shared props listed in Table B-2. It also takes one additional required prop, listed in Table B-3.

*Table B-3. Additional props required by `StaticImage`*

| Prop | Type | Description |
|---|---|---|
| `src` (required) | `string` | The source image, processed at build time; can be a path relative to the source file, or an absolute URL |

The images are loaded and processed at build time, so there are restrictions on how you pass props to the component. The values need to be statically analyzed at build time, which means you can't pass them as props from outside the component, or use the results of function calls, for example. You can either use static values, or use variables within the component's local scope:

```
export function Dino() {
  // Local variables are fine
  const width = 300
  return <StaticImage src="trex.png" width={width} />
}
```

If you find yourself wishing you could use a prop for the image src, then it's likely that you should be using a dynamic image:

```
// A variable in the same file is fine
const width = 300
export function Dino() {
  // This works because the value can be statically analyzed
  const height = (width * 16) / 9
  return <StaticImage src="trex.png" width={width} height={height} />
}
```

> The StaticImage component does not support higher-order components, which includes the styled function from libraries such as Emotion and Styled Components. The parser relies on being able to identify StaticImage components in the source, and passing them to a function means this is not possible. For more information about this limitation, consult the Gatsby documentation's section on using StaticImage with CSS-in-JS libraries (*https://oreil.ly/I3kp6*).

## GatsbyImage

This component accepts all the shared props listed in Table B-2, as well as the one in Table B-4. These props are passed directly to the component, and are not to be confused with image options, which are passed to the GraphQL resolver when using dynamic images.

*Table B-4. Additional props required by GatsbyImage*

| Prop | Type | Description |
| --- | --- | --- |
| image (required) | GatsbyImageData | The image data object, returned from the gatsbyImageData resolver |

# Image Options

There are a few differences in how you specify options for `StaticImage` and `Gatsby Image`:

- When using `StaticImage`, options are passed as props to the component, whereas for the `GatsbyImage` component they are passed to the `gatsbyImageData` GraphQL resolver.
- In the `StaticImage` component, props such as `layout` and `placeholder` take a string, while the resolver takes a GraphQL enum, which is uppercase by convention and is not quoted like a string. Both syntaxes are shown in the following table.

 For dynamic images, these options are for the `gatsbyImageData` resolver on `sharp` nodes. If you are using `gatsbyImageData` from a different plugin, such as a CMS or image host, you should refer to that plugin's documentation for the options, as they will differ. Static images use `sharp` under the hood, so these options apply when using the `StaticImage` component too.

Table B-5 lists the options available to both static and dynamic images. We'll look at these in more detail in the following sections.

*Table B-5. Image options*

| Option | Default string/enum value | Description |
| --- | --- | --- |
| `layout` | `"constrained"` or `CONSTRAINED` | Determines the size of the image and its resizing behavior |
| `aspectRatio` | Source image aspect ratio | Forces a specific ratio between the image's width and height |
| `width/`<br>`height` | Source image size | Changes the size of the image |
| `placeholder` | `"dominantColor"` or `DOMI`<br>`NANT_COLOR` | Sets the style of temporary image shown while the full image loads |
| `formats` | `["auto","webp"]` or `[AUTO,WEBP]` | File formats of the images generated |
| `transform`<br>`Options` | `{fit: "cover", cropFocus:`<br>`"attention"}` or `{fit: COVER,`<br>`cropFocus: ATTENTION}` | Options to pass to sharp to control cropping and other image manipulations |

## layout

The image components support three types of layout, which determine the image sizes that are generated, as well as the resizing behavior of the image itself in the browser (see Table B-6).

*Table B-6. layout options for StaticImage and DynamicImage*

| Layout | Component prop value | Resolver prop value | Description |
|---|---|---|---|
| Constrained | "constrained" | CONSTRAINED | This is the default layout. It displays the image at the size of the source image, or you can set a maximum size by passing in width or height. If the screen or container size is less than the width of the image, the component scales it down to fit, maintaining its aspect ratio. The component generates smaller versions of the image so that a mobile browser doesn't need to load the full-size image. |
| Fixed | "fixed" | FIXED | Use this for fixed-size images. The image will always display at the same size, and will not shrink to fit its container. The size is either the size of the source image, or the size set by the width and height props. Use this only if you are certain that the container will never need to be narrower than the image. |
| Full width | "fullWidth" | FULL_WIDTH | Use this for images that are always displayed at the full width of the screen, such as banners or hero images. Like with the constrained layout, the image will be resized to fit the container. It is not restricted to a maximum size, so it will grow to fill the container, however large it is, maintaining its aspect ratio. The component generates several smaller image sizes for different screen breakpoints, so that the browser only needs to load one large enough to fit the screen. You can pass a breakpoints prop if you want to specify the sizes to use, though in most cases you can allow it to use the default. |

To set the layout of a static image, pass in the type to the layout prop:

```
<StaticImage
  src="./dino.png"
  alt="A dinosaur"
  layout="fixed"
/>
```

For a dynamic image, pass it to the resolver:

```
dino {
  childImageSharp {
    gatsbyImageData(layout: FIXED)
  }
}
```

## width and height

The width and height props are available in the fixed and constrained layouts:

- For a fixed layout, these define the size of the image displayed onscreen.
- For a constrained image, these define the maximum size, as the image will scale down to fit smaller containers if needed.

Size props are optional in GatsbyImage and StaticImage. Because the images are processed at build time, the plugin knows the size of the source image and can add the correct width and height to the <img> tag, so it displays correctly with no layout jumping. However, if you want to change the display size you can use the size options to do this.

If you set just one of these, the source image is resized to that width or height while maintaining its original aspect ratio. If you include both, then it is also cropped if needed to ensure it is that exact size.

## aspectRatio

The aspectRatio prop forces an image to the specified aspect ratio, cropping it if needed. The value is a number, but can be clearer to express as a fraction: e.g., aspectRatio={16/9}. This prop is available in the fixed, constrained, and fullWidth layouts:

- For fixed and constrained images, you can also optionally pass either width or height, and it will use that to calculate the other dimension. For example, if you pass width={800} aspectRatio={4/3}, then height will be set to the width divided by the aspect ratio: so, 600. Passing 1 as the aspectRatio will crop the image to a square. If you don't pass a width or height, then it will use the source image's width.
- For fullWidth images you don't specify width or height, as this layout resizes the image to fit the screen width. Passing aspectRatio will crop the image if needed, and the height will scale according to the width of the screen. For example, if you set aspectRatio to 16/9, then when the image is displayed full width on a screen that is 1,280 pixels (px) wide, the image will be 720 px high.

 There are several advanced options that you can pass to control the cropping and resizing behavior. For more details, see "transformOptions" on page 469.

## placeholder

Gatsby image components are lazy-loaded by default, which means that if they are offscreen they are not loaded by the browser until they come into view. To ensure that the layout does not jump around, a placeholder is displayed before the image loads. You can choose one of three types of placeholder, listed in Table B-7, or not use a placeholder at all.

*Table B-7. placeholder values*

| Placeholder | Component prop value | Resolver prop value | Description |
|---|---|---|---|
| Dominant color | `"dominant Color"` | `DOMINANT _COLOR` | The default placeholder. This calculates the dominant color of the source image and uses it as a solid background color. |
| Blurred | `"blurred"` | `BLURRED` | This generates a very low-resolution version of the source image and displays it as a blurred background. |
| Traced SVG | `"tracedSVG"` | `TRACED_SVG` | This generates a simplified, flat SVG version of the source image, which it displays as a placeholder. This works well for images with simple shapes or that include transparency. |

## formats

The Gatsby Image plugin supports four output formats: JPEG, PNG, WebP, and AVIF. The default component prop value is `["auto", "webp"]`, and the default resolver prop value is `[AUTO, WEBP]`; this means that by default the plugin generates images in the same format as the source image, as well as WebP. For example, if your source image is a PNG, it will generate PNG and WebP images.

In most cases, you should not change this. However, in some cases you may need to manually set the formats. One reason for doing so is if you want to enable support for AVIF images. AVIF is a new image format that results in significantly smaller file sizes than alternative formats. It currently has limited browser support, but this is likely to increase. It is safe to include as long as you also generate fallbacks for other browsers, which the Image plugin does automatically by default.

## transformOptions

The options listed in Table B-8 can be passed in as an object to `transformOptions`, either as a prop to `StaticImage`, or to the resolver for dynamic images. They are advanced settings that most people will not need to change. Any provided object is merged with the defaults listed here.

 For more information about `trim`, `cropFocus`, and `fit`, consult the Sharp documentation (*https://oreil.ly/F8ytR*).

*Table B-8. transformOptions options*

| Option | Default | Description |
|---|---|---|
| grayscale | false | Converts the image to grayscale. |
| duotone | false | Adds a duotone effect. Pass false for no duotone, or an options object containing {highlight: *string*, shadow: *string*, opacity: *number*}. |
| rotate | 0 | Rotates the image. The value is provided in degrees. |
| trim | false | Trims "boring" pixels. |
| cropFocus | "attention" or ATTENTION | Controls crop behavior. |
| fit | "cover" or COVER | Controls behavior when resizing an image and providing both width and height. |

# Helper Functions

There are a number of utility functions to help you work with gatsbyImageData objects. Gatsby strongly recommends that you do not try to access the internals of these objects directly, as the format could change; instead, use the functions described in the following sections.

### getImage

Use the getImage function to safely get a gatsbyImageData object. It accepts several different sorts of objects and is null-safe, returning undefined if the object passed or any intermediate children are undefined.

If passed a File object, this function will return file?.childImageSharp?.gatsby ImageData. If passed a node such as a ContentfulAsset that includes a gatsbyImage Data field, it will return the gatsbyImageData object. If passed a gatsbyImageData object itself, it will return the same object. For example:

```
import { getImage } from "gatsby-plugin-image"

const image = getImage(data.avatar)
// This is the same as:
const image = data?.avatar?.childImageSharp?.gatsbyImageData
```

### getSrc

Use the getSrc function to get the default image src as a string. This will be the fall-back, so usually jpg or png. This function accepts the same types as getImage. For example:

```
import { getSrc } from "gatsby-plugin-image"

// ...
const src = getSrc(data.hero)
return <meta property="og:image" content={src} />
```

## getSrcSet

Use the `getSrcSet` function to get the default image `srcset`. This will be the fallback, so usually `jpg` or `png`.

## withArtDirection

By default, the Image plugin displays different image resolutions at different screen sizes, but it also supports *art direction*, which is where a visually different image is displayed at different sizes. Example usages include displaying a simplified logo or a tighter crop on a profile picture when viewing on a small screen. To enable this, you can use the `withArtDirection` function. You need both images available from GraphQL in the case of a replacement image, and you should be able to write a media query for each size.

The first argument this function takes is the default image. This is displayed when no media queries match, but it is also used to set the layout, size, placeholder, and most other options. You then pass an array of art-directed images, which are objects with `media` and `image` values:

```
import { GatsbyImage, getImage, withArtDirection } from "gatsby-plugin-image"

export function MyImage({ data }) {
  const images = withArtDirection(getImage(data.largeImage), [
    {
      media: "(max-width: 1024px)",
      image: getImage(data.smallImage),
    },
  ])

  return <GatsbyImage image={images} />
}
```

When the screen is less than 1,024 px wide, it will display `smallImage`. Otherwise, it will display `largeImage`.

> For more information about this helper function and how to use it with CSS media queries, consult the Gatsby documentation's section on `withArtDirection` (*https://oreil.ly/OLLz4*).

# Gatsby Configuration APIs

Gatsby provides several configuration APIs that are used to allow for arbitrary configuration of your Gatsby site as well as to adjust how the site works in the browser and how it is handled during server-side rendering and the build process. In this appendix, we'll take a tour of Gatsby's Config and Node APIs.

> Gatsby also provides other APIs, namely its Browser APIs (*https://oreil.ly/dOZnG*) (to modify Gatsby's behavior in the browser) and Server-Side Rendering APIs (*https://oreil.ly/fU4iU*) (to modify Gatsby's server-side rendering behavior), as well as actions (*https://oreil.ly/Jahy7*) and Node API helpers (*https://oreil.ly/2hGKC*) that are outside the scope of these appendixes.

## Config APIs

The *gatsby-config.js* file defines your site's metadata, plugins, and other broad configuration and must be located in the root directory of your Gatsby site. All sites created with the `gatsby new` command come with a Gatsby configuration file already populated on your behalf.

The file should export a JavaScript object containing a variety of configuration options, as seen in the following example:

```
// gatsby-config.js
module.exports = {
  siteMetadata: {
    title: `Gatsby`,
  },
  plugins: [
    `gatsby-transform-plugin`,
    {
```

```
        resolve: `gatsby-plugin-name`,
        options: {
          optionA: true,
          optionB: `Another option`,
        },
      },
    ],
  }
```

The Gatsby configuration file allows the following configuration options to be set, which are defined in this section:

- siteMetadata (object)
- plugins (array)
- flags (object)
- pathPrefix (string)
- polyfill (Boolean)
- mapping (object)
- proxy (object)
- developMiddleware (function)

## siteMetadata

To reuse common pieces of data across the entire Gatsby site (such as the site title), you can house that data in the siteMetadata object:

```
// gatsby-config.js
module.exports = {
  siteMetadata: {
    title: `Gatsby`,
    siteUrl: `https://www.gatsbyjs.com`,
    description: `Blazing fast modern site generator for React`,
  },
}
```

## plugins

In Gatsby, plugins are Node.js packages that implement Gatsby APIs. The Gatsby configuration file accepts an array of plugins. While some plugins need to be listed only by name, many require configuration options, which are catalogued in each plugin's respective documentation.

Installing a plugin using a package manager such as NPM or Yarn *does not* enable that plugin in your Gatsby site. The final step to ensure a Gatsby plugin functions in your site is to include the plugin in the `plugins` array within the Gatsby configuration file, as seen in the following example, which shows a plugin without options:

```
// gatsby-config.js
module.exports = {
  plugins: [`gatsby-plugin-name`],
}
```

When adding multiple plugins, these need to be comma-separated in the `plugins` array.

Many plugins require or allow configuration options, which may be mandatory or optional. When specifying configuration options, instead of a simple string as seen in the preceding example, the plugin must be configured as an object with its name all its options, as shown here:

```
// gatsby-config.js
module.exports = {
  plugins: [
    {
      resolve: `gatsby-plugin-name`,
      options: {
        optionA: true,
        optionB: `Another option`,
      },
    },
  ],
}
```

# flags

The `flags` object allows Gatsby sites to enable experimental or coming changes that are not yet ready for release or remain in testing. For example:

```
// gatsby-config.js
module.exports = {
  flags: {
    QUERY_ON_DEMAND: true,
  },
}
```

> For a full list of currently available Gatsby flags, consult the Gatsby source code on GitHub (*https://oreil.ly/BAx7m*).

## pathPrefix

Gatsby sites are commonly hosted in locations other than the root of their domains. To prefix a Gatsby site located at *example.com/blog* such that */blog* is the path prefix respected across the Gatsby site, configure a path prefix as follows:

```
// gatsby-config.js
module.exports = {
  pathPrefix: `/blog`,
}
```

For more information about configuring path prefixes, consult the Gatsby documentation (*https://oreil.ly/qyxSH*).

## polyfill

Because Gatsby depends on the ES6 `Promise` API, which some browsers do not support, Gatsby includes a `Promise` polyfill by default. You can also configure your own `Promise` polyfill by setting the `polyfill` key to `false`:

```
// gatsby-config.js
module.exports = {
  polyfill: false,
}
```

For more information about Gatsby browser support and polyfills, consult the documentation's guide to browser support in Gatsby (*https://oreil.ly/W9auM*).

## mapping

Gatsby provides a feature for advanced use cases that permits the creation of mappings between distinct node types for reference in the GraphQL API. Mappings can be used to link between a node type containing a field and a node type containing another field that represents the same type of data, as seen in the following example:

```
// gatsby-config.js
module.exports = {
  mapping: {
    "MarkdownRemark.frontmatter.author": `AuthorYaml`,
  },
}
```

Creating this mapping enables GraphQL queries that look like the following, where the fields contained in the second node type can be accessed from a different node type that creates a reference to those fields, such as an author whose fields are located in an AuthorYaml type but need to be accessed from a MarkdownRemark field that originally contains only the author name:

```
query($slug: String!) {
  markdownRemark(fields: { slug: { eq: $slug } }) {
    html
    fields {
      slug
    }
    frontmatter {
      title
      author {
        # This now links to the author object
        id
        bio
        twitter
      }
    }
  }
}
```

Mappings can also be used to map an array of identifiers to any other arbitrary collection of data, and to supply references between Markdown files.

 Gatsby v2.2 introduced a new approach to creating foreign key relationships between node types using the @link GraphQL extension (*https://oreil.ly/RDzUY*). For more information and more detailed examples about mappings, consult the Gatsby documentation (*https://oreil.ly/LgR5i*).

## proxy

The proxy configuration option, which accepts an object, is used to instruct the gatsby develop server to proxy any unknown requests to a specified server, as shown here:

```
// gatsby-config.js
module.exports = {
  proxy: {
    prefix: "/api",
    url: "http://examplesite.com/api/",
  },
}
```

For more information, consult the Gatsby documentation's guide to proxying API requests in development (*https://oreil.ly/DauDk*).

## developMiddleware

The `developMiddleware` configuration option accepts a function that describes further granularity or flexibility in the development server provided by Gatsby, where you can add Express middleware as needed:

```
const { createProxyMiddleware } = require("http-proxy-middleware") // v1.x.x
// Use implicit require for v0.x.x of 'http-proxy-middleware'
// const proxy = require('http-proxy-middleware')
// Be sure to replace 'createProxyMiddleware' with 'proxy' where applicable
module.exports = {
  developMiddleware: app => {
    app.use(
      "/.netlify/functions/",
      createProxyMiddleware({
        target: "http://localhost:9000",
        pathRewrite: {
          "/.netlify/functions/": "",
        },
      })
    )
  },
}
```

For more information about advanced proxying in development and self-signed certificates, consult the Gatsby documentation (*https://oreil.ly/3yJ6O*).

# Node APIs

Gatsby's Node APIs are implemented in the *gatsby-node.js* file, which is executed once when Gatsby builds your site. These APIs include capabilities to generate pages programmatically, add data into the GraphQL API, and respond to particular events in the build lifecycle. The *gatsby-node.js* file must be located in the root of your Gatsby project, and any APIs you wish to use need to be exported in the file.

Each Gatsby Node API is passed a series of helper functions. These allow you to access methods like reporting or actions that are often more fine-grained than Gatsby's Node APIs.

Some plugins require operations to be performed asynchronously rather than synchronously. These include operations like disk I/O, database access, and remote API queries that require asynchronicity. To write a plugin with asynchronous behavior implementing the Node APIs, you must either return a promise (explicitly through the `Promise` API or implicitly using the `async` and `await` keywords) or use the callback passed to the third argument. This is because Gatsby needs to be aware of when plugins are finished doing their work, as some APIs require previous API implementations to have concluded first. Here's an example of this syntax:

```
// Async/await
exports.createPages = async () => {
  // do async work
  const result = await fetchExternalData()
}

// Promise API
exports.createPages = () => {
  return new Promise((resolve, reject) => {
    // do async work
  })
}

// Callback API
exports.createPages = (_, pluginOptions, cb) => {
  // do async work
  cb()
}
```

> For more information about handling synchronous and asynchronous operations in Gatsby's Node APIs, consult the documentation's guide to debugging asynchronous lifecycles (*https://oreil.ly/3tsAd*).

# createPages

Implementing this API creates pages dynamically. This extension point is invoked only after the initial sourcing and transformation of nodes and the creation of the GraphQL schema are both complete, so that you can query data to create pages. The `createPages` API also allows you to fetch data from remote or local sources to create pages.

> See also the Gatsby documentation's guide to the `createPage` action (*https://oreil.ly/JKTCh*).

## Parameters

- Destructured object (see the Node API helpers section of the documentation (*https://oreil.ly/enp6l*))

  — `action` (actions)

    — `createPage` (function)

  — `graphql` (function): Queries the GraphQL API.

  — `reporter` (GatsbyReporter): Log issues using `GatsbyReporter`.

## Return value

`Promise<void>`

No return value specified, but the caller will `await` any promise that is returned.

## Example

```
const path = require(`path`)

exports.createPages = ({ graphql, actions }) => {
  const { createPage } = actions
  const blogPostTemplate = path.resolve(`src/templates/blog-post.js`)
  // Query for markdown nodes to use in creating pages.
  // You can query for whatever data you want to create pages for e.g.
  // products, portfolio items, landing pages, etc.
  // Variables can be added as the second function parameter
  return graphql(`
    query loadPagesQuery ($limit: Int!) {
      allMarkdownRemark(limit: $limit) {
        edges {
          node {
            frontmatter {
              slug
            }
          }
        }
      }
    }
  `, { limit: 1000 }).then(result => {
    if (result.errors) {
      throw result.errors
    }

    // Create blog post pages.
    result.data.allMarkdownRemark.edges.forEach(edge => {
      createPage({
        // Path for this page — required
        path: `${edge.node.frontmatter.slug}`,
        component: blogPostTemplate,
        context: {
```

```
              // Add optional context data to be inserted
              // as props into the page component.
              //
              // The context data can also be used as
              // arguments to the page GraphQL query.
              //
              // The page "path" is always available as a GraphQL
              // argument.
            },
          })
        })
      })
  }
```

# createPagesStatefully

Like the previous API, implementing this API creates pages programmatically, but it is oriented toward plugins that need to manage the creation and deletion of pages themselves in response to changes in data that are not managed by Gatsby. Plugins implementing `createPages` will be regularly invoked to recompute page information as Gatsby's data changes, but those implementing `createPagesStatefully` will not.

> See the `gatsby-plugin-page-creator` plugin (*https://oreil.ly/ ElMR6*) for an example of usage of this extension point.

# createResolvers

Implementing this API adds custom field resolvers to the GraphQL schema and allows logic to add new fields to types by providing field configurations or adding resolver functions to new fields. Here are some things to keep in mind when using this API:

- Overriding field types is disallowed in favor of the `createTypes` action. In the case of types added from third-party schemas, where this is impossible, overriding field types is allowed.

- New fields will be unavailable on `filter` and `sort` input types. Extend types defined with `createTypes` if you need this.

- In field configurations, types can be referenced as strings.

- When extending a field with an existing field resolver, the original resolver function is available from `info.originalResolver`.

- The `createResolvers` API is invoked as the final step in schema generation. Therefore, an intermediate schema is made available on the `intermediateSchema` property. In resolver functions themselves, it is recommended to access the final built schema from `info.schema`.

- Gatsby's data layer, including all internal query capabilities, is exposed via `context.nodeModel`. The node store can be queried directly with `getAllNodes`, `getNodebyId`, and `getNodesByIds`, while more advanced queries can be composed with `runQuery`. Note that `runQuery` will invoke field resolvers before querying, so foreign key fields, for instance, will be expanded to full nodes. The other methods on `nodeModel` do not do this.

- It is possible to add fields to the root `Query` type.

- When using the first resolver argument (`source` in the following example, often also known as `parent` or `root`), be aware of the fact that field resolvers can be invoked more than once in a query, for instance when the field is present both in the input filter and in the selection set. This means that foreign key fields on `source` can be either resolved or not resolved.

> For more complete examples, consult the Using Type Definitions example codebase (*https://oreil.ly/COecH*).

### Parameters

- Destructured object
  - `intermediateSchema` (GraphQLSchema): The current GraphQL schema.
  - `createResolvers` (function): Adds custom resolvers to GraphQL field configurations.
- `$1` (object)
  - `resolvers` (object): An object map of GraphQL type names to custom resolver functions.
  - `options` (object): Optional `createResolvers` actions.
    - `ignoreNonexistentTypes` (object): Silences the warning when trying to add resolvers for types that don't exist. Useful for optional extensions.

## Example

```
exports.createResolvers = ({ createResolvers }) => {
  const resolvers = {
    Author: {
      fullName: {
        resolve: (source, args, context, info) => {
          return source.firstName + source.lastName
        }
      },
    },
    Query: {
      allRecentPosts: {
        type: [`BlogPost`],
        resolve: (source, args, context, info) => {
          const posts = context.nodeModel.getAllNodes({ type: `BlogPost` })
          const recentPosts = posts.filter(
            post => post.publishedAt > Date.UTC(2018, 0, 1)
          )
          return recentPosts
        }
      }
    }
  }
  createResolvers(resolvers)
}
```

# createSchemaCustomization

Implementing this API customizes Gatsby's GraphQL schema by creating type definitions or field extensions, or adding third-party schemas. The createTypes, create
FieldExtension, and addThirdPartySchema actions are available only in this API.
The createSchemaCustomization API executes immediately before schema generation. To modify the generated schema, for instance to customize added third-party
types, use the createResolvers API.

## Parameters

- Destructured object
  — actions (object)
    — createTypes (object)
    — createFieldExtension (object)
    — addThirdPartySchema (object)

## Example

```
exports.createSchemaCustomization = ({ actions }) => {
  const { createTypes, createFieldExtension } = actions

  createFieldExtension({
    name: 'shout',
    extend: () => ({
      resolve(source, args, context, info) {
        return String(source[info.fieldName]).toUpperCase()
      }
    })
  })

  const typeDefs = `
    type MarkdownRemark implements Node @dontInfer {
      frontmatter: Frontmatter
    }
    type Frontmatter {
      title: String!
      tagline: String @shout
      date: Date @dateformat
      image: File @fileByRelativePath
    }
  `

  createTypes(typeDefs)
}
```

# onCreateBabelConfig

Implementing this API allows plugins to extend or mutate the site's Babel configuration by invoking setBabelPlugin or setBabelPreset.

## Parameters

- Destructured object
  - — stage (string): The current build stage. One of desktop, develop-html, build-javascript, or build-html.
  - — actions (object)
- options (object): The Babel configuration.

## Example

```
exports.onCreateBabelConfig = ({ actions }) => {
  actions.setBabelPlugin({
    name: `babel-plugin-that-i-like`,
    options: {}
  })
}
```

# onCreateDevServer

This API executes when the Gatsby development server is started. It can be used to add proxies or Express middleware to the server.

## Parameters

- Destructured object
  — app (Express): The Express app used to run the server.

## Example

```
exports.onCreateDevServer = ({ app }) => {
  app.get('/hello', function (req, res) {
    res.send('hello world')
  })
}
```

# onCreateNode

This API is called when a new node is created. Plugins wishing to extend or transform nodes created by other plugins should implement the onCreateNode API. See also the createNode and createNodeField actions.

## Example

```
exports.onCreateNode = ({ node, actions }) => {
  const { createNode, createNodeField } = actions
  // Transform the new node here and create a new node or
  // create a new node field.
}
```

# onCreatePage

This API is called when a new page is created. It's useful for programmatically manipulating pages created by other plugins, for example if you need paths without trailing slashes. There is a mechanism available in Gatsby to prevent calling onCreatePage for pages created by the same *gatsby-node.js* to avoid infinite loops and callbacks.

# onCreateWebpackConfig

This API allows plugins to extend and mutate the site's Webpack configuration. See also the setWebpackConfig action (*https://oreil.ly/zswYL*).

### Parameters

- Destructured object
  - `stage` (string): The current build stage. One of `develop`, `develop-html`, `build-javascript`, or `build-html`.
  - `getConfig` (function): Returns the current Webpack configuration.
  - `rules` (object): A set of preconfigured Webpack configuration rules.
  - `loaders` (object): A set of preconfigured Webpack configuration loaders.
  - `plugins` (object): A set of preconfigured Webpack configuration plugins.
  - `actions` (object)

### Example

```
exports.onCreateWebpackConfig = ({
  stage, getConfig, rules, loaders, actions
}) => {
  actions.setWebpackConfig({
    module: {
      rules: [
        {
          test: 'my-css',
          use: [loaders.style(), loaders.css()]
        },
      ],
    },
  });
}
```

# onPostBootstrap

This API is called at the end of the bootstrap process after all other extension APIs have been called.

# onPostBuild

This is the last extension point called after all other parts of the build process are complete.

# onPreBootstrap

This API is called when Gatsby has initialized itself and is ready to bootstrap your site.

# onPreBuild

This is the first extension point called during the build process. It's called after the bootstrap has completed but before the build steps start.

# onPreExtractQueries

This API is run before GraphQL queries and fragments are extracted from JavaScript files and is useful for plugins to add more JavaScript files with queries and fragments, for example from `node_modules`.

 See the `gatsby-transformer-sharp` (*https://oreil.ly/OosOl*) and `gatsby-source-contentful` (*https://oreil.ly/mO5Fn*) plugins for examples of implementations of this API.

# onPreInit

This is the first API called during Gatsby execution. It runs as soon as plugins are loaded, before cache initialization and bootstrap preparation.

# pluginOptionsSchema

This API is run during the bootstrap phase. Plugins can use this to define a schema for their options, using Joi to validate the options users pass to the plugin.

### Parameters

- Destructured object
  - — `Joi` (object): The instance of Joi to define the schema.

### Example

```
exports.pluginOptionsSchema = ({ Joi }) => {
  return Joi.object({
    // Validate that the anonymize option is defined by the user and is a
    // Boolean
    anonymize: Joi.boolean().required(),
  })
}
```

# preprocessSource

Implementing this API asks compile-to-JavaScript plugins to process source code to JavaScript so the query runner can extract out GraphQL queries for running.

## resolvableExtensions

Implementing this API allows plugins implementing support for other compile-to-JavaScript plugins to add to the list of "resolvable" file extensions. Gatsby supports *.js* and *.jsx* by default.

## setFieldsOnGraphQLNodeType

This API is called during the creation of the GraphQL schema and allows plugins to add new fields to the types created from data nodes. It will be called separately for each type. `setFieldsOnGraphQLNodeType` should return an object in the shape of `GraphQLFieldConfigMap`, which will be appended to fields inferred by Gatsby from data nodes.

Many transformer plugins implement this API to add fields that accept arguments. For example:

- `gatsby-transformer-remark` adds an `excerpt` field where the user when writing a query can specify how many characters to prune the Markdown source to.

- `gatsby-transformer-sharp` exposes many image transformation options as GraphQL fields.

 For more information about `GraphQLFieldConfigMap`, consult the GraphQL documentation (*https://oreil.ly/ESlng*). Import GraphQL types from *gatsby/graphql*, and refrain from adding the `graphql` package to your project or plugin dependencies to avoid "Schema must contain unique named types but contains multiple types named" errors. *gatsby/graphql* exports all built-in GraphQL types as well as the `GraphQLJSON` type.

### Parameters

- Destructured object

    — `type` (object): An object containing `name` and `nodes`.

### Example

```
import { GraphQLString } from "gatsby/graphql"

exports.setFieldsOnGraphQLNodeType = ({ type }) => {
  if (type.name === `File`) {
    return {
      newField: {
        type: GraphQLString,
        args: {
```

```
        myArgument: {
          type: GraphQLString,
        }
      },
      resolve: (source, fieldArgs) => {
        return `Id of this node is ${source.id}.
              Field was called with argument: ${fieldArgs.myArgument}`
      }
    }
  }
}

// by default return empty object
return {}
}
```

# sourceNodes

This API is an extension point called during the Gatsby bootstrap sequence that instructs plugins to source nodes. It's called exactly once per plugin (and once for your site's *gatsby-config.js* file). If you define this hook in *gatsby-node.js*, it will be called exactly once after all of your source plugins have finished creating nodes.

 See also the createNode action (*https://oreil.ly/CN0g3*).

### Example

```
exports.sourceNodes = ({ actions, createNodeId, createContentDigest }) => {
  const { createNode } = actions

  // Data can come from anywhere, but for now create it manually
  const myData = {
    key: 123,
    foo: `The foo field of my node`,
    bar: `Baz`
  }

  const nodeContent = JSON.stringify(myData)

  const nodeMeta = {
    id: createNodeId(`my-data-${myData.key}`),
    parent: null,
    children: [],
    internal: {
      type: `MyNodeType`,
      mediaType: `text/html`,
      content: nodeContent,
```

```
      contentDigest: createContentDigest(myData)
    }
  }

  const node = Object.assign({}, myData, nodeMeta)
  createNode(node)
}
```

# unstable_onPluginInit

This API is executed in each process (once per process) and is used to store actions and other information for later use.

## Example

```
let createJobV2
exports.unstable_onPluginInit = ({ actions }) => {
  // Store job creation action to use it later
  createJobV2 = actions.createJobV2
}
```

# unstable_shouldOnCreateNode

This API is called before scheduling an onCreateNode callback for a plugin. If it returns falsely, then Gatsby will not schedule the onCreateNode callback for this node for this plugin.

 This API does not receive the regular api that other callbacks get as the first argument.

## Example

```
exports.unstable_shouldOnCreateNode = (
  {node},
  pluginOptions
) => node.internal.type === 'Image'
```

# Index

## About the Author

**Preston So** is a product architect and strategist, digital experience futurist, innovation lead, developer advocate, three-time SXSW speaker, and author of *Decoupled Drupal in Practice* (Apress, 2018). At Gatsby, Preston led the product and design teams for the general availability release of Gatsby Cloud, one of the most anticipated Jamstack product launches of 2019.

## Colophon

The animal on the cover of *Gatsby: The Definitive Guide* is a lesser galago, or bush-baby (*Galago senegalensis*), one of the world's smallest primates. Native to sub-Saharan Africa, bushbabies measure just 5 to 7 inches and weigh 3 to 10 ounces. They typically live three to four years in the wild. When in danger, they will cry out, sounding similar to human babies.

The animal's soft, thick fur varies in color, including brown, black, gray, and white, with hints of red, orange, yellow, and even green. Their ears move independently and have no fur. Bushbabies have huge round eyes, oversized ears, and tails longer than the rest of their bodies. These traits help them navigate trees and vegetation at night when they hunt down insects, pick fruit and leaves, and build or occupy nests to retreat to come daylight. Bushbabies sometimes adopt abandoned nests of birds and unoccupied beehives. These primates hop, leap, and climb, and are able to clear 30 feet in seconds.

The population of bushbabies is decreasing due to human activities. While their habitat encompasses a broad array of environments across Africa, bushbaby populations are suffering from human encroachment on their habitat. Many of the animals on O'Reilly's covers are endangered; all of them are important to the world.

The cover illustration is by Karen Montgomery, based on a black and white engraving from *Natural History of Mammals*. The cover fonts are Gilroy Semibold and Guardian Sans. The text font is Adobe Minion Pro; the heading font is Adobe Myriad Condensed; and the code font is Dalton Maag's Ubuntu Mono.

Lightning Source UK Ltd.
Milton Keynes UK
UKHW031809251021
392803UK00008B/25